Assessment of Trauma in Youths

Assessment of Trauma in Youths: Understanding issues of age, complexity, and associated variables is a collection of articles by well-known specialists in the field of childhood trauma. The articles describe developmental issues in addition to others that are important to the assessment of trauma-exposed youth, to the on-going refinement of trauma-related diagnoses for children, and to understanding PTSD and more complicated reactions to trauma for young people.

The book explores trauma in very young to middle childhood aged children, trauma in adolescents, childhood complicated trauma, and childhood complicated grief. It considers PTSD and Reactive Attachment Disorder as well as discussing disorders that are under continued study such as Developmental Trauma Disorder, Prolonged Grief Disorder, and Traumatic Grief. In the second half of the book, chapters look at the associated features of childhood traumatic response such as genetics and personality, cortisol, poly-victimization, and guilt and shame. Variables such as cortisol reactivity and guilt/shame may influence or follow traumas in children.

This book was originally published as a special issue of the *Journal of Child and Adolescent Trauma.*

Dr. Kathleen Nader is a national and international consultant/trainer who has provided specialized interventions following shootings, bombings, disasters, and war or terrorism. She has written and co-authored publications, assessment scales, and videotapes regarding youth trauma, treatment, and school interventions. Previous publications include *Honoring Differences: Cultural Issues in the Treatment of Trauma and Loss* (1999), *Understanding and Assessing Trauma in Children and Adolescents* (2008), and *School Rampage Shootings and Other Youth Problem*s (2012).

Assessment of Trauma in Youths

Understanding issues of age, complexity, and associated variables

Edited by
Kathleen Nader

Routledge
Taylor & Francis Group
LONDON AND NEW YORK

First published 2014
by Routledge
2 Park Square, Milton Park, Abingdon, Oxon, OX14 4RN

Simultaneously published in the USA and Canada
by Routledge
711 Third Avenue, New York, NY 10017

Routledge is an imprint of the Taylor & Francis Group, an informa business

British Library Cataloguing in Publication Data
A catalogue record for this book is available from the British Library

ISBN13: 978-0-415-63481-6

Typeset in Times New Roman
by Taylor & Francis Books

Publisher's Note
The publisher accepts responsibility for any inconsistencies that may have arisen during the conversion of this book from journal articles to book chapters, namely the possible inclusion of journal terminology.

Contents

Citation Information

The following chapters were originally published in the *Journal of Child and Adolescent Trauma*, volume 4, issues 3 and 4 (2011). When citing this material, please use the original page numbering for each article, as follows:

Chapter 1
Trauma in Children and Adolescents: Issues Related to Age and Complex Traumatic Reactions
Kathleen Nader
Journal of Child and Adolescent Trauma, volume 4, issue 3 (2011) pp. 161-180

Chapter 2
PTSD in Children Younger Than the Age of 13: Towards Developmentally Sensitive Assessment and Management
Michael S. Scheeringa
Journal of Child and Adolescent Trauma, volume 4, issue 3 (2011) pp. 181-197

Chapter 3
Clinical Considerations in Assessing Trauma and PTSD in Adolescents
Mandy Habib and Victor Labruna
Journal of Child and Adolescent Trauma, volume 4, issue 3 (2011) pp. 198-216

Chapter 4
Assessing Child and Adolescent Complex Traumatic Stress Reactions
Julian Ford
Journal of Child and Adolescent Trauma, volume 4, issue 3 (2011) pp. 217-232

Chapter 5
Complicated Grief Reactions in Children and Adolescents
Kathleen Nader and Alison Salloum
Journal of Child and Adolescent Trauma, volume 4, issue 3 (2011) pp. 233-257

Chapter 6
The Assessment of Associated Features Important to Understanding Childhood Trauma
Kathleen Nader
Journal of Child and Adolescent Trauma, volume 4, issue 4 (2011) pp. 259-273

Chapter 7
Attachment and Trauma in Early Childhood: A Review
Angela S. Breidenstine, Letia O. Bailey, Charles H. Zeanah and Julie A. Larrieu
Journal of Child and Adolescent Trauma, volume 4, issue 4 (2011) pp. 274-290

Chapter 8
Polyvictimization in Developmental Context
David Finkelhor, Anne Shattuck, Heather A. Turner, Richard Ormrod and Sherry L. Hamby
Journal of Child and Adolescent Trauma, volume 4, issue 4 (2011) pp. 291-300

Chapter 9
Genetic and Environmental Influences on Posttrauma Adjustment in Children and Adolescents: The Role of Personality Constructs
Josh M. Cisler, Ananda B. Amstadter and Nicole R. Nugent
Journal of Child and Adolescent Trauma, volume 4, issue 4 (2011) pp. 301-317

Chapter 10
Understanding and Assessing Cortisol Levels in Children and Adolescents
Kathleen Nader and Carl F. Weems
Journal of Child and Adolescent Trauma, volume 4, issue 4 (2011) pp. 318-338

Chapter 11
Understanding and Assessing Traumatic Responses of Guilt, Shame, and Anger among Children, Adolescents, and Young Adults
Kenneth E. Fletcher
Journal of Child and Adolescent Trauma, volume 4, issue 4 (2011) pp. 339-360

Preface

This book is a collection of articles from a two journal special series on understanding and assessing trauma in children and adolescents. The series updates some aspects of materials presented in 2008 (Nader, 2008). Part I explores issues related to age and complex traumatic reactions. Part II examines some of the variables associated with traumatic reactions. PTSD is a core posttrauma response (Scheeringa, Chapter 2). This book discusses the nature and assessment of posttrauma reactions in youth.

As will be discussed in the final chapter, a number of changes were proposed for DSM-V. Ongoing field studies hope to elaborate aspects of posttrauma reactions in youth—e.g., developmental trauma disorder (DTD). Other field studies have confirmed recommendations (e.g., for preschool age children; see Chapter 2) for inclusion of new diagnoses or changes in existing trauma-related diagnoses (see also Chapter 4 and the update for Chapter 7). Recent genetic studies have provided new information related to stress sensitivity and suggest increased vulnerability for certain genotypes to psychopathological reactions (see Chapter 12).

Chapter 1 (Nader) presents issues related to development and their importance to understanding and assessing traumatic reactions in children. Age differences have been identified in the emergence of particular youth skills, in trauma's disruption of development, and in the onset of disorders. Youth's understanding and ability to report aspects of their reactions vary by age. Additionally, trauma may disrupt the ability to report symptoms and emotions. A body of evidence has substantiated the need for adjustments to the adult version of posttraumatic stress disorder (PTSD) and other posttrauma reactions (see also Chapters 2–5 and 12). The structure of PTSD has also been examined and a number of structural revisions in the categorical model as well as a continuous model have shown some superiority to the DSM-IV model (see also Chapters 2 and 12). Although most often associated with prolonged, intense or early traumas, individuals exposed to single traumatic events also have reported complicated traumatic reactions. More study is needed to determine the variables associated with such reactions and the variations in response for different types of exposure that might induce traumatic reactions. A number of factors that may complicate grief reactions have been described as well (see also Chapter 5).

Scheeringa (Chapter 2) discusses the difficulties of trying to apply the DSM-IV PTSD diagnosis to children under the age of 12. For reporting adults and children, reporting children's subjective symptoms may be difficult. Symptoms are particularly difficult to establish in very young children who do not have the verbal ability of older youth and adults. Contrary to earlier beliefs, children do not simply grow out of PTSD reactions and may have a more unremitting and chronic course than adults. Also in contrast to previous interpretations of findings, Dr. Scheeringa found evidence of more responsive parenting by parents of traumatized children compared to parents of children without PTSD. Because of rapid brain development, PTSD persistence is particularly salient for young children. Age differences in response and reporting have implications for assessment and treatment. Evidence suggests the importance for examining the severity of symptoms and the vulnerability factors of respondents when comparing populations and when examining the specificity of PTSD diagnostic criteria. For children, the issue has more often been lack of sensitivity or under-recognition of trauma. Although a new disorder (DTD)—most commonly applied to interpersonal and chronic trauma—has been proposed, no one has yet documented that the signs and symptoms of chronic trauma are not adequately represented by PTSD (see Chapter 12). Scheeringa suggests that, with careful interview, it should not be difficult to identify PTSD even in the presence of comorbidity, and it has been possible to distinguish PTSD from other disorders such as MDD and GAD. Additionally, symptomatic children without diagnosable PTSD by DSM IV standards have been as functionally impaired as children who received the diagnosis. Dr. Scheeringa makes suggestions relevant to changes in the diagnosis for young children. As will be discussed in Chapter 12, a new diagnosis of PTSD for preschool children has been proposed for inclusion in DSM-V.

In Chapter 3, Habib and Labruna explore the particular challenges of understanding and assessing trauma in adolescents. Although revised for DSM-V, DSM-IV PTSD Criterion A2 required trauma-engendered emotions that adolescents might not identify, especially in response to an ongoing trauma that is considered a routine part of life. In addition to increased opportunities for exposure to traumas through new experiences (e.g., driving, dating, access to controlled substances), youth are more prone to sensation or reward seeking, have a sense of invulnerability, and have not yet fully developed impulse control. At the same time, they may be more affectively and physiologically reactive. Some adolescents tend to minimize their posttrauma reactions for a variety of reasons, including those related to increased self-consciousness among peers, heightened shame proneness or need to preserve self-image, low trust of adults, stress avoidance, faulty appraisal of danger or symptoms, and/or fear of consequences for candid revelation. Recommendations for assessment are provided.

Ford (Chapter 4) provides a framework for assessing youths' complicated traumatic reactions as forms of impaired self-regulation, including affect dysregulation, dissociation, somatization, suicidality, eating and body-image disorders, sleep disorders, substance use disorders, conduct/externalizing behavior disorders, and physical health problems. Secure attachments are requisite to infant self-regulation, which elaborates with age and development and permits prosocial relationships and productive behaviors. Ford discusses measures for assessing a number of types and aspects of self-regulation. DSM-IV PTSD does not fully capture the symptoms associated with complex trauma histories. Chapter 4 examines the need for a separate diagnosis for complex reactions. The proposed disorder, DTD, is currently undergoing testing (see Chapter 12).

In Chapter 5, Nader and Salloum examine theoretical constructs related to complicated forms of grief and discuss proposed forms of complicated grief (e.g., prolonged grief, traumatic grief, grief with depression; see also Chapter 1). Notably, failure to integrate the loss, factors that interfere with integration, and negative beliefs and/or expectations may be important underlying constructs for more than one type of grief. For example, trauma, the relationship to the deceased or the prospect of life without him/her, other disorders, lack of match between grieving style and grief processing, lack of resilience, or discoveries associated with betrayal may interfere with grief processing and resolution. Trauma-associated loss is significantly linked to increased trauma symptoms and complicated grieving. Symptom levels are moderated by a number of variables including, for example, the child's adaptive functioning and family environment. For DSM-V, a diagnosis of adjustment disorder related to bereavement has been proposed. More study has been recommended related to the different forms of complicated grief and the relationship of age and development to complicated grieving (see Chapter 12).

Part II examines the trauma-associated variables of attachment, polyvictimization, genetics, cortisol, and trauma-related emotions—shame, guilt, and anger. Chapter 6 introduces this section with a brief discussion of multidimensionality and synergistic influence (e.g., of multiple genetic and environmental factors) of mediating and moderating variables that are associated with posttrauma outcomes. For example, aspects of self-regulation evolve across development, are influenced by child and environmental factors, may be affected by traumatic experience, and may impact other outcomes. Examining relevant variables and appropriate variable groupings influences findings. Chapter 6 briefly summarizes aspects of the variables described in the chapters to follow.

Attachment style has robustly predicted resilience or vulnerability as well as interactional and other behavioral patterns across life. In Chapter 7, Breidenstine et al. provide a brief summary of attachment theory, including phases in the development of attachment and attachment classifications in children and adults. Chapter 7 details aspects of the relationship between trauma and attachment, highlighting disorganized attachments, which may be trauma related. The nature and assessment of two types of Reactive Attachment Disorder—*Reactive Attachment Disorder* (RAD) in infancy or early childhood and *Disinhibited Social Engagement Disorder* (DSED)—are discussed. An update related to DSM-V can be found in the update to Chapter 7.

Given its part in explaining the severity of reactions to single and "complex traumas" for children of all age groups, the assessment of polyvictimization (Chapter 8; Finkelhor et al.) is essential to understanding PTSD and complicated traumatic reactions. Exposure to multiple forms of trauma is common. The tendency to focus on only one kind of victimization may be among reasons for mixed findings for a number of variables. Stresses/adversities may combine and interact/transact in different ways, and multiple traumas may have varying influences on the nature of symptoms. For example, negative expectations toward self, others, and the world—a part of proposed DSM-V Criterion D—is, likely, more difficult to resist with multiple victimizations. Finkelhor and colleagues examine polyvictimization in each of four developmental cohorts.

Cisler et al. (Chapter 9) examine the importance of personality and genetics on posttraumatic exposure and outcomes. Genetic and personality effects may be influenced by a number of mediating and moderating, environmental or youth factors. For example, possibly with age variation, genetics may influence personality (e.g., neuroticism, behavioral inhibition), which, in turn, is associated with increased likelihood of PTSD (and other anxiety or depressive disorders) after traumatic exposure. Difficult temperament children who tend to exhibit more externalizing problems may also be vulnerable to PTSD because of increased exposure to traumas. PTSD or its symptoms have been related to specific genetic polymorphisms (e.g., serotonin, dopamine; see also Chapter 12). Environmental factors such as social support and parenting appear to influence outcomes.

Trauma is associated with alterations in cortisol activity and reactivity. In Chapter 10, Nader & Weems examine trauma-associated and laboratory findings for cortisol. Following traumas, variations in cortisol reactivity have been related to time since the trauma, peritraumatic emotions, developmental age, and controllability of the stressor. For normal children (Chapter 10, Tables 1 and 2), the situations that elicit cortisol elevation vary by age. In general, for individuals over age 4, unpredictability and uncontrollability under social evaluation (e.g., feeling judged; shame or embarrassment) amplify threat and increase the HPA response thereby increasing cortisol levels. A natural phase of hyporesponsivity occurs at puberty. Gender differences that follow may be explained by differences in the timing of maturation. Early cortisol exposure may influence reactivity (Chapters 10 and 12). Cortisol exposure has been associated with a number of problems that affect individuals across life (e.g., reduced brain volume, health problems). Cortisol levels have been differentially related to disorders and traits.

Chapter 11 (Fletcher) discusses the role of guilt, shame, and anger in traumatic reactions and recovery and discusses methods of assessing them. Peritraumatic guilt, shame, and anger have been associated with increased posttraumatic reactions. Posttraumatic guilt and shame are commonly reported after traumas and play a role in complex traumatic reactions. The "reasons for" and "nature of" guilt or shame vary across development and for different situations. An individual can experience all three emotions in response to a single trauma or type of trauma. Shame may turn into anger. Anger may mediate the effects of trauma and of shame on adjustment and may influence revictimization.

Chapter 12 provides updated information related to proposed changes in DSM-V and some of the issues discussed in earlier chapters. For example, new findings related to genetics, sometimes in combination with other variables, may influence future versions of PTSD.

Introduction

Trauma in Children and Adolescents: Issues Related to Age and Complex Traumatic Reactions

KATHLEEN NADER

Two Suns

Accurate assessment is important to treatment selection, and following traumas is particularly important for children. Traumas may undermine a child's developmental progression as well as emotional health and functioning. A number of developmental issues influence the nature and accurate assessment of traumatic reactions in children and adolescents. Youth reactions and reporting differ from those of adults, which suggest the need for diagnostic criteria and assessment measures specifically designed for varying developmental age groups. This introductory article discusses trauma-related developmental issues and the structure and nature of posttraumatic stress disorder now debated for adults and children. Also addressed are children's complicated trauma-related disorders, which are still being tested and for which measures are newly developed or undergoing revision.

In anticipation of the fifth edition of the *Diagnostic and Statistical Manual of Mental Disorders* (*DSM-V*), child-focused researchers and clinicians have been examining the nature and structure of posttraumatic stress disorder (PTSD), the need for PTSD alterations that reflect developmental differences, and the nature of complicated posttraumatic reactions in youths. The field continues to study and elaborate for youths, variations in types of reactions that may be related to development, personality, genetic predisposition, family background, other child or environmental variables, event variations, and variable combinations. The first part of this two-journal special series on understanding and assessing trauma in children and adolescents examines issues related to age and development as well as complex trauma reactions. It highlights articles that address age differences in the manifestation and reporting of PTSD (Scheeringa, this issue; Habib & Labruna, this issue), as well as a discussion of complex traumatic and grief reactions (Ford, this issue; Nader & Salloum, this issue). The following is a discussion of some of the developmental issues relevant to assessment and treatment of trauma in youths.

Trauma and Development

Many professionals have come to believe that all psychopathology is most appropriately viewed in developmental terms (Costello, Foley, & Angold, 2006; Emde & Spicer, 2000). Developmental psychology seeks to understand children's symptoms and reactions to adversity in relationship to normative adaptation at different developmental stages and to biological, psychological, and social-contextual systems (Costello et al., 2006). Accordingly, clearly defining the nature of youth reactions to trauma requires an understanding of developmental differences and normal aspects of adaptation.

Age and the Emergence of Skills, Traits, and Symptoms

Age and development influence the emergence and levels of youth's skills (e.g., self-control, perspective-taking), the development of resilience and risk factors (e.g., self-esteem, lifetime adversities), and the effect of exposure to adverse events on a child or adolescent's life (Nader, 2008). If all goes well in the course of development, children become increasingly less helpless and more skilled, for example, in problem solving, self-regulation, goal attainment, as well as in self-awareness and other-awareness. Periods of proliferation of brain synapses in the first 3 years of life and again at puberty onset mark disorganization, interruption of quantitative developmental improvements, and pruning of unused brain connections (Blakemore & Choudhury, 2006). Working memory increases from infancy onward. Working memory permits delayed imitation of observed behaviors, vicarious learning, and the combining of memories (e.g., of observations or experiences) toward innovation or other goal-directed behaviors (see Barkley, 2001). Increases in verbal and nonverbal working memory assist such skills as social interaction, self-defense, inhibition, and other self-regulation (e.g., memory of pain or of someone's bad outcome may inspire inhibition of a strong urge to react).

Timing and Analysis of Traumatic Reactions

When only variable-centered versus person-centered approaches are used to assess mental health outcomes, the multiple pathways to that outcome are indistinguishable (Laird, Jordan, Dodge, Pettit, & Bates, 2001). Although individual and subgroup trajectories may differ across time, overall patterns of development may be similar (e.g., between risk groups) or may highlight important differences (e.g., between the genders or in environmental living conditions; Nader, 2008). For example, the peaks in synaptic proliferation (Blakemore & Choudhury, 2006) and in aspects of event-related potential (an electroencephalogram index of attentional resources; Iacano & McGue, 2006) occur earlier for girls than for boys. For example, sociocognitive and behavioral risk factors for aggression occur earlier for boys than for girls, and aggression manifests differently across age groups (Aber, Brown, & Jones, 2003; Rutter, 2003). In young children, acts of physical aggression peak at ages 2 to 3 years and then decline (Tremblay, 2004). In middle childhood, youth engage in a wide range of activities and make judgments increasingly in accordance with gender stereotypes (Steele & Steele, 2005). Youth subgroups (e.g., boys, low socioeconomic status, minorities) demonstrate initial higher risk and higher rates of linear growth on measures of aggression between ages 6 and 12 years. Lower risk youths (e.g., girls, Caucasian) reach similar levels of measured variables by age 12 years (Aber et al., 2003). Normally, children's self-concepts become more negative or less unrealistically positive in middle childhood (ages 7 to 8 years) and again in early adolescence (followed by a slow increase in self-esteem in later adolescence; Geiger & Crick, 2001; Twenge &

Campbell, 2001). Evidence suggests that boys recover self-esteem during high school, and girls recover it during college. As a consequence, some studies have shown a large gender gap in self-esteem during high school. Differences in these trajectories are important for assessment and treatment of youth.

The timing of traumas is important to brain development. Studies that have examined children across time (in comparison with themselves and with groups) must take into account variations in stress sensitivity and manifestation of skills and symptoms by age or stage. For example, animals and human studies have demonstrated the brain's particular sensitivity to stress during early childhood, adolescence, and old age (Blakemore & Choudhury, 2006; Carrion, Weems, Richert, Hoffman, & Reiss, 2010; De Bellis, 2002; Lupien, McEwen, Gunnar, & Heim, 2009). Exposure to early-life stress has been associated with increased reactivity to stress and cognitive deficits in adulthood. The adolescent prefrontal cortex may be particularly vulnerable to extreme stress. The prefrontal cortex is critically involved in inhibiting the stress response as well as in attention, organization, self-regulation, and planning (Rothbart & Rueda, 2005; Stevens, Kiehl, Pearlson, & Calhoun, 2007).

Development and Psychopathology

Disorders once deemed typically as adult disorders are often reported to have had their onsets during childhood and adolescence (Angold & Egger, 2007). The time of onset of disorders varies among individuals, and prevalence varies by age group. For example, most depressed adolescent boys were probably not depressed as preschool students. Moreover, many disordered preschool students will later be quite well. Evidence has suggested a peak onset for major depression, mania, obsessive-compulsive disorder, phobias, and drug and alcohol disorders in childhood or adolescence (Costello et al., 2006). Disorders that are primarily childhood onset include attention-deficit/hyperactivity disorder (ADHD), autism and non–autistic pervasive developmental disorder, separation anxiety, specific phobia, and oppositional defiant disorder (Costello et al., 2006). Disorders that are primarily adolescent onset disorders include social phobia, panic, substance abuse, depression, anorexia nervosa, and bulimia nervosa. For boys, some studies have suggested that childhood-onset antisocial behavior has antecedents and a course that are different from adolescent-onset deviance (Costello et al., 2006; McBurnett, King, & Scarpa, 2003). Most childhood-onset disorders have more male cases than female cases, whereas most of the adolescent disorders have more female cases than male cases.

Trauma's Impact on Development

Traumatic events may disrupt a youth's brain development, developmental skills, talents, personality development, and functioning. Complex traumatic reactions, in particular, result in compromises in a youth's self-development, which includes self-regulation, self-integrity, and/or ability to experience relationships as nurturing and reliable (Ford & Courtois, 2009). Functional impairment, developmental disruptions, and dangerous symptoms such as suicidality may occur from a subset of trauma symptoms (Nader, 2008; Olfson, Hellman, Blanco, Guardino, & Struening, 2001). Posttrauma changes (e.g., in personality) may influence interrelationships and selection for opportunities at school or in life. For example, *agreeableness* describes prosocial traits such as politeness, cooperation, and compassion at one end of the continuum, and antisocial traits such as callousness and aggression at the other end (DeYoung et al., 2010). Agreeableness is linked to the mechanisms that allow the understanding of others' emotions, intentions, and mental states (e.g., empathy, theory of mind) and may be undermined by trauma.

Age and Assessing Traumatic Reactions

A number of researchers have pointed out the need for caution in simply "down-aging" existing adult DSM diagnoses in describing a disorder as it applies to children (Meiser-Stedman, Smith, Glucksman, Yule, & Dalgleish, 2008, p. 1326; Nader & Layne, 2009). Identifying age-related differences is a daunting task because of individual variations in the timing of skill development and puberty onset, mixed research findings, and the complexity of variable interrelationships. More study is needed to confirm and specify which events differ among age groups and to separate the effects of, for example, grieving from the effects of trauma. In addition, the importance of including multiple sources of information (e.g., youth, male and female caregiver, teacher/sitter, clinician), different contexts (e.g., home, school, laboratory), and different methods of assessment (e.g., interview, form completion, play methods, observation) has been well established (Egger & Angold, 2006; Kerr, Lunkenheimer, & Olsen, 2007).

Children of the same chronological age vary widely in their functioning age levels (Becker-Weidman, 2009; Nader, 2008). The gap between chronological and functioning age may be especially great among traumatized youths (Becker-Weidman, 2009). For example, some adopted and foster children age 9 or 10 years may function at an age of 4 or 5 years. Because of developmental and functional age-related differences in reporting style, self- and interpersonal skills, coping resources, the ability to label and report affective states, and the nature of reactions, the need for age-related changes in PTSD diagnostic criteria are clear. In addition to changing the PTSD diagnostic criteria are the proposal for *developmental trauma disorder* and forms of complicated grief reactions in the *DSM-V*, which are discussed later in this article and series.

Multiple assessment-related factors have influenced outcomes of youth studies. Location (home or laboratory), duration and number of assessment periods, interrelationship variables between child and caregiver or interviewer/observer, the focus of interpretation, and the level of distress produced during the assessment session may all influence findings (Nader, 2008; Rosen & Rothbaum, 1993). For example, in scripted laboratory procedures, Kochanska, Aksan, Penney, and Doobay (2007) found that young children's positive emotionality (e.g., surgency/extraversion, affiliativeness/agreeableness, approach, pleasure, sociability, and positive anticipation) related negatively to self-regulation, whereas in mother–child interactions, it related positively to self-regulation. Similarly, self-reports of some traits (e.g., empathy) differ from observations (Grynberg, Luminet, Corneille, Grèzes, & Berthoz, 2010). As mentioned earlier, using multiple sources of information is advisable. The importance of including child self-reports when possible is well established. Although most self-report measures are worded for children age 8 years and older (Briere, 2005), researchers have successfully and directly assessed younger children (see Table 1). It is clear that the manner of analysis influences findings. For example, despite correlations between complicated grief (CG) and PTSD, exploratory factor analyses have confirmed the distinctness between CG and PTSD and/or depression for adults (Boelen, van de Schoot, van den Hout, de Keijser, & van den Bout, 2010; Golden, Dalgleish, & Mackintosh, 2007) and for children (Dillen, Fontaine, & Verhofstadt-Denève, 2008, 2009; Melhem et al., 2004). Alternatively, confirmatory factor analyses have found significant overlap between CG and PTSD, especially in reexperiencing (O'Connor, Lasgaard, Shevlin, & Guldin, 2010).

Table 1
Assessment methods for three age groups

Age group	Types of assessment
Young children	• Infants and toddlers – observational methods to assess attachment relationships with caregivers (Ainsworth, Blehar, Waters, & Wall, 1978) • Age 3 years and older and autistic children – observational methods (Angold & Egger, 2007; Lord, Rutter, DiLavore, & Risi, 2003) such as preschool or classroom observations (e.g., Reynolds & Kamphaus, 1998), general play observation (Mogford-Bevan, 2000; K. H. Rubin, 1989), traumatic play observation (Nader, Stuber, & Fletcher, 2005; Scheeringa, Peebles, Cook, & Zeanah, 2001), and videotape observation (Soloman & George, 1999) • Ages 4 or 5 years – coded responses to story stems, dollhouse scenarios or doll play tasks, and puppet-based assessments (Granot & Mayseless, 2001; Stadelmann, Perren, Von Wyl, & Von Klitzing, 2007) • First-grade students – self-report questionnaires (Angold & Egger, 2007; Ialongo, Edelsohn, & Kellam, 2001; Ialongo, Edelsohn, Werthamer-Larsson, & Kellam, 1995) • Age 6 years and older – drawing and symptom descriptions (Angold & Egger, 2007; Valla, Bergeron, & Smolla, 2000)
Middle childhood	• See also methods used for young children • Younger and middle childhood – combination of play and narrative methods (Nader & Mello, 2008; Pearlman et al., 2010; Pynoos & Eth, 1986) • Age 8 or 9 years and older – child self-report questionnaires (most such questionnaires are developed for this age group) • Age 8 or 9 years and older – a variety of scales are available (e.g., to assess a variety of symptoms; Achenbach & Rescorla, 2001; Reynolds & Kampaus, 1998), disorders (e.g., Angold, Cox, Prendergast, Rutter, & Simonoff, 2008; Reich & Todd, 2002), traits (e.g., Murphy & Meisgeier, 1987; Oakland, Glutting, & Horton, 1996; Reynolds & Richmond, 2000), single disorders (e.g., Amaya-Jackson, McCarthy, Newman, & Cherney, 1995; Nader et al., 2004), and types and aspects of exposure (e.g., Finkelhor, Ormrod, & Turner, 2007; Fletcher, 2010; Ford et al., 2005)
Adolescents	• Adolescent – specifically worded questionnaires and interviews (Habib & Labruna, this issue) • Adult scales – used with adolescents even though adolescents have a different mindset, processing capacity, and cognitive style than adults (Blakemore & Choudhury, 2006; Habib & Labruna, this issue) • Face-to-face interviews – may assist with a tendency to minimize or avoid offering information (Habib & Labruna, this issue; Nader, 2008)

Assessing Trauma in Young Children

Because many PTSD symptoms are experienced internally, their detection in young children is sometimes difficult (Scheeringa, this issue). For pre- or barely verbal children, the *DSM-IV* (American Psychiatric Association [APA], 2000) PTSD Criterion A2 requirement for fear, helplessness, or horror may not be known, and for subsequent criteria, distress or avoidance may not be obvious. Research has suggested the need for wording changes and additional items in the diagnosis of PTSD in young children. In addition, the *or rule* or the *either-or rule* refers to counting a symptom as present if it is reported by the caregiver, teacher, or child (Angold & Egger, 2007). Using combined reports has provided relatively stronger predictive power, suggesting the importance of aggregating data across different informants (Meiser-Stedman et al., 2008; Scheeringa, Wright, Hunt, & Zeanah, 2006). It is possible that when children cannot provide symptom information for themselves, prevalence rates of posttraumatic stress are underestimated (Scheeringa et al., 2006). Thus, the structure of *DSM-IV* PTSD has been questioned for adults and youths (see "The Structure of PTSD" section). A body of evidence has suggested the appropriateness of using an alternative diagnostic algorithm for young children (Meiser-Stedman et al., 2008; Scheeringa, this issue; Scheeringa, Peebles, Cook, & Zeanah, 2001).

Assessing Trauma in Middle Childhood

Studies of children place middle childhood as young as 7 or 8 years and as old as 11 years. As will be discussed later, children younger than 12 years of age may have difficulty reporting some PTSD symptoms such as avoidance, but this age group is generally able to report their symptoms. In addition to self-report measures, doll play and narrative methods either separately or together (Steele & Steele, 2005) as well as some of the observational methods described for younger children in Table 1 have been used to assess children in middle childhood. Doll-play tasks permit reenactment of experiences and relationships, including traumas. They have been used with story completion (narrative) methods to assess attachment (Granot & Mayseless, 2001; Kerns, Abraham, Schlegelmilch, & Morgan, 2007; Steele & Steele, 2005) and combined with trauma narratives for diagnostic and therapeutic purposes (Nader & Mello, 2008; Pearlman, Schwartz, & Cloitre, 2010; Pynoos & Eth, 1986).

Assessing Trauma in Adolescents

Adult scales have sometimes been used to assess adolescents. Older adolescents' reactions may be similar to those of adults following traumatic exposure, yet youths can have a decidedly different presentation and reporting style as well as a different mindset and processing style (Habib & Labruna, this issue; House, 2002). Habib and Labruna point out the importance of recognizing adolescents' tendency to minimize exposure and symptoms and to avoid offering information. They recommend face-to-face interviews and avoiding terms such as *rape* or *abuse* in favor of behavioral descriptors in order to operationalize the experience.

The Nature of Traumatic Reactions in Youths

Skills such as the ability to focus and sustain attention, label and calm emotions, plan and maintain goal-directed behavior, monitor errors, and inhibit behavioral responses develop normally across time and are important to normal functioning (Ford, this issue; Posner & Rothbart, 2007). Because trauma may interrupt development, future assessments of a variety of adversities (and not only complex traumas) may include evaluations of specific developmental skills such as self-regulation, attention, interpersonal skills, and adaptive functioning, as well as brain development and neurochemical reactivity in addition to PTSD symptoms. Significant disturbances in any of these realms may have dire consequences for youths.

The Nature of PTSD

A number of issues complicate the assessment of PTSD in youths (Scheeringa, this issue). These include the need to tie symptoms to an event, the role of avoidance in influencing memory, the numbers of symptoms in the disorder that are required for each criterion, the internal nature of many symptoms, the reactivation of symptoms in response to traumatic reminders that may not be obvious to an outside observer, the differences in symptom manifestations in different age groups, the possibility of hypo- or hyperresponses, and the chance that traumatized youths may have a more complicated set of reactions without having PTSD. In addition, symptoms may change in nature across time and in relationship to the age at occurrence. These and other issues have not been adequately studied.

The applicability of Criterion A, the numbers and wording of symptoms required for a diagnosis of PTSD in youths, and the structure of PTSD continue to undergo scrutiny. Compared to PTSD in adults, the course of PTSD may be more chronic and unremitting for children (Scheeringa, this issue). As noted, trauma may disrupt brain and normal skill and trait development, and children may have functional impairment without meeting the algorithms for a full PTSD diagnosis (Broman-Fulks et al., 2009; Scheeringa, this issue).

DSM-IV PTSD Criterion A (Exposure Criterion)

For youth, DSM-IV PTSD requires an "actual or threatened death or serious injury, or a threat to the physical integrity of self or others" and (A2) "the person's response involved intense fear, helplessness, or horror . . . [or] disorganized or agitated behavior" (APA, 1994, pp. 427–428). However, evidence has suggested that the types of events that cause stress response activation vary for different age groups (Habib & Labruna, this issue; Nader & Weems, in press; Scheeringa, this issue). For example, prolonged or ongoing separations may be traumatic for children up to the age of 4, whereas stressors that involve shame and humiliation may be more potent for older children and adults (Nader & Weems, in press). It is notable that events not defined by *DSM-IV* Criterion A1 are among those that may induce long-term psychosocial and biological stress reactivity. As Ford and Courtois (2009) pointed out, emotional abuse may not be life-threatening or a violation of physical integrity, but it nevertheless poses a threat to self-integrity and may lead to ongoing, severe problems in self-regulation (Teicher, Samson, Polcari, & McGreenery, 2006). Emotional abuse is associated with increased feelings of isolation, negative self-esteem, an external locus of control, and depressive symptomatology, as well as with aggression and/or increased sexual risk-taking or abuse behaviors (Younge et al., 2010; Zurbriggen, Gobin, & Freyd, 2010). Childhood emotional abuse is associated with paranoid, schizotypal, borderline, and cluster C personality disorders, and emotional neglect is associated with histrionic and borderline personality disorder in adults (Lobbestael, Arntz, & Bernstein, 2010). In addition, the unexpected death of a relative or close friend or the severe illness of self or significant other has been linked to adult and adolescent trauma (Breslau & Kessler, 2001; Kilpatrick, Resnick, & Acierno, 2009). As the events of September 11, 2001, and other terrorist or war events have demonstrated, media exposure may result in long-term consequences for adults (Breslau, Lanius, Novac, Schnyder, & Galea, 2009) and children (see Nader, 2010). Kilpatrick and colleagues (2009) recommended that Criterion A1 be retained but should acknowledge that listed events are not exhaustive, thereby permitting flexibility to include other types of stressors. Breslau and colleagues (2009) suggested that allowance must be made for variability in stress reactivity when considering the stressor criterion.

Criterion A2 is also problematic for youths, perhaps particularly but not only in relation to complex traumatic reactions. Very young children are unable to report the emotions required in Criterion A2 (Scheeringa, this issue). Reporting A2 responses may also be difficult either for youths who are not adept at labeling or communicating their emotions (Steele & Steele, 2005), or for adolescents who minimize or have become accustomed to their experiences (Habib & Labruna, this issue). Strong arguments have been made against the limited number of responses included in A2 (Breslau et al., 2009). For adults, research has found an association between shame, anger, and PTSD and found that shame and anger has effects on later PTSD independent from those of intense peritraumatic fear, helplessness, or horror (Brewin, Andrews, & Rose, 2000; Fletcher, in press). Proposed as a new disorder for the *DSM-V*, developmental trauma disorder identifies a sense of betrayal, fear, rage, shame, resignation, or defeat among its Criterion A2 experiences (van der Kolk, 2005). Emotions such as rage and shame or humiliation may be of particular importance to adolescents as well as to complexly traumatized youths. A number of researchers have suggested the expansion of the range of peritraumatic emotions included in Criterion A2 (Kilpatrick et al., 2009).

PTSD Algorithms and Wording

Especially for young children, using an alternative algorithm for parent-reported PTSD is a more sensitive predictor than *DSM-IV* PTSD or acute stress disorder algorithms of later onset psychopathology (Scheeringa, this issue). Algorithm changes have been recommended for older children as well (La Greca & Prinstein, 2002). Proposed changes in the structure of PTSD may address the need for changes in PTSD algorithms (see later section, "The Structure of PTSD"). *Alexithymia*, or the difficulty identifying and labeling emotional feelings and a tendency toward externally oriented thinking, may be a symptom of PTSD (Frewen, Dozois, Neufeld, & Lanius, 2008) and may interfere with reporting accuracy. Proposed changes in the wording and algorithms of Criterion C numbing and avoidance symptoms demonstrate some of the problems in applying the current PTSD diagnostic algorithms and wording to youths. Studies have confirmed the need to reduce the number of Criterion C symptoms to only one for children under age 6 or 7 years (Meiser-Stedman et al., 2008; Scheeringa et al., 2006) as well as younger than age 12 years (La Greca & Prinstein, 2002; Scheeringa, this issue). Children are less able than adults to control whether or not they avoid people, places, things, and situations (Nader, 2008; Pynoos et al., 2009). Therefore, asking whether they avoid these things instead of whether they wish to avoid them may elicit false negatives. Criterion C7 (sense of a foreshortened future; does not expect career, marriage, family, or normal lifespan) may be better worded to suggest the emergence of negative cognitions toward the world, the future, and/or self (Meiser-Stedman et al., 2009), such as increased pessimism.

The Structure of PTSD

Confirmatory factor analyses have been used to assess the underlying categorical structure of PTSD. Taxometric assessments study the fit of a categorical versus a dimensional or continuous model. The following factor and no-factor models have been proposed and have proven successful (Elhai et al., 2009; Kasam-Adams, Marsac, & Cirilli, 2010; see Table 2): (a) 4-factor models (*emotional numbing*; King, Leskin, King, & Weathers, 1998; *dysphoria*; Simms, Watson, & Doebbeling, 2002), (b) 3 primary factors plus a secondary factor (*hierarchical*; Anthony et al., 2005), and (c) 2-factor (Spitzer, First, & Wakefield, 2007). Mixed evidence has suggested the possible influence of interview focus (i.e., focus on a specific trauma versus focus on global trauma exposure) on findings related to PTSD structure (Elhai et al., 2009; Naifeh, Elhai, Kashdan, & Grubaug, 2008). Although findings have been somewhat mixed (Armour et al., 2011; Elhai et al., 2009), studies of adults and a few adolescent studies have provided little support for the *DSM-IV* model of the structure of PTSD (Armour et al., 2011; Ford, Elhai, Ruggiero, & Frueh, 2009). For 8–17-year-olds, however, Kassam-Adams et al. (2010) found that the *DSM-IV* 3-factor model was a relatively good fit, although other models were as good or better. As is true with *DSM-IV* PTSD, some adaptation is required for youths in other models. For example, although Ford and colleagues (2009) found that the 2-factor model demonstrated a superior structural fit compared to the 4-factor or *DSM-IV* models, using the four-symptom threshold for Criterion C/D recommended for adults rather than a three-symptom threshold substantially lowered the prevalence of PTSD, suggesting possible underdetection of as many as 40–45% of clinically impaired adolescents.

In contrast to categorical models of PTSD, a dimensional model of posttraumatic stress reactions recognizes that most people experience some form of trauma with some resulting symptoms (Broman-Fulks et al., 2009). Even without diagnosable PTSD, many individuals seek help for their reactions to trauma or demonstrate some level of dysfunction (Broman-Fulks et al., 2009; Carrion, Weems, Ray, & Reiss, 2002; Daviss et al., 2000; Nader, 2008). Taxometric research supports a dimensional model of PTSD (Broman-Fulks et al., 2009). This model recognizes the additive or graded and multidetermined etiology of PTSD—that no single, environmental, genetic, or other personal factor is responsible for symptoms. In addition, some research has suggested that assessing latent class analysis of dimensional/continuous diagnoses permits the examination of differential intervention needs, for example, for severe/high, moderate, low, intermediate, and baseline/normative classes (Bornovalova, Levy, Gratz, & Lejuez, 2010).

The Nature of Complicated Traumatic Reactions

Complicated traumatic and grief reactions have been studied and proposed for inclusion in the *DSM-V*. Additional study of these reactions is needed. As will be discussed, although the currently proposed developmental trauma disorder (DTD) requires exposure to interpersonal traumas, it is important to avoid excluding youths who may have complicated reactions without exposure to interpersonal traumas and to avoid narrowing the range of symptoms before extensive study.

Complicated Traumatic Reactions

By 2005, clinicians had documented a high incidence of specific problems for youth who were victims of prolonged interpersonal traumas, particularly when the trauma was early

Table 2
The structure of PTSD: Analysis and findings

Type of analysis	Model of PTSD
Taxometric research	**Graded Dimensionality** • Confirms PTSD as a continuous rather than categorical group of symptoms for adults and adolescents (Broman-Fulks et al., 2009) – recognizes that experiencing some symptoms of PTSD, rather than a diagnosis, can result in psychosocial and academic or occupational dysfunction (Broman-Fulks et al., 2009; Carrion et al., 2002; Daviss et al., 2000; Nader, 2008)
Latent class analysis	**Dimensional/continuous class or subgroup structure** • Permits the delineation of classes for dimensional/categorical diagnoses – such as severity levels or risk type
Confirmatory factor analysis	**Symptom Deletion** (2-factor model; Spitzer et al., 2007) • Reexperiencing (as per *DSM-IV*) • C/D – includes C1, avoidance of thoughts; C2, avoidance of reminders; C5, social detachment; C6, emotional numbing; C7, sense of foreshortened future; D4; hypervigilance, and D5, exaggerated startle response [removes symptoms that overlap with major depressive episode and generalized anxiety disorder (C4, anhedonia; D1, irritability/anger; D3 difficulty concentrating) or have questionable validity (C3, psychogenic amnesia – may indicate normal age-related changes or fit with dissociative disorders)] ***DSM-IV* PTSD** (3-factor model; APA, 2004) • Reexperiencing • Numbing/avoidance • Hyperarousal **Hierarchical Model** (Anthony et al., 2005) • Three first-order factors – combined intrusion and effortful avoidance; numbing; arousal • A second-order factor – general PTSD factor **Dysphoria Model** (4-factor; Simms, Watson, & Doebbeling, 2002) • Reexperiencing • Avoidance • Hyperarousal • Dysphoria – numbing and three hyperarousal symptoms – trouble sleeping, irritability, difficulty concentrating – comprise the dysphoria criterion, a general distress factor **Emotional Numbing Model** (4-factor; King, Leskin, King, & Weathers, 1998) • Reexperiencing • Avoidance • Emotional numbing • Arousal

Note. PTSD = posttraumatic stress disorder; *DSM-IV* = *Diagnostic and Statistical Manual of Mental Disorders* (4th edition).

in the life cycle. These problems were in the following areas: (a) regulation of affect and impulses, (b) memory and attention, (c) self-perception, (d) interpersonal relations, (e) somatization, and (f) systems of meaning (van der Kolk, Roth, Pelcovitz, Sunday, & Spinazzola, 2005). Proposed for the *DSM-V*, originally DTD requires multiple or chronic exposures to developmentally adverse interpersonal traumas and the subjective experience of rage, betrayal, resignation, fear, defeat, or shame. DTD symptoms include persistent, cue-related dysregulation—of affect, somatization, cognition, behavior, relationships, and self-attribution—as well as altered or negative attributions and expectations toward self, caretakers, social agencies, and others (van der Kolk, 2005). The conceptualization of DTD is currently undergoing study and shaping (see Ford, this issue). Findings on polyvictimization (Finkelhor, Ormrod, & Turner, 2009) have indicated the importance of assessing the number of types of trauma exposures in examining the nature of posttrauma reactions. In addition, wording of DTD exposure requirements will need to allow for such experiences as the impact of multiple foster placements (Becker-Weidman, 2009; Rubin, O'Reilly, Luan, & Localio, 2007) and emotional abuse (Bornovalova et al., 2010), as well as the reporting difficulties for youths whose responses reflect peritraumatic freezing, numbing of emotions, self-contempt rather than shame, failure or inability to label relevant emotions, or feeling that traumas are normal (Frewen et al., 2008; Habib & Labruna, this issue). Study is needed to examine the child traits (e.g., genes, temperament) and/or environments that may contribute to complex reactions (Cisler, Amstadter, & Nugent, in press).

Complex traumas. The term *complex trauma* has been applied to such traumas as maltreatment, abandonment by caregiver(s), domestic violence, gruesome injuries as a result of community violence, terrorism, or war, and prolonged coercive internment under degrading conditions (Ford, 2005, 2009; Herman, 1992/1997). Although complicated trauma reactions have been reported by individuals exposed to natural disasters without a history of interpersonal traumas (van der Kolk et al., 2005), single traumas engender complex traumatic reactions less often and are not listed among types of trauma considered to be complex traumas. As will be discussed in the next issue of this series, findings related to polyvictimization (exposure to multiple types of trauma) may influence the perception of what constitutes a complex trauma.

Complicated Grief

Normal grief in youth is associated with a range of short-term difficulties including increased risk for illness, internalizing and externalizing symptoms, and academic underachievement, among others (Abdelnoor & Hollins, 2004; Luecken, 2008; Nader & Layne, 2009). A number of variables may complicate grieving. For example, youths' grief reactions may be complicated by the traumatic nature of a loss, the significance of the deceased to the youth's life, or the presence of other disturbances in combination with grief (Nader & Salloum, this issue; Pearlman et al., 2010). Complicated grief may prolong and intensify reactions as well as include additional symptom sets. For youths, such effects may be cumulative over time.

Current conceptualizations of CG are numerous (see Table 3). Some researchers have suggested the examination of grief as a continuous set of possible reactions (Holland, Neimeyer, Boelen, & Prigerson, 2009); others have defined specific types of CG or have highlighted variables that complicate grieving (Nader & Salloum, this issue; see Table 3). In addition, some clinicians have proposed the likelihood of complicated grief occurring after non–death-related losses, such as loss of home and family or an idealized image of

Table 3
Types of complicated grief (CG) reactions

Type of CG	Description and references
Adaptive versus maladaptive	Grief viewed on a continuum between normal and maladaptive grieving. Pathology might be measured by the number of symptoms/reactions, the intensity and/or duration of symptoms, and/or their interference with normal functioning – personal, interpersonal, and/or academic or career functioning (Holland, Neimeyer, Boelen, & Prigerson, 2009; Nader & Layne, 2009).
Bereavement-related depression (studied primarily in adults)	Bereavement is among stressors that increase the likelihood of major depression in vulnerable individuals (Corruble, Chouinard, Letierce, Gorwood, & Chouinard, 2009; Zisook & Shear, 2009; Zisook, Shear, & Kendler, 2007; Zisook, Reynolds et al., 2010). At present, in *DSM-IV* but not ICD-10; major depression is not a valid diagnosis in the early phases of grief.
Grief combined with other disturbances	From an intervention perspective, "simple grief" may combine with (i.e., be complicated by) other disturbances such as anxiety, depression, and/or behavioral problems (Pearlman et al., 2010). Accordingly, treatment must vary on the basis of the specific needs of the child and family as well as on the specific complicating factors (e.g., addition of narrative methods for posttraumatic stress disorder; addition of parent and child interventions toward regulation of behaviors for conduct disturbances).
Posthumous disillusionment (observed in adults)	Revelation of distressing events and/or behaviors of the now deceased person prior to death may change a core set of beliefs about and interpretations of the person who has died and consequently may change the perception of the nature of the relationship with the deceased (Stalfa, 2010). A sense of betrayal may be prominent.
Prolonged grief (PG) disorder	PG includes normal grief symptoms that are persistent and exacerbated (Boelen, van den Hout, & van den Bout, 2006; Prigerson et al., 2009; Prigerson, Vanderwerker, & Maciejewski, 2008; Shear, Jackson, Essock, Donahue, & Felton, 2006; see Table 2 in Nader & Salloum, this issue). A primary focus is the griever's attachment to the deceased and difficulties adjusting to life without the deceased. PG disorder has been studied and proposed for *DSM-V* (Prigerson et al., 2009). More testing and additional item listings have been proposed by other researchers (Zisook, Simon et al., 2010).
Traumatic grief (TG)	TG focuses on grief related to a death that occurs or is perceived to occur under traumatic circumstances or in a traumatic way (see Nader & Salloum, this issue). Traumatic reactions or the automatic segue from grief to trauma reexperiencing and other trauma reactions may interfere with adaptive grieving.

Note. See Nader (2010). *ISTSS loss and grief special interest group information pages* (www.istss.org). *DSM-IV* = *Diagnostic and Statistical Manual of Mental Disorders* (4th edition); ICD-10 = International Classification of Diseases-10.

home and parental love as a result of maltreatment. Among the most discussed types of CG are *prolonged grief* and *traumatic grief* (Nader & Salloum, this issue). Prolonged grief includes symptoms of grief that are persistent and exacerbated (Boelen, van den Hout, & van den Bout, 2006; Prigerson et al., 2009). For prolonged grief, emphasis is on the griever's attachment to the deceased. In contrast, traumatic grief focuses on the traumatic circumstances of a death and trauma-related interference with adaptive grieving processes. An additional conceptualization examines differences in treatment needs for grief versus grief combined with anxiety, depression, and/or behavioral problems (Pearlman et al., 2010). For clarity, revisers of current youth scales must find ways to include all relevant youth reactions and adaptations for developmental and cultural groups.

Conclusions

Evolving definitions of youths' posttrauma reactions have often begun with adult constructs of trauma. However, the potential long-term consequences of trauma in childhood indicate the importance of employing a developmental perspective to the conceptualization of trauma, beyond adult constructs. Changes to the *DSM-IV* classification of PTSD are clearly indicated for youths. Several types of trauma-related disorders have been proposed for the new *DSM-V* (van der Kolk, 2005). The newly proposed developmental trauma disorder is currently under evaluation.

Trauma may interrupt the development of normal skills that are essential to social, emotional, and academic or career functioning. Even the disruption of some seemingly less important skills may have an important effect on youths' lives. For example, humor assists youths in social and personal functioning. The ability to engage in humor may permit a child to relieve tension, regulate emotions, enhance relationships, increase or maintain group cohesion, save face, attract or maintain attention, express views otherwise difficult to communicate, or express aggression in a socially acceptable way (Semrud-Clikeman & Glass, 2010). The significant interruption of some skills (e.g., self-regulation of emotions and behaviors, coping and social skills) may drastically undermine personal and interpersonal functioning. Consequently, it is important to assess the impact of trauma on developing skills for single as well as complex traumas.

Evidence has suggested differences in treatment needs for cumulative traumas and/or complicated traumatic reactions (Ford & Courtois, 2009; Kira, 2010). Referring to some traumas as complex traumas rather than using the term specifically for outcomes can be confusing. Given that some individuals exposed to single, noninterpersonal traumas develop complex reactions, further study is needed to determine whether specific variable combinations are associated with such reactions for these youths. For example, research and observation have suggested the importance of the following in impacting trauma outcomes: (a) exposure to other life adversities (e.g., household dysfunction; Anda et al., 2006), (b) the number of deaths during a disaster (Lobb et al., 2010), (c) the length and nature of life threats and/or multiple exposures during a single event, (d) the level of support experienced, (e) specific child characteristics and circumstances (e.g., attachment issues, personality, genetics), and (f) access to basic resources (e.g., food, shelter). For example, the likelihood of single-event complicated reactions may be greater when a youth has also been exposed to inner-city conditions and distressed parenting (Scaramella, Sohr-Preston, Callahan, & Mirabile, 2008) or is genetically and psychologically vulnerable. In addition, preliminary adult findings have suggested that the duration of exposure makes a small, significant contribution to initial posttrauma clinical status (Kaysen, Rosen, Bowman, & Resick, 2010). It will be important to determine whether different disorder algorithms or treatment needs exist for youths complexly traumatized by individual events that are not interpersonal in nature. If in the future, childhood trauma disorders are defined as dimensional (i.e., a continuous model), it is likely that reactions rather than the trauma itself will define complexity.

Acknowledgments

The Editor of the *Journal of Child & Adolescent Trauma* and the guest editor of this special issue would like to acknowledge and express thanks to Teri Arnold, MSW, Assistant Editor of the *Journal of Child & Adolescent Trauma,* for providing feedback and editing for this special issue.

References

Abdelnoor, A., & Hollins, S. (2004). The effect of childhood bereavement on secondary school performance. *Educational Psychology in Practice*, *20*(1), 43–54.

Aber, J., Brown, J., & Jones, S. (2003). Developmental trajectories toward violence in middle childhood: Course, demographic differences, and response to school-based intervention. *Developmental Psychology*, *39*, 324–348.

Achenbach, T., & Rescorla, L. (2001). *Manual for the ASEBA school-age forms & profiles*. Burlington: University of Vermont, Research Center for Children, Youth, & Families.

Ainsworth, M., Blehar, M., Waters, E., & Wall, S. (1978). *Patterns of attachment: A psychological study of the strange situation*. Hillsdale, NJ: Erlbaum.

Amaya-Jackson, L., McCarthy, G., Newman, E., & Cherney, M. (1995). *Child PTSD Checklist*. Durham, NC: Duke University Medical Center.

American Psychiatric Association. (1994). *Diagnostic and statistical manual of mental disorders* (4th ed.). Washington, DC: Author.

American Psychiatric Association. (2000). *Diagnostic and statistical manual of mental disorders* (text rev.). Washington, DC: Author.

Anda, R., Felitti, V., Bremner, J., Walker, J., Whitfield, C., Perry, B. D., et al. (2006). The enduring effects of abuse and related adverse experiences in childhood: A convergence of evidence from neurobiology and epidemiology. *European Archives of Psychiatry and Clinical Neuroscience*, *256*, 174–186.

Angold, A., Cox, A., Prendergast, M., Rutter, M., & Simonoff, E. (2008). *Child and adolescent psychiatric assessment*. Unpublished manuscript, Center for Developmental Epidemiology, Department of Psychiatry and Behavioral Sciences, Duke University Medical Center, Durham, NC.

Angold, A., & Egger, H. (2007). Preschool psychopathology: Lessons for the lifespan. *Journal of Child Psychology and Psychiatry*, *48*, 961–966.

Anthony, J., Lonigan, C., Vernberg, E., La Greca, A., Silverman, W., & Prinstein, M. (2005). Multisample crossvalidation of a model of childhood posttraumatic stress disorder symptomatology. *Journal of Traumatic Stress*, *18*, 667–676.

Armour, C., Layne, C., Naifeh, J., Shevlin, M., Duraković-Belko, E., Djapo, N., et al. (2011). Assessing the factor structure of posttraumatic stress disorder symptoms in war-exposed youths with and without Criterion A2 endorsement. *Journal of Anxiety Disorders*, *25*, 80–87.

Barkley, R. (2001). The executive functions and self-regulation: An evolutionary neuropsychological perspective. *Neuropsychology Review*, *11*(1), 1–29.

Becker-Weidman, A. (2009). Effects of early maltreatment on development: A descriptive study using the Vineland Adaptive Behavior Scales-II. *Child Welfare*, *88*, 137–161.

Blakemore, S., & Choudhury, S. (2006). Development of the adolescent brain: Implications for executive function and social cognition. *Journal of Child Psychology and Psychiatry*, *47*, 296–312.

Boelen, P., van den Hout, M., & van den Bout, J. (2006). A cognitive-behavioral conceptualization of complicated grief. *Clinical Psychology Science and Practice, 13*, 109–128.

Boelen, P. van de Schoot, R., van den Hout, M., de Keijser, J., & van den Bout, J. (2010). Prolonged grief disorder, depression, and posttraumatic stress disorder are distinguishable syndromes. *Journal of Affective Disorders, 125*, 374–378.

Bornovalova, M., Levy, R., Gratz, K., & Lejuez, C. (2010). Understanding the heterogeneity of BPD symptoms through latent class analysis: Initial results and clinical correlates among inner-city substance users. *Psychological Assessment*, *22*, 233–245.

Breslau, N., & Kessler, R. (2001). The stressor criterion in *DSM-IV* posttraumatic stress disorder: An empirical investigation. *Biological Psychiatry*, *50*, 699–704.

Breslau, C., Lanius, R., Novac, A., Schnyder, U., & Galea, S. (2009). Reformulating PTSD for *DSM-V*: Life after Criterion A. *Journal of Traumatic Stress*, *22*, 366–373.

Brewin, C. R., Andrews, B., & Rose, S. (2000). Fear, helplessness, and horror in posttraumatic stress disorder: Investigating *DSM-IV* Criterion A2 in victims of violent crime. *Journal of Traumatic Stress*, *13*, 499–509.

Briere, J. (2005). *Trauma Symptom Checklist for Young Children* (TSCYC). Odessa, FL: Psychological Assessment Resources.

Broman-Fulks, J., Ruggiero, K., Green, B., Smith, D., Hanson, R., Kilpatrick, D., et al. (2009). The latent structure of PTSD among adolescents. *Journal of Traumatic Stress*, *22*, 146–152.

Carrion, V., Weems, C., Ray, R., & Reiss, A. (2002). Toward an empirical definition of pediatric PTSD: The phenomenology of PTSD symptoms in youth. *Journal of the American Academy of Child and Adolescent Psychiatry*, *41*, 166–173.

Carrion, V., Weems, C., Richert, K., Hoffman, B., & Reiss, A. (2010). Decreased prefrontal cortical volume associated with increased bedtime cortisol in traumatized youth. *Biological Psychiatry*, *68*, 491–493.

Cisler, J., Amstadter, A., & Nugent, N. (in press). Genetic and environmental influences on post-trauma adjustment in children and adolescents: The role of personality constructs. *Journal of Child & Adolescent Trauma.*

Corruble, E., Chouinard, V., Letierce, A., Gorwood, P., & Chouinard, G. (2009). Is *DSM-IV* bereavement exclusion for major depressive episode relevant to severity and pattern of symptoms? A case-control, cross-sectional study. *Journal of Clinical Psychiatry*, *70*, 1091–1097.

Costello, E., Foley, D., & Angold, A. (2006). 10-year research update review: The epidemiology of child and adolescent psychiatric disorders: II. Developmental epidemiology. *Journal of the American Academy of child and Adolescent Psychiatry*, *45*, 8–25.

Daviss, W., Mooney, D., Racusin, R., Ford, J., Fleischer, A., & McHugo, G. (2000). Predicting posttraumatic stress after hospitalization for pediatric injury. *Journal of American Academy of Child and Adolescent Psychiatry*, *59*, 576–583.

De Bellis, M. (2002). Developmental traumatology: A contributory mechanism for alcohol and substance use disorders. *Psychoneuroendocrinology*, *27*, 155–170.

DeYoung, C., Hirsh, J., Shane, M., Papademetris, X., Rajeevan, N., & Gray, J. (2010). Testing predictions from personality neuroscience: Brain structure and the big five. *Psychological Science*, *21*, 820–828.

Dillen, L., Fontaine, J., & Verhofstadt-Denève, L. (2008). Are normal and complicated grief different constructs? A confirmatory factor analytic test. *Clinical Psychology and Psychotherapy*, *15*, 386–395.

Dillen, L., Fontaine, J., & Verhofstadt-Denève, L. (2009). Confirming the distinctiveness of complicated grief from depression and anxiety among adolescents. *Death Studies*, *33*, 437–461.

Egger, H., & Angold, A. (2006). Common emotional and behavioral disorders in preschool children: Presentation, nosology, and epidemiology. *Journal of Child Psychology and Psychiatry*, *47*, 313–337.

Elhai, J., Engdahl, R., Palmieri, P., Naifeh, J., Schweinle, A., & Jacobs, G. (2009). Assessing posttraumatic stress disorder with or without reference to a single, worst traumatic event: Examining differences in factor structure. *Psychological Assessment*, *21*, 629–634.

Emde, R., & Spicer, P. (2000). Experience in the midst of variation: New horizons for development and psychopathology. *Development and Psychopathology*, *12*, 313–331.

Finkelhor, D., Ormrod, R., & Turner, H. (2007). Poly-victimization: A neglected component in child victimization. *Child Abuse & Neglect*, *31*, 7–26.

Finkelhor, D., Ormrod, R., & Turner, H. (2009). Lifetime assessment of poly-victimization in a national sample of children & youth. *Child Abuse & Neglect*, *33*, 403–411.

Fletcher, K. (2010). *Dimensions of Stressful Events (DOSE-R3)*. Unpublished measure, Boston, MA.

Fletcher, K. (in press). Assuming responsibility: Understanding and assessing traumatic responses of guilt, shame, and anger among children, adolescents, and adults. *Journal of Child & Adolescent Trauma*.

Ford, J. (2005). Treatment implications of altered neurobiology, affect regulation and information processing following child maltreatment. *Psychiatric Annals*, *35*, 410–419.

Ford, J. (2009). Neurobiological and developmental research: Developmental implications. In C. Courtois & J. Ford (Eds.), *Treating complex traumatic stress disorders: An evidence-based guide* (pp. 31–58). New York: Guilford Press.

Ford, J., & Courtois, C. (2009). Defining and understanding complex trauma. In C. Courtois & J. Ford (Eds.), *Treating complex traumatic stress disorders: An evidence-based guide* (pp. 13–30). New York: Guilford Press.

Ford, J., Elhai, J., Ruggiero, K., & Frueh, B. (2009). Refining posttraumatic stress disorder diagnosis: Evaluation of symptom criteria with the National Survey of Adolescents. *Journal of Clinical Psychiatry*, *70*, 748–755.

Ford, J., Ghosh Ippen, C., Wolpaw, J., Racusin, R., Rogers, K., Ellis, C, et al. (2005). *Traumatic Events Screening Inventory for Children (TESI-C)*. Dartmouth, VT: National Center for PTSD and Dartmouth Child Psychiatry Research Group.

Frewen, P., Dozois, D., Neufeld, R., & Lanius, R. (2008). Meta-analysis of alexithymia in posttraumatic stress disorder. *Journal of Traumatic Stress*, *21*, 243–246.

Geiger, T., & Crick, N. (2001). A developmental psychopathology perspective on vulnerability to personality disorders. In R. E. Ingram & J. M. Price (Eds.), *Vulnerability to psychopathology: Risk across the lifespan* (pp. 57–102). New York: Guilford Press.

Golden, A., Dalgleish, T., & Mackintosh, B. (2007). Levels of specificity of autobiographical memories and of biographical memories of the deceased in bereaved individuals with and without complicated grief. *Journal of Abnormal Psychology*, *116*, 786–795.

Granot, D., & Mayseless, O. (2001). Attachment security and adjustment to school in middle childhood. *International Journal of Behavioral Development*, *25*, 530–541.

Grynberg, D., Luminet, O., Corneille, O., Grèzes, J., & Berthoz, S. (2010). Alexithymia in the inter-personal domain: A general deficit of empathy? *Personality and Individual Differences*, *49*, 845–850.

Herman, J. (1992/1997). Complex PTSD: A syndrome in survivors of prolonged and repeated trauma. *Journal of Traumatic Stress*, *5*, 377–391.

Holland, J., Neimeyer, R., Boelen, P., & Prigerson, H. (2009). The underlying structure of grief: A taxometric investigation of prolonged and normal reactions to loss. *Journal of Psychopathology and Behavioral Assessment*, *31*, 190–201.

House, A. E. (2002). *The first session with children and adolescents: Conducting a comprehensive mental health evaluation*. New York: Guilford Press.

Iacono, W., & McGue, M. (2006). Association between P3 event-related brain potential amplitude and adolescent problem behavior. *Psychophysiology*, *43*, 465–469.

Ialongo, N., Edelsohn, G., & Kellam, S. (2001). A further look at the prognostic power of young children's reports of depressed mood and feelings. *Child Development*, *72*, 736–747.

Ialongo, N., Edelsohn, G., Werthamer-Larsson, L., & Kellam, S. (1995). The significance of first graders' self-reports of anxious symptoms: Prediction to adaptive functioning and anxious symptoms in fifth grade. *Journal of Child Psychology and Psychiatry*, *36*, 427–437.

Kassam-Adams, N., Marsac, M., & Cirilli, C. (2010). Posttraumatic stress disorder symptom structure in injured children: Functional impairment and depression symptoms in a confirmatory factor analysis. *Journal of the American Academy of Child and Adolescent Psychiatry*, *49*, 616–625.

Kaysen, D., Rosen, G., Bowman, M., & Resick, P. (2010). Duration of exposure and the dose-response model of PTSD. *Journal of Interpersonal Violence*, *25*(1), 63–74.

Kerns, K., Abraham, M., Schlegelmilch, A., & Morgan, T. (2007). Mother–child attachment in later middle childhood: Assessment approaches and associations with mood and emotion regulation. *Attachment & Human Development*, *9*(1), 33–53.

Kerr, D., Lukenheimer, E., & Olsen, S. (2007). Assessment of child problem behaviors by multiple informants: A longitudinal study from preschool to school entry. *Journal of Child Psychology and Psychiatry*, *48*, 967–975.

Kilpatrick, D., Resnick, H., & Acierno, R. (2009). Should PTSD Criterion A be retained? *Journal of Traumatic Stress*, *22*, 374–383.

King, D., Leskin, G., King, L., & Weathers, F. (1998). Confirmatory factor analysis of the Clinician-Administered PTSD Scale: Evidence for the dimensionality of posttraumatic stress disorder. *Psychological Assessment*, *10*, 90–96.

Kira, I. (2010). Etiology and treatment of post-cumulative traumatic stress disorders in different cultures. *Traumatology*, *16*, 128–141.

Kochanska, G., Aksan, N., Penney, S., & Doobay, A. (2007). Early positive emotionality as a heterogeneous trait: Implications for children's self-regulation. *Journal of Personality and Social Psychology*, *93*, 1054–1066.

La Greca, A., & Prinstein, M. (2002). Hurricanes and earthquakes. In A. La Greca, W. Silverman, E. Vernberg, & M. Roberts (Eds.), *Helping children cope with disasters and terrorism* (pp. 107–138). Washington, DC: American Psychological Association Press.

Laird, R. D., Jordan, K. Y., Dodge, K. A., Pettit, G. S., & Bates, J. E. (2001). Peer rejection in childhood, involvement with antisocial peers in early adolescence, and the development of externalizing behavior problems. *Development and Psychopathology*, *13*, 337–354.

Lobb, E., Janson, L., Aoun, S., Monterosso, L., Halkett, G., & Davies, A. (2010). Predictors of complicated grief: A systematic review of empirical studies. *Death Studies*, *34*, 673–698.

Lobbestael, J., Arntz, A., & Bernstein, D. (2010). Disentangling the relationship between different types of childhood maltreatment and personality disorders. *Journal of Personality Disorders*, *24*, 285–295.

Lord, C., Rutter, M., DiLavore, P. C., & Risi, S. (2003). *Autism Diagnostic Observation Schedule (ADOS)*. Los Angeles: Western Psychological Services.

Luecken, L. (2008). Long-term consequences of parental death in childhood: Psychological and physiological manifestations. In M. Stroebe, R. Hansson, H. Schut, & W. Stroebe (Eds.), *Handbook of bereavement research and practice: Advances in theory and intervention* (pp. 397–416). Washington, DC: American Psychological Association.

Lupien, S., McEwen, B., Gunnar, M., & Heim, C. (2009). Effects of stress throughout the lifespan on the brain, behaviour and cognition. *Neuroscience*, *10*(1), 1–12.

McBurnett, K., King, J., & Scarpa, A. (2003). The hypothalamic-pituitary-adrenal system (HPA) and the development of aggressive, antisocial, and substance abuse disorders. In D. Cicchetti & E. Walker (Eds.), *Neurodevelopmental mechanisms in psychopathology* (pp. 324–344). Cambridge, England: Cambridge University Press.

Meiser-Stedman, R., Smith, P., Bryant, R., Salmon, K., Yule, W., Dalgleish, T., et al. (2009). Development and validation of the Child Post-Traumatic Cognitions Inventory (CPTCI). *Journal of Child Psychology and Psychiatry*, *50*, 432–440.

Meiser-Stedman, R., Smith, P., Glucksman, E., Yule, W., & Dalgleish, T. (2008). The posttraumatic stress disorder diagnosis in preschool- and elementary school-age children exposed to motor vehicle accidents. *American Journal of Psychiatry*, *165*, 1326–1337.

Melhem, N., Day, N., Shear, M. K., Day, R., Reynolds, C., III, & Brent, D. (2004). Traumatic Grief among adolescents exposed to a peer's suicide. *American Journal of Psychiatry*, *161*, 1411–1416.

Mogford-Bevan, K. (2000). The Play Observation Kit (POKIT): An observational assessment technique for young children. In K. Gitlin-Weiner, A. Sandgrund, & C. Schaefer (Eds.), *Play diagnosis and assessment* (2nd ed., pp. 262–299). New York: Wiley.

Murphy, E., & Meisgeier, C. (1987). *Murphy-Meisgeier Type Indicator for Children*. Palo Alto, CA: Consulting Psychologists Press.

Nader, K. (2008). *Understanding and assessing trauma in children and adolescents: Measures, methods, and youth in context*. New York: Routledge.

Nader, K. (2010). Children and adolescent's exposure to the mass violence of war and terrorism: Role of the media. In N. B. Webb (Ed.), *Helping bereaved children* (3rd ed., pp. 215–239). New York: Guilford Press.

Nader, K., & Layne, C. (2009). Maladaptive grieving in children and adolescents: Discovering developmentally linked differences in the manifestation of grief. *Traumatic Stress Points*, *23*(5), 12–16.

Nader, K., & Mello, C. (2008). Interactive trauma/grief focused therapy. In N. Coady & P. Lehmann (Eds.), *Theoretical perspectives for direct social work practice: A generalist eclectic approach* (2nd ed., pp. 493–519). New York: Springer.

Nader, K., Newman, E., Weathers, F., Kaloupek, D., Kriegler, J., & Blake, D. (2004). *Clinician-Administered PTSD Scale for children and adolescents (CAPS-C)*. Los Angeles: Western Psychological Press.

Nader, K., Stuber, M., & Fletcher, K. (2005). *The Traumatic Play Observation Scale (TPOS)*. Austin: Two Suns.

Nader, K., & Weems, C. (in press). Understanding and assessing cortisol levels in children and adolescents. *Journal of Child & Adolescent Trauma.*

Naifeh, J., Elhai, J., Kashdan, T., & Grubaugh, A. (2008). The PTSD Symptom Scale's latent structure: An examination of trauma-exposed medical patients. *Journal of Anxiety Disorders*, *22*, 1355–1368.

Oakland, T., Glutting, J., & Horton, C. (1996). *Student Styles Questionnaire: Star qualities in learning, relating, and working*. San Antonio: The Psychological Corporation, Harcourt Brace.

O'Connor, M., Lasgaard, M., Shevlin, M., & Guldin, M. (2010). A confirmatory factor analysis of combined models of the Harvard Trauma Questionnaire and the Inventory of Complicated Grief-Revised: Are we measuring complicated grief or posttraumatic stress? *Journal of Anxiety Disorders*, *24*, 672–679.

Olfson, M., Hellman, F., Blanco, C., Guardino, M., & Struening, E. (2001). Comorbidity, impairment, and suicidality in subthreshold PTSD. *American Journal of Psychiatry*, *158*, 1467–1473.

Pearlman, M., Schwartz, K., & Cloitre, M. (2010). *The varied manifestations of grief: Assisting a child and caregiver after the loss of a parent*. Washington, DC: American Psychological Association.

Posner, M., & Rothbart, M. (2007). *Educating the human brain*. Washington, DC: American Psychological Association.

Prigerson, H., Horowitz, M., Jacobs, S., Parks, C. M., Aslan, M., Goodkin, K, et al. (2009). Prolonged grief disorder: Psychometric validation of criteria proposed for *DSM-V* and ICD11. *PLoS Medicine*, *6*(8), e1000121.

Prigerson, H., Vanderwerker, L., & Maciejewski, P. (2008). A case for inclusion of prolonged grief disorder in *DSM-V*. In M. Stroebe, R. Hansson, H. Schut, & W. Strobe (Eds.), *Handbook of bereavement research and practice: Advances in theory and intervention* (pp. 165–186). Washington, DC: APA Books.

Pynoos, R., & Eth, S. (1986). Witness to violence: The child interview. *Journal of the American Academy of Child Psychiatry*, *25*, 306–319.

Pynoos, R., Steinberg, A., Layne, C., Briggs, B., Ostrowski, S., & Fairbank, J. (2009). *DSM-V* PTSD diagnostic criteria for children and adolescents: A developmental perspective and recommendations. *Journal of Traumatic Stress*, *22*, 391–398.

Reich, W., & Todd, R. (2002). *Missouri Assessment of Genetics Interview for Children specifications manual*. St. Louis, MO: Washington University School of Medicine.

Reynolds, C., & Kamphaus, R. (1998). *Behavior Assessment System for Children manual*. Circle Pines, MN: American Guidance Service.

Reynolds, C., & Richmond, B. (2000). *Revised Children's Manifest Anxiety Scale manual*. Los Angeles: Western Psychological Services.

Rosen, K. S., & Rothbaum, F. (1993). Quality of parental caregiving and security of attachment. *Developmental Psychology*, *29*, 358–367.

Rothbart, M., & Rueda, M. (2005). The development of effortful control. In U. Mayr, E. Awh, & S. W. Keele (Eds.), *Developing individuality in the human brain: A festschrift honoring Michael I. Posner* (pp. 167–188). Washington, DC: American Psychological Association.

Rubin, D., O'Reilly, A., Luan, X., & Localio, A. (2007). The impact of placement stability on behavioral well-being for children in foster care. *Pediatrics, 119*, 336–344.

Rubin, K. H. (1989). *The Play Observation Scale (POS)*. Waterloo, Ontario, Canada: University of Waterloo.

Rutter, M. (2003). Commentary: Causal processes leading to antisocial behavior. *Developmental Psychology, 39*, 372–378.

Scaramella, L., Sohr-Preston, S., Callahan, K., & Mirabile, S. (2008). A test of the family stress model on toddler-aged children's adjustment among Hurricane Katrina impacted and nonimpacted low-income families. *Journal of Clinical Child & Adolescent Psychology, 37*, 530–541.

Scheeringa, M., Peebles, C., Cook, C., & Zeanah, C. (2001). Toward establishing procedural, criterion, and discriminant validity for PTSD in early childhood. *Journal of the American Academy of Child and Adolescent Psychiatry, 40*(1), 52–60.

Scheeringa, M., Wright, M., Hunt, J., & Zeanah, C. (2006). Factors affecting the diagnosis and prediction of PTSD symptomatology in children and adolescents. *American Journal of Psychiatry, 163*, 644–651.

Semrud-Clikeman, M., & Glass, K. (2010). The relation of humor and child development: Social, adaptive, and emotional aspects. *Journal of Child Neurology, 25*, 1248–1260.

Shear, K., Jackson, C., Essock, S., Donahue, S., & Felton, C. (2006). Screening for complicated grief among Project Liberty service recipients 18 months after September 11, 2001. *Psychiatric Services, 57*, 1291–1297.

Simms, L., Watson, D., & Doebbeling, B. (2002). Confirmatory factor analyses of posttraumatic stress symptoms in deployed and nondeployed veterans of the Gulf War. *Journal of Abnormal Psychology, 111*, 637–647.

Solomon, J., & George, C. (1999). The measurement of attachment security in infancy and childhood. In J. Cassidy & P. R. Shaver (Eds.), *Handbook of attachment: Theory, research, and clinical applications* (pp. 287–316). New York: Guilford Press.

Spitzer, R., First, M., & Wakefield, J. (2007). Saving PTSD from itself in *DSM-V*. *Journal of Anxiety Disorders, 21*, 233–241.

Stadelmann, S., Perren, S., Von Wyl, A., & Von Klitzing, K. (2007). Associations between family relationships and symptoms/strengths at kindergarten age: What is the role of children's parental representations? *Journal of Child Psychology and Psychiatry, 48*, 996–1004.

Stalfa, F. (2010). "Posthumous disillusionment" as a type of complicated grief. *The Journal of Pastoral Care and Counseling, 64*(2), 71–78.

Steele, H., & Steele, M. (2005). The construct of coherence as an indicator of attachment security in middle childhood: The friends and family interview. In K. Kerns & R. Richardson (Eds.), *Attachment in middle childhood* (pp. 137–160). New York: Guilford Press.

Stevens, M., Kiehl, K., Pearlson, G., & Calhoun, V. (2007). Functional neural networks underlying response inhibition in adolescents and adults. *Behavioural Brain Research, 181*, 12–22.

Teicher, M., Samson, J., Polcari, A., & McGreenery, C. (2006). Sticks, stones and hurtful words: Relative effects of various forms of childhood maltreatment. *American Journal of Psychiatry, 163*, 993–1000.

Tremblay, R. E. (2004). The development of human physical aggression: How important is early childhood? In L. Leavitt & D. Hall (Eds.), *Social and moral development: Emerging evidence on the toddler Years* (pp. 221–238). Brunswick, NJ: Johnson & Johnson Pediatric Institute.

Twenge, J. M., & Campbell, W. K. (2001). Age and birth cohort differences in self-esteem: A cross-temporal meta-analysis. *Personality and Social Psychology Review, 5*, 321–344.

Valla, J., Bergeron, L., & Smolla, N. (2000). The Dominic-R: A pictorial interview for 6- to 11-year-old children. *Journal of the American Academy of Child and Adolescent Psychiatry, 39*, 85–93.

van der Kolk, B. (2005). Developmental trauma disorder: Toward a rational diagnosis for children with complex trauma histories. *Psychiatric Annals*, *35*, 401–408.

van der Kolk, B., Roth, S., Pelcovitz, D., Sunday, S., & Spinazzola, J. (2005). Disorders of extreme stress: The empirical foundation of a complex adaptation to trauma. *Journal of Traumatic Stress*, *18*, 389–399.

Younge, S., Salazar, L., Sales, J., DiClemente, R., Wingood, G., & Rose, E. (2010). Emotional victimization and sexual risk-taking behaviors among adolescent African American women. *Journal of Child & Adolescent Trauma*, *3*(2), 79–94.

Zisook, S., Reynolds, C., Pies, R., Simon, N., Lebowitz, B., Madowitz, J., et al. (2010). Bereavement, complicated grief, and DSM, Part 1: Depression. *Journal of Clinical Psychiatry*, *71*, 955–956.

Zisook, S., & Shear, K. (2009). Grief and bereavement: What psychiatrists need to know. *World Psychiatry*, *9*, 67–74.

Zisook, S., Shear, K., & Kendler, K. (2007). Validity of the bereavement exclusion criterion for the diagnosis of major depressive episode. *World Psychiatry*, *6*, 102–107.

Zisook, S., Simon, N., Reynolds, C., Pies, R., Lebowitz, B., Tal-Young, I., et al. (2010). Bereavement, complicated grief, and DSM, Part 2: Complicated grief. *Journal of Clinical Psychiatry*, *71*, 1097–1098.

Zurbriggen, E., Gobin, R., & Freyd, J. (2010). Childhood emotional abuse predicts late adolescent sexual aggression perpetration and victimization. *Journal of Aggression, Maltreatment & Trauma*, *19*, 204–223.

Developmental Issues

PTSD in Children Younger Than the Age of 13: Toward Developmentally Sensitive Assessment and Management

MICHAEL S. SCHEERINGA
Tulane University School of Medicine

Posttraumatic stress disorder can be more difficult to assess compared to other disorders. The complicated nature of the symptoms contributes to underdetection of the diagnosis in children. The most substantial proposal for the diagnostic criteria is to lower the Criterion C requirement from three to one symptom. Comorbid disorders tend to complicate the clinical picture, but research is reviewed showing that posttraumatic stress disorder is the core, well-defined posttrauma syndrome. Early longitudinal studies have suggested that the course may be more chronic in children than in adults. Caution is urged about how to view the effects of parent–child relationships on children's symptomatology following trauma. The author organizes advice for interviewing respondents into seven practical suggestions and discusses treatment implications.

Ever since posttraumatic stress disorder (PTSD) was first defined in the *Diagnostic and Statistical Manual* (*DSM*; American Psychiatric Association [APA], 1980), there has been controversy in general about the diagnosis. This has included skepticism about the existence of the diagnosis in children (Benedek, 1985); however, this is no longer debatable. Previous iterations of *DSM* criteria for PTSD were published throughout three editions with few data available from studies that examined diagnostic algorithms in children younger than 18 years of age and almost no data on children younger than 12 years of age. Fortunately, a substantial number of studies have examined diagnostic algorithms, and other types of studies have been conducted in the past 15 years to establish the diagnostic validity of PTSD in preschool and school-age children. However, detecting PTSD in children in clinical settings is time-consuming and difficult. The challenges in assessing infant, preschool, and school-age children have only recently been described and still have far to go in terms of adequate application in clinical settings.

Assessment of PTSD is Relatively More Difficult Compared to Other Disorders

The current diagnostic criteria for PTSD require that children have experienced, witnessed, or learned of a traumatic event, which is defined as one that is terrifying, shocking, and potentially threatening to life, safety, or physical integrity of self or other. Children must also meet at least one reexperiencing criteria, three avoidant/numbing criteria, and two increased arousal criteria. Children must meet minimal duration criteria of at least one month, and they must show functional impairment in an important area (e.g., school, peers, family). Relative to most other disorders, this is a difficult threshold for at least seven reasons.

1. PTSD is one of the rare disorders in the *DSM-IV* (APA, 1994) that requires an etiological component. Before asking about any symptoms of PTSD, one must go through a menu of all possible traumatic experiences, because many children have experienced more than one traumatic event. In a community representative sample of 1,420 children, 37% had been exposed to more than one traumatic event (Copeland, Keeler, Angold, & Costello, 2007). The need to inventory trauma exposure is time-consuming, relatively invasive, and may run counter to efforts to build rapport.
2. There are 17 possible symptoms in the *DSM-IV* criteria for PTSD (APA, 1994). This is more than double the number found in nearly all other disorders, with the exception of attention-deficit/hyperactivity disorder (ADHD) and conduct disorder. At a practical level, this more than doubles the amount of time needed to conduct an assessment per disorder. For this article, data were extracted post hoc from an existing study (Posttraumatic Stress Disorder in Preschool Children, National Institute of Mental Health, 5 R01 MH065884) to document how long it takes to interview for PTSD compared to other common disorders. In this assessment study, 3–6-year-old trauma-exposed children were assessed with the Preschool Age Psychiatric Assessment (Egger et al., 2006), which is an interview for caregivers about children. Twelve interviews were sampled in a quasi-random selection process. The durations required for each disorder were 52.4 min for PTSD, 25.6 min for major depressive disorder (MDD), 13.3 min for ADHD, 10.3 min for oppositional defiant disorder (ODD), 8.0 min for phobias, 6.5 min for separation anxiety disorder (SAD), and 4.3 min for generalized anxiety disorder (GAD).
3. Each one of the 17 symptoms has to be tied back to an event/date of onset. It is insufficient to establish that only one of the 17 PTSD symptoms developed immediately after a traumatic event. This process is, again, time-consuming and also poses unique technical challenges. Many of these inquiries require multistep connections for the interviewer and the respondent—identify the symptom, connect it back in time to a past event, and recognize that the current manifestations are similar to the past experiences.
4. Memory is a unique and key aspect of PTSD not present in any other disorder. Memory of a traumatic event is required for the disorder, and memory to connect present symptoms to past experiences is required to discuss symptoms in an assessment. Yet, these memories and symptoms are, by definition, unpleasant. The interviewer attempts to solicit descriptions of events that the respondent may want to forget. This issue is closely tied to two of the seven symptoms in Criterion C (avoidance and numbing symptoms) that are about avoidance of reminders of past events. It is particularly challenging to ask respondents to report avoidance symptoms, because the nature of the symptom is to actively avoid talking or thinking about the issue (Cohen & Scheeringa, 2009). Respondents can be prone to reply, "I don't want to talk about it" or "I don't want to

think about it." The former response puts up a roadblock that sensitive clinicians may fear crossing, and the latter response sounds like a denial when it may actually be an endorsement. In each case, the response contains insufficient information. A clinician must probe further to determine whether any of these children may be actively avoidant and may have significant PTSD symptoms. Arguably, patients with other types of disorders also find it unpleasant to discuss their symptoms, but the inherent embeddedness of unpleasant memory in PTSD is unlike any other disorder.

A further complication to this challenge is a basic misunderstanding of PTSD symptomatology. Oftentimes, avoidance has been incorrectly dismissed as adaptive learning from experience. The reasoning is that if children incurred harm from past experiences (e.g., being hit by a car while crossing a street) and subsequently act fearful when placed in a similar situation that reminds them of the past event (e.g., when crossing streets), then it is only logical and appropriate versus being a symptom. What this assertion fails to acknowledge is that caution is a normative reaction for children when crossing busy streets, but fear is not. The spirit of the PTSD symptom is that new distress is coupled with avoidant behavior, which is different from simply acting with normative apprehension.

5. Many PTSD symptoms are highly internalized, which makes them difficult for parents to observe and difficult for children to express with developing language and narrative capacities. Internalized symptoms include the following: (a) avoidance of internalized reminders of past traumas, (b) inability to recall events (as a result of psychogenic blocking of painful memories), (c) sense of a foreshortened future, (d) feelings of detachment or estrangement from people, (e) certain types of psychological distress from reminders of traumas, (f) physiological reactivity to reminders of traumas, (g) dissociative experiences, (h) intrusive recollections, and (i) nightmares. In addition to the obvious problem of making these symptoms difficult to discover, this presents a practical challenge in that it often requires more probing to assess these symptoms comprehensively, which takes more time.
6. Because most persons have never had PTSD, caregivers may have no common frame of reference from which to report on their children's feelings. Contrast this with other types of disorders, such as depression, ADHD, or ODD. Nearly everyone intuitively understands and recognizes sadness, hyperactivity, and defiance; these are easily observable and require little in the way of verbalizations and self-recognitions from children in order for caregivers to be aware of them. A lack of familiarity with PTSD symptoms adds to the time and complexity of the interview process, because a proper interview must educate the respondent about each symptom while concurrently asking about each symptom.
7. Many PTSD symptoms manifest differently at different developmental stages. For example, the symptom of intrusive recollections is manifest in school-age children primarily through verbalizations, but it is manifest in many preschool-age children as reenactments in their play, which relies less heavily on verbalizations. Avoidance behaviors, restricted range of affect, diminished interest in activities, detachment from loved ones, difficulty concentrating, and irritability/outbursts of anger may also have systematic differences in presentations on the basis of age. This requires awareness on the part of the interviewer of developmental differences and flexibility in interviewing. A single stock question is not sufficient for all age periods or even for one child. Multiple ways of asking about a symptom may be needed, which again, requires time and effort.

Diagnostic Validity, Sensitivity, Specificity, and Comorbidity: Evidence for PTSD as the Core Trauma Response

The tenor of past controversies around PTSD seem to have been extreme, because PTSD is one of the rare disorders with an etiologic event, and because many claims for diagnoses have been in the context of claims for disability, financial gain, and legal manipulations. However, putting those diversions aside, the case for the validity of PTSD as a distinct diagnostic construct is as strong as for any other psychiatric disorder. PTSD is one of the most well-studied and validated disorders in longitudinal, neurobiological, and treatment response studies. Some clinicians, scholars, and other observers may be dissatisfied with the complexity and messiness of posttraumatic responses, but the data do not support a wholesale deconstruction of PTSD on the basis of false negatives or false positives. Not all of the diagnostic validity evidence can be reviewed in this space, but several major issues of practical clinical assessment are reviewed.

For a larger context in which to view assessment of children, it is worth noting that the most frequent criticism about PTSD in adults is a lack of specificity, or concerns that persons who do not really have the disorder may be diagnosed (too many false positives). For example, in one study of patients enrolling in treatment studies for depression, the group with true trauma events and the group with minor traumas both had nearly 80% rates of PTSD on the basis of structured interviews (Bodkin, Pope, Detke, & Hudson, 2007). That is, the minor trauma subjects endorsed enough Criteria B, C, and D symptoms from their events to qualify for the diagnosis. However, the authors paid only glancing attention to the issue that this was a highly selective help-seeking, depressed sample that may have had greater vulnerability to developing symptoms in reaction to minor trauma. Furthermore, no attempt was made to comparatively grade the severity of PTSD within each of those groups to explore the possibility that the minor trauma group may have had relatively less severe PTSD than did the trauma group.

Another fact that drives some concerns about specificity is the overlap between diagnostic criteria for PTSD and other internalizing disorders. Four PTSD diagnostic criteria (decreased interest in activities, sleep disturbance, restricted range of affect, and decreased concentration) overlap with MDD. Three symptoms of PTSD (decreased concentration, irritability, and sleep disturbance) overlap with GAD.

Speculating from concerns about overlap and studies such as Bodkin et al. (2007), Spitzer First, and Wakefield (2007) proposed modified diagnostic criteria for PTSD in an effort to restrict who could receive the diagnosis. The main suggestion was to eliminate five symptoms that overlapped with other disorders. In addition, the requirements for three out of seven symptoms from Criterion C plus two out of five symptoms from Criterion D were replaced with a single Criterion (Criteria C and D collapsed) of seven possible symptoms, of which four symptoms were required. These changes were unfortunately proposed in the absence of empirical data. Elhai, Grubaugh, Kashdan, and Frueh (2008) reviewed the data of 5,692 participants in the National Comorbidity Survey Replication and found that these recommendations made an insignificant effect. The recommendations only lowered the rate of PTSD from 6.81% to 6.42%. Elhai et al. (2008) concluded that "little difference was found between the criteria sets in diagnostic comorbidity and disability, structural validity, and internal consistency" (p. 597).

In contrast, the prominent concern in the child literature has not been about specificity, because historically, the issue in the clinical trenches is that children have been underrecognized as having internalizing symptoms and not overdiagnosed. In other words, the concern has been lack of sensitivity rather than lack of specificity. When PTSD was first being recognized in adults, disbelief was expressed at the notion that children could also manifest the disorder (Benedek, 1985). This phenomenon could have been the result of misunderstandings on the part of adult clinicians about the true developmental capacities of children. However, even among trained child clinicians, recognition of PTSD in clinics can be lacking or slow. One can speculate that this is partly because one cannot look at a child and tell that he or she has PTSD. Returning again to the analogy of the more observable disorders of ADHD, ODD, and MDD, which one can fairly obviously see in a mental status exam (or in a classroom or a living room), PTSD is relatively less obvious. The key and pathognomonic symptoms are triggered by trauma reminders and can be uncommon. In addition, the seriousness of PTSD seems to be underestimated because victims were normal or without PTSD symptoms before the traumatic events, thus suggesting that they can simply revert back to normal with the passage of time. An analogy is memories of unpleasant personal experiences or bone fractures; people have faith that these will fade or heal with time. However, evidence presented later indicates that PTSD symptoms often do not fade with time.

PTSD is also challenged by claims that children who have been chronically exposed to interpersonal trauma in early childhood either cannot qualify for PTSD or need a better diagnosis than PTSD (van der Kolk, 2005). It has been suggested that when they are diagnosed with PTSD plus the inevitable comorbid disorder(s), this purportedly misleads clinicians to treat comorbid conditions rather than the trauma syndrome and "may run the risk of applying treatment approaches that are not helpful" (van der Kolk, p. 406). A new syndrome, *developmental trauma disorder*, was proposed, but without preliminary validity data (van der Kolk, 2005). At this point, it has not yet achieved face validity. It is interesting to note that no one has documented that the signs and symptoms in chronically and repeatedly traumatized youngsters are not adequately represented by PTSD.

Underlying these concerns about sensitivity and specificity is the high degree of comorbidity of other disorders with PTSD. In adult and child populations, PTSD occurs with at least one other disorder 80–90% of the time (Kessler, Sonnega, Bromet, Hughes, & Nelson, 1995; Scheeringa & Zeanah, 2008; Scheeringa, Zeanah, Myers, & Putnam, 2003). Implicit in the arguments made by Spitzer et al. (2007) is that comorbidity is clouding the picture; specifically, that non-PTSD symptoms are being misidentified as part of PTSD because they overlap. In adults, the common comorbid conditions include depression, anxiety, and substance abuse (Kessler et al., 1995). In one study with children 1–6 years old who had experienced heterogeneous types of trauma events, the comorbid frequencies with PTSD were 75% for ODD and 63% for SAD (Scheeringa et al., 2003). In a second study involving children who had suffered a hurricane disaster, the comorbid rates were 61% for ODD and 21% for SAD (Scheeringa & Zeanah, 2008). The types of comorbid disorders in older children and adolescents are less well-documented.

Nevertheless, there are at least three reasons why comorbidity is neither a dense conundrum nor an issue of slipshod taxonomy. First, despite the overlap of some PTSD symptoms with other disorders, there are pathognomonic symptoms of PTSD that make it distinct. No diagnoses other than acute stress disorder (ASD)include trauma-specific items such as Criteria B 1–5 (specific to traumatic reexperiencing symptoms) or Criteria C 1–3 (specific to traumatic avoidance and numbing). Thus, 8 out of 17, or nearly half of the PTSD diagnostic criteria, are unique to PTSD or partly shared by ASD. It is impossible to be diagnosed with PTSD without trauma-specific Criterion B symptoms. If one conducts a careful interview, it should not be difficult to diagnose PTSD even in the presence of other disorders.

Second, Keane, Taylor, and Penk (1997) conducted a study explicitly to address this question. They asked 340 clinicians to rate a 90-item form with items meant to reflect PTSD,

MDD, and GAD. MDD and GAD were chosen because they were supposedly two categories with which PTSD was commonly confused. The clinicians were asked to rate the extent to which each item reflected each of the three disorders on Likert scales. The findings were clear that clinicians had little difficulty distinguishing PTSD from MDD or GAD.

Third, most prior studies have had at least one of two shortcomings limiting their ability to demonstrate the precise relationship between comorbid disorders and PTSD. The first shortcoming has been a failure to ask about the temporal relationships between non-PTSD disorders and traumatic events. The second shortcoming has been a failure to consider individuals with any PTSD symptoms as PTSD cases, so therefore their posttrauma non-PTSD disorders would appear to have arisen in the absence of PTSD symptoms. For example, if an individual developed MDD and six symptoms of PTSD after a trauma, but the PTSD symptoms were not in the correct algorithm for the diagnosis, this individual would not have been counted as a PTSD case and the new MDD disorder would not have been considered as a comorbid disorder, when it should be. This could have led some observers to assume that the non-PTSD disorders developed after traumas in the absence of PTSD, when plainly this individual had substantial PTSD symptoms. A study by McMillen, North, Mosley, and Smith (2002) rectified those shortcomings by studying 162 adult flood survivors and carefully tracking the onset of all symptoms. Of all individuals that developed new, non-PTSD disorders following the flood, they all developed either full PTSD or significant PTSD symptoms. Thus, a PTSD syndrome seems to be the core posttrauma response. Comorbid disorders may or may not develop in individuals for different reasons. This finding was replicated subsequently with preschool children and with their caregivers following Hurricane Katrina (Scheeringa & Zeanah, 2008).

It is also worth noting that not all of the comorbid disorders develop following trauma. Findings from studies that have examined subjects prospectively prior to exposure to traumatic events have shown that a proportion of the comorbid conditions predate and perhaps serve as vulnerability factors for the development of PTSD. For example, when studied prior to traumatic events, 100% of 26-year-old adults who had PTSD in the last year met criteria for another mental disorder between the ages of 11 and 21 years (Koenen et al., 2008).

Age Differences in Criteria and Algorithms

Infant and preschool children. Ten studies have examined PTSD symptoms in young children using developmentally sensitive criteria (Bogat, DeJonghe, Levendosky, Davidson, & von Eye, 2006; Ghosh-Ippen, Briscoe-Smith, & Lieberman, 2004; Levendosky, Huth-Bocks, Semel, & Shapiro, 2002; Meiser-Stedman, Smith, Glucksman, Yule, & Dalgleish, 2008; Ohmi et al., 2002; Scheeringa, Peebles, Cook, & Zeanah, 2001; Scheeringa & Zeanah, 2008; Scheeringa, Zeanah, Drell, & Larrieu, 1995; Scheeringa et al., 2003; Stoddard et al., 2006) compared to two studies that have examined alternative diagnostic algorithms in school-age children and adolescents (Meiser-Stedman et al., 2008; Scheeringa, Wright, Hunt, & Zeanah, 2006). Thus, the field of PTSD is in an unusual place in that diagnostic validity has been more meticulously studied in young children than in school-age and adolescent children. On the basis of findings from these studies, PTSD can be reliably detected in young children, and an alternative diagnostic algorithm appears more developmentally sensitive and valid than the *DSM-IV* criteria. Also, longitudinal studies have indicated that children do not simply grow out of PTSD symptoms and may have a more unremitting course than adults (McFarlane, 1987; Scheeringa, Zeanah, Myers, & Putnam, 2005; Shaw, Applegate, & Schorr, 1996).

One main challenge with infant and preschool children is that symptomatology depends on verbalizations from the individuals, which makes them difficult to detect in preverbal or barely verbal children. For example, detection of the item *avoidance of thoughts, feelings, or conversations associated with the traumatic event* requires children to verbalize that they experienced these phenomena. This item may be detected somewhat from behavioral observations of avoidance, but this requires an adult's presence to observe, infer, and report on the child's behavioral reactions. A second main challenge is that symptoms that are experienced internally are difficult or impossible to detect, even when an adult is present to observe. This holds true even for young children who have developed narrative language capacities. This capacity to self-report on any internalized symptomatology gradually emerges with age, but it is not yet a mature skill in young children.

It was clear from reviewing signs and symptoms of highly symptomatic, traumatized young children that they could not meet the algorithm for the *DSM-IV* diagnosis of PTSD (Scheeringa et al., 1995). This was largely due to the requirement for three avoidance and numbing (Criterion C) items. The seven avoidance and numbing items are also the most internal of the 17 possible PTSD criteria. If the requirement for the numbing and avoidance items were lowered to one item, then young children could qualify for the diagnosis at reasonable rates (Scheeringa et al., 1995; Scheeringa et al., 2001; Scheeringa et al., 2003).

The algorithm change is the main change, but the following changes in wording of five items have also been proposed (see Table 1).

1. Do not require the Criterion A2 item that the child's response at the time of the traumatic event involved helplessness, fear, or horror. This transient reaction cannot be known if children are preverbal or adults were not present to witness the children's reactions. The next four modifications are minor wording changes that enhance the face validity of the items for young children, but do not alter the intent of the original *DSM-IV* items.
2. For the symptom *recurrent and intrusive distressing recollections of the event*, include a note that the distress may not be obvious. Some young children spontaneously talk

Table 1
Proposed changes to wording for five *DSM-IV* Posttraumatic Stress Disorder items

DSM-IV #	*DSM-IV* wording	Proposed change
A.2	Person's response at the time of the event involved helplessness, fear, or horror	For young children, make this optional if there was no adult present to witness the children's reactions
B.1	Recurrent and intrusive distressing recollections of the event	Note: For young children, distress not required
C.4	Markedly diminished interest or participation in significant activities	Note: For young children, significant activities may be play, social interactions, and daily routines
C.5	Feeling of detachment or estrangement from others	Note: For young children, may appear as social withdrawal from loved ones or acquaintances
D.2	Irritability or outbursts of anger	Add: or new temper tantrums

about or play out their intrusive traumatic recollections, but they do not appear obviously distressed. The reason for this is unclear. The initial intuitive interpretation may be to assume that children who do not show distress are less severe overall. However, there is some evidence from maltreated children that appearing less distressed may reflect a worse prognosis. In a study of adolescent and young adult women who had experienced sexual abuse, those who expressed positive affect when discussing their abuse had poorer long-term social adjustment than did those who expressed negative affect (Bonanno et al., 2007).

3. For the item *markedly diminished interest or participation in significant activities*, it makes relatively more sense to ask about significant activities in terms of play, social interactions, and daily routines.
4. The item *feeling of detachment or estrangement from others* (a highly internal phenomenon) should be asked in more behavioral terms such as social withdrawal from loved ones or acquaintances.
5. When asking about the item *irritability or outbursts of anger*, it makes reasonable sense to include inquiry about new or extreme temper tantrums.

Using an alternative algorithm and sets of criteria that were similar to the wording changes recommended above, seven studies have now calculated rates of PTSD in head-to-head comparisons with the *DSM-IV* rules (see Table 2). The last column of Table 2 also reports the mean number of PTSD symptoms for five of the studies. The frequencies of

Table 2

Head-to-head comparisons of DSM-IV and alternative algorithm frequencies of diagnoses in six studies of young children

	Age range (years)	*DSM-IV* diagnosis frequency (%)	Alternative algorithm[a] frequency (%)	Mean number of PTSD symptoms in alternative algorithm cases
Scheeringa et al., 1995; $n = 12$ (clinic)	1–4	13	69	Not reported
Scheeringa et al., 2001; $n = 15$ (clinic)	1–3	20	60	9.9
Ohmi et al., 2002; $n = 32$	2–6	0	25	6.1
Scheeringa et al., 2003; $n = 62$	1–6	0	26	6.1
Meiser-Stedman et al., 2008; $n = 156$	2–6	1.7	10	10.0
Scheeringa et al., 2008; $n = 70$	3–6	15.7	50	7.8
Levendosky et al., 2002; $n = 62$	3–5	3	26	Not reported

[a]Scheeringa et al. (1995), Scheeringa et al. (2001), Levendosky et al. (2002), and Ohmi et al. (2002) used an earlier algorithm that required a total of four symptoms: one Criterion B reexperiencing, one Criterion C numbing/avoidance, one Criterion D increased arousal, and one from a new criterion consisting of three items (new fears not related to the trauma, new separation anxiety, and new aggression. Criterion C included a new item called *developmental regressions*. The three later studies used an algorithm that also required a total of four symptoms but in a different algorithm: one from Criterion B, one from Criterion C, and two from Criterion D.

PTSD in young children identified by using the *DSM-IV* rules are considerably lower than the frequencies identified by using the alternative algorithm. When coupled with the observation that children diagnosed by the alternative rules were highly symptomatic (6.1 to 10.0 symptoms), this suggests that *DSM-IV* criteria require some modification for use in young children. Note that lowering the threshold for Criterion C has been suggested even for adults, because highly symptomatic and impaired adults could not be given the diagnosis if they had only two but not three Criterion C symptoms (Kilpatrick & Resnick, 1993).

One additional note is that research has also identified four items of symptomatology that were commonly shown by young children but were not present in the *DSM-IV*. These four items are (a) regression in skills (e.g., verbal skills, dressing skills, toileting), (b) new onset separation anxiety, (c) new onset aggression, and (e) new onset of fears of things not related to the trauma (e.g., the dark, going to the bathroom alone). Including these items in the diagnostic criteria did not increase the diagnostic sensitivity (Scheeringa et al., 2003). Regardless, these items still may have other uses, such as for constituents of dimensional symptom checklists or treatment outcome measures.

School-age and adolescent children. The two studies that examined diagnostic algorithms in school-age children also found suggestive evidence that the *DSM-IV* algorithm was not sensitive enough to diagnose children who were highly symptomatic and functionally impaired. A small study of 11 acute injury victims ages 7 to 11 years found a frequency of PTSD diagnosis of 18.2% by the alternative 1B/1C/2D algorithm versus 9.1% by *DSM-IV* criteria (Scheeringa et al., 2006). A study of 52 motor vehicle accident victims ages 7 to 10 years found a frequency of diagnosis of 18.8% by the 1B/1C/2D algorithm versus 2.1% by *DSM-IV* criteria (Meiser-Stedman et al., 2008); the 1B/1C/2D cases had a mean of 11.6 *DSM-IV* symptoms (by combined parent and child reports). Again, it seems implausible that children who have so many PTSD symptoms and impairment should not meet the diagnostic threshold for PTSD.

Course

Most individuals who experience truly life-threatening traumas show some symptoms of PTSD within the first month (Davidson, Hughes, Blazer, & George, 1991), but most of these individuals are resilient and do not experience enduring symptoms. Approximately 70% lose those symptoms over the first month, and only 30% tend to have enduring symptoms (Kessler et al., 1995). This fits fairly well with the *DSM-IV* requirement that symptoms must be present for 1 month before a diagnosis is made (keeping in mind, however, that those who eventually qualify for the diagnosis have been symptomatic the entire first month and could have been receiving treatment). Thus, most individuals exposed to life-threatening events do not develop PTSD. In particular, longitudinal studies have demonstrated four trajectories of symptoms: (a) a resilient group of people who develop symptoms but show quick recovery within the first month following severe trauma, or show no symptoms in the first month following less-severe traumas; (b) those who develop symptoms but show substantial naturalistic recovery over the first 1 to 2 years (symptoms with recovery); (c) those who develop unremitting symptoms (chronic PTSD) ; and (d) those with delayed onset (Bonanno, Rennicke, & Dekel, 2005).

These trajectories indicate that for those who develop PTSD, it becomes a chronic illness in approximately 50% of patients (Davidson & Fairbank, 1993). Despite this course, the majority of longitudinal studies in adults have shown significant naturalistic reduction in mean symptoms over time, even if the signs and symptoms do not completely disappear.

In children, prospective studies are not yet common, but the early studies have suggested a pattern of relatively more unremitting and chronic PTSD. Scheeringa et al. (2005) studied 62 children ages 1 to 6 years with mixed traumatic experiences and found significant stability of symptoms over two years. The group that had been diagnosed by the 1B/1C/2D algorithm at Time 1 had an estimated mean of 6.1 PTSD symptoms, which did not diminish by as much as one symptom over two years. In a prospective design, Meiser-Stedman and colleagues (2008) found that 69% of preschool children diagnosed with the 1B/1C/2D algorithm at 2 to 4 weeks posttrauma retained the diagnosis six months later. A prospective study of 808 Australian schoolchildren (mean age = 8.2 years) showed no decrease in stress symptoms 26 months after a bushfire (McFarlane, 1987). Last, 70% of a sample of children ages 6 to 11 years (n = 30) were still in the moderate to severe category of posttraumatic stress symptoms 21 months after surviving Hurricane Andrew (Shaw, Applegate, & Schorr, 1996).

Unremitting PTSD takes on new salience in early childhood during a time of uniquely rapid brain development. Given the speculations about potentially permanent alterations in the developing brain from early traumas (Perry, Pollard, Blakley, Baker, & Vigilante, 1995), these preliminary data raise concerns about the chronicity of PTSD symptomatology in young children. It should be important to identify the risk factors for chronic PTSD in children, but progress on this issue is underdeveloped. At this point, data can only be extrapolated from adult studies that have preliminarily identified factors that predict chronic PTSD (as opposed to developing PTSD that remits naturally to some degree). Unfortunately, just as the development of PTSD does not appear to be accounted for by only a few risk factors, chronic PTSD also appears to be multifactorial. For example, in a prospective study of 205 assault victims who were assessed using one of the more comprehensive and well-chosen batteries of 13 potential predictor variables, eight of the variables significantly predicted PTSD after 6 months (Kleim, Ehlers, & Glucksman, 2007). The combination of the best three predictors (mental defeat, rumination about the trauma, and prior psychological problems) accounted for only 47% of the variance.

Parenting and PTSD

Scheeringa and Zeanah (2001) reviewed 17 studies that met the following inclusion criteria: (a) children had been exposed to a *DSM-IV* level trauma, (b) the children and parents were assessed concurrently, and (c) the studies used measures that were standardized and replicable. All but one of those studies found a significant association between an aspect of poor parental functioning and less adaptive child outcome. The poor child outcomes most often were PTSD symptoms. The parental variables included PTSD, depression, anxiety, overprotectiveness, less family cohesion, family chaos, and perceived less supportiveness. In a study of sexually abused preschool children treated with cognitive behavioral therapy, higher parental emotional distress and depression symptoms at the beginning of treatment predicted which children improved less (Cohen & Mannarino, 1996). Because of the acknowledged importance of the parent–child relationship for a variety of functions, it is tempting to speculate from these studies that parents who are more symptomatic are less able to protect their children, who then experience more intense symptomatology.

However, a study involving 95 children ages 7 to 12 years (the first to use an observational rating of parenting in relation to domestic violence) showed no simple direction of influence (Levendosky & Graham-Bermann, 2000). After statistical control for demographics, past abuse toward the mother, maternal depression, and observed maternal warmth did not predict child outcomes. Observed maternal authority-control was predictive of child behavior, but the chicken-or-the-egg question could not be answered by this study design. In other words, children may not have been reacting to their parent's rearing style, but the parent's rearing style might have been a reaction to their children's characteristics.

In addition, other data with preschool children have failed to support the notion that parents affect children's symptoms following trauma. In the study mentioned earlier by Scheeringa et al. (2003), parents and children were observed while interacting in structured and unstructured activities, including 5 min of free play, 1–2 min of clean-up, and 20 min for four structured puzzle tasks (Crowell, Feldman, & Ginsberg, 1988). The final tasks increased in difficulty so that the third and fourth tasks were too difficult for the child to complete alone, thus increasing the demand for dyadic collaboration. Two raters were trained to reliability with an expert rater. Caregivers were rated on a 7-point Likert scale (with higher scores meaning better qualities) on the following variables: (a) behavioral responsiveness, (b) emotional responsiveness, (c) positive affect, (d) withdrawal/depression, (e) irritability/anger, (f) verbal aggression, (g) positive discipline during clean-up, and (h) negative discipline during clean up.

These previously unpublished observational data were available on 14 children diagnosed with PTSD by the 1B/1C/2D algorithm, 38 children who had symptoms of PTSD but not enough for the diagnosis (trauma/no PTSD group), and 61 non–trauma-exposed controls. As expected, the caregivers of the PTSD children were significantly more symptomatic for PTSD and depression. Contrary to expectations, the caregivers of the PTSD children scored highest on emotional responsiveness (see Figure 1). In addition, the caregivers of the PTSD children showed higher positive affect that was marginally significant, which was again contrary to expectations. There were no differences on the other variables.

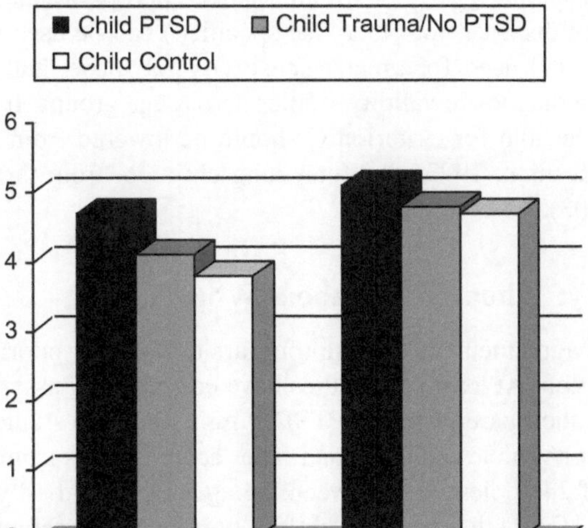

Figure 1. Observed parenting qualities of caregivers with children with posttraumatic stress disorder (child PTSD), caregivers with children with PTSD symptoms but not PTSD (trauma/no PTSD), and caregivers of nonexposed children (child control). Child PTSD diagnosed by the alternative 1B/1C/2D algorithm. Caregivers of the child PTSD group scored significantly higher emotional responsiveness than did caregivers of the child control group in a Wilcoxon rank-sum pairwise test ($p < .05$) after a significant three-group Kruskal-Wallis test. Caregivers of the child PTSD group showed marginally significant higher positive affect than did the other caregivers (Kruskal-Wallis test $p = .06$).

Therefore, it would be difficult to conclude from these data that negative parenting led to more severe children's PTSD symptoms.

These first observational data of parent–child interaction for children with PTSD symptoms provide a different perspective than the 17 self-report studies reviewed by Scheeringa and Zeanah (2001). These findings serve as a gentle caution in drawing premature conclusions about the directionality of effects before the data are in. The direction of effects caused by parent–child relationships on children's and parents' symptomatology following trauma is still unknown.

Symptomatic and Impaired, But Not Diagnosed

Like any medical or psychiatric diagnosis in which symptomatology exists on a continuum of severity (Angold, Costello, & Farmer, 1999), a PTSD diagnosis dichotomy underestimates the number of children with symptom-related functional impairment. Children with interpersonal trauma ages 7 to 14 years who met PTSD diagnostic criteria in only two out of the three Criteria B, C, and D had the same level of functional impairment as did children who had full PTSD diagnoses (Carrion, Weems, Ray, & Reiss, 2002). When preschool children who suffered heterogeneous types of trauma were reassessed one year after their first assessment, significantly more were functionally impaired in at least one domain (48.9%) versus those who had the full diagnosis of PTSD (23.4%; $n = 47$); the gap was even greater after 2 years (74.3% impaired vs. 22.9% diagnosed; $n = 35$; Scheeringa et al., 2005).

Current practice parameters have recommended that children with clinically significant impairment levels of PTSD symptoms, regardless of diagnostic status, should be provided with evidence-supported treatment options (Cohen & American Academy of Child & Adolescent Psychiatry, 1998). An alternative appropriate diagnosis (e.g., adjustment disorder; anxiety disorder not otherwise specified) can be used if PTSD diagnostic criteria are not met. This need for greater sensitivity for those that need treatment has also been supported in diagnostic validity studies across age groups. It has been suggested that for adults, the threshold for Criterion C should be lowered from three to two symptoms (Kilpatrick & Resnick, 1993) and for young children, from three to one symptom (Scheeringa et al., 2003).

Procedural Validity: Whom to Ask about What?

Children and parental agreement about symptoms are notoriously poor; however, each provides unique information. At least two studies have concurrently assessed the frequencies at which children and their parents report PTSD symptoms. Both studies sampled children who experienced motor vehicle accidents and other acute injuries from emergency departments. In a sample of 24 adolescents between the ages of 12 and 18 years, 8.3% met the threshold for the 1B/1C/2D diagnosis by child report, 4.2% by parent report, and 37.5% by combined report (Scheeringa et al., 2006). In a sample of 51 children between the ages of 7 and 10 years, 17.8% met the 1B/1C/2D diagnosis by child report, 18.8% by parent report, and 40.0% by combined report (Meiser-Stedman et al., 2008).

Given this well-established finding that parents and children each contribute unique information about children's psychopathology, for which the combination of information is significantly greater than each separately, the ideal assessment of young children should include both informants. Unfortunately, interviewing children younger than 7 years of age is not feasible, because they have not yet mastered multiple types of skills needed for this task. Despite some advances in this area with 5- and 6-year-old children, most notably with the Berkeley Puppet Interview (Measelle, Ablow, Cowan, & Cowan, 1998), there is little reason to believe that children younger than 5 years would have sufficient skills, and there have been no known studies with children younger than 7 years on their accuracy to self-report in relation to diagnoses. Therefore, assessments of disorders in young children using current techniques are practically dependent on interviews of their caregivers.

An attempt was made to systematically elicit PTSD symptom information from 1- to 3-year-old children in a study with structured and unstructured interaction formats (Scheeringa et al., 2001). The interactions were designed to be those that could be realistically used in a clinic assessment setting (e.g., caregiver–child free play, or examiner-guided trauma reenactment play). Only 12% of the children's symptoms that were reported from parental interviews could be detected from observations and interactions with them.

Even when relying on caregivers' reports, there is cause for concern that interviews about young children may be less reliable and/or valid compared to older age groups for which there are more established norms for problem behaviors. Nevertheless, when examined empirically, the first reported psychometrics for an early childhood diagnostic instrument showed promising results (Scheeringa et al., 2001). The parents of 15 children ages 1 to 3 years were interviewed with the Posttraumatic Stress Disorder Semi-Structured Interview and Observational Record for Infants and Young Children (Scheeringa & Zeanah, 2005). When two clinicians rated videotapes of these interviews, the inter-rater reliability was substantial, with a Cohen's kappa of 0.74. Subsequently, the largest demonstration of the feasibility of interviewing caregivers of young children has come from a study with the Preschool Age Psychiatric Assessment (PAPA; Egger et al., 2006), which was the first multidisorder instrument with published psychometric properties. The PAPA was used to interview caregivers of 307 children ages 2 to 5 years recruited from a general pediatric clinic for 12 disorders (Egger et al., 2006). Categorical agreement for PTSD was good with a Cohen's kappa of .73, and continuous agreement was good with an intraclass correlation coefficient of .56.

Interviewing Method

The aforementioned implications for interviewing respondents are organized into the following practical suggestions.

1. Professionals must be aware that young children can develop PTSD. Only then can appropriate screening and assessment referrals be triggered.
2. Even with older children, self-reports of symptoms are rarely spontaneous; only systematic probing will successfully elicit accurate data.
3. When conducting assessments, developmentally appropriate measures and criteria must be used so as not to miss the diagnosis.
4. When new-onset comorbid disorders arise following trauma (typically ODD and SAD in young children), this should trigger a full assessment for PTSD.
5. While the *DSM-IV* criteria do not restrict making the diagnosis on the basis of a single traumatic event, standardized instruments for PTSD often ask respondents to select the worst traumatic event that he or she experienced and to rate all PTSD symptoms in relation to that specific event. However, one recent study indicated that 37% of all children in the United States have experienced more than one potentially traumatic event (Copeland et al., 2007). It is often difficult for children—young children in particular—to select only one traumatic event as the worst that they have experienced. Because it

does not make sense clinically to restrict attention to only a portion of children's PTSD symptoms, it seems logical that an instrument should be comprehensive and assess all PTSD symptoms from all past events.

6. To minimize false positives and false negatives, one must conduct a comprehensive, standardized, and rigorous interview for all 17 symptoms of PTSD. In particular, one must ask from a menu of probes and ask for examples, onsets, durations, and frequencies. This means using a structured instrument.
7. Most important, clinicians must probe further than asking, "Does your child have *x* symptom?" A simple yes/no response can mean almost anything. One has to obtain examples. If the respondent cannot provide examples, the interviewer must provide possible examples. This type of educational interviewing gives respondents a frame of reference for the internalized and abstract items that comprise signs of PTSD. This is in contrast to other types of symptomatology, such as hyperactivity or depression, which are readily observable and intuitively obvious to most people. PTSD symptoms are not intuitively obvious or experienced by most people. Concerns that this type of interviewing is inappropriate because it leads the witness who will then endorse symptoms that do not exist are typically unjustified. Such concerns that respondents endorse symptoms that do not exist are justified for malingerers, but there is little evidence that this occurs in general practice, especially in respect to young children. Also, there is the failsafe technique that the gathering of examples will always be able to support or disprove a respondent's answer.

Treatment Implications

Evidence-based treatments now exist for children with PTSD of nearly all ages. The major issue is not whether these treatments work, but whether children who need them receive access to them, as they are undoubtedly underused. For example, rapid-needs assessments conducted immediately after the September 11th attacks (Herman, Felton, & Susser, 2002) and the Hurricane Katrina disaster (Dalton, Scheeringa, & Zeanah, 2008) estimated that 520,000 and 260,612 individuals respectively would develop PTSD. Treatment capacity could never treat that many children, but even if it could, the assessment challenges and obstacles to disorder recognition noted earlier would prevent many thousands from getting treatment.

Despite the well-known phenomenon of comorbid disorders with PTSD from all types of traumatic events (Scheeringa et al., 2003) and claims of cases receiving inappropriate treatment for their comorbid disorders (van der Kolk, 2005), there is little evidence that comorbid disorders themselves cause incorrect treatment decisions. Instead, it is more likely that if inappropriate treatment decisions are being made, it is because clinicians are not appropriately assessing for PTSD. If confusion exists from the presence of comorbidity, it is not inherently a flaw of the taxonomy system in general or PTSD in particular. Good history-taking about the timing of symptom onset and understanding that PTSD is the underlying basis of new disorders after trauma exposure should contribute substantially to accurate diagnosis and treatment planning.

There are few data on whether having a second (or third) disorder makes it more difficult to treat PTSD, or vice versa, whether having PTSD makes it more difficult to treat a coexisting disorder. It would be intuitive to hypothesize that a cumulative load of disorders predicts greater chronicity and greater treatment resistance. This is an important area of research that may help identify subsets of children with different courses and different biomarker profiles who would require alternative treatment modalities in order to achieve equivalent effect sizes.

Although the brief data presented earlier on parenting issues suggests an important direction for assessing parent and family issues, as well as for attempting to understand more clearly the effect of those issues on child behavior, caution is warranted in attributing directionality. There is no evidence that children cannot improve when treated with evidence-based therapy, regardless of the degree of parental symptomatology or family dynamics. The number of controlled studies investigating the addition of parents to children's treatment has been extremely limited and has generally not supported adding parental components to therapy (Deblinger, Steer, & Lippmann, 1999). It is also noteworthy that even in the Cohen et al. (1996) study mentioned earlier, which suggested that young children who had more depressed parents at the beginning of therapy improved less than children with less depressed parents, the children who had more depressed parents still improved substantially with therapy. In other words, having relatively more depressed parents did not prevent the young children from improving overall. It would be premature, for example, to withhold or delay treatment for children while parents are referred to their own treatment; however, more research is needed on combined parent treatment trials and other treatment methods to target parent–child relationship issues that might facilitate treatment for young children.

References

American Psychiatric Association. (1980). *Diagnostic and statistical manual of mental disorders* (3rd ed.). Washington, DC: Author.

American Psychiatric Association. (1994). *Diagnostic and statistical manual of mental disorders* (4th ed.). Washington, DC: Author.

Angold, A., Costello, E., & Farmer, E. (1999). Impaired but undiagnosed. *Journal of the American Academy of Child and Adolescent Psychiatry*, *38*, 129–137.

Benedek, E. P. (1985). Children and psychic trauma: A brief review of contemporary thinking. In S. Eth & R. S. Pynoos (Eds.), *Post-traumatic stress disorder in children* (pp. 1–16). Washington, DC: American Psychiatric Publishing.

Bodkin, J. A., Pope, H. G., Detke, M. J., & Hudson, J. I. (2007). Is PTSD caused by traumatic stress? *Journal of Anxiety Disorders*, *21*, 176–182.

Bogat, G., DeJonghe, E., Levendosky, A., Davidson, W., & von Eye, A. (2006). Trauma symptoms among infants exposed to intimate partner violence. *Child Abuse and Neglect*, *30*, 109–125.

Bonanno, G. A., Colak, D. M., Keltner, D., Shiota, M. N., Papa, A., Noll, J. G., et al. (2007). Context matters: The benefits and costs of expressing positive emotion among survivors of childhood sexual abuse. *Emotion*, *7*, 824–837.

Bonanno, G. A., Rennicke, C., & Dekel, S. (2005). Self-enhancement among high-exposure survivors of the September 11th terrorist attack: Resilience or social maladjustment? *Journal of Personality and Social Psychology*, *88*, 984–999.

Carrion, V. G., Weems, C. F., Ray, R., & Reiss, A. L. (2002). Toward an empirical definition of pediatric PTSD: The phenomenology of PTSD symptoms in youth. *Journal of the American Academy of Child and Adolescent Psychiatry*, *41*, 166–173.

Cohen, J., & American Academy of Child & Adolescent Psychiatry. (1998). Practice parameters for the assessment and treatment of children and adolescents with posttraumatic stress disorder. *Journal of the American Academy of Child and Adolescent Psychiatry*, *37*, 4S–26S.

Cohen, J., & Mannarino, A. (1996). Factors that mediate treatment outcome of sexually abused preschool children. *Journal of the American Academy of Child and Adolescent Psychiatry*, *35*, 1402–1410.

Cohen, J., & Scheeringa, M. (2009). Post-traumatic stress disorder diagnosis in children: challenges and promises. *Dialogues in Clinical Neuroscience*, *11*(1), 91–99.

Copeland, W. E., Keeler, G., Angold, A., & Costello, E. J. (2007). Traumatic events and posttraumatic stress in childhood. *Archives of General Psychiatry*, *64*, 577–584.

Crowell, J. A., Feldman, S. S., & Ginsberg, N. (1988). Assessment of mother–child interaction in preschoolers with behavior problems. *Journal of the American Academy of Child and Adolescent Psychiatry*, *27*, 303–311.

Dalton, R., Scheeringa, M. S., & Zeanah, C. H. (2008). Did the prevalence of PTSD following Hurricane Katrina match a rapid needs assessment prediction? A template for future public planning after large-scale disasters. *Psychiatric Annals*, *38*, 134–141.

Davidson, J., & Fairbank, J. (1993). The epidemiology of posttraumatic stress disorder. In J. Davidson & E. Foa (Eds.), *Posttraumatic stress disorder: DSM-IV and beyond* (pp. 147–169). Washington, DC: American Psychiatric Press.

Davidson, J., Hughes, G., Blazer, D., & George, L. (1991). Posttraumatic stress disorder in the community: An epidemiologic study. *Psychological Medicine*, *21*, 713–721.

Deblinger, E., Steer, R. A., & Lippmann, J. (1999). Two-year follow-up study of cognitive behavioral therapy for sexually abused children suffering post-traumatic stress symptoms. *Child Abuse and Neglect*, *23*, 1371–1378.

Egger, H. L., Erkanli, A., Keeler, G., Potts, E., Walter, B. K., & Angold, A. (2006). Test–retest reliability of the Preschool Age Psychiatric Assessment (PAPA). *Journal of the American Academy of Child and Adolescent Psychiatry*, *45*, 538–549.

Elhai, J. D., Grubaugh, A. L., Kashdan, T. B., & Frueh, B. C. (2008). Empirical examination of a proposed refinement to *DSM-IV* posttraumatic stress disorder symptom criteria using the National Comorbidity Survey Replication data. *Journal of Clinical Psychiatry*, *69*, 597–602.

Ghosh-Ippen, C. G., Briscoe-Smith, A., & Lieberman, A. F. (2004, November). *PTSD symptomatology in young children.* Paper presented at the International Society for Traumatic Stress Studies 20th Annual Meeting, New Orleans, LA.

Herman, D., Felton, C., & Susser, E. (2002). Mental health needs in New York State following the September 11th attacks. *Journal of Urban Health*, *79*, 322–331.

Keane, T. M., Taylor, K. L., & Penk, W. E. (1997). Differentiating post-traumatic stress disorder (PTSD) from major depression (MDD) and generalized anxiety disorder (GAD). *Journal of Anxiety Disorders*, *11*, 317–328.

Kessler, R., Sonnega, A., Bromet, E., Hughes, M., & Nelson, C. (1995). Posttraumatic stress disorder in the National Comorbidity Survey. *Archives of General Psychiatry*, *52*, 1048–1060.

Kilpatrick, K., & Resnick, H. (1993). Posttraumatic stress disorder associated with exposure to criminal victimization in clinical and community populations. In J. Davidson & E. Foa (Eds.), *Posttraumatic stress disorder: DSM-IV and beyond* (pp. 113–143). Washington, DC: American Psychiatric Press.

Kleim, B., Ehlers, A., & Glucksman, E. (2007). Early predictors of chronic post-traumatic stress disorder in assault survivors. *Psychological Medicine*, *37*, 1457–1467.

Koenen, K. C., Mofitt, T. E., Caspi, A., Gregory, A., Harrington, H., & Poulton, R. (2008). The developmental mental disorder histories of adults with posttraumatic stress disorder: A prospective longitudinal birth cohort study. *Journal of Abnormal Psychology*, *117*, 460–466.

Levendosky, A., & Graham-Bermann, S. (2000). Behavioral observations of parenting in battered women. *Journal of Family Psychology*, *14*(1), 80–94.

Levendosky, A. A., Huth-Bocks, A. C., Semel, M. A., & Shapiro, D. L. (2002). Trauma symptoms in preschool-age children exposed to domestic violence. *Journal of Interpersonal Violence*, *17*, 150–164.

McFarlane, A. (1987). Posttraumatic phenomena in a longitudinal study of children following a natural disaster. *Journal of the American Academy of Child and Adolescent Psychiatry*, *26*, 764–769.

McMillen, C., North, C., Mosley, M., & Smith, E. (2002). Untangling the psychiatric comorbidity of posttraumatic stress disorder in a sample of flood survivors. *Comprehensive Psychiatry*, *43*, 478–485.

Measelle, J. R., Ablow, J. C., Cowan, P. A., & Cowan, C. P. (1998). Assessing young children's views of their academic, social, and emotional lives: An evaluation of the self-perception scales of the Berkeley Puppet Interview. *Child Development, 69*, 1556–1576.

Meiser-Stedman, R., Smith, P., Glucksman, E., Yule, W., & Dalgleish, T. (2008). The posttraumatic stress disorder diagnosis in preschool- and elementary school-age children exposed to motor vehicle accidents. *American Journal of Psychiatry, 165*, 1326–1337.

Ohmi, H., Kojima, S., Awai, Y., Kamata, S., Sasaki, K., Tanaka, Y., et al. (2002). Post-traumatic stress disorder in pre-school aged children after a gas explosion. *European Journal of Pediatrics, 161*, 643–648.

Perry, B., Pollard, R., Blakley, T., Baker, W., & Vigilante, D. (1995). Childhood trauma, the neurobiology of adaptation, and "use-dependent" development of the brain: How "states" become "traits." *Infant Mental Health Journal, 16*, 271–291.

Scheeringa, M. S., Peebles, C. D., Cook, C. A., & Zeanah, C. H. (2001). Toward establishing procedural, criterion, and discriminant validity for PTSD in early childhood. *Journal of the American Academy of Child and Adolescent Psychiatry, 40*(1), 52–60.

Scheeringa, M. S., & Zeanah, C. H. (2001). A relational perspective on PTSD in early childhood. *Journal of Traumatic Stress, 14*, 799–815.

Scheeringa, M. S., & Zeanah, C. H. (2005). *Posttraumatic Stress Disorder Semi-Structured Interview and Observational Record for Infants and Young Children, Version 1.4*. New Orleans, LA: Tulane University Health Sciences Center.

Scheeringa, M. S., & Zeanah, C. H. (2008). Reconsideration of harm's way: Onsets and comorbidity patterns in preschool children and their caregivers following Hurricane Katrina. *Journal of Clinical Child and Adolescent Psychology, 37*, 508–518.

Scheeringa, M. S., Zeanah, C. H., Drell, M. J., & Larrieu, J. A. (1995). Two approaches to the diagnosis of posttraumatic stress disorder in infancy and early childhood. *Journal of the American Academy of Child and Adolescent Psychiatry, 34*, 191–200.

Scheeringa, M. S., Zeanah, C. H., Myers, L., & Putnam, F. W. (2003). New findings on alternative criteria for PTSD in preschool children. *Journal of the American Academy of Child and Adolescent Psychiatry, 42*, 561–570.

Scheeringa, M. S., Zeanah, C. H., Myers, L., & Putnam, F. W. (2005). Predictive validity in a prospective follow-up of PTSD in preschool children. *Journal of the American Academy of Child and Adolescent Psychiatry, 44*, 899–906.

Scheeringa, M. S., Wright, M., Hunt, J., & Zeanah, C. H. (2006). Factors affecting the diagnosis and prediction of PTSD symptomatology in children and adolescents. *American Journal of Psychiatry, 163*, 644–651.

Shaw, J., Applegate, B., & Schorr, C. (1996). Twenty-one-month follow-up study of school-age children exposed to Hurricane Andrew. *Journal of the American Academy of Child and Adolescent Psychiatry, 35*, 359–364.

Spitzer, R. L., First, M. B., & Wakefield, J. C. (2007). Saving PTSD from itself in *DSM-V*. *Journal of Anxiety Disorders, 21*, 233–241.

Stoddard, F., Saxe, G., Ronfeldt, H., Drake, J., Burns, J., Edgren, C., et al. (2006). Acute stress symptoms in young children with burns. *Journal of the American Academy of Child and Adolescent Psychiatry, 45*(1), 87–93.

van der Kolk, B. (2005). Developmental trauma disorder. *Psychiatric Annals, 35*, 401–408.

Clinical Considerations in Assessing Trauma and PTSD in Adolescents

MANDY HABIB AND VICTOR LABRUNA

North Shore University Hospital and Hofstra – North Shore LIJ School of Medicine

The developmental tasks and underlying neurobiological development associated with adolescence result in high rates of traumatization and posttraumatic stress disorder for this age group. Although the development of new measures is ongoing, assessing traumatized adolescents continues to present challenges. This article outlines some of the issues complicating an accurate assessment of trauma and posttraumatic stress disorder. Inaccuracies inherent in reporting traumatic exposure and associated sequelae are confounded by varying definitions of trauma, chronicity or multiplicity of exposure, and developmental factors unique to adolescence. Considerations in conducting thorough assessments are reviewed, with a focus on understanding the factors underlying the unintentional minimization and/or active concealment of traumatic events and trauma symptoms. Suggestions for enhancing assessment accuracy are offered, and treatment implications are discussed.

Prevalence Rates

Rates of exposure to violence in children and adolescents are alarmingly high, with survivors oftentimes experiencing multiple layers of traumatic exposure. In a national survey of more than 2,000 children and youth, 71% had experienced at least one form of victimization within the past year, with three incidences on average (Finkelhor, Ormrod, & Turner, 2007a). In a large community sample of 1,420 adolescents followed longitudinally, approximately 68% had experienced at least one traumatic event by the age of 16 years (Copeland, Keeler, Angold, & Costello, 2007). Findings from a national survey of more than 4,000 adolescents placed lifetime prevalence rates of posttraumatic stress disorder (PTSD) at 8.1% for youth between the ages of 12 and 17 years (Kilpatrick & Saunders, 2003), with greater lifetime prevalence observed among older adolescents. International studies have also found high rates of traumatization and PTSD in adolescents (Elklit & Petersen, 2008). These rates increase substantially with the inclusion of subclinical symptoms or partial PTSD (Copeland et al., 2007).

It is not surprising that research has indicated that the experience of chronic trauma (i.e., number of incidences of the same type of trauma) as well as multiple types of victimization (e.g., physical abuse, sexual abuse, witnessing domestic violence, community violence, bullying) predicts symptom severity (Finkelhor, Ormrod, & Turner, 2007b;

Ford, Stockton, Kaltman, & Green, 2006) and symptom complexity (i.e., greater number of symptom types; Briere, Kaltman, & Green, 2008). While youth exposed to trauma frequently develop PTSD, symptoms often extend beyond diagnostic criteria for post-traumatic stress and include a range of comorbid conditions such as conduct disorder, depressive disorders, anxiety disorders, and substance abuse, as well as other functional difficulties not captured by a discrete diagnostic category (Copeland et al., 2007). These symptoms, which often include significant behavioral and affective dysregulation, problems with self-perception and identity, somatic complaints, and dissociative symptoms, can derail normal developmental processes and result in poor academic and social functioning (Cook et al., 2005). Significant relational difficulties associated with trust are common and are oftentimes magnified by struggles finding a purpose and meaning in life as well as worldviews that make it difficult for adolescents to see a future for themselves.

In 2001, the Substance Abuse and Mental Health Services Administration of the U.S. Department of Health and Human Services funded the National Child Traumatic Stress Network(NCTSN). This network of academic centers and community agencies is dedicated to improving the quality of trauma-informed care. As part of a clinical treatment pilot involving numerous agencies within the NCTSN, our trauma treatment center collected information on more than 400 traumatized adolescents referred for treatment (*M* age = 15.8 years; 76% female, 24% male). Of adolescents, 72% reported difficulties in the clinical range on a standardized self-report measure of general functioning, with the majority reporting significant problems in areas related to inattention and hyperactivity, anxiety and depression, conduct problems, and high-risk psychiatric symptoms. Most notable is that nearly 80% endorsed interpersonal problems related to difficulties with trust and aggression. A subset of these adolescents completed the UCLA PTSD Reaction Index for *DSM-IV* (Pynoos, Rodriguez, Steinberg, Stuber, & Frederick, 1998), with approximately 30% meeting criteria for probable PTSD, and at least 60% exhibiting significant subclinical symptoms. These findings mirror data gathered by the National Center for Child Traumatic Stress on more than 10,000 children and adolescents. In this large sample drawn from community clinics nationwide, 25% met full criteria for PTSD with greater comorbidity associated with the experience of more traumas (Briggs-King, 2009).

PTSD Criterion A in Adolescents

When considering a diagnosis of PTSD, the *Diagnostic and Statistical Manual of Mental Disorders* (*DSM-IV-TR*; American Psychiatric Association [APA], 2000) requires the conjunctive satisfaction of a two-part definition of trauma. *Criterion A1* involves actual or threatened exposure to serious injury or violation of physical integrity to self or others, whereas *Criterion A2* refers to the individual's subjective response of extreme fear, helplessness, or horror. There is considerable debate regarding the standard that Criterion A establishes for what qualifies as a traumatic event (Spitzer, First, & Wakefield, 2007). Views range from the belief that it is too narrowly defined (e.g., it excludes emotional abuse and neglect) to the contention that it is too broadly defined, thereby allowing the possible inclusion of events not previously defined as traumatic (e.g., sexual harassment; see Rosen, Spitzer, & McHugh, 2008). These arguments are relevant to the extent that they affect the assessment of trauma exposure and the types of experiences that would meet criteria for a diagnosis of PTSD.

Many children who have experienced traumatic events do not meet criteria for PTSD (Copeland et al., 2007), a finding which may be related to the definition as well as the chronicity and frequency of trauma exposure. Children exhibiting trauma-related symptoms of reexperiencing (Criterion B), avoidance (Criterion C), and hyperarousal (Criterion D), may not meet diagnostic criteria simply because they have not experienced a stressor consistent with the A1 Criterion (e.g., if their symptoms were related to separation from a caregiver). Meanwhile, adolescents exposed to an A1 trauma may not experience the event with the requisite emotions defined in Criterion A2. For example, in the case of ongoing physical abuse, some adolescents fail to identify the abuse as traumatic if it is part of their routine life. It is not surprising that they may not exhibit threshold levels of PTSD symptoms in each of the three symptom areas. Therefore, while children and adolescents exposed to chronic or multiple traumas are more likely to develop PTSD than individuals experiencing a single-incident trauma (Copeland et al., 2007), many others experience severe trauma but do not respond with the requisite helplessness or horror, and thus do not develop PTSD. This is consistent with findings that the absence of A2 predicts the absence of PTSD (Bedard-Gilligan & Zoellner, 2008) and has led some to suggest that Criterion A may be entirely superfluous to the diagnosis, and therefore, possibly expendable (Kraemer, Wittmann, Jenewein, Maier, & Schnyder, 2009; Maier, 2006).

However, as with Criterion A1, others have posited a more expanded definition of Criterion A2, one which would reflect a more phenomenologically driven approach that includes alternate possible reactions to the stressor, such as feelings of betrayal, rage, shame, resignation, or defeat (Courtois & Ford, 2009). It is unclear how, if at all, an expansion of Criterion A would affect the presence of PTSD in adolescents. The majority of the research regarding the utility of Criterion A has been conducted with adult samples and does not address whether a broader definition of trauma would result in changes in the prevalence and accuracy of PTSD diagnoses in youth, or whether adolescents experiencing an A1 level trauma in the absence of an A2 response exhibit subthreshold levels of PTSD (i.e., partial PTSD) meriting clinical attention.

Understanding traumatic reactions in adolescents involves an understanding of PTSD, as well as trauma symptoms that do not reach threshold levels or that extend beyond PTSD. Many youth who have experienced multiple traumas do not meet full criteria for PTSD, but they do exhibit a range of cognitive, behavioral, and affective symptoms that significantly affect their lives. To that end, it is necessary to consider the nature of the traumatic exposure and the adolescent's subjective experience of each event (irrespective of whether it meets Criterion A2), as well as the range and severity of ensuing symptoms (Taylor & Weems, 2009), within and beyond a diagnosis of PTSD. This article highlights the importance of assessing the sequelae of trauma exposure in a manner that considers current definitions of *posttraumatic stress disorder* and underscores developmental factors that may complicate an accurate assessment and understanding of trauma in adolescence.

Why Are Adolescents at Greater Risk for Trauma Exposure and PTSD?

The major developmental tasks of adolescence, including separation and individuation, and the onset of more adult behaviors such as driving, dating, and substance use, result in many adolescents being exposed to a significant number of potentially dangerous situations. Although adolescents are neurobiologically wired to engage in greater sensation-seeking, they do not fully develop the capacity for impulse control until adulthood (Steinberg, 2007; Stevens, Kiehl, Pearlson, & Calhoun, 2007). This may explain why Reyna and Farley (2006) found that adolescents continue to engage in dangerous behaviors even when they understand the risks they are taking. Paraphrasing Dahl (2001, p. 69), Steinberg and colleagues (2008) describe the process as "akin to starting the engine without a skilled driver behind the wheel" (p. 1764).

Along with a growing need for autonomy, adolescents' sense of invulnerability, which has been described in the literature for decades, has recently been linked to increased risk-taking (Alberts, Elkind, & Ginsberg, 2007). Others believe that perceptions of invulnerability actually reflect the neurobiological process described earlier, wherein adolescents' reward-seeking behavior begins to accelerate at a time when the cognitive-control system is not fully mature (Steinberg, 2007). This results in what appears to be a sense of invulnerability among adolescents. Whether due to changes occurring on a neurobiological level, a desire to project an image of strength and maturity, or judgments that do not code situations as dangerous, adolescents are notorious for placing themselves in danger. For these myriad reasons, rates of trauma exposure increase dramatically from early to late adolescence (Kilpatrick & Saunders, 2003).

Unfortunately, at the same time that adolescents are more likely to experience extremely stressful events, they may also be affected more intensely by those events. Adolescents have been found to exhibit increased physiological and affective reactivity to stressful or emotional stimuli (Dahl & Gunnar, 2009; Silk et al., 2009; Stroud et al., 2009). Although these are normal developmental processes intended to help adolescents respond and adapt to new environments and experiences, they may also lead to a greater risk for PTSD (Spear, 2009).

Considerations in the Assessment of Trauma Exposure and Symptoms

Inaccuracies in gathering information regarding trauma-related symptoms and the experience of traumatic events occur for a variety of conscious and unconscious reasons on the part of youth and interviewers. These are further confounded by developmental considerations unique to adolescence, as well as complex trauma histories in which chronic victimization is the norm. During the course of the treatment pilot described earlier, clinicians completing an assessment checklist reported that at least 10% of the 400 adolescents they screened minimized the extent of their trauma exposure and the severity of their symptoms. This minimization was significant enough that the assessments (which included a combination of interview and self-report questionnaires) were considered invalid as they did not reflect an accurate assessment of the adolescent's history or current functioning. Reasons that may result in difficulty obtaining a clear trauma history are discussed subsequently. Where relevant, they are discussed within the context of adolescent development.

Considerations in Assessment: Trauma Exposure

Peer influence. Increased capacity for formal operational thought is often accompanied by a heightened self-consciousness in which adolescents become preoccupied with what they imagine others are thinking about them (Elkind, 1967). The growing importance of the adolescent's peer group takes on greater salience for the traumatized teenager who already struggles with tremendous shame and guilt. Shame in particular is often quite debilitating, and has been linked to aggression and self-harm in multiple traumatized populations (Dyer et al., 2009). Traumatized individuals often experience themselves as permanently damaged and different from everyone else, as if no one could ever really know or understand them. Adolescence, a period during which children are already preoccupied with how they look and sound, and whether they fit in, is further complicated with traumas such as physical or sexual abuse. Newly emerging conceptions of gender roles may affect disclosures of sexual abuse—in particular for boys—for fear of inferences regarding sexuality. It is not surprising that some adolescents prefer to conceal traumatic experiences from others out of concern that people will look at them differently if they found out. However, a thorough and well-conducted trauma history interview can be validating if the clinician highlights just how common many of these traumatic events are.

Avoiding restrictions or consequences. In a survey of first-year Ivy League college students, many participants reported having engaged in a variety of reckless, potentially dangerous activities. They further reported that their parents were unaware of these activities, which included high-risk sexual conduct and life-threatening behavior while intoxicated (Garbarino & deLara, 2002). Overwhelming evidence suggests that adolescence is a period during which youth begin to seek out novel and exciting experiences, an observation substantiated by the finding that the onset of puberty is accompanied by an increase in sensation-seeking (Steinberg et al., 2008). Adolescents engaging in high-risk, thrill-seeking behaviors are unlikely to share the nature of their extracurricular activities with parents or adults who are in a position to either restrict their activities or impose punishments. Efforts to conceal participation in activities viewed as risky or dangerous by adults may result in inaccuracies in the reporting of exposure to traumatic events (e.g., a sexual assault occurring in the context of substance use).

Trust. A burgeoning desire for independence during adolescence creates an environment in which adults and adolescents are necessarily at odds, with adolescents striving toward autonomy, and adults struggling to protect them from harm. In addition to concerns that adults may impede their participation in risky activities or impose consequences, adolescents are in general more cautious in their interactions with adults than are younger children, a dynamic that is compounded in those individuals victimized by adults. Multiply traumatized individuals— in particular those experiencing interpersonal traumas—may develop a view of relationships as unstable, at times exploitive, and as alternating between loving and potentially dangerous. A general cautiousness or distrust of authority during adolescence coupled with a history of interpersonal violence may affect the tenor of a trauma history interview (Courtois, 1996), particularly if the adult administering the assessment is viewed as an authority figure or extension of the person or agency requesting the assessment. Although clarification regarding confidentiality is a critical first step in establishing trust, it is often not in itself sufficient to engage youth with complex trauma histories. Whether the adolescent presents as compliant or oppositional, youth with extensive trauma histories may retain a level of suspicion that can influence what they are willing to share.

Avoiding distress related to memories of the event. There are varying levels of awareness and intentionality regarding the avoidance of disclosing victimization or minimizing the details of a traumatic event. For example, an adolescent who forgets or does not recall a significant traumatic experience and a young man who knowingly omits critical information regarding a traumatic event are both providing an inaccurate trauma history. In both cases, the omissions represent an attempt to avoid experiencing painful feelings; one unknowingly and the other intentionally. To expect that trauma survivors will not engage in some level of avoidance is counterintuitive, given that avoidance is a hallmark of PTSD. Although avoidance or minimization regarding the nature of a traumatic event can be an adaptive response, it can interfere with clinical assessment. It is helpful to reassure youth that they do not need to share details of their past if they are not comfortable. Moreover, they need not even share the exact nature of the event (this is discussed in further detail later). Providing youth with an opportunity to disclose the occurrence of a traumatic event without relaying any of the associated details limits the clinician's ability to assess the nature and severity of the event (i.e., the ability to make a determination regarding Criterion A1); however, it also improves the likelihood that adolescents report important information rather than conceal it for fear that they will be forced to talk about painful experiences.

Varying perceptions of danger and trauma. The tendency for adolescents to minimize real risks, coupled with life experiences in which repeated victimization is the norm, often results in the intentional or unintentional failure to accurately report trauma histories. As an example, during a 45-minute trauma history interview at our center, a 16-year-old girl revealed numerous incidences of trauma exposure, including a severe assault by her grandmother that resulted in an extended hospitalization. The girl reported that the incident was isolated and that her grandmother, her primary caretaker, had never beaten her before. The interviewer, curious about what would make this seemingly nonviolent woman inflict serious physical harm on her granddaughter, continued to gently question the girl. With the interview drawing to a close and no additional insight into this reported solitary occurrence, the interviewer again asked about a history of violence between the girl and her grandmother, to which she responded, "Oh! Yeah! She hit me all the time! She beat me at least a couple of times a week. I thought you were asking how many times she *almost beat me to death*. That only happened once."

In this case, it was clear to the interviewer that the youth, who was forthcoming and engaged throughout the interview, had not previously reported this routine household violence because she simply did not view it as unusual. Failure to disclose abuse did not stem from an intentional or unintentional avoidance of traumatic events or difficult memories, nor did it represent an effort to mislead the interviewer. She simply did not report these common incidences of aggression because it was a trauma interview, and these events did not, in her mind, rise to the level of being traumatic. Although the interviewer had asked about past abuse, she simply had not phrased the questions in the precise manner needed to elicit the information. For many children and adolescents, physical abuse, sexual abuse, community violence, or domestic violence is part of everyday life and no more noteworthy than life's other routine occurrences. In the absence of an alternate worldview, children and adolescents make psychological adaptations in order to survive. Reality accommodates the violence such that events, perceived by others as traumatic, are normalized.

Similarly, the myth of invulnerability so common to adolescence may result in appraisals of potentially dangerous situations as ordinary, a faulty perception that is further compounded by histories of repeated victimization wherein violence is normal. An 18-year-old girl with an extensive trauma history stormed away from her boyfriend after an argument at a New York City nightclub. Dressed in skimpy club attire, she walked the 90 blocks back to her college dorm room at 1 a.m. Upon arriving home two hours later, she was baffled to find her boyfriend and her roommates awake and furious with her. She was, after all, safe. Moreover, she had not felt scared or perceived herself to be in danger at any time. Six months later she was date-raped by an acquaintance, an event that she disclosed detachedly years later to her therapist during the course of a trauma history interview. She described how the night began, who she was with, where they went, then, skipping over crucial details (in this case, that an assault had taken place), she concluded with, "So then I left." The therapist, looking at her with confusion, surmised, "So nothing happened . . . .?" at which point she returned the therapist's confused expression with one of her own. Hadn't she just told him? This smart, college-educated and oftentimes insightful young woman had unknowingly and unintentionally minimized what others would perceive as a trauma to the point where her therapist was unable to recognize that a sexual assault had occurred. Like many other of her life experiences, she did not perceive herself to have been exposed to serious threat or injury (Criterion A1), nor did she react with intense fear, helplessness, or horror (Criterion A2). Her response undoubtedly represents a complex interplay between an extensive trauma history and developmental factors that affect judgment and perceptions of risk.

Considerations in Assessment: Trauma Symptoms

Preserving self-image. Individuals experiencing repeated victimization often have a frame of reference in which violence is the norm. This worldview creates an expectation that "bad things happen and you move on." Significant trauma symptoms may be viewed by the survivor as a weakness or personal defect. For trauma survivors who do recognize that difficulties associated with their experience are common, they may experience shame or a sense of defeat if they cannot resolve these symptoms within an oftentimes self-imposed time frame (Nader, 2008). As a result, survivors may conceal or minimize the frequency, range, or severity of their symptoms. This is particularly relevant for adolescents who are already invested in being perceived as strong, self-sufficient, and able to take care of themselves.

Trust. The experience of any traumatic event, even single-incident traumas such as a robbery, car accident, or natural disaster, can affect an individual's sense of safety and can result in problems in relationships. As stated previously, repeated interpersonal victimization in particular results in problems with trust, which are further magnified during adolescence, a period that for some youth is already marked by a degree of guardedness and suspicion of authority figures. As with assessing trauma exposure, issues related to trust may also result in inaccuracies when reporting the presence or severity of symptoms.

Peer influence. As the influence of one's peer group begins to take on new proportions, it becomes more important than ever to fit in. Although this may result in a tendency to conceal traumatic events and associated symptoms, it can also have the opposite effect. Adolescents may underreport or exaggerate symptoms depending on who they are talking to and whether it will enhance their social status or solidify their membership in a particular peer group (Nader, 2008). For example, in a residential facility in California, one adolescent, upon observing the self-inflicted cut on another youth's arm, commented, "That's nothing," and proceeded to show her the object she had self-embedded deep beneath her skin. While certain dramatic tendencies are evident in the way teenagers describe others ("Oh, she's anorexic" or "He's bipolar"), they also highlight the stigma associated with mental health difficulties. Consequently, the typical clinical presentation is one in which youth make efforts to minimize any psychological difficulties they may be having, particularly if they are socially undesirable to others (Nader, 2008). As an example, adolescents who engage in parasuicidal behaviors such as cutting, burning, biting, or embedding generally do so in private and do not disclose their actions to adults or to peers unless they are in an environment where such behavior is socially accepted. It should be noted that while self-injurious behavior (which is linked to childhood trauma and PTSD; Yates, 2004) often represents a method to cope with or escape from painful feelings, it may at times also reflect an attempt to fit in or an effort to gain attention. Understanding the reasons that underlie inaccuracies in reporting provides the clinician with strategies for engaging youth and enhancing the accuracy of the information gathered. For example, if the clinician senses that the adolescent is "faking good" in an effort to minimize differences and fit in with other teens, the clinician may use this as an opportunity to normalize the symptoms as a common reaction to traumatic events.

Failure to recognize symptoms as symptoms. Survivors of trauma may not recognize associated behavioral and affective symptoms as being related to past events; rather, the symptoms are simply just part of who they are. While traumatic events often result in problems modulating a range of emotions including anxiety, anger, and depression (Cook et al., 2005), symptoms may not be recognized as such for a variety of reasons. During a trauma symptom interview conducted by one of our colleagues, a young man was asked, "Has there ever been a time when having someone comfort you made you uncomfortable? For example, when you were upset, did you avoid letting someone hug you?" This question sparked first-time disclosure of additional abuse that later became the focus of treatment. In being asked the question, the young man gained new insight regarding current relational problems connected to a history of abuse. He had not previously recognized the difficulties he'd been experiencing as symptoms of posttraumatic stress related to an extensive trauma history. He did not consider his emotional and behavioral lability to be unusual. Chaotic relationships were viewed as typical of most relationships rather than the consequence of trauma-triggered responses; as such, depending on how the question was framed, he may not have reported them as symptoms.

At times, symptoms may actually be perceived as positive traits or strengths rather than symptoms. For example, a client who views explosive, verbally aggressive outbursts as "being real" or honest may not view her behavior as problematic, and consequently may deny symptoms of emotional or behavioral dysregulation. However, she might endorse symptoms if asked more concretely, "In the past month, how often have you yelled or cursed at people or called them names?" Rather than intentionally minimizing or denying symptoms that may be viewed as weak, the failure to recognize symptoms as problematic represents a less intentional attempt to reframe trauma-related symptoms. In doing so, symptoms become characterological idiosyncrasies (i.e., "Oh, that's just how I am. I tell it like it is.") or even strengths (e.g., permitting only superficial relationships as a sign of independence and self-sufficiency). Adolescents' growing desire for autonomy can intensify the need to feel and be perceived as strong. Therefore, in conducting an assessment, concerns that adolescents will minimize symptoms because they do not trust others may be compounded by the risk that ego-syntonic symptoms will not be reported.

Conducting Assessments: What Are We Assessing and How?

Measures of Exposure and Posttraumatic Stress

Given the complexity of posttraumatic stress symptom presentations, structured or semi-structured interviews are the most reliable and valid method of assessing PTSD, especially when detailing reactions to numerous traumatic events. There are several widely used PTSD interviews for adolescents, including the Clinician-Administered PTSD Scale for Children and Adolescents (Nader et al., 2004), which is currently considered the standard tool for assessing PTSD in this age group. Broad diagnostic interviews that include PTSD modules, such as the Missouri Assessment Genetics Interview for Children (Reich & Todd, 1999), are also appropriate. Self-report measures such as the Reactions of Adolescents to Traumatic Stress Questionnaire (Bean et al., 2006) and the UCLA PTSD Reaction Index (Pynoos et al., 1998), which can also be administered as an interview, can be completed relatively quickly and yield symptom severity scores that can be used to track treatment progress. A well-constructed symptom inventory contains specific, objectively framed questions that will capture current functioning in a manner that includes the adolescent's subjective experience but does not rely solely on subjective experience in determining symptom presence or absence. Issues related to the unintentional failure to report or recognize symptoms become more salient in the context of an unstructured interview or an assessment that does not contain sufficient objective, measurable indicators.

Because many adolescents have trauma symptoms that extend beyond a diagnosis of PTSD, it is important to use assessments of comorbid conditions and other trauma-related symptoms. Trauma symptoms including anxiety, depression, anger, and dissociation may be assessed using self-report instruments such as the Trauma Symptom Checklist for Children (Briere, 1996) or semi-structured interviews such as the Structured Interview for Disorders of Extreme Stress (SIDES; Pelcovitz et al., 1997). The latter has been used to assess the sequelae of complex trauma exposure in adults and is in development for use with adolescents (Habib, Sonnenklar, Labruna, Sunday, DeRosa, & Pelcovitz, 2005). Given the frequent comorbidity found in adolescents with trauma-related disorders (Kilpatrick et al., 2003), it is likely that traumatized teenagers will require, at a minimum, a broad-based screening that includes anxiety, depression, substance abuse, and conduct problems. Clinically relevant and scientifically valid instruments, although integral in the assessment of symptomatology, are beyond the scope of this article. For a more detailed review of instruments assessing comorbidity and a range of trauma-related symptoms in youth, see Nader (2008). Courtois and Ford (2009) reviewed measures assessing complex trauma, and Mash and Barkley (2007) provided a comprehensive discussion regarding the psychometric properties and application of a variety of child and adolescent trauma measures.

Regarding the assessment of trauma exposure, there are a variety of instruments assessing a range of moderate- and high-magnitude events. Among these are the Traumatic Events Screening Inventory (Ford et al., 2005) and the Young Adults Upsetting Times Checklist (Fletcher, 1992), both of which are reliable, with the former being an interview and the latter being a self-report measure of general functioning, with good validity (see Mash & Barkely, 2007, for a list of existing instruments). The Dimensions of Stressful Events Ratings Scale (Fletcher, 1996) assesses the severity of exposure rather than the type, and further includes variables related to the youth's subjective experience of the traumatic event. Last, the Adolescent Trauma History Checklist and Interview (Habib & Labruna, 2006), which is described in greater detail subsequently, contains very specific, concrete questions regarding trauma exposure.

In the following section, we focus on issues related to the assessment of trauma exposure and the expression of posttraumatic stress symptoms within the context of adolescent development. We begin with a discussion of the factors complicating an accurate assessment of trauma exposure in adolescence.

Assessing Exposure: The Use of a Trauma History Interview

Advances in the assessment of trauma symptoms have not been matched by progress in evaluating trauma exposure (Weathers & Keane, 2007). Concerns are varied and center on issues related to Criterion A of PTSD as well as on the method of assessment. Whether to apply a narrow versus more inclusive definition of what is or is not trauma depends on the purpose of the assessment. Establishing a diagnosis would dictate a rigid application of the *DSM-IV* PTSD Criteria. However, a broader conceptualization of trauma, on the basis of the adolescent's subjective experience of the event, may be more informative in terms of treatment planning than knowing whether or not the stressor rose to the level of a trauma as defined by the *DSM-IV*. Further, methods for assessing exposure are varied and may range from completion of a brief self-report checklist of traumatic events to a comprehensive semi-structured interview lasting several hours depending on the individual's trauma history. Although the level of depth required depends on the intended purpose of the assessment, in general an interview is recommended over a self-report.

Challenges in conducting an assessment of trauma, although inevitable, can be minimized by using a thorough trauma interview and adhering to a structured format in which questions are not only concrete and objectively framed, but also consider the youth's subjective experience of a particular event. For example, the question, "Has anyone ever raped you?" is neither concrete nor objective. Depending on the context, definitions of rape may be cultural, personal, or legal. Alternately, asking, "Has anyone ever touched you sexually in a way that made you feel uncomfortable or when you didn't want them to?" is entirely subjective and in and of itself does not provide enough information for the interviewer to determine whether or not the event meets criteria for an A1 trauma. Although difficulties in assessment occur for a variety of reasons ranging from the active concealment of distressing events to the unintentional minimization that occurs outside of the client's awareness, the end result may be an incomplete, inaccurate assessment of a client's trauma history. Consequently, a thorough trauma assessment necessarily begins with a comprehensive trauma exposure interview that balances structure and flexibility in order to accommodate the myriad reasons people conceal, distort, forget, or avoid.

A detailed trauma history screen should include a fairly exhaustive list of possible traumatic experiences, ranging from exposure to or direct experience with domestic violence, community violence, physical and sexual abuse, natural disasters, serious accidents, life-threatening illnesses, and less commonly experienced traumas such as kidnapping and stalking.

As part of collaborations with agencies across the country, we provide consultation regarding the use the Adolescent Trauma History Checklist & Interview (Habib & Labruna, 2006), a trauma history exposure screen developed by our center. We routinely hear anecdotal stories about clients who had been in treatment for years, disclosing abuse during the interview for the first time simply because no one had ever asked them specific exposure questions before. This has borne out in our own clinical practice as well. In one case, a clinician learned that a woman who had been in treatment for 6 months had 2 years earlier discovered her husband's body after he had committed suicide. She had never mentioned this event when she presented for treatment of trauma-related symptoms stemming from a different trauma. Unless clients are specifically asked about discrete events, they oftentimes do not report their complete trauma history (Franklin, Sheeran, & Zimmerman, 2002), because there are too many to share, they don't consider the experiences to be traumatic, or they simply forget amid the chaos in their lives.

When included as part of a diagnostic interview for PTSD, an assessment of lifetime exposure should not only include a range of potentially traumatic events, but should provide sufficient information to determine whether the event rises to the level of a trauma as defined by the *DSM-IV*. For example, clients may endorse having been in a fire, but there is a difference between experiencing a small cooking fire that can be quickly extinguished and being trapped in a burning room. We have also found it useful to include an item that allows individuals to endorse a traumatic experience without revealing more than they are comfortable sharing. For example, "Is there anything else really scary or very upsetting that has happened to you that I haven't asked you about? Sometimes people have something in mind, but they're not comfortable talking about the details. Is that true for you?" This approach has been especially helpful when working with traumatized adolescents whose developmental struggles with issues related to identity and self-perception are compounded by the shame and secrecy shrouding traumatic events. Clients should be encouraged to endorse items and decline elaboration, rather than provide inaccurate information.

For clinical and scientific purposes, a thorough assessment of trauma exposure must consider objectively defined criteria (i.e., "Has anyone ever hit you with an object like a belt?") as well as subjectively defined experiences. When considering a diagnosis of PTSD, the objectively framed questions typically relate to the A1 Criterion about exposure to potentially life-threatening events, whereas the A2 Criterion questions regarding how the event was experienced (i.e., "Was it horrifying?") tend to be more subjective (Weathers & Keane, 2007). However, in certain circumstances, both of these criteria are subject to personal interpretation depending on the individual's trauma history and developmental stage. Questions regarding exposure to life-threatening or dangerous situations (Criterion A1) are interpreted and answered through the same developmental lens that enables adolescents to engage in high-risk behaviors such as reckless driving, unprotected sex, hitchhiking, and *subway surfing* (i.e., riding on the roof of subway cars). Simply put, adolescents' perceptions of risk are far different from those of adults, as are cost-benefit analyses regarding the risks they take. For adolescents, potentially life-threatening events become ordinary or acceptable risks. For this reason, the adolescent version of the SIDES considers the adolescent's interpretation of risk by asking if the adolescent has ever *knowingly* engaged in dangerous behaviors, has ever *unknowingly* engaged in dangerous behaviors (and then later realized the danger), or has ever engaged in acts *other people* would consider dangerous. Although a multitude of reasons underlie inaccuracies in gathering information about trauma exposure, administering a trauma history screen as an interview rather than self-report addresses many of the issues related to the active, or unknowing minimization or avoidance of particular traumatic events.

Use of Interviews Versus Self-Report

Risk-taking adolescents are unlikely to disclose reckless behavior to their parents, and to the extent that their psychological difficulties are not socially desirable, are also less likely to share details of their trauma symptoms with others for fear of not fitting in. As a result, self-report instruments and reports by others are limited by the adolescent's willingness to share. A skilled interviewer can help adolescents feel comfortable discussing details of potentially traumatic events and concomitant difficulties in functioning. While the use of a good, flexibly applied, semi-structured interview can enhance accuracy, self-report questionnaires afford some measure of detachment and emotional distance not afforded by an interview. For particularly guarded adolescents, disclosing information in the absence of an adult who could ask follow-up questions serves as an opportunity to talk about it without actually talking. As with most other conditions, a complete assessment includes a synthesis of information gathered from multiple sources using a variety of methods (e.g., self-report, interview, direct observation, review of relevant records such as academic, medical, and juvenile justice). This is especially important given adolescents' tendencies to minimize the potential risk of dangerous situations, coupled with their desire to fit in and be like everyone else.

Use of Adolescent Report Versus Report by Others

There has been ongoing discussion regarding the utility of parent report in the diagnosis of PTSD and trauma-related disorders. Adolescents are generally considered to be the best reporters of their own symptoms, in particular internalizing symptoms such as reexperiencing, avoidance, and hyperarousal (Nader, 2008). However, the issues described in this paper highlight some of the difficulties in relying solely on reports provided by adolescents. Unfortunately, there are limitations to parent reports as well. Recent research has revealed that there is only poor to moderate agreement between the self-reported PTSD symptoms of injured adolescents and the ratings provided by their parents (Ghesquiere et al., 2008). In particular, parents with their own diagnoses of PTSD appear to overreport symptoms in their adolescents. Overall, findings suggest that parental reports should be interpreted with some caution and may be the most useful when considered in conjunction with adolescents' self-reports.

In our unpublished analyses of more than 400 traumatized adolescents, clinicians indicated that approximately 5% of adolescents reported symptoms in a manner that was extremely inaccurate and "did not correspond to what was reported or observed by clinicians." These numbers are likely an underrepresentation of the level of minimization that occurs in reporting symptoms, because they do not consider less severe levels of underreporting. Furthermore, inaccuracies could only be detected when the referral source had independent knowledge of the adolescent's functioning—information that most of the clinicians did not have before treatment.

As discussed, there are many reasons why adolescents may inaccurately report symptom presence or severity, including a level of distrust of the adult requesting the information and a desire to fit in with peers and be viewed as normal. Consequently, it has been our experience that clients reporting subclinical difficulties before treatment sometimes report greater symptom levels following treatment. In these cases, clinicians have indicated that the adolescents began to view their symptoms as less stigmatizing and also felt more comfortable disclosing difficulties over time. Unfortunately, this results in the appearance that some clients are more symptomatic following treatment, when they are simply more comfortable talking about what they have been through and the symptoms they experience. Given that the severity of symptoms may not be accurately reported, it is helpful to conduct assessments at multiple time points, because the forces driving inaccurate reporting will likely change the presentation of the clinical picture over time once good rapport has been established. Although these findings highlight the importance of using multiple informants whenever possible, adolescents remain the best reporters of their own trauma symptoms (Nader, 2008), especially when the barriers to accurate reporting are understood and steps are taken to lessen their influence.

Treatment Implications of the Assessment Process

A thorough and accurate assessment of symptoms serves as an important prelude to trauma-informed therapy. Conducted in a supportive manner and at a pace that is not retraumatizing, the assessment begins the process of exploring the adolescent's memories of potentially traumatic experiences, and in some cases, may represent first steps in understanding how past experiences relate to current functioning. In the example of the young man described earlier, it was during a trauma interview that he began to make the connection between his relationship difficulties and his history of childhood abuse. The level of distress exhibited during an assessment provides important information regarding the adolescent's readiness to participate in a range of trauma-focused therapies (including exposure-based treatments). This guides treatment planning in a way that balances treatment needs with the adolescent's willingness and ability to fully participate.

Understanding the etiology of inaccuracies in reporting trauma exposure and symptoms is clinically essential when working with traumatized populations. Is the failure to disclose abuse an active avoidance of reminders of the trauma (thereby suggesting the use of an exposure-based intervention)? Or, do distortions in reporting represent an unconscious minimization of events resulting from a worldview in which violence is the norm? With regard to the latter, treatment planning might target the client's belief system and help him or her understand connections between past interpersonal events and current relational functioning.

While developmental factors may complicate a trauma assessment, they also present clinicians with a window of opportunity in treatment. Fortunately, as adolescents shift to formal operational thought, their increased capacity for insight and abstract thinking leads them to ponder questions about themselves and the world and ask, "Why?" and "What if?" As adolescents begin to consider existential issues, they are better able to make connections between past traumas and their effect on current functioning, and understand how their history shapes the values and beliefs that drive their behavior and worldview.

Conclusion

Adolescence is a period of great physical, psychological, and physiological change, with neurological developments rivaled only by those that occur during the neonatal period (Schore, 2001). The developmental changes associated with adolescence present a unique set of vulnerabilities which, if not protected, place the traumatized adolescent at even greater risk during a period that can already be confusing and challenging. The relationship between adolescent victimization and negative long-term outcomes is extensive and well-documented (Kilpatrick & Saunders, 2003). The social, psychological, educational, occupational, and health-related problems associated with childhood trauma exposure affect the individual and societal level, with policy implications across a range of local and national agencies (Kendall-Tackett, 2003).

The clinical and scientific community has become more adept at assessing symptoms of posttraumatic stress in adult populations (Weathers & Keane, 2007). However, we continue to struggle with assessing PTSD in children and adolescents (Mash & Barkley, 2007) and are only just beginning to assess other trauma-related symptoms in youth (Nader, 2008). Given the high rates of PTSD and comorbidity among traumatized samples and the prevalence of other trauma-related symptoms, an accurate assessment includes an understanding of the extent of exposure to potentially traumatizing events (in terms of frequency, severity, and type) and of the adolescent's interpretation of and response to each event.

Efforts to attenuate the effect of trauma should begin with an accurate and comprehensive assessment of trauma exposure and corresponding sequelae. The selection of appropriate trauma-informed interventions should be informed by a thorough assessment that addresses *DSM-IV* criteria as well as other trauma-related symptoms, and must include a phenomenological understanding of the adolescent's experience.

Acknowledgments

The authors acknowledge members of the National Child Traumatic Stress Network who shared valuable insights and anecdotes regarding their experiences in assessing trauma in adolescents.

References

Alberts, A., Elkind, D., & Ginsberg, S. (2007). The personal fable and risk-taking in early adolescence. *Journal of Youth and Adolescence*, *37*, 71–76.

American Psychiatric Association. (2000). *Diagnostic and statistical manual of mental disorders* (text rev.). Washington, DC: Author.

Bean, T., Derluyn, I., Eurelings-Bontekoe, E., Broekaert, E., & Spinhoven, P. (2006). Validation of the multiple language versions of the Reactions of Adolescents to Traumatic Stress Questionnaire. *Journal of Traumatic Stress*, *19*, 241–255.

Bedard-Gilligan, M., & Zoellner, L. (2008). The utility of the A1 and A2 criteria in the diagnosis of PTSD. *Behaviour Research and Therapy*, *46*, 1062–1069.

Briere, J. (1996). *The Trauma Symptom Checklist for Children*. Odessa FL: Psychological Assessment Resources.

Briere, J., Kaltman, S., & Green, B. (2008). Accumulated childhood trauma and symptom complexity. *Journal of Traumatic Stress*, *21*, 223–226.

Briggs-King, E. (2009, March). *Highlights from the core data set*. Paper presented at the All Network Conference of the National Child Traumatic Stress Network, Orlando, FL.

Cook, A., Spinazzola, J., Ford, J., Lanktree, C., Blaustein, M., Cloitre, M., et al. (2005). Complex trauma in children and adolescents. *Psychiatric Annals*, *35*, 390–398.

Copeland, W., Keeler, G., Angold, A., & Costello, E. J. (2007). Traumatic events and posttraumatic stress in childhood. *Archives of General Psychiatry*, *64*, 577–584.

Courtois, C. (1996). *Healing the incest wound: Adult survivors in therapy*. New York: Norton.

Courtois, C., & Ford, J. (2009). *Treating complex traumatic stress disorders: An evidence-based guide*. New York: Guilford Press.

Dahl, R. (2001). Affect regulation, brain development, and behavioral/emotional health in adolescence. *CNS Spectrums*, *6*, 60–72.

Dahl, R., & Gunnar, M. (2009). Heightened stress responsiveness and emotional reactivity during pubertal maturation: Implications for psychopathology. *Development and Psychopathology*, *21*, 1–6.

Dyer, K., Dorahy, M., Hamilton, G., Corry, M., Shannon, M., MacSherry, A., et al. (2009). Anger, aggression, and self-harm in PTSD and complex PTSD. *Journal of Clinical Psychology*, *65*, 1099–1114.

Elkind, D. (1967). Egocentrism in adolescence. *Child Development*, *38*, 1025–1033.

Elklit, A., & Petersen, T. (2008). Exposure to traumatic events among adolescents in four nations. *Torture*, *18*, 2–11.

Finkelhor, D., Ormrod, R., & Turner, H. (2007a). Poly-victimization: A neglected component in child victimization. *Child Abuse and Neglect*, *31*, 7–26.

Finkelhor, D., Ormrod, R., & Turner, H. (2007b). Polyvictimization and trauma in a national longitudinal cohort. *Development and Psychopathology*, *19*, 149–166.

Fletcher, K. (1996). Psychometric review of Dimensions of Stressful Events (DOSE) Ratings Scale. In B. H. Stamm (Ed.), *Measurement of stress, trauma, and adaptation* (pp. 144–151). Lutherville, MD: Sidran Press.

Fletcher, K. (1992). *Young Adult Upsetting Times Checklist (YAUTC)*. Unpublished measure, Psychiatry Department, University of Massachusetts Medical Center.

Ford, J., Ghosh-Ippen, C., Wolpaw, J., Racusin, R., Rogers, K., Ellis, C., et al. (2005). *Traumatic Events Screening Inventory for Children (TESI-C) Version 8.5*. Dartmouth, VT: National Center for PTSD and Dartmouth Child Psychiatry Research Group.

Ford, J., Stockton, P., Kaltman, S., & Green, B. (2006). Disorders of extreme stress (DESNOS) symptoms are associated with type and severity of interpersonal trauma exposure in a sample of healthy young women. *Journal of Interpersonal Violence*, *21*, 1399–1416.

Franklin, C., Sheeran, T., & Zimmerman, M. (2002). Screening for trauma history, posttraumatic stress disorder, and subthreshold PTSD in psychiatric outpatients. *Psychological Assessment*, *4*, 467–471.

Garbarino, J., & deLara, E. (2002). *And words can hurt forever: How to protect adolescents from bullying, harassment, and emotional violence*. New York: The Free Press.

Ghesquiere, A., Fan, M., Berliner, L. Rivara, F., Jurkovich, G., Russo, J., et al. (2008). Adolescents' and parents' agreement on posttraumatic stress disorder symptoms and functioning after adolescent injury. *Journal of Traumatic Stress, 21*, 487–491.

Habib, M., & Labruna, V. (2006). *The Adolescent Trauma History Checklist and Interview*. Copyrighted scale, North Shore University Hospital.

Habib, M., Sonnenklar, J., Labruna, V., Sunday, S., DeRosa, R., & Pelcovitz, D. (2005). *Structured Interview for Disorders of Extreme Stress- Adolescent Version (SIDES-A)*. Unpublished measure; North Shore University Hospital.

Kendall-Tackett, K. (2003). *Treating the lifetime health effects of childhood victimization*. Kingston, NJ: Civic Research Institute.

Kilpatrick, D., Ruggiero, K., Acierno, R., Saunders, B., Resnick, H., & Best, C. (2003). Violence and risk of PTSD, major depression, substance abuse-dependence, and comorbidity: Results from the national survey of adolescents. *Journal of Consulting and Clinical Psychology, 71*, 692–700.

Kilpatrick, D., & Saunders, B. (2003). *Prevalence and consequences of child victimization: Results from the National Survey of Adolescents*. Final Report to the U.S. Department of Justice. National Crime Victims Research and Treatment Center, Department of Psychiatry and Behavioral Sciences, Medical University of South Carolina, Charleston, South Carolina.

Kraemer, B., Wittmann, L., Jenewein, J., Maier, T., & Schnyder, U. (2009). Is the stressor criterion dispensable? *Psychopathology, 42*, 333–336.

Maier, T. (2006). Post-traumatic stress disorder revisited: Deconstructing the A-criterion. *Medical Hypotheses, 66*, 103–106.

Mash, E., & Barkley, R. (2007). *Assessment of childhood disorders* (4th ed.). New York: Guilford Press.

Nader, K. (2008). *Understanding and assessing trauma in children and adolescents: Measures, methods, and youth in context*. New York: Routledge.

Nader, K., Newman, E., Weathers, F., Kaloupek, D., Kriegler, J., & Blake, D. (2004). *Clinician-Administered PTSD Scale for children and adolescents (CAPS- C)*. Los Angeles: Western Psychological Press.

Pelcovitz D., van der Kolk, B., Roth, S., Mandel, F., Kaplan, S., & Resick, P. (1997). Development of a criteria set and a structured interview for disorders of extreme stress. *Journal of Traumatic Stress, 10*, 3–16.

Pynoos, R., Rodriguez, N., Steinberg, A., Stuber, M., & Frederick, C. (1998). *UCLA PTSD Index for DSM-IV*. Copyrighted scale, UCLA Neuropsychiatric Institute.

Reich, W., & Todd, R. (1999). *Missouri Assessment of Genetics Interview for Children (MAGIC)*. St. Louis, MO: Washington University School of Medicine.

Reyna, V., & Farley, F. (2006). Risk and rationality in adolescent decision making: Implications for theory, practice, and public policy. *Psychological Science in the Public Interest, 7*, 1–44.

Rosen, G., Spitzer, R., & McHugh, P. (2008). Problems with the post-traumatic stress disorder diagnosis and its future in *DSM-V*. *The British Journal of Psychiatry, 192*, 3–4.

Schore, A. (2001). Effects of a secure attachment relationship on right brain development, affect regulation, and infant mental health. *Infant Mental Health Journal, 22*, 7–66.

Silk, J., Siegle, G., Whalen, D., Ostapenko, L., Ladouceur, C., & Dahl, R. (2009). Pubertal changes in emotional information processing: Pupillary, behavioral, and subjective evidence during emotional word identification. *Developmental Psychopathology, 21*, 7–26.

Spear, L. (2009). Heightened stress responsivity and emotional reactivity during pubertal maturation: Implications for psychopathology. *Development and Psychopathology, 21*, 87–97.

Spitzer, R., First, M., & Wakefield, J. (2007). Saving PTSD from itself in *DSM-V*. *Journal of Anxiety Disorders, 21*, 233–241.

Steinberg, L. (2007). Risk-taking in adolescence: New perspectives from brain and behavioral science. *Current Directions in Psychological Science, 16*, 55–59.

Steinberg, L., Albert, D., Cauffman, E., Banich, M., Graham, S., & Woolard, J. (2008). Age differences in sensation seeking and impulsivity as indexed by behavior and self-report: Evidence for a dual systems model. *Developmental Psychology*, *44*, 1764–1777.

Stevens, M., Kiehl, K., Pearlson, G., & Calhoun, V. (2007). Functional neural networks underlying response inhibition in adolescents and adults. *Behavioural Brain Research*, *181*, 12–22.

Stroud, L., Foster, E., Handwerger, K., Papandonatos, G. D., Granger, D., Kivlighan, K. T., et al. (2009). Stress response and the adolescent transition: Performance versus peer rejection stress. *Development and Psychopathology*, *21*, 47–68.

Taylor, L., & Weems, C. (2009). What do youth report as a traumatic event? Toward a developmentally informed classification of traumatic stressors. *Psychological Trauma: Theory, Research, Practice, and Policy*, *1*, 91–106.

Weathers, F., & Keane, T. (2007). The criterion A problem revisited: Controversies and challenges in defining and measuring psychological trauma. *Journal of Traumatic Stress*, *20*, 107–121.

Yates, T. M. (2004). The developmental psychopathology of self-injurious behavior: Compensatory regulation in posttraumatic adaptation. *Clinical Psychological Review*, *24*, 35–74.

Appendix

Recommendations for obtaining accurate information in the assessment of trauma exposure and symptoms in adolescents

Guidelines	Specific recommendations/example
• It is ideal to use interview and self-reports.	• When assessing exposure, an interview is generally recommended over a self-report. • Include self-report assessments with adolescents who are guarded or reluctant to share information about exposure and symptoms face-to-face. • When making diagnostic decisions, structured or semi-structured interviews are recommended.
• Consider the role of developmental factors that may contribute to minimization (e.g., struggles with fitting in, identity, and independence).	• Provide information regarding the prevalence of trauma. • Normalize symptoms in the context of the event. "I've worked with lots of teenagers who've gone through similar things as you [have]. They also [have] had a hard time sleeping. Sometimes they'd feel really high-strung, other times they felt really numbed out. Does that ever happen to you?" • Reinforce that it takes courage to discuss difficult things.
• Ask, ask, ask! • Do not assume adolescents will volunteer every traumatic experience. This is true in particular for adolescents with complex trauma histories.	• Use a comprehensive trauma history screen that includes questions about severity, duration, and frequency on a broad range of traumatic events.
• When assessing trauma exposure, avoid relying on labels and terms such as *rape* and *abuse*. • Use concrete, objective language to avoid confusing terminology. Elicit behavioral descriptors to operationalize the event. • Consider the adolescent's subjective experience and interpretation of the event.	• For example, begin with, "Has anyone ever touched you sexually in a way that made you feel uncomfortable or when you didn't want them to?" instead of, "Has anyone ever raped you?" Follow up with, "Where did they touch you?" and "How?" etc. • Instead of statements that may be open to interpretation such as, "Did your parents abuse you?" ask, "How do they punish you? Do they ever use a belt or a spoon?" • Use the adolescent's language when possible, to get objective and clear information. "You said that sometimes your grandmother 'disciplined' you; can you tell me how?"

(*Continued*)

Appendix
(Continued)

Guidelines	Specific recommendations/example
• Subjective interpretations, although clinically relevant, may skew the accuracy of symptoms reported.	• For example, a teenage boy who reports he is "always in control" may not recognize a violent, triggered outburst as a loss of control.
• When assessing trauma symptoms, include objectively framed questions. Note subjective interpretations (because they have important assessment and treatment implications).	• For example, instead of asking, "Do you ever lose control?" ask "In the past month, how often have you thrown or broken something when you're mad? Have you ever hit anyone when you were upset?"
• Do not assume that the most objectively severe trauma is the most significant trauma to the adolescent. • When screening for PTSD in multiply traumatized clients, if possible, identify the most significant trauma. • If the adolescent cannot identify which trauma is the most upsetting, assess PTSD symptoms separately for each significant trauma identified.	• Ask, "What is the thing that bothers you the most right now?" "What's the one thing you really don't like thinking about?" or "Which of these things pops into your head when you least expect it?" • Ask, "We talked about your father coming into your room at night when you were little. We also talked about seeing your mother's boyfriend beat her with a bat a couple of years ago. Of those things, which bothers you the most?" • For example, "It sounds like both of these things bother you equally, for now I'm going to ask you about nightmares and thoughts you have about the time your mother was attacked by her boyfriend. Afterward, I'll ask you the same questions about your father. Is that ok?"
• When screening for PTSD using a self-report, ensure that the adolescent has identified an appropriate A1 stressor. If necessary, assist without choosing for the client. • Do not assume that the "thing that bothers him or her the most right now" is even a trauma.	• For example, "I know you're really upset about breaking up with your boyfriend. For this questionnaire, though, we need to choose something from that list of things we talked about earlier" (refer back to trauma exposure screen).

(*Continued*)

Appendix
(Continued)

Guidelines	Specific recommendations/example
• Provide the opportunity to disclose trauma without having to discuss details.	• Ask, "Is there anything else really scary or very upsetting that has happened to you that I haven't asked you about? You don't have to say what happened if you don't want to, just let me know if there is something else. Sometimes people have something in mind, but they're not comfortable talking about the details. Is that true for you?"
• Provide the opportunity to report exposure without fear of punishment or restriction for high-risk activities that may have contributed to trauma exposure.	• Clearly define parameters of confidentiality and the extent to which their responses may result in negative consequences. • This is especially important if the interview is being conducted by someone with whom the adolescent does not have a therapeutic relationship.
• Assess for PTSD and beyond PTSD.	• Use an assessment battery that includes disorders frequently occurring with PTSD, such as conduct disorder, depressive disorders, anxiety disorders, and substance abuse. • In particular with chronically traumatized adolescents, assess behavioral and affective dysregulation, problems with self-perception and identity, somatic complaints, relational difficulties, and dissociative symptoms and sense of purpose and future.

Note. PTSD = posttraumatic stress disorder.

Complicated Forms of Trauma-Related Reactions

Assessing Child and Adolescent Complex Traumatic Stress Reactions

JULIAN D. FORD

University of Connecticut Health Center

Children and adolescents exposed to traumatic stressors may develop severe and persistent complex traumatic stress reactions. A framework for conceptualizing and assessing children's and adolescents' complex traumatic stress reactions as forms of impaired self-regulation is described. Psychometric measures for the assessment of posttraumatic dysregulation of emotion, cognition, behavior, and bodily functioning are also described. The question of whether children and adolescents who are experiencing complex traumatic stress reactions would benefit from the establishment of a distinct syndrome and psychiatric diagnosis is discussed in light of recent findings suggesting that existing psychiatric diagnoses do not fully account for the impairment suffered by such youth.

Complex traumatic stress reactions extend beyond the primary symptoms of anxiety and dysphoria that characterize posttraumatic stress disorder (PTSD) and include alterations in emotional regulation, information processing, biological self-regulation, and relational engagement (Cook et al., 2005). Such exposure includes not only physical abuse, sexual abuse, and neglect, but also other forms of victimization (Finkelhor, Turner, Ormrod, & Hamby, 2010). Complex traumatic stress reactions may contribute not only to the risk and severity of psychological and psychiatric problems over the lifespan, but also to stress-related medical illnesses (e.g., cardiovascular, metabolic, immunologic). Therefore, in addition to assessing exposure to complex traumatic stressors (e.g., polyvictimization, Finkelhor et al., 2010) it is important clinically and scientifically to assess complex posttraumatic reactions.

A number of approaches have been proposed for the conceptualization and assessment of child and adolescent complex traumatic stress reactions. Several approaches are described in the second part of this special issue and will not be discussed here. The focus of the present article is on recent scientific and clinical assessment studies of complex traumatic stress reactions in childhood and adolescence that involve impaired self-regulation. This includes affect dysregulation, dissociation, somatization, suicidality, eating and body-image disorders, sleep disorders, substance use disorders, conduct/externalizing behavior disorders, and physical health problems. These complex traumatic stress reactions lead to and exacerbate functional impairment in core areas of child and adolescent development and functioning that require careful assessment. These areas of impairment include the following: (a) attachment with primary caregivers, (b) peer relationships, (c) information processing (attention and concentration, working, procedural, and narrative memory, executive functions), (d) safety and legal status, and (e) school/work performance. Whether complex traumatic stress reactions and the associated functional impairments warrant a diagnosis distinct from PTSD (e.g., developmental trauma disorder; van der Kolk, 2005) will be discussed.

Self-Regulation in Childhood and Adolescence

Assessment of complex traumatic stress reactions in childhood and adolescence inevitably involves the assessment of failures in biopsychosocial self-regulation. However, self-regulation is a multifaceted construct that has many different meanings (Kim & Hamann, 2007). There is a relatively clear consensus that self-regulation involves a set of adaptive capacities, or "an integrated set of abilities or skills that draw from both executive function and emotion regulation capacities, which are invoked in the service of accomplishing both proximal and distal goals" (Buckner, Mezzacappa, & Beardslee, 2009, p. 19).

Self-regulation begins in infancy with primarily biologically driven adaptations that enable neonates to adjust their level of physiological arousal so as to achieve basic goals (e.g., feeding when hungry, contact with caregivers, soothing distress, and exploring the environment while titrating levels of sensory/perceptual stimulation; Calkins, 2007). From these first days of life, self-regulation involves the modulation of stress-related reactivity by the nervous system through a combination of central (i.e., vagal nerve) and peripheral (i.e., the parasympathetic branch of the body's autonomic nerves) activity that is associated with adaptive heart rate rhythmicity and reduced peripheral sympathetic nervous system output (Porges, 2009). Secure maternal-child attachment appears to be a prerequisite for infant self-regulation (Sbarra & Hazan, 2008).

In toddlerhood and the early school years, physiologically based self-regulation elaborates into an integrated set of psychological "processes of attentional engagement and disengagement, emotional regulation, and . . . behavioral regulation and executive cognitive control" (Calkins, 2007, p. 267). In childhood, an array of affective, cognitive, and behavioral self-regulatory competencies (see Table 1) emerge as the child develops and sustains prosocial family and peer relationships and productive involvement and achievement in school and avocations (Blair & Diamond, 2008; Hemenover et al., 2008). In adolescence, the core self-regulation competencies remain largely unchanged (Raffaelli, Crockett, & Shen, 2005). Adolescent self-regulation continues to reflect the individual's stable temperament and character. However, the life challenges of adolescence require greater sophistication, automaticity, and cross-domain coordination of self-regulation than earlier in childhood (Lewis, Granic, & Lamm, 2006).

In studies with children and adolescents, self-regulation has been found to be concurrently or retrospectively associated with higher levels of social, academic, and psychological competence and achievement, and lower levels of physical/mental health symptoms and distress. One study by Buckner and colleagues (2009) used Q-sort measures of executive functioning (i.e., impulse inhibition, attentional focusing/shifting, working memory, proactive goal-directed planning) and emotion regulation (i.e., tolerance of and recovery from frustration/distress, emotion expression appropriate to context) to show that

Table 1
Self-regulation competencies

Affective Self-Regulation
• Recognizing, labeling, and expressing discrete emotions Selectively enhancing or reducing affect states
• Maintaining affect intensity within a tolerable "window"
Cognitive Self-Regulation
• Focusing and sustaining attention selectively
• Encoding information in and retrieving information from procedural/situational and verbal/declarative/narrative memory
• Organizing and reconstructing information in working memory
• Formulating and evaluating the enactment and outcomes of goals and plans with optimism and willingness to disengage from unattainable goals
• Reflectively observing thought processes ("mentalizing"; Fonagy & Target, 2006)
Behavioral Self-Regulation
• Sustaining goal-directed behavior (task persistence)
• Shifting task focus and action strategy flexibly
• Error monitoring Inhibiting impulsive and aggressive behavior
Bodily Self-Regulation
• Recognizing somatic state-markers (e.g., tension/relaxation, energy/fatigue, pain/comfort)
• Maintaining physical arousal within a tolerable "window"
• Using bodily states to inform and guide affective, cognitive, and behavioral self-regulation

self-regulation was consistently associated with low-income children's social competence, behavioral and legal problems, anxiety and depression symptoms, and intellectual and academic functioning. Self-regulation capacities were also inversely related to anxiety and externalizing problems more so for girls (who had higher levels of self-regulatory skills) than for boys.

McEwen and Flouri's (2009) study of low-income British teens found that adverse events were associated with emotion regulation difficulties. In a prospective study of children from more affluent families and a cross-sectional sample of low-income children (i.e., Ayduk et al., 2000), self-regulation as assessed by a delay of gratification paradigm was related to fewer interpersonal problems in childhood and in early adulthood, in particular for individuals with high levels of sensitivity to rejection. In a sample of 11- to 13-year-old youth involved in 4-H clubs, self-regulation was assessed by a measure of the ability to "select, optimize, and compensate" was associated with adaptive functioning (Gestsdottir & Lerner, 2007, p. 508). Thus, across a range of populations and measures, self-regulation has been found to be an important contributor and/or indicator of children's and adolescents' adaptive psychosocial functioning.

Complex Traumatic Stress Reactions as Forms of Self-Dysregulation

Several lines of evidence suggest that complex traumatic stress reactions can be understood as instances of a breakdown or failure of self-regulation. First, self-dysregulation has been found to be related to a variety of psychological problems in childhood and adolescence, including depression (Buckner et al., 2009; Crockett, Moilanen, Raffaelli, &

Randall, 2006; Dishion & Connell, 2006), generalized anxiety (Roemer et al., 2009), eating disorders (Czaja, Rief, & Hilbert, 2009), substance use disorders (Dorard, Berthoz, Phan, Corcos, & Bungener, 2008), aggression (Ayduk, Rodriguez, Mischel, Shoda, & Wright, 2007; Bates, Goodnight, Fite, & Staples, 2009; Lewis et al., 2006), antisocial behavior (Dishion & Connell, 2006), risk-taking (Ben-Zur & Zeidner, 2009), self-harm (Buckner et al., 2009; Crockett et al., 2006; Dishion & Connell, 2006; Messer & Fremouw, 2008), and suicidality (Crowell, Beauchaine, & Linehan, 2005; Liu, Sun, & Yang, 2008).

Second, exposure to complex traumatic stressors places children and adolescents at risk for self-dysregulation. Maughan and Cicchetti's (2002) study of children with and without histories of maltreatment found that the maltreated children were twice as likely (80% vs. 37%) to exhibit dysregulated emotion patterns (i.e., undercontrolled/ambivalent and overcontrolled/unresponsive types); in addition, emotional dysregulation was associated with problems with depression and anxiety, and it mediated the relation between maltreatment and depression/anxiety. Polyvictimized children and adolescents in large population samples have been shown to have poorer interpersonal and school functioning (Finkelhor et al., 2010; Ford, Elhai, Connor, & Frueh, 2010) and an increased likelihood of juvenile justice involvement (Finkelhor et al., 2010; Ford et al., 2010) compared to children with more limited or no trauma histories. Abused children tend to selectively attend and react to stimuli that signal potential threat (Ayoub et al., 2006) as do children with anxiety disorders (Pine, 2007), thus limiting their capacities to self-regulate attention, emotion, and social involvement.

Third, the consistently documented sequelae of exposure to complex traumatic stressors in childhood and adolescence (e.g., PTSD, internalizing, externalizing symptoms) are associated with self-dysregulation (Cook et al., 2005). In a sample of toddlers from an urban low-income population, exposure to potential traumatic events was related to problems with emotion regulation, social functioning, and internalizing and externalizing symptoms, especially for those whose mothers observed dramatic behavior changes afterwards (Mongillo, Briggs-Gowan, Ford, & Carter, 2009).

A study by Amone-P'olak, Garnefski, and Kraaij (2007) of Ugandan youth who had been abducted during war found that self-reported cognitive and emotion regulation strategies were associated with posttraumatic stress as well as internalizing and externalizing problems. A population sample of Israeli adolescents exposed to ongoing terrorism violence showed that risky behavior was associated with more severe PTSD symptoms, both of which were related to discontinuing normal routines (Pat-Horenczyk, Schiff, & Doppelt, 2006) and functional impairment in social and school domains (Pat-Horenczyk et al., 2007). Thus, although self-regulation and its psychobiological components (Cicchetti & Curtis, 2005; Loizzo, 2009) have received limited scientific study in relation to children's and adolescents' posttraumatic stress reactions, there is a growing body of indirect evidence indicating that dysregulation and self-regulation may provide a useful framework for the assessment of the sequelae of complex forms of exposure to traumatic stressors (Koenen, 2006).

Assessing Self-Regulation and Dysregulation with Complexly Traumatized Children and Adolescents

A range of clinical and research psychometric questionnaires and structured interviews have been developed to assess trauma-related dysregulation and relevant self-regulation competences (Briere & Spinazzola, 2009; Nader, 2008). However, relatively few protocols have been identified for assessing the sequelae of exposure to complex traumatic stressors with children or adolescents (see, e.g., Briere & Spinazzola, 2009, pp. 108–110; Nader,

Table 2

Recommendations for assessment and treatment of complex trauma with children

1. Assess complex trauma history using developmentally validated self-report and caregiver report
   - Traumatic Events Screening Instrument (Daviss et al., 2000; Ford et al., 2000b)
   - UCLA PTSD Reaction Index (Steinberg, Brymer, Decker, & Pynoos, 2004)
   - Dimensions of Stressful Events (Fletcher, 1996)
   - Parent–Child Conflict Tactics Scale (Straus, Hamby, Finkelhor, Moore, & Runyan, 1998)
2. Assess affect regulation and dysregulation using norm-referenced measures
   - Five Factor Personality Inventory for Children (Kroes, Veerman, & De Bruyn, 2005)
   - Minnesota Multiphasic Personality Inventory for Adolescents (Stokes et al., 2009)
   - Personality Inventory for Youth/Personality Inventory for Children-Revised (Lachar & Gruber, 1993)
   - Affect Intensity and Reactivity measure for Youth (Jones et al., 2009)
   - Abbreviated Dysregulation Inventory (Mezzich et al., 2001)
3. Assess cognitive regulation and dysregulation using norm-referenced measures
   - Attentional focusing/shifting (Langenecker, Zubieta, Young, Akil, & Nielson, 2007)
   - Working memory (Mangeot et al., 2002)
   - Verbal/declarative and procedural memory (Poreh, 2005; Prehn-Kristensen et al., 2009)
   - Narrative memory (Miniscalco, Hagberg, Kadesjo, Westerlund, & Gillberg, 2007)
   - Higher order conceptual thinking and problem solving (Miniscalco et al., 2007; Poreh, 2005)
   - Adult-rated executive dysfunction: Achenbach System of Empirically Based Assessment (Achenbach et al., 2008); Behavior Assessment System for Children-2 (Kamphaus et al., 1999); Personality Inventory for Youth/Personality Inventory for Children-Revised (Lachar & Gruber, 1993)
   - Abbreviated Dysregulation Inventory Cognitive Scale (Mezzich et al., 2001)
   - Social information processing vignettes (Dodge, Greenberg, & Malone, 2008) Child Dissociative Checklist (Wherry et al., 2009)
   - Adolescent Dissociative Experiences Scale (ADES; Martinez-Taboas et al., 2006)
   - Trauma Symptom Checklist for Children (Wolpaw, Ford, Newman, Davis, & Briere, 2005), Trauma Symptom Checklist Young Children (Briere et al., 2001) dissociation subscales
4. Assess behavioral regulation and dysregulation using norm-referenced measures
   - Five-Factor Personality Inventory for Children Conscientiousness scale (Kroes et al., 2005)
   - Achenbach System of Empirically Based Assessment Social Competence scale (Achenbach et al., 2008)
   - Behavior Assessment System for Children-2 Activities of Daily Living, Adaptability, Leadership, Functional Communication, Social Skills, and Study Skills scales (Kamphaus et al., 1999)
   - Perceived Competence Scales for Children (Harter & Whitesell, 2003)
   - Abbreviated Dysregulation Inventory, Behavior Scale (Mezzich et al., 2001)
   - Trauma Symptom Checklist for Children (Wolpaw et al., 2005), Trauma Symptom Checklist Young Children (Briere et al., 2001) Sexual Concerns and Anger/Aggression subscales
   - Child Sexual Behavior Inventory (Friedrich et al., 2001)

(Continued)

Table 2
(Continued)

5. Assess somatic regulation and dysregulation
   - Achenbach System of Empirically Based Assessment Somatic Distress scale (Achenbach et al., 2008)
   - Behavior Assessment System for Children-2 Somatic Complaints scales (Kamphaus et al., 1999)
   - MMPI-A Hypochondriasis and Hysteria scales (Stokes et al., 2009)
   - Personality Inventory for Youth/Personality Inventory for Children-Revised Somatic Concern scale (Lachar & Gruber, 1993)
   - Trauma Symptom Checklist for Children (Wolpaw et al., 2005), Trauma Symptom Checklist Young Children (Briere et al., 2001), Somatic Complaints subscale

Note. MMPI-A = Minnesota Multiphasic Personality Inventory for Adolescents; UCLA PTSD = University of California at Los Angeles Posttraumatic Stress Disorder.

2008, pp. 263–264, 279). Table 2 provides a summary of measures of child and adolescent self-regulation and trauma-related dysregulation with recommendations for assessment of complex trauma and dysregulation.

Measures of Affect Regulation and Dysregulation

The Five-Factor Personality Inventory for Children (FFPI-C; Kroes, Veerman, & De Bruyn, 2005) is an omnibus self-report questionnaire that provides a well-normed, reliable, and validated Emotion Regulation subscale. The subscale does not assess affect dysregulation but rather its downstream byproducts (i.e., anger/hostility, anxiety, dysphoria, impulsivity, perceived vulnerability). Two other omnibus self-report measures, the Minnesota Multiphasic Personality Inventory for Adolescents (MMPI-A; Stokes, Pogge, Sarnicola, & McGrath, 2009) and the Personality Inventory for Youth/Personality Inventory for Children-Revised (PIY/PIC-R;Lachar & Gruber, 1993), have several similar subscales. The FFPI-C also has subscales reflecting specific competences, including Agreeableness (e.g., altruism, trust, tender mindedness), Extraversion (warmth, excitement seeking, positive emotions), and Openness to Experience (e.g., aesthetics, feelings, values).

A more direct measure of a subset of affect regulation competences (i.e., positive and negative affect intensity and affect reactivity) is provided by a briefer self-report questionnaire, the Affect Intensity and Reactivity Measure for Youth (AIR-Y; Jones, Leen-Feldner, Olatunji, Reardon, & Hawks, 2008). For an assessment of a broader range of affect regulation competences and types of affect dysregulation, the Dysregulation Inventory is a 92-item questionnaire (with a 30-item abbreviated version [ADI] selected using item response theory analyses to maximize discriminative efficiency) for children and adolescents 10 to 18 years old (Mezzich, Tarter, Giancola, & Kirisci, 2001). The ADI has self-, parent-, and teacher-report versions and includes a subscale for affect dysregulation with items tapping difficulty with anger (e.g., "I fly off the handle for no good reason"), anxiety (e.g., "I lose sleep because I worry"), hyperarousal (e.g., "There are days when I'm on edge all the time"), mood lability (e.g., "My mood goes up and down without reason"), and loss of control (e.g., "Often I am afraid I will lose control of my feelings"). The affect dysregulation subscale of the ADI correlates with measures of emotional distress and dysregulated behavior distinct from the callous and unemotional style associated with psychopathy (Mezzichet al., 2001; Pardini, Lochman, & Frick, 2003).

Two affect dysregulation measures developed and validated primarily with adults may be cautiously used with older adolescents. The Inventory of Altered Self-Capacities (IASC; Briere & Rickards, 2007) is a multiscale self-report questionnaire with subscales for affect dysregulation and tension reduction. Studies have shown evidence of validity for these IASC subscales in relation to measures of childhood trauma and abuse history, interpersonal problems, suicidality, and substance abuse history (Briere & Rickards, 2007). The Generalized Expectancies for Negative Mood Regulation (NMR; Christiansen, Copeland, & Stapert, 2008) is a 30-item questionnaire assessing affect modulation and distress tolerance that appears feasible for use with children with reading levels at or above the fifth-grade level.

Measures of Cognitive Regulation and Dysregulation

Neuropsychological tests of executive functions provide well-validated reliable assessments of children's and adolescents' cognitive regulation capacities, including attentional focusing/shifting, working memory, verbal/declarative and procedural memory, narrative memory, and higher order conceptual thinking/problem solving. However, neuropsychological testing requires specialized training and is time-intensive. Scales on omnibus self-, parent-, and teacher-report measures such as the Achenbach System of Empirically Based Assessment (ASEBA; formerly known as the Child Behavior Checklist, or CBCL; Achenbach et al., 2008) and the Behavior Assessment System for Children-2 (BASC-2; Kamphaus et al., 1999) as well as briefer parent or teacher rating scales (Mangeot, Armstrong, Colvin, Yeates, & Taylor, 2002; Trillingsgaard et al., 2004) have been developed as screening instruments to identify children or adolescents with clinically significant executive dysfunction. The PIY/PIC-R and ADI have scales for cognitive (achievement, learning, memory problems) and attentional (distractibility) impairment. Also, tests involving oral or written responses to simulated social vignettes have been validated as measures of social information processing, with children who have been maltreated or exposed to familial or neurotoxic adversity demonstrating deficits or problematic patterns (see Table 2).

Although substantial evidence supports an association between abuse or severe adversity and deficits or alterations in cognitive processing (Dodge, Greenberg, & Malone, 2008; McGee et al., 2009; Pollak, 2005), few measures exist to assess the range of cognitive self-regulation capacities beyond specialized tests for neuropsychological and intellectual functioning assessment (Sameroff & Rosenblum, 2006). Environmental factors such as family, peer, or neighborhood support (DuMont, Widom, & Czaja, 2007) have been shown to be predictors of resilience and recovery from childhood adversity, but the role of cognitive self-regulation remains to be studied. One promising measure is the psychometrically robust cognitive self-regulation subscale of the Dysregulation Inventory (Mezzich et al., 2001), which taps several important cognitive competences (e.g., "I develop a plan for all my important goals," "I think about the future consequences of my actions," "Failure at a task or in school makes me work harder," "I stick to a task until it is finished").

Dissociation is a sequela of cognitive dysregulation that has been found among children and adolescents to be associated with a history of exposure to complex traumatic stressors (Becker-Blease, Freyd, & Pears, 2004; Chu & DePrince, 2006; Kaplow, Dodge, Amaya-Jackson, & Saxe, 2005). Two validated psychometric scales have been developed to assess dissociation in childhood or adolescence: (a) the observer-rated Child Dissociative Checklist (CDC; Wherry, Neil, & Taylor, 2009) and (b) the self-rated Adolescent Dissociative Experiences Scale (ADES; Martinez-Taboas, Canino, Wang, Garcia, & Bravo, 2006), as well as a detailed but unvalidated clinical assessment measure, the Dissociative Features Profile (Silberg, 2000; see Nader, 2008, pp. 354–355, for descriptions and psychometric summaries). Two omnibus measures, the self- or caregiver-rated Trauma Symptom Checklist for Children (TSCC; Wolpaw, Ford, Newman, Davis, & Briere, 2005) and the caregiver-rated Trauma Symptom Checklist Young Children (TSCYC; Briere et al., 2001), include normed subscales for dissociation.

It is interesting to note that recent findings have suggested that dissociation may have a stronger relationship with behavioral rather than cognitive dysregulation in childhood (as it does in adulthood). Dissociation (assessed by foster parent ratings on the CDC) was shown to be associated with deficits in tasks requiring impulse inhibition but not those involving higher order cognitive planning, strategy, or multiple rule sets (Cromer, Stevens, DePrince, & Pears, 2006), using the Developmental Neuropsychological Assessment (NEPSY; Mosconi, Nelson, & Hooper, 2008). Moreover, whether pathological posttraumatic dissociation can be distinguished from normative anxiety-related dissociation in childhood is not known (Tolmunen et al., 2007). Thus, dissociation in childhood may be related to cognitive dysregulation, but until dissociation itself has been better defined and operationalized in childhood, their relationship is unclear.

Assessment of Behavioral Self-Regulation and Dysregulation

Behavioral self-regulation may be assessed by subscales from psychometrically robust child- and parent- or teacher-rated omnibus measures such as the FFPI-C Conscientiousness subscale and the AESBA Social Competence subscale. The BASC-2 extensively covers positive behavioral self-regulation, with subscales for activities of daily living, adaptability, leadership, functional communication, social skills, and study skills subscales. The self-report Perceived Competence Scales for Children (PCSC; Harter & Whitesell, 2003) reliably and validly assesses behavioral, peer, and physical competence in early childhood (i.e., age 4 to 7 years, with a pictorial version), and athletic, scholastic, behavioral, friendship, romantic relationship, and job competence in latency and adolescence.

With regard to dysregulation, the ADI behavior scale assesses hyperactivity (e.g., "I have difficulty remaining seated at school or at home during dinner"), argumentativeness ("I get into arguments when people disagree with me"), boredom ("I get bored easily"), and impulsivity ("I spend money without thinking about it first"). The ASEBA, BASC-2, MMPI-A, and PIY/PIC-2 indirectly assess behavioral dysregulation with subscales for aggression, hyperactivity, withdrawal, and conduct problems, as do other briefer self-report measures for those domains.

Children or adolescents who have been exposed to complex traumatic stressors are at risk for severe problems with aggression and sexuality (Cook et al., 2005). The TSCC and TSYCC have well-normed, reliable, and validated subscales for two types of behavioral dysregulation associated with exposure to sexual trauma (Sexual Concerns) and violence or physical abuse (Anger/Aggression). The Child Sexual Behavior Inventory (CSBI; Friedrich et al., 2001) provides a detailed and well-normed, reliable, and validated assessment of several highly specific types of dysregulated sexual motivation and behavior (e.g., intrusiveness, voyeurism, exhibitionism, self-stimulation).

Assessment of Somatic Self-Regulation and Dysregulation

Although self-regulation begins during infancy with somatic functions (Manian & Bornstein, 2009) that serve as a foundation for all other forms of self-regulation (Supplee, Skuban, Shaw, & Prout, 2009), standardized approaches to assessing children's and adolescents' ability to modulate physical arousal and hedonic tone could not be located. Omnibus measures (e.g., ASEBA; BASC-2; MMPI-A; PIY/PIC-2) have psychometrically robust subscales for somatic complaints that may serve as indirect indices of somatic dysregulation. Briefer self-report questionnaires have been developed for or used with adolescents to assess fatigue, somatic complaints, and the associated problem of alexithymia (van de Putte, Engelbert, Kuis, Kimpen, & Uiterwaal, 2007).

Children's Complex Traumatic Stress Reactions: Is a New Diagnosis Needed?

Self-regulation and complex posttraumatic dysregulation in childhood and adolescence take many forms that are not fully assessed by any single measure or battery of tests. In addition to pointing to the need for a more comprehensive approach to developing and validating assessment instruments for children's complex traumatic stress reactions, this review raises a further question: Do the existing conceptual and nosological (diagnostic) systems for child psychopathology require revision or expansion to address the full range of complex traumatic stress reactions? This question is of particular relevance at this time, because the American Psychiatric Association [APA] is considering the nature of and evidence for existing and new psychiatric disorder diagnoses in preparation for a major fifth revision of the *Diagnostic and Statistical Manual of Mental Disorders* (APA, 2008).

Features of PTSD (e.g., psychological and physiological distress in reaction to reminders of traumatic events, avoidance of such reminders and the associated distress, emotional numbing, hyperarousal) are evident in children's complex traumatic stress reactions. However, posttraumatic dysregulation in children does not always take the form of classic PTSD and often involves problems that lead to other comorbid (or alternative) diagnoses—notably reactive attachment disorder (Lyon, Coffey, & Silva, 2008), anxiety disorders (Pine, 2007), bipolar disorder (Romero et al., 2009), psychotic disorders (Hlastala & McClellan, 2005), dissociative disorders (Diseth & Christie, 2005), externalizing behavior disorders (Ford et al., 2000), eating disorders (Ohmann et al., 2008), and personality disorders (Ohmann et al., 2008). Although it is possible that childhood exposure to developmentally adverse interpersonal trauma may contribute to these disorders' etiology or course (e.g., exacerbating symptom severity), the plethora of clinical outcomes and presentations is likely to lead to wide variability and limited success in conceptualizing and treating complex traumatic stress reactions in childhood and adolescence (as well as subsequently in adulthood; Cook et al., 2005). Compared to the enormous estimated costs of the epidemic of posttraumatic neurodevelopmental injuries (more than that for all cancers combined), limited resources have been allocated for scientific research and evidence-based treatment for the millions of affected children and youth (Kaffman, 2009). Systematic approaches are therefore urgently needed for conceptualizing, assessing, and diagnosing (van der Kolk, 2005) the forms of biopsychosocial dysregulation that result from what Kaffman (2009) aptly described as posttraumatic neurodevelopmental injuries.

However, before a new diagnosis is contemplated, research is needed to empirically test the clinical utility (First et al., 2004) of existing diagnoses in accounting for and guiding clinicians in successfully treating children and adolescents with complex traumatic stress histories. Ford, Connor, and Hawke's (2009) study with psychiatrically impaired children in residential treatment found that, as expected, these children had substantial histories of early life adversity (Rutter, 2005), as operationalized by indices of documented physical or sexual abuse, impaired parents, and out-of-home placements. Cluster analyses revealed distinct subgroups representing different complexities of exposure to these potentially traumatic adversities and showed that the severity of internalizing and externalizing problems could not be fully accounted for by the fourth edition of the *Diagnostic and Statistical Manual of Mental Disorders* (*DSM-IV*; APA, 2000) psychiatric diagnoses (nor by age or gender). Two subgroups with complex trauma histories were identified that had severe teacher-rated behavior problems and clinician-rated psychosocial impairment independent of substance abuse, developmental disorders, and externalizing behavior disorder diagnoses. Moreover, substance use disorders were unrelated to behavior problems when the effect of complex trauma was included, and externalizing disorders were associated with impulsivity and hyperactivity only after the effect of a core component of complex trauma—multiple out-of-home placements—was accounted for. Thus, the study findings suggested that differential levels of severity of externalizing problems among seriously emotionally disturbed children are related to complex trauma exposure over and above the effect of *DSM-IV* psychiatric diagnoses.

Although these findings do not demonstrate that children with severe psychiatric impairment and complex trauma histories require a new diagnosis, they suggest that existing *DSM-IV* diagnoses do not fully account for the symptoms and impairment associated with complex trauma histories (Lieberman & Knorr, 2007). Thus, *DSM-IV* diagnoses may fail to identify a highly symptomatic and impaired subgroup of children who have extensive histories of parental impairment, abuse, and out-of-home placements.

Ford and colleagues' (2009) study also found that multiple out-of-home placements contributed to the severity of behavior problems beyond the effects of demographics, psychiatric diagnoses, documented abuse, and parental impairment. This is consistent with the presumed etiology of reactive attachment disorder (RAD), as well as with evidence that children who lose (or never acquire) stable attachment relationships as a result of abuse or impaired parenting are at risk for long-lasting (at least into early adulthood) problems with affect regulation, disorganized attachment working models, and dissociation (Lyons-Ruth, Dutra, Schuder, & Bianchi, 2006). Thus, children with RAD and adolescents with dysregulation similar to RAD warrant assessment for complex traumatic stress histories and reactions in order to guide treatment planning.

Although Ford et al. (2009) identified a subgroup that was particularly likely to have experienced sexual abuse (typically in combination with physical abuse), this subgroup in general did not differ in regards to symptom severity, psychosocial impairment, parental impairment, or out-of-home placements from children with primary histories of physical abuse. Sexual abuse appears to have a distinct course and sequelae in comparison to physical abuse, but it commonly occurs along with physical abuse, emotional abuse, and family violence (Putnam, 2003). While sexual abuse may warrant assessment of survivors' unique experiences of betrayal (Freyd, DePrince, & Gleaves, 2007), it does not appear to warrant a unique diagnostic classification in psychiatrically impaired children.

Physically abused children are reported by independent observers and caregivers (Crittenden, Claussen, & Sugarman, 1994) as well as peers (Salzinger, Feldman, Ng-Mak, Mojica, & Stockhammer, 2001) to be more verbally and physically assaultive than other children. However, the results of Ford et al.'s (2009) study suggest that it may not be abuse per se but a larger array of potentially traumatic conditions that arise in the context of abuse, including parental impairment and out-of-home placements. Moreover, the sequelae of physical abuse and associated adversities may lead youth to be labeled psychopathic or *callous and unemotional* (CU) and viewed as intractably antisocial. A study of girls in juvenile detention found that affect dysregulation as measured by the Dysregulation Inventory was unrelated to endorsing CU beliefs (Marsee & Frick, 2007), and a study with boys in juvenile detention identified a subgroup who endorsed callous and unemotional beliefs but reacted to cues of emotional distress (i.e., showing signs of empathy albeit on a relatively preconscious level) and tended to have histories of abuse (Kimonis, Frick, Munoz, & Aucoin, 2008). Similarly, further analyses of the sample of psychiatrically impaired children described earlier showed that physical abuse was associated with reactive but not proactive aggression (Ford, Fraleigh, & Connor, 2010). Thus, aggressive behavior and apparently CU attitudes among abused youth may be better understood and treated as complex traumatic stress reactions rather than as conduct disorder.

Although it requires replication with other clinical and nonclinical populations, the findings of these studies with psychiatrically impaired and juvenile justice–involved youth suggest that existing psychiatric diagnoses may not fully (nor in some cases accurately) account for the severe problems in multiple domains of self-regulation that occur following exposure to complex trauma (Cook et al., 2005; Kaffman, 2009; van der Kolk, 2005). While advances in theory, research, and clinical practice proceed and inform the development of diagnostic nosology, assessment instrumentation and procedures, and treatment for children with complex trauma histories, it is incumbent upon practitioners to proactively address the self-regulation problems and needs of these children, regardless of their past or current diagnoses. Sensitive inquiry concerning trauma history (see Nader, 2007; Table 1) should be standard practice for all mental health providers. Moreover, a thorough evaluation with well-validated measures of self-regulation and dysregulation in the affective, cognitive, behavioral, and somatic domains is essential for all children.

Ultimately, clinical assessment and conceptualization/diagnosis is useful primarily through informing treatment planning and delivery. In the past decade, several therapeutic models have been designed or adapted to address the core self-regulation problems associated with complex trauma (see Ford & Cloitre, 2009; Table 1). As the toolkit for assessment of complex trauma and self-regulation/dysregulation has grown, the need for and potential benefits of treatments that correspondingly focus on complex trauma and self-regulation has become evident. Regardless of the specific diagnostic profile of each child, which understandably varies greatly on the basis of biological and environmental differences for each individual child, a complex trauma perspective provides clinicians with two key therapeutic opportunities. The first challenge is to determine whether complex trauma has been a part of the child's developmental experience, and the second is to determine how enhancing self-regulation can be accomplished in a therapeutic manner so as to improve the child's ability to develop fully and overcome otherwise debilitating psychiatric and psychosocial problems.

References

Achenbach, T. M., Becker, A., Dopfner, M., Heiervang, E., Roessner, V., Steinhausen, H. C., et al. (2008). Multicultural assessment of child and adolescent psychopathology with ASEBA and SDQ instruments: Research findings, applications, and future directions. *Journal of Child Psychology and Psychiatry*, *49*, 251–275.

America Psychiatric Association. (2000). *Diagnostic and statistical manual of mental disorders* (text rev.). Washington, DC: Author.

American Psychiatric Association. (2008). *DSM-V: The future manual.* Retrieved from http://www.psych.org/dsmv.asp

Amone-P'olak, K., Garnefski, N., & Kraaij, V. (2007). Adolescents caught between fires: Cognitive emotion regulation in response to war experiences in Northern Uganda. *Journal of Adolescence, 30*, 655–669.

Ayduk, O., Mendoza-Denton, R., Mischel, W., Downey, G., Peake, P. K., & Rodriguez, M. (2000). Regulating the interpersonal self: Strategic self-regulation for coping with rejection sensitivity. *Journal of Personality and Social Psychology, 79*, 776–792.

Ayduk, O., Rodriguez, M. L., Mischel, W. R., Shoda, Y. I., & Wright, J. (2007). Verbal intelligence and self-regulatory competencies: Joint predictors of boys' aggression. *Journal of Research in Personality, 41*, 374–388.

Ayoub, C. C., O'Connor, E., Rappolt-Schlichtmann, G., Fischer, K. W., Rogosch, F. A., Toth, S. L., et al. (2006). Cognitive and emotional differences in young maltreated children: A translational application of dynamic skill theory. *Development & Psychopathology, 18*(3), 679–706.

Bates, J. E., Goodnight, J. A., Fite, J. E., & Staples, A. D. (2009). Behavior regulation as a product of temperament and environment. In S. L. Olson & A. J. Sameroff (Eds.), *Biopsychosocial regulatory processes in the development of childhood behavioral problems* (pp. 116–143). New York: Cambridge University Press.

Becker-Blease, K. A., Freyd, J. J., & Pears, K. C. (2004). Preschoolers' memory for threatening information depends on trauma history and attentional context: Implications for the development of dissociation. *Journal of Trauma & Dissociation, 5*(1), 113–131.

Ben-Zur, H., & Zeidner, M. (2009). Threat to life and risk-taking behaviors: A review of empirical findings and explanatory models. *Personality and Social Psychology Review, 13*(2), 109–128.

Briere, J., Johnson, K., Bissada, A., Damon, L., Crouch, J., Gil, E., et al. (2001). The Trauma Symptom Checklist for Young Children (TSCYC): Reliability and association with abuse exposure in a multi-site study. *Child Abuse and Neglect, 25*, 1001–1014.

Briere, J., & Rickards, S. (2007). Self-awareness, affect regulation, and relatedness: Differential sequels of childhood versus adult victimization experiences. *Journal of Nervous & Mental Disease, 195*, 497–503.

Briere, J., & Spinazzola, J. (2009). Assessment of complex posttraumatic reactions. In C. A. Courtois & J. D. Ford (Eds.), *Treating complex traumatic stress disorders: An evidence-based guide* (pp. 104–121). New York: Guilford Press.

Buckner, J. C., Mezzacappa, E., & Beardslee, W. R. (2009). Self-regulation and its relations to adaptive functioning in low income youths. *American Journal of Orthopsychiatry, 79*(1), 19–30.

Calkins, S. D. (2007). The emergence of self-regulation. In C. A. Brownell & C. B. Kopp (Eds.), *Socioemotional development in the toddler years: Transitions and transformations* (pp. 261–284). New York: Guilford Press.

Christiansen, L. M., Copeland, E. P., & Stapert, E. B. (2008). Predictors of somatic symptoms in younger rural adolescents. *Adolescence, 43*, 791–806.

Chu, A., & DePrince, A. P. (2006). Development of dissociation. *Journal and Trauma & Dissociation, 7*(4), 75–89.

Cicchetti, D., & Curtis, W. J. (2005). An event-related potential study of the processing of affective facial expressions in young children who experienced maltreatment during the first year of life. *Development & Psychopathology, 17*, 641–677.

Cook, A., Spinazzola, P., Ford, J., Lanktree, C., Blaustein, M., Cloitre, M., et al. (2005). Complex trauma in children and adolescents. *Psychiatric Annals, 35*, 390–398.

Crittenden, P. M., Claussen, A. H., & Sugarman, D. P. (1994). Physical and psychological maltreatment in middle childhood and adolescence. *Development & Psychopathology, 6*, 145–164.

Crockett, L. J., Moilanen, K. L., Raffaelli, M., & Randall, B. A. (2006). Psychological profiles and adolescent adjustment. *Developmental Psychopathology, 18*, 195–214.

Cromer, L. D., Stevens, C., DePrince, A. P., & Pears, K. (2006). The relationship between executive attention and dissociation in children. *Journal of Trauma & Dissociation, 7*, 135–153.

Crowell, S. E., Beauchaine, T. P., & Linehan, M. M. (2009). A biosocial developmental model of borderline personality. *Psychological Bulletin*, *135*, 495–510.

Czaja, J., Rief, W., & Hilbert, A. (2009). Emotion regulation and binge eating in children. *International Journal of Eating Disorders*, *42*, 356–362.

Daviss, W. B., Mooney, D., Racusin, R., Ford, J. D., Fleischer, A., & McHugo, G. J. (2000). Predicting posttraumatic stress after hospitalization for pediatric injury. *Journal of the American Academy of Child & Adolescent Psychiatry*, *39*, 576–583.

Diseth, T. H., & Christie, H. J. (2005). Trauma-related dissociative (conversion) disorders in children and adolescents: An overview of assessment tools and treatment principles. *Nordic Journal of Psychiatry*, *59*, 278–292.

Dishion, T. J., & Connell, A. (2006). Adolescents' resilience as a self-regulatory process: promising themes for linking intervention with developmental science. *Annals of the New York Academy of Science*, *1094*, 125–138.

Dodge, K. A., Greenberg, M. T., & Malone, P. S. (2008). Testing an idealized dynamic cascade model of the development of serious violence in adolescence. *Child Development*, *79*, 1907–1927.

Dorard, G., Berthoz, S., Phan, O., Corcos, M., & Bungener, C. (2008). Affect dysregulation in cannabis abusers. *European Child and Adolescent Psychiatry*, *17*, 274–282.

DuMont, K. A., Widom, C. S., & Czaja, S. J. (2007). Predictors of resilience in abused and neglected children grown-up: The role of individual and neighborhood characteristics. *Child Abuse and Neglect*, *31*, 255–274.

First, M. B., Pincus, H. A., Levine, J. B., Williams, J. B. W., Ustun, B., & Peele, R. (2004). Clinical utility as a criterion for revising psychiatric diagnoses. *American Journal of Psychiatry*, *161*, 946–954.

Finkelhor, D., Turner, H., Ormrod, R., & Hamby, S. L. (2010). Trends in childhood violence and abuse exposure: Evidence from 2 national surveys. *Archives of Pediatric and Adolescent Medicine*, *164*(3), 238–242.

Fletcher, K. (1996). Psychometric review of Dimensions of Stressful Events (DOSE) Ratings Scale. In B. Stamm (Ed.), *Measurement of stress, trauma, and adaptation* (pp. 144–151). Lutherville, MD: Sidran Press.

Fonagy, P., & Target, M. (2006). The mentalization-focused approach to self pathology. *Journal of Personality Disorders*, *20*, 544–576.

Ford, J. D., & Cloitre, M. (2009). Best practices in psychotherapy for children and adolescents. In C. A. Courtois & J. D. Ford (Eds.), *Treating complex traumatic stress disorders: An evidence-based guide* (pp. 59–81). New York: Guilford.

Ford, J. D., Connor, D. F., & Hawke, J. (2009). Complex trauma among psychiatrically impaired children. *Journal of Clinical Psychiatry*, *70*, 1155–1163.

Ford, J. D., Elhai, J. D., Connor, D. F., & Frueh, B. C. (2010). Poly-victimization and risk of posttraumatic, depressive, and substance use disorders and involvement in delinquency in a national sample of adolescents. *Journal of Adolescent Health*, *46*, 545–552.

Ford, J. D., Fraleigh, L. A., & Connor, D. F. (2010). Child abuse and aggression among psychiatrically impaired children. *Journal of Clinical Child and Adolescent Psychology*, *39*, 25–34.

Ford, J. D., Racusin, R., Ellis, C. G., Daviss, W. B., Reiser, J., Fleischer, A., et al. (2000). Child maltreatment, other trauma exposure, and posttraumatic symptomatology among children with oppositional defiant and attention deficit hyperactivity disorders. *Child Maltreatment*, *5*, 205–217.

Freyd, J. J., DePrince, A. P., & Gleaves, D. H. (2007). The state of betrayal trauma theory: Reply to McNally—Conceptual issues and future directions. *Memory*, *15*, 295–311.

Friedrich, W. N., Fisher, J. L., Dittner, C. A., Acton, R., Berliner, L., Butler, J., et al. (2001). Child Sexual Behavior Inventory. *Child Maltreatment*, *6*(1), 37–49.

Gestsdottir, S., & Lerner, R. M. (2007). Intentional self-regulation and positive youth development in early adolescence. *Developmental Psychology*, *43*, 508–521.

Harter, S., & Whitesell, N. R. (2003). Beyond the debate: Why some adolescents report stable self-worth over time and situation, whereas others report changes in self-worth. *Journal of Personality*, *71*, 1027–1058.

Hemenover, S. H., Augustine, A. A., Shulman, T., Tran, T. Q., & Barlett, C. P. (2008). Individual differences in negative affect repair. *Emotion, 8*, 468–478.

Hlastala, S. A., & McClellan, J. (2005). Phenomenology and diagnostic stability of youths with atypical psychotic symptoms. *Journal of Child and Adolescent Psychopharmacology, 15*, 497–509.

Jones, R. E., Leen-Feldner, E. W., Olatunji, B. O., Reardon, L. E., & Hawks, E. (2009). Psychometric properties of the Affect Intensity and Reactivity Measure adapted for Youth (AIR-Y). *Psychological Assessment, 21*, 162–175.

Kaffman, A. (2009). The silent epidemic of neurodevelopmental injuries. *Biological Psychiatry, 66*, 624–626.

Kamphaus, R. W., Petoskey, M. D., Cody, A. H., Rowe, E. W., Huberty, C. J., & Reynolds, C. R. (1999). A typology of parent rated child behavior for a national U.S. sample. *Journal of Child Psychology and Psychiatry, 40*, 607–616.

Kaplow, J. B., Dodge, K. A., Amaya-Jackson, L., & Saxe, G. N. (2005). Pathways to PTSD, part II: Sexually abused children. *American Journal of Psychiatry, 162*(7), 1305–1310.

Kim, S. H., & Hamann, S. (2007). Neural correlates of positive and negative emotion regulation. *Journal of Cognitive Neuroscience, 19*, 776–798.

Kimonis, E. R., Frick, P. J., Munoz, L. C., & Aucoin, K. J. (2008). Callous-unemotional traits and the emotional processing of distress cues in detained boys. *Development & Psychopathology, 20*, 569–589.

Koenen, K. C. (2006). Developmental epidemiology of PTSD: Self-regulation as a central mechanism. *Annals of the New York Academy of Sciences, 1071*, 255–266.

Kroes, G., Veerman, J. W., & De Bruyn, E. E. (2005). The impact of the Big Five personality traits on reports of child behavior problems by different informants. *Journal of Abnormal Child Psychology, 33*, 231–240.

Lachar, D., & Gruber, C. P. (1993). Development of the Personality Inventory for Youth: A self-report companion to the Personality Inventory for Children. *Journal of Personality Assessment, 61*(1), 81–98.

Langenecker, S. A., Zubieta, J. K., Young, E. A., Akil, H., & Nielson, K. A. (2007). A task to manipulate attentional load, set-shifting, and inhibitory control. *Journal of Clinical and Experimental Neuropsychology, 29*, 842–853.

Lewis, M. D., Granic, I., & Lamm, C. (2006). Behavioral differences in aggressive children linked with neural mechanisms of emotion regulation. *Annals of the New York Academy of Science, 1094*, 164–177.

Lieberman, A. F., & Knorr, K. (2007). The impact of trauma: A development framework for infancy and early childhood. *Psychiatric Annals, 37*, 416–422.

Liu, X., Sun, Z., & Yang, Y. (2008). Parent-reported suicidal behavior and correlates among adolescents in China. *Journal of Affective Disorders, 105*(1–3), 73–80.

Loizzo, J. (2009). Optimizing learning and quality of life throughout the lifespan. *Annals of the New York Academy of Sciences, 1172*, 186–198.

Lyon, G. J., Coffey, B., & Silva, R. (2008). Posttraumatic stress disorder and reactive attachment disorder. *Journal of Child and Adolescent Psychopharmacology, 18*, 641–646.

Lyons-Ruth, K., Dutra, L., Schuder, M. R., & Bianchi, I. (2006). From infant attachment disorganization to adult dissociation. *Psychiatric Clinics of North America, 29*, 63–86.

Mangeot, S., Armstrong, K., Colvin, A. N., Yeates, K. O., & Taylor, H. G. (2002). Long-term executive function deficits in children with traumatic brain injuries. *Child Neuropsychology, 8*, 271–284.

Manian, N., & Bornstein, M. H. (2009). Dynamics of emotion regulation in infants of clinically depressed and nondepressed mothers. *Journal of Child Psychology and Psychiatry, 50*, 1410–1418.

Marsee, M. A., & Frick, P. J. (2007). Exploring the cognitive and emotional correlates to proactive and reactive aggression in a sample of detained girls. *Journal of Abnormal Child Psychology, 35*, 969–981.

Martinez-Taboas, A., Canino, G., Wang, M. Q., Garcia, P., & Bravo, M. (2006). Prevalence and victimization correlates of pathological dissociation in a community sample of youths. *Journal of Traumatic Stress*, *19*, 439–448.

Maughan, A., & Cicchetti, D. (2002). Impact of child maltreatment and interadult violence on children's emotion regulation abilities and socioemotional adjustment. *Child Development*, *73*, 1525–1542.

McEwen, C., & Flouri, E. (2009). Fathers' parenting, adverse life events, and adolescents' emotional and eating disorder symptoms: The role of emotion regulation. *European Child and Adolescent Psychiatry*, *18*(4), 206–216.

McGee, C. L., Bjorkquist, O. A., Price, J. M., Mattson, S. N., & Riley, E. P. (2009). Social information processing skills in children with histories of heavy prenatal alcohol exposure. *Journal of Abnormal Child Psychology*, *37*(6), 817–830.

Messer, J. M., & Fremouw, W. J. (2008). A critical review of explanatory models for self-mutilating behaviors in adolescents. *Clinical Psychology Review*, *28*, 162–178.

Mezzich, A., Tarter, R., Giancola, P., & Kirisci, L. (2001). The Dysregulation Inventory. *Journal of Child and Adolescent Substance Abuse*, *10*, 35–43.

Miniscalco, C., Hagberg, B., Kadesjo, B., Westerlund, M., & Gillberg, C. (2007). Narrative skills, cognitive profiles and neuropsychiatric disorders in 7–8-year-old children with late developing language. *International Journal of Language and Communication Disorders*, *42*, 665–681.

Mongillo, E. A., Briggs-Gowan, M., Ford, J. D., & Carter, A. S. (2009). Impact of traumatic life events in a community sample of toddlers. *Journal of Abnormal Child Psychology*, *37*, 455–468.

Mosconi, M., Nelson, L., & Hooper, S. R. (2008). Confirmatory factor analysis of the NEPSY for younger and older school-age children. *Psychological Reports*, *102*, 861–866.

Nader, K. (2008). *Understanding and assessing trauma in children and adolescents: Measures, methods, and youth in context*. New York: Routledge.

Ohmann, S., Schuch, B., Konig, M., Blaas, S., Fliri, C., & Popow, C. (2008). Self-injurious behavior in adolescent girls. *Psychopathology*, *41*, 226–235.

Pardini, D. A., Lochman, J. E., & Frick, P. J. (2003). Callous/unemotional traits and social-cognitive processes in adjudicated youths. *Journal of the American Academy of Child and Adolescent Psychiatry*, *42*, 364–371.

Pat-Horenczyk, R., Peled, O., Miron, T., Brom, D., Villa, Y., & Chemtob, C. M. (2007). Risk-taking behaviors among Israeli adolescents exposed to recurrent terrorism: provoking danger under continuous threat? *American Journal of Psychiatry*, *164*(1), 66–72.

Pat-Horenczyk, R., Schiff, M., & Doppelt, O. (2006). Maintaining routine despite ongoing exposure to terrorism: A healthy strategy for adolescents? *Journal of Adolescent Health*, *39*, 199–205.

Pine, D. S. (2007). Research review: A neuroscience framework for pediatric anxiety disorders. *Journal of Child Psychology and Psychiatry*, *48*, 631–648.

Pollak, S. D. (2005). Early adversity and mechanisms of plasticity: Integrating affective neuroscience with developmental approaches to psychopathology. *Development & Psychopathology*, *17*(3), 735–752.

Poreh, A. (2005). Analysis of mean learning of normal participants on the Rey Auditory-Verbal Learning Test. *Psychological Assessment*, *17*, 191–199.

Porges, S. W. (2009). The polyvagal theory. *Cleveland Clinical Journal of Medicine*, *76*(Suppl. 2), S86–S90.

Prehn-Kristensen, A., Goder, R., Chirobeja, S., Bressmann, I., Ferstl, R., & Baving, L. (2009). Sleep in children enhances preferentially emotional declarative but not procedural memories. *Journal of Experimental Child Psychology*, *104*(1), 132–139.

Putnam, F. W. (2003). Ten-year research update review: Child sexual abuse. *Journal of the American Academy of Child and Adolescent Psychiatry*, *42*, 269–278.

Raffaelli, M., Crockett, L. J., & Shen, Y. L. (2005). Developmental stability and change in self-regulation from childhood to adolescence. *Journal of Genetic Psychology, 166*(1), 54–75.

Roemer, L., Lee, J. K., Salters-Pedneault, K., Erisman, S. M., Orsillo, S. M., & Mennin, D. S. (2009). Mindfulness and emotion regulation difficulties in generalized anxiety disorder. *Behavior Therapy, 40*, 142–154.

Romero, S., Birmaher, B., Axelson, D., Goldstein, T., Goldstein, B. I., Gill, M. K., et al. (2009). Prevalence and correlates of physical and sexual abuse in children and adolescents with bipolar disorder. *Journal of Affective Disorders, 112*, 144–150.

Rutter, M. (2005). Environmentally mediated risks for psychopathology: Research strategies and findings. *Journal of the American Academy of Child & Adolescent Psychiatry, 44*(1), 3–18.

Salzinger, S., Feldman, R. S.,Ng-Mak, D. S., Mojica, E., & Stockhammer, T. F. (2001). The effect of physical abuse on children's social and affective status. *Development & Psychopathology, 13*, 805–825.

Sameroff, A. J., & Rosenblum, K. L. (2006). Psychosocial constraints on the development of resilience. *Annals of the New York Academy of Science, 1094*, 116–124.

Sbarra, D. A., & Hazan, C. (2008). Coregulation, dysregulation, self-regulation. *Personality & Social Psychology Review, 12*, 141–167.

Silberg, J. L. (2000). Fifteen years of dissociation in maltreated children. *Child Maltreatment, 5*, 119–136.

Steinberg, A. M., Brymer, M. J., Decker, K. B., & Pynoos, R. S. (2004). The University of California at Los Angeles Post-traumatic Stress Disorder Reaction Index. *Current Psychiatry Report, 6*(2), 96–100.

Stokes, J., Pogge, D., Sarnicola, J., & McGrath, R. (2009). Correlates of the MMPI-A Psychopathology Five (PSY-5) facet scales in an adolescent inpatient sample. *Journal of Personality Assessment, 91*(1), 48–57.

Straus, M. A., Hamby, S. L., Finkelhor, D., Moore, D. W., & Runyan, D. (1998). Identification of child maltreatment with the Parent–Child Conflict Tactics Scales: Development and psychometric data for a national sample of American parents. *Child Abuse and Neglect, 22*, 249–270.

Supplee, L. H., Skuban, E. M., Shaw, D. S., & Prout, J. (2009). Emotion regulation strategies and later externalizing behavior among European American and African American children. *Developmental Psychopathology, 21*, 393–415.

Tolmunen, T., Maaranen, P., Hintikka, J., Kylma, J., Rissanen, M. L., Honkalampi, K., et al. (2007). Dissociation in a general population of Finnish adolescents. *Journal of Nervous & Mental Disease, 195*, 614–617.

Trillingsgaard, A., Damm, D., Sommer, S., Jepsen, J. R., Ostergaard, O., Frydenberg, M., et al. (2004). Developmental profiles on the basis of the FTF (Five to Fifteen) questionnaire. *European Child and Adolescent Psychiatry, 13*(Suppl. 3), 39–63.

van de Putte, E. M., Engelbert, R. H., Kuis, W., Kimpen, J. L., & Uiterwaal, C. S. (2007). Alexithymia in adolescents with chronic fatigue syndrome. *Journal of Psychosomatic Research, 63*, 377–380.

van der Kolk, B. A. (2005). Developmental trauma disorder. *Psychiatric Annals, 35*, 401–408.

Wherry, J. N., Neil, D. A., & Taylor, T. N. (2009). Pathological dissociation as measured by the child dissociative checklist. *Journal of Child Sexual Abuse, 18*(1), 93–102.

Wolpaw, J. M., Ford, J. D., Newman, E., Davis, J. L., & Briere, J. (2005). Trauma Symptom Checklist for Children. In T. Grisso, G. Vincent, & D. Seagrave (Eds.), *Mental health screening and assessment in juvenile justice* (pp. 152–165). New York: Guilford Press.

Complicated Grief Reactions in Children and Adolescents

KATHLEEN NADER[1] AND ALISON SALLOUM[2]

[1]Two Suns
[2]University of South Florida

An understanding of complicated grief in youth is incomplete, because the full range of observed, theorized, and studied symptoms and reactions has not yet been examined in different age groups. Until recently, scales to assess complicated grief in youth were based on adult constructs of complicated grief and did not include many of the symptoms and reactions proposed for posttrauma grief. Much can be learned from adult theories and findings. Nevertheless, future prospective studies are needed that include children from different age groups and with different personal traits, environmental conditions, relationships with the deceased, and circumstances of loss.

In the late 1900s, researchers and clinicians observed that when someone died traumatically, youth who were traumatized by the event and/or the nature of the loss were often unable to grieve normally. Since then, a number of theories have emerged related to the traits, circumstances, and conditions that influence maladaptive or *complicated grief* (CG) reactions and the persistence of symptoms in bereaved individuals (see Nader & Layne, 2009). Although maladaptive (pathological) grief reactions are addressed briefly in the 4th edition of the *Diagnostic and Statistical Manual of Mental Disorders* (*DSM-IV*; American Psychiatric Association [APA], 1994, 2000), and different types of CG reactions have been theorized and sometimes studied, the exact nature of CG in children and adolescents has yet to be defined. Much can be learned from the examination of theories and findings for adults. Nevertheless, developmental differences in youths' understanding of death and other aspects of loss, the nature and progression of emerging skills (e.g., self-regulation, identity formation, coping capacity), and brain growth suggest the likelihood of differences in the impact of loss, grief presentation, and treatment needs for varying age groups.

Numerous questions require clarification in order for there to be an understanding of CG reactions in youth. With some overlap, theories of CG emphasize aspects of the griever, the nature of the loss, or the relationship with the deceased (Nader & Layne, 2009; Pearlman, Schwartz, & Cloitre, 2010). For example, losses have sometimes been classified by griever traits or by whether deaths occurred under circumstances that were considered traumatic, specifically violent, personally devastating, or involving a close relationship. On the one hand, researchers and clinicians have proposed specific types of CG (e.g., prolonged grief and traumatic grief; Nader & Layne, 2009; Prigerson et al., 2009). They have also suggested that a continuum of symptoms from adaptive to maladaptive is a more accurate measure of CG than assessment of the discrete criteria proposed for different types of CG (Nader & Layne, 2009). Lack of clarity on CG in youth is related to the need for (a) large enough prospective studies, which assess the full range of symptoms/reactions theorized and observed in youth of different ages; and (b) studies with a broad enough range of influencing variables, to discover some of the complex interrelationships among variables and the developmental age group differences in reactions. Assessment measures that include symptoms/reactions of each of the main theories discussed in relation to traumatic events have only recently become available.

This article summarizes a number of theories and related findings for normal and complicated (maladaptive) forms of grief and presents some of the assessment issues and tools important to the study of CG. Theories that are developed primarily on the basis of observations and findings for adult grief reactions are discussed first for their implications for childhood CG. Normal grief in youth and published descriptions and discussions of traumatized youths' grief reactions follow.

Theories and Findings on the Basis of Adult Grief Reactions

Numerous studies have examined theories that were originally based on observations and findings with bereaved adults. Although these studies examined a number of variables, the theories and findings presented here are organized as those that emphasized the nature of grief, aspects of grievers, and the relationship with the deceased (see the "Types of Complicated Grief" section for the latter).

Nature of Grief

Researchers have examined normal grief and prolonged grief reactions in adults and youth. A full understanding of CG requires examination of additional forms of CG reactions (e.g., traumatic grief) as well. Nevertheless, adult-based observations and findings suggest distinctions (e.g., between chronic grief and chronic depression), variables, and variations in treatment needs that should be considered in the conceptualization and study of CG in youth. For example, the nature of grief, aspects of the griever, the nature of the loss, and the relationship with the deceased are important in the study of CG.

Cognitive-Behavioral Conceptualization

Boelen, van den Hout, and van den Bout (2006) suggested that although other variables may influence CG, three processes are crucial to its development and maintenance: "(a) poor elaboration and integration of the loss into the database of autobiographical knowledge, (b) negative global beliefs and misinterpretations of grief reactions, and (c) anxious and depressive avoidance strategies" (p. 111). In theory, the interactions among the three processes account for the intensity and persistence of CG. Although background variables (including traumas and traits) are not believed to produce CG, they may influence the three main processes, the nature and content of grieving, and emotional problems after bereavement. In this theory, some of the proposed symptoms of CG are seen as driving forces in the condition.

Failure of elaboration and integration. In normal grief, the mourner processes the permanence of the separation and its implications and meaning to his or her life. Over time, reminders of the loss become less disruptive, and grief and despair are replaced by a range of more balanced emotions (Boelen, van den Hout et al., 2006). In addition, fragmented memories of the deceased become a part of a coherent story about the relationship, with a beginning and an end. In contrast, for the individual with CG, the loss continues to be experienced as an unreal event. The mourner has difficulty admitting that the separation is permanent. Consequently, attachment reactions (proximity seeking/searching) may persist.

Negative beliefs and misinterpretations. Negative beliefs are likely to intensify a mourner's propensity to dwell on what is lost, thereby interfering with integration of the loss (e.g., by keeping attention away from the present and future; Boelen, van den Hout et al., 2006). Negative beliefs, such as the worthlessness of self, meaninglessness of life, and hopelessness of the future, may contribute to depressive avoidance. In addition, mistaken beliefs that emotional pain will be intolerable, that the intensity of sadness may signal loss of control, that vivid intrusions reflect insanity, and/or that numbness is depression may contribute to anxious avoidance. Negative beliefs may fuel emotions associated with CG such as yearning and anger. Misinterpretations may engender discomfort and fear. Importantly, either negative beliefs, misinterpretations, or both may contribute to the development of CG.

Avoidance strategies. Mourners may avoid people, places, and things that remind them of the loss (Boelen, van den Hout et al., 2006). Avoidance is not always detrimental; temporary escape from sorrow can be protective. However, persistent avoidance is likely to interfere with integration and adjustment. When using anxious avoidance strategies, mourners may anxiously suppress painful memories, deflect undesired thoughts and feelings, and find ways to escape admitting the loss and associated emotions. Some mourners may approach reminders but avoid confrontations with the fact that the deceased is dead and gone. Depressive avoidance is characterized by behavioral patterns of inactivity and withdrawal. Consequently, the normal reinforcers of healthy behavior, such as seeking support, are absent. Both forms of avoidance may contribute to detachment, numbness, and problems imagining a fulfilling life and future.

Implications. A failure to integrate the loss, along with the interference to integration that results from anxious and/or depressive avoidance and negative beliefs and/or misinterpretations may be important underlying constructs for more than one type of grief and their treatment. As will be discussed, although a failure of processing and integration underlies traumatic grief (TG) and prolonged grief (PG; see the "Types of Grief" section), the manner in which this occurs differs for each type of CG. Trauma may result in anxious and/or depressive avoidance as well as in negative self-appraisals, negative beliefs, and unrealistic, fearful cognitions. Differences in the trauma-related nature of avoidance, negative thoughts, and interference with integration, however, reportedly correspond to some differences in treatment needs. In particular, trauma clinicians have observed the need to process aspects of the trauma before grief work can be successfully begun or accomplished. Traumatized youth may experience devastation from loss of the relationship with the deceased and/or experience traumatization because of the traumatic nature of a death. Making a distinction among these three groups—traumatized grievers, grievers who are devastated by the loss but not traumatized, and grievers who are devastated and traumatized—may be important to understanding the nature of reactions and the success of treatment methods. Additional research is needed to determine the importance of this distinction.

Categorical CG *Versus a Continuum of Symptoms/Reactions*

Although evidence has confirmed different types of CG, grief continuums have been discussed as well. Rather than there being discrete stages of grief (Kubler-Ross, 1969), research has suggested that reactions underlying the psychological construct of grief such as disbelief, yearning, anger, and sadness are highly correlated. On average, for normal grief reactions, these reactions peak at around 6 months after the death (Prigerson & Maciejewski, 2008). As grief diminishes, acceptance of the loss increases, suggesting that grief and acceptance are two ends of a continuum. Prigerson and Maciejewski (2008) suggested that acceptance may represent the tranquility and sense of peace that follows letting go of the struggle to regain what is lost. In addition, for adults, Holland, Neimeyer, Boelen, and Prigerson (2009) found little support for a categorical conceptualization of CG, but instead found support that normal and complicated grief fall along different ends of a continuum. They suggested that it may be best to define CG by the severity of grief symptoms. Even though a continuum of symptoms/reactions may also provide a measure of severity in grieving youth, different types of CG appear to correspond to some differences in treatment needs.

Qualities of the Griever

Grieving styles and trajectories are presented in this section (see Table 1 for additional details).

Grieving Style

Martin and Doka (2000) theorized that grieving styles are characterized by culturally and personally influenced idiosyncratic strategies (i.e., idiosyncratic use of cognitive, behavioral, and affective strategies in adapting to loss). Styles can be found on a continuum from intuitive to instrumental patterns, with blended patterns located along the continuum (Doughty, 2009). The intuitive grieving style is marked by a heightened experience and expression of emotion (i.e., sadness, anguish, and tears that may persist long after the death). In contrast, the instrumental grieving style is marked by a more cognitive-behavioral, problem-solving approach (i.e., affect under control, a desire to manage emotions rather than express them openly, focus on problem-solving activities rather than on the pain of the loss). All types of grievers may seek social support. Although the more prevalent blended grievers naturally experience and express grief in both cognitive and affective ways, one style is typically more dominant. It is notable that individuals may try to grieve in ways deemed socially, culturally, personally, or religiously acceptable/advisable. In theory, difficulties arise when an individual tries to use a grieving style that does not fit his/her natural style. For adults, these proposed factors appear to have been confirmed by a panel of clinicians (Doughty, 2009).

Implications. Many questions must be answered in the treatment of grieving children and adolescents. Martin and Doka (2000) proposed that individuals with an instrumental grieving style were more likely to construct memorials and volunteer. Although grieving style was not assessed, Brown et al. (2008) assessed three different groups of children of different demographics from three different locations exposed to different traumas. Only the New York group exposed to the September 11th terrorist attacks reported

Table 1
Variables that may influence grief reactions

Variable	Risk	Protection	References
Attachment Young Children	• A succession of caretakers; prolonged absence of the mother	• Presence of a sibling and/or a single ongoing caretaker, especially one introduced by the mother beforehand	Bowlby, 1969/1982
Adults with Childhood Losses	• Poor relationship with deceased; surviving parent emotionally unavailable; lack of support after death; unassessed factors related to lack of childhood resolution of the loss	• Good relationship with deceased and surviving parent; open communication about the deceased and the death; good support system	Hurd, 1999 (Q-sort; some subgroups were small)
Nature of the Loss	• Suicide: death of child, adults report *stigmatization* (e.g., feeling a social outcast, lack of concern and support, avoided and gossiped about), depression, and suicidal thinking	• Natural death (e.g., illness): reported less stigma, strain, and perceived harmful responses from others (rejection and shunning)	Feigelman et al., 2009
	• Traumatic death (suicide, homicide, accident, ambiguous circumstances): reported more stigma, strain, and preceived harmful responses from others	• Suicide (traumatic) or natural death survivors: feeling closer to family and others who were helpful after the death (instead of finding unhelpfulness where solace & support were expected)	Feigelman et al., 2009
	• Simultaneous occurrences of trauma and grief: *increased trauma symptoms* when grief was reported;		Nader et al., 1990; 1993; Pfefferbaum et al., 1999, 2001; Pynoos et al., 1987a, b
	• *Correlation* between trauma and grief (separate factor structure for trauma and grief)		Brown & Goodman, 2005; Brown et al., 2008; Melhem, Day, Shear, Day, Reynolds, & Brent, 2004

(*Continued*)

Table 1
(Continued)

Variable	Risk	Protection	References
Grieving Style	*Because of social expectations, beliefs, or other reasons:* • Intuitive grievers do not express grief openly; avoid talking about the loss, crying, and/or connecting with others regarding their experience • Instrumental grievers feel they must openly express emotions and share feelings with others; do not use a cognitive, problem solving approach and/or take constructive actions such as memorializing and volunteering to honor the loved one	*Grievers feel free to grieve in line with their personal style:* • Intuitive grievers openly express grief emotions and talk and connect with others about the loss and their experience for as long as needed after the death • Instrumental grievers use a more cognitive, behavioral, problem-solving approach to the loss; keep affect under control; manage and seek to master their emotions rather than express them openly; when seeking social support, talk about problems associated with the loss rather than feelings; construct a memorial or volunteer for an organization that was meaningful to their loved one • Blended grievers experience and express grief in both cognitive and affective ways, feeling free to use their dominant and nondominant style (intuitive or instrumental)	Martin & Doker, 2000 (see Doughty, 2009) (based on adults)

Grief Trajectories	• *Chronic grievers* (low pre-loss depression, persistent high post-loss depression) good marriage before the death; high personal dependency and dependency on the relationship with the deceased; spouse healthy before the death (less likely to have anticipated the death) • *Chronically depressed* (high pre and post-loss depression) high dependency; high levels of marital conflict; ongoing psychological problems	• *Resilient* grievers (low pre and post-loss depression) more happy or peaceful feelings when thinking or talking about deceased, low avoidance and distraction, and fewest regrets of behavior with the deceased spouse; less troubled by attributing meaning to the death; belief in a just world; acceptance of the death; and have an instrumental support system. • *Improved during bereavement* (high pre-loss and low post-loss depression) poorest quality marriages; higher levels of ambivalence toward the spouse 3 years before the death; higher neuroticism, perceived personal injustice, and introspection, low ability to find comfort from memories of deceased, but improved ability to find comfort from talking and thinking about deceased over time; high levels of positive affect during bereavement	Bonanno, 2004; Bonanno et al., 2008 (based on adults)

increased symptoms in association with attending memorial services. Three months after the September 11th attacks, kindergarten through sixth-grade children in Washington, D.C., who engaged in patriotic gestures or volunteer efforts reported increased feelings of shaken safety (Phillips, Prince, & Schiebelhut, 2004). These findings suggest the importance of studying personal style and traits as well as the type of event in assessments of youth's reactions and treatment needs.

Trajectories of Grief

The majority of grief-stricken adults remain relatively stable while grieving and exhibit short-lived grief reactions (Bonanno, Boerner, & Wortman, 2008). Research has suggested that minimal or absent grief reactions are prevalent, whereas delayed reactions are rare. Bonanno and colleagues assessed grief and depression in older married adults, 3 years before the death of a spouse and 6, 18, and 48 months after the death (Bonanno et al., 2002; Bonanno et al., 2008). At 18 months post-loss, they identified five trajectories of grief: (a) *common grief/recovery*, or low preloss depression and high postloss depression improved by 18 months post-loss (11% of the sample); (b) *resilience/stable low distress*, or low pre- and postloss depression (46%); (c) *depression that improved during bereavement*, or high preloss depression and low postloss depression (10%); (d) *chronic grief*, or low preloss depression and persistent high postloss depression (16%); and (e) *chronic depression*, or high preloss depression that persists post-loss (8%). A period of intense yearning and pangs of intense grief in the early months after the loss as well as intrusive thoughts of the deceased shortly after the loss were common even among resilient groups. Chronic grievers were unlikely to have anticipated the loss (i.e., the spouse was healthy). Chronic grievers, in contrast with chronically depressed individuals, did not report conflicted marriages or ambivalence toward the deceased before death. Dependency before loss was an important predictor of grief reactions for both groups.

Implications. It is likely that issues of resiliency, dependency, and prior depression may also significantly influence the trajectory of grief for youth. For example, some grievers may benefit from treatment that assists in finding meaning in the loss; others may need assistance with issues implicated in ongoing depression, lack of social support, poor coping skills, and/or poor emotional self-regulation (Bonanno et al., 2008). Longitudinal studies on grief reactions with bereaved youth are needed.

Types of Grief

The International Society for Traumatic Stress Studies, Loss and Grief Special Interest Group recently conferred about two forms of CG reactions, PG and TG. The literature on PG at first focused primarily on adults, whereas TG literature focused primarily on children. Although originally based on findings for adults related to the loss of a long-time partner, in the past decade, PG has been studied in trauma-exposed youth as well.

Prolonged Grief

Prolonged grief disorder (PGD), proposed for the *DSM-V* (see Table 2), is a complicated form of bereavement that occurs after a significant interpersonal loss (Gray, Prigerson, &

Table 2
Theories of grief

Theory[a]	Basis/description of grief response	Influence on grieving
Normal grief Bonanno, Goorin, & Coifman, 2008; Crenshaw, 2007; Dominick et al., 2009; Prigerson & Jacobs, 2001; Stroebe, Schut, & Stroebe, 2007	Affective reactions – dominated by sadness but including other negative affects (e.g., anger, guilt) and positive states (sometimes even relief and emancipation) Physical/somatic difficulties – such as insomnia, loss of appetite, headaches, and nausea Cognitive reactions such as ruminations, poor concentration, a sense of the deceased's presence, and attempts to rationalize or cognitively explain the death Behavioral reactions may be present in the form of crying, social withdrawal, increased substance use, accidents or clumsiness, changes in physical activity, and activities that provide a connection to the deceased Spiritually there may be a loss of faith and/or an existential search for meaning, increased focus on rituals, or changes in spiritual practices At least temporary impairment in functioning (e.g., social, occupational and/or academic) Majority will adapt within the first 2–6 months after a loss 10–15% of bereaved experience a more complicated and prolonged form of grief	Quality and nature of support after the death Personal effect and meaning of loss Coping and ability to reconstruct meaning and identity Grieving style and expression Avoidance or interruption of grieving

(Continued)

Table 2
(Continued)

Theory[a]	Basis/description of grief response	Influence on grieving
Prolonged grief (proposed disorder) Boelen & Prigerson, 2007; Dillen et al., 2008, 2009; Melham et al., 2004; Melham, Moritz, Walker, & Shear, 2007; Prigerson, 2004; Prigerson et al., 2008; Shear et al., 2007; Shear & Shair, 2005	One of the following symptoms of separation distress daily or to an intense disruptive degree: (a) intrusive thoughts related to the deceased (b) intense pangs of separation distress (c) distressingly strong yearnings for the deceased Five of the following: (a) confusion about his or her role in life or a diminished sense of self (feeling a part of oneself has died) (b) difficulty accepting the loss (c) avoidance of reminders of the reality of the loss (d) an inability to trust others since the loss (e) bitterness or anger related to the loss (f) difficulty moving on with life (g) numbness of emotions since the loss (h) feeling life is unfulfilling, empty, and meaningless since the loss (i) feeling stunned, dazed, or shocked At least 6 months after the death for a diagnosis Disturbance causes clinically significant impairment Disorder not better accounted for by major depressive disorder, generalized anxiety disorder, or posttraumatic stress disorder	Attachment relationship with deceased Avoidance Failure of integration of permanence of the loss into autobiographical knowledge base Beliefs related to grief and self Influence by nature of event/death, postloss sequelae, and personality Risk: pronounced avoidance; intense negative affect in the initial grief period Protection: A reducing magnitude of oscillations between attention away from and attention toward the deceased; positive emotions during bereavement

Traumatic grief Theories in need of testing	Reexperiencing (a) Repeatedly experiences intrusions of observed or imagined images, thoughts, or other sensory experiences related to the manner of the death (b) Grief-related dreaming may turn into general bad dreams or traumatic dreams; may have bad dreams about the deceased (c) Reenacts in behaviors or activities the circumstances of the death or other death-related repetitions (e.g., repeated death-related play, death-related rhymes, and/or repeated talk about death and dying) (d) Experiences intense physiological reactions to reminders of the deceased or the manner of death	Need for some trauma resolution in order to be able to grieve adaptively May be influenced by trauma-related failure of integration or processing of the loss, postloss sequelae, nature of the event, child circumstances, and personality Distinguish between trauma and grief reexperiencing
	Avoidance/numbing (a) Attempts to avoid reminders of the deceased in order to avoid reminders of the traumatic nature of the death (b) Attempts to avoid people, things, places and activities that remind of the deceased because remembering the deceased reminds of the manner of death and triggers cue-conditioned fear and/or other trauma symptoms (c) Attempts to avoid thoughts, feelings, and/or conversations related to the deceased in order to avoid intense emotions or other trauma symptoms (d) Social withdrawal (e) Changes in expectations of the future related to the loss	Rule out avoidance related to superstitious thinking about the contagion of death or avoiding acknowledging the loss Children may have difficulty reporting a reason for avoidance Distinguish between grief- and trauma-related changes in expectations
	Arousal Distinguish between grief- and trauma-related arousal	

[a]For the proposed *DSM-V*, adjustment disorder related to bereavement and the bereavement-related disorder, see http://www.dsm5.org/proposedrevision/pages/proposedrevision.aspx?rid=367#

Litz, 2004; Jacobs, 1999; Prigerson, Vanderwerker, & Maciejewski, 2008). The primary focus in PG reactions is the griever's attachment to the deceased. Some evidence has suggested that the intensity of grief may increase with the intensity of the attachment (Shear & Shair, 2005). Jacobs (1999) pointed out that a prolonged grief reaction may be triggered when the loss is personally devastating, with or without the occurrence of a traumatic event. In such cases, the loss itself may be experienced or perceived as traumatic. Prigerson (2004) described PG as a condition in which individuals are stuck in a state of chronic mourning. Although symptoms of PG occur transiently in many mourners (normal grief), in PG, these symptoms are persistent and exacerbated (Boelen, van den Hout, & van den Bout, 2006).

Findings. Many studies have examined and provided evidence for the symptoms of PG in adults (Prigerson et al., 2009; Shear, Jackson, Essock, Donahue, & Felton, 2006; Stroebe, Hansson, Stroebe, & Schut, 2008). Compared to those who do not meet criteria for PGD, adults with PGD have been shown to be at increased risk for major depressive disorder, posttraumatic stress disorder (PTSD), generalized anxiety disorder, functional disability, diminished quality of life, health problems, and suicidal ideation months to years after experiencing a loss (Lannen, Wolfe, Prigerson, Onelov, & Keicbergs, 2008; Prigerson & Maciejewski, 2008). For adults, researchers have found that PG reactions are structurally distinct from normal grief (Boelen & van den Bout, 2008). Although some findings need replication, evidence has suggested the following risk factors for PG: (a) experiencing the death as unexpected (Goldsmith, Morrison, Vanderwerker, & Prigerson, 2008), (b) negative cognitions and misinterpretations about grief reactions (Boelen et al. 2006), and (c) avoidance (Shear et al., 2007). Differences within and between racial/ethnic groups and the influence of associated variables such as socioeconomic status, culture, and social support need to be examined to further identify potential groups at risk for PG (Goldsmith et al., 2008). Intrusive images are common among mourners, regardless of the nature of the death (Boelen & Huntjens, 2008), and they vary somewhat by age and time since a death. Four types of intrusive images include (a) images of the deceased, (b) images of moments surrounding the death (the death event), (c) reenactment fantasies (unbidden fantasies of what the decedent experienced before dying), and (d) unpleasant images of the future. Boelen and Huntjens (2008) found that high levels of the four types of intrusive images coincided with higher levels of PG, anxiety, and depression. Positive intrusive memories of the lost person were associated with PG but not with depression and anxiety. Intrusive images of moments surrounding the death were linked to anxiety but not to PG and depression.

Using scales adapted from adult PG scales or developed primarily on the basis of PG symptoms, researchers have confirmed some findings for youth exposed to traumatic events. Although PG, depression, and PTSD were correlated, factor analytic methods found that PG is factorially distinct (i.e., belonging to distinct factors in factor analysis) from normal grief in older adolescents (Boelen & van den Bout, 2008; Dillen, Fontaine, & Verhofstadt-Denève, 2008) and factorially distinct from PTSD, anxiety, or depression in youth (Dillen, Fontaine, & Verhofstadt-Denève, 2009; Melhem et al., 2004). When deaths were by violent means, adolescents had higher levels of anxiety, depression, and PG than for nonviolent deaths (Dillen et al., 2009). Nevertheless, the three-factor structure was invariant across groups. Melham, Moritz, Walker, and Shear (2007) found that PG reactions were significantly associated with functional impairment even after controlling for other disorders (i.e., depression, anxiety, and PTSD).

Findings related to PG and the nature of a traumatic event are also mixed. Some evidence suggests that feeling that others were accountable for the death is associated with higher PG scores (Melham et al., 2007). Melham and colleagues (2007) discovered no differences in outcome on the basis of types of death (i.e., suicide, accident, or sudden natural parental death), nor did they find differences on the basis of exposure to aspects of the death (i.e., knowledge of details of the death, seeing the death scene, attending the funeral, or helping to remove the deceased's personal effects). In contrast, Brown et al. (2008) found some differences in the reactions of youth in different locations with different demographics and exposed to different events. Dillen et al. (2009) found higher anxiety, depression, and PG levels for violent versus nonviolent deaths and when the deceased was a first-degree relative (e.g., mother, father, or sibling).

Childhood Traumatic Grief

TG, described in the child trauma literature since the 1980s, is a form of complicated grief that may follow a death that occurs in a traumatic way or during a traumatic event (Brown & Goodman, 2005; Cohen, Mannarino, Greenberg, Padlo, & Shipley, 2002; Eth & Pynoos, 1985; Layne, Savjak, Saltzman, & Pynoos, 2001; Nader, 1997; Raphael, Martinek, & Wooding, 2004). In contrast to PG, which emphasizes the loss of a significant attachment figure, TG focuses on the traumatic circumstances of a death and trauma-related interference with adaptive grieving processes (see Table 2). The deceased may or may not be perceived as significant to the traumatized individual's survival or ability to function in life.

Theories of TG. On the basis of clinical observations and assessments of posttrauma grief in youth, TG theorists have suggested that grief and treatment may be complicated by the interplay of trauma and grief: (a) this interplay may intensify symptoms common to both trauma and grief; (b) thoughts of the deceased may lead to traumatic recollections and may trigger PTSD reactions; (c) traumatic aspects of the death may hinder or complicate issues of bereavement including, for example, the ability to recover from shock related to the loss, reminiscing, grief-related dreaming, aspects of the relationship with the deceased, issues of identification, and the processing of anger and rage; and (d) a sense of posttraumatic estrangement or aloneness may interfere with healing interactions (Cohen et al., 2002; Nader, 1997). It has been proposed that a child's perception of a death as being traumatic (whether others agree) or concern about a significant other during a traumatic event even without direct exposure are sufficient to result in TG reactions.

Findings. Researchers long ago documented higher levels of trauma symptoms associated with concurrent grief reactions after traumatic deaths. Before the advent of scales designed to measure CG, youth exposed to war (Nader, Pynoos, Fairbanks, Al-Ajeel, & Al-Asfour, 1993), violence (Nader, Pynoos, Fairbanks, & Frederick, 1990; Pynoos, Frederick et al., 1987; Pynoos, Nader, Frederick, Gonda, & Stuber, 1987), or terrorism (Pfefferbaum, Call, et al., 2001; Pfefferbaum, Nixon, et al., 1999) who endorsed symptoms of grief or relationships to individuals who died under those traumatic circumstances were more likely to have higher levels of posttraumatic stress symptoms. After youth CG measures emerged at the beginning of this decade, trauma researchers found a correlation between scores on these scales and PTSD (Brown et al., 2008; Brown & Goodman, 2005; Melham et al., 2004), anxiety (Brown & Goodman, 2005), and depression (Brown et al., 2008; Brown & Goodman, 2005) but found them to be factorially distinct. In theory, TG may not be as distinct from PTSD as PG. Further research including additional TG items is needed. Boelen and Huntjens (2008) found that high levels of positive intrusive memories of the lost person were associated with PG but not with depression and anxiety, and intrusive images of moments surrounding the death were linked to anxiety but not to PG and depression. This finding may provide some evidence of differences in TG and PG. To determine any distinctness of TG from PTSD or from PG, scales and methods must be used that assess all symptoms/reactions proposed for TG as well as reactions proposed and found for other types of grief (Nader & Layne, 2009).

Grief Reactions in Children and Adolescents

Researchers and clinicians have recognized the importance of including a developmental perspective in assessing disorders in youth (Costello, Foley, & Angold, 2006; Emde & Spicer, 2000). Developmental issues are important in the manifestation of normal versus complicated childhood reactions to stressors. In addition, CG may undermine development and functioning for children and adolescents, may persist for years if unresolved, and may require treatment distinct from normal grief work that may vary by age group (Melhem et al., 2007; Nader & Layne, 2009).

Normal Bereavement from a Developmental Perspective

Evidence has indicated that the nature, expression, and experience of grief vary across life stages as well as in response to different contexts, individual differences, and among different cultures (Baker & Sedney, 1996; Corr & Corr, 1996; Oltjenbruns, 2007). At different ages, children differ in their understanding of the universality, inevitability, unpredictability, irreversibility, bodily nonfunctionality, and causality of death (Corr, 2008; Speece & Brent, 1996; see Table 3). Despite increasing understanding with age of the physical aspects of death, a child simultaneously may hold more than one idea about the characteristics of death (Corr, 2008). For example, an 11-year-old boy who knew that heart attacks were not contagious held his breath every time he walked through the hall where his nanny had “dropped dead.” Even though he did not believe in ghosts, he wondered if her spirit was there whenever he walked near her room. Symptom presentations, death-related preoccupations, and the developmental tasks that might be disrupted by grief vary among age groups (see Table 3). For example, regressive behaviors such as bedwetting, thumb-sucking, fear that others will die, magical thinking-related guilt (e.g., believing that wishing someone would go away could kill the person), and the expectation that death is temporary and reversible are more common in early childhood (Himebauch, Arnold, & May, 2008; Oltjenbruns, 2007). Adolescents may fear what others are thinking and saying about them or feel different, lonely, and/or preoccupied with issues of personal mortality.

Studies of grief in children have found ethnicity, religion, and socioeconomic status to be of little consequence in youths’ understanding of death (Speece & Brent, 1996). In contrast, cultural differences, previous death-related experiences, intelligence, and having a life-threatening illness all affect children’s conceptualizations of the bioscientific aspects of death (Hunter & Smith, 2008; Speece & Brent, 1996). Findings related to normal childhood grief have been obscured by the nature of assessments. Corr (2008) pointed out that findings are confusing because of the “lack of precision and agreement about the terms and definitions used for various components of the concept of death” (p. 11). Early studies of grief in children failed to separate groups of children by the context or nature of the loss—for example, whether the loss occurred under traumatic circumstances or was expected and occurred under peaceful circumstances. Consequently, children who are now considered to have complicated grief were among children assessed in defining normal grief.

Table 3

Age and understanding of grief (varies by experience and maturity)

Age	Understanding of death	Some of the possible grief reactions
Infant (0–2 years)	No cognitive understanding of death Expect the person to return	Can grieve but have difficulty identifying or dealing with the loss Crying excessively, fretting persistently; may ultimately become nonaffective and withdrawn Separation anxiety Irritability Regression Changes in feeding and sleeping patterns May mirror caregiver reactions
Toddler (2–4 years)	Think death is temporary and reversible May think death is just sleeping Magical thinking about causes of death	Questions reflect a concrete and literal interpretation of the world Separation anxiety Regression; loss of skills and abilities May have trouble concentrating and with memory May be irritable; may have more than are normal tantrums May fear going to sleep May have nightmares Prone to living in the moment; may move in and out of grieving
Preschool age (4–6 years)	Some children begin to understand that death is irreversible, makes people nonfunctional, and is universal; others do not	May experience some of the possible grief reactions listed for toddlers Self-blame; may feel like they caused the death Regression

(*Continued*)

Table 3
(Continued)

Age	Understanding of death	Some of the possible grief reactions
	Magical thinking about causes of death (e.g., wishing someone would go away can kill the person)	Aggression
School age (6–8 years)	In general, recognize that death is final and irreversible and the deceased is nonfunctional Do not believe that death is universal or that it could happen to them	Anger at deceased or someone believed to have been able to save them Anxiety Depression Somatic complaints Fears about safety of or deaths of other loved ones May see self as different from other children and feel stigmatized May feel loss of control May have concerns about isolation
Preadolescent (8–12 years)	Understand that death is final, irreversible, and a natural part of life Have an increased understanding of the cause of death and of what life might be like without the deceased	May intellectualize death May have morbid curiosity or want to understand the details of the death May have an interest in religious and cultural traditions related to death May feel guilt May have difficulty identifying and dealing with feelings May fear dying Will be aware that they are different from some or most other children

Adolescent (12–17 years)	An increasing capacity for abstract reasoning; may be interested in the existential implications of the death Can understand the reality of thousands of deaths and some of the complexities of life without the person who died Developing an understanding of the meaning and/or greater effect of a traumatic or other death-related event	May become more preoccupied with their own thought processes May resent sequelae of the loss (e.g., demands after parent loss) Concerns about how others are thinking and speaking about them. May feel different, lonely, and/or preoccupied with issues of their personal mortality (may engage in high-risk activities) May reject adult rituals and support May feel no one understands them May have difficulty identifying and expressing feelings Normal mood swings may exacerbate emotions of grief; grief may exacerbate struggles for independence and/or identity May idealize deceased and demonize survivor (e.g., parent)

Note. See Corr, 2008; Corr and Corr, 1996; Diareme et al., 2007; Galonos, 2007; Himebauch, Arnold, & May, 2008; Hunter & Smith, 2008; Oltjenbruns, 2007; Speece & Brent, 1996.

Theories and Findings Related to Specific Variables and CG

Multiple factors influence a youth's grief reactions. Personal variables, history and background variables, and event variables may complexly influence reactions (Brown et al., 2008; Crenshaw, 2007; Webb, 2002). Risk and protective factors tend to occur in combination (Shapiro, 2008). Poverty, for example, may combine with unsafe neighborhoods, inadequate schools, and housing instability, and may vary with circumstances. A few of the traits and circumstances that may result in complicated forms of grieving are presented here (see Table 2).

Child Variables

Child-related variables such as hardiness/resilience versus vulnerability factors, gender, ethnicity, adaptive functioning (e.g., avoidance, problem solving, coping), cognitive processing, history of stressors, and peritraumatic emotional states are important to assess in the discovery of developmental variations in grief. For example, in the study of trauma, evidence suggests that the intensity of emotions during a traumatic event with loss is associated with increased reactions (Lengua, Long, Smith, & Meltzoff, 2005; Pfefferbaum et al., 2003). Evidence for adult CG and preliminary evidence for youth CG suggests that avoidance is associated with increased symptoms (Crenshaw, 2007; Melham et al., 2007; Shear et al., 2007).

Environmental Variables

Environmental issues such as the nature of attachments and other support systems are important to grief reactions. Among the identified risk and protective factors for CG are parenting, home conditions, and social support (Brown et al., 2008; Saldinger, Porterfield, & Cain, 2004). Brown et al. (2008) found an association between CG and caregivers' emotional reactions, sadness in the home, and anger. Factors identified as protective in relation to loss included increased levels of support, child-centered parenting, and adaptive functioning.

Attachment. Bowlby (1969/1982) pointed out that after prolonged separation from their mothers, very young children proceed through phases of protest, despair, and detachment, and they may stay in a state of alternation from one phase to the next for days or weeks. It is notable that whether mourning was healthy or unhealthy depended on the family environment—the relationship with the deceased parent and with the surviving parent, communication about the death among the surviving family members, the child's participation in memorialization, and the extent of support from family and others (Hurd, 1999). Although important additional variables such as personality were not measured, Hurd provided preliminary evidence that middle-aged adults whose parent had died in their childhood had more positive adult outcomes (positive self-assessment, absence of depression) if they had a good relationship with the deceased and the surviving parent, open communication, and good support (see Table 1).

Interactions between infants and caregivers shape the ultimate growth and architecture of the brain, and reciprocal interactions between parent and child help the infant to learn to psychobiologically modulate positive states (e.g., joy and excitement) as well as negative states (e.g., stress, aggression, and fear; Nader, 2008; Schore, 2003; Siegel, 2003). Grief in infancy can disrupt the basis of a number of skills, including self-regulatory skills. The death of grandparents, to whom the child has not developed an attachment, can have long-term consequences in that the mother's grief may result in a disorganized attachment (Hesse, Main, Abrams, & Rifkin, 2003). Disorganized attachments have been linked to aspects of psychopathology from middle childhood to late adolescence (Hesse et al., 2003; Liotti, 2004).

Support and other environmental issues. Support from others has been an important protective factor for trauma and grief (Feigelman, Gorman, & Jordan, 2009; Hurd, 1999; Silver, Holman, McIntosh, Poulin, & Gil-Rivas, 2002). Feigelman et al. (2009) suggested that traumatic deaths (e.g., suicide, homicide, drug overdose, vehicular accident) in general evoke specific responses from others. Such losses may elicit fear (e.g., "It could happen to us"), dread, and/or a feeling of not knowing how to respond (lack of social norms for response), and consequently, avoidance responses from members of a person's social network.

Assessing Complicated Grief Reactions

A number of issues may complicate the assessment of CG, whether examined as a continuous variable or as a specific form of CG. Some of these issues and measures to assess CG are presented briefly here.

Factors That Complicate Determining the Nature of Childhood Grieving

Delineating the different manifestations of complicated grief across age groups may be a difficult task for a number of reasons. The complexity of variable interrelationships may influence the nature of grief reactions (Nader, 2008). Grieving includes many types of reactions (i.e., physical, psychological, social, and cognitive) and an individual set of mitigating factors (Sanders, 1989). Unlike adults, children may grieve in spurts and can grieve again when new developmental stages enhance their understanding of death or the nature of a death (Himebauch et al., 2008). In addition, normal grief reactions can have at least temporarily problematic and developmentally significant consequences for children and adolescents (Abdelnoor & Hollins, 2004; Luecken, 2008; Nader & Layne, 2009; Silverman & Worden, 1992). It is important to note that some of the symptoms of CG are the same as symptoms of normal grief, which makes them difficult to distinguish. Only their persistence and intensity may distinguish them from normal reactions. To determine distinctions among types of grief and their relationship with trauma may require determining whether symptoms such as bad dreams, revenge or intervention fantasies, avoidance, and changed views of the future, differ in their relationship with trauma, grief, loss of attachment figures, and a combination of these precursors.

Bereaved individuals demonstrate enormous diversity in their emotional responses (Bonanno, 2004; Shapiro, 2008). Although some research has focused on specific types of loss (e.g., loss of a strong-attachment figure; deaths during PTSD traumas; anticipated death), youth exposed to the same type of loss may have different reactions, and youth exposed to different types of loss may have similar reactions (Shapiro, 2008). In addition, the lower levels of stress associated with one type of loss may be increased by other circumstances related to the death or to the youth's nature and circumstances. The benefits of being able to anticipate a death as a result of illness, for example, may be diminished by added stressors such as the strain on resources and the problems of having attention diverted away from other family and personal concerns (e.g., undermining of child-centered parenting, disruptions to normal concentration).

Measuring Complicated Grief Reactions and Associated Variables

Most current youth CG scales assess grief types. Among PG items are normal grief reactions that may become problematic in their persistence and intensity (Boelin, van den Hout et al., 2006). PG is assessed by the Inventory of Complicated Grief, Revised (Melhem et al., 2007; Prigerson et al., 1995) and the Inventory of Complicated Grief for Children (Dyregrov et al., 2001). The Extended Grief Inventory (Layne et al., 2001) includes PG/grief items and several theorized TG reactions (Brown & Goodman, 2005; Goodman & Brown, 2008). A new scale, the Complicated Grief Assessment for Children and Adolescents – Long Form (Nader & Prigerson, 2009), includes grief, *DSM-IV* pathological grief, proposed TG, and PG items. Scale revisions in progress are aimed at providing a broader range of developmentally sensitive items. In addition, the Texas Revised Inventory of Grief (Faschingbauer, Zisook, & Devaul, 1987) is an adult measure also used to assess normal grief reactions in adolescents.

Conclusions

Until recently, scales have not been available that assess the full range of theorized grief symptoms/reactions in youth. A clear picture of complicated grieving in youth populations will not be possible until the full range of theorized symptoms and variables are studied in different youth age groups (Nader & Layne, 2009). Until studies assess all of the hypothesized symptoms of each of the types of grief proposed and a possible continuum of grief reactions from adaptive to maladaptive, a meaningful distinction cannot be made between TG and PG, TG and normal grief, TG and PTSD, or TG's relationship with other theories of CG.

Since the preparation of this article, the *DSM-V* workgroup has considered the research related to prolonged grief disorder and traumatic grief and has proposed that a bereavement-related disorder not be included in the *DSM-V*, but rather that the proposed bereavement disorder be included as an appendix for further study. The proposed bereavement-related disorder includes many of the symptoms of the proposed prolonged grief disorder and allows one to specify if the bereavement is traumatic bereavement due to deaths resulting from homicide, suicide, disaster, or accident. In addition, the workgroup has proposed that adjustment disorder allow one to specify if the adjustment is related to bereavement, which includes at least 12 months of the identified behaviors and symptoms after the death. More research will be needed to ensure that the proposed criteria include developmentally specific symptoms pertaining to childhood bereavement (American Psychiatric Association, 2010).

Numerous unanswered questions remain in the discussion of childhood CG reactions (see International Society for Traumatic Stress Studies Loss and Grief Special Interest Group information pages; Nader & Layne, 2009; see Table 3). Among them are those related to the nature of CG in youth of different age groups, the mediators and moderators of CG, and the best methods of examining aspects of CG and its associated variables. For example, the prevalence of intrusive imagery regardless of the nature of the death suggests the need for methods to examine the qualities (e.g., persistence, nature) of some reactions (e.g., intrusive imagery) that may make them relevant to types of CG or their treatment. Although researchers have examined symptoms of PG in youth in relation to PTSD and depression, until recently, CG scales have not asked the full range of proposed or theorized TG symptoms. Further research to understand and assess childhood complicated grief and its associations with protective and risk factors, other disorders, and the trajectories of grief within a developmental context will help practitioners to tailor treatment needs.

Clearly determining the nature of childhood grieving necessitates examining the contributions of such factors as the child's nature (e.g., personality, genetics, gender), skills (e.g., coping skills; experience with death and grieving), environment (e.g., culture, socioeconomic status, support systems), developmental age, and grieving style, as well as the type of loss or cause of death (e.g., traumatic, tranquil), time since death (e.g., possible differences in the "phase of grieving" or changes in grief over time; Doka, 2005/2006; Sanders, 1989, 1992), and the relationship to the deceased (e.g., family vs. acquaintance; degree of closeness and/or nature of attachment; Bowlby, 1969/1982; Hurd, 1999). In addition, decisions must be made about when and how reactions are to be considered maladaptive—for example, when they interfere with functioning, persist, or reach certain numbers and/or levels of intensity (Nader & Layne, 2009).

Information is available about developmental differences in youth's understanding of death. More information is needed about developmental differences in the immediate and long-term outcomes of childhood bereavement and in the relationship of additional variables with grief reactions. Studies need to do the following:

- assess the full range of possible grief reactions in youth on the basis of findings, observations, and theories;
- compare and contrast trajectories of postloss adjustment in different age groups bereaving under varying circumstances: (a) loss not perceived as traumatic (e.g., an expected, tranquil death); (b) loss that took place under Criterion A–type traumatic circumstances (e.g., during natural disaster, homicide, war, violent accident, suicide); (c) loss of a significant attachment figure perceived as important to life and functioning (i.e., feeling personally devastated by the loss of a significant person as a result of causes not described by the *DSM-IV* or proposed for the *DSM-V* Criterion A); and (d) losses strongly characterized by elements in (b) and (c);
- examine the interplay of additional variables with grief reactions, their nature, persistence, intensity, and ability to interfere with functioning.

References

Abdelnoor, A., & Hollins, S. (2004). The effect of childhood bereavement on secondary school performance. *Educational Psychology in Practice*, *20*(1), 43–54.

American Psychiatric Association. (1994). *Diagnostic and statistical manual of mental disorders* (4th ed.). Washington, DC: Author.

American Psychiatric Association. (2000). *Diagnostic and statistical manual of mental disorders* (text rev.). Washington, DC: Author.

American Psychiatric Association. (2010). DSM-V *development: G 06 adjustment disorders*. Retrieved from http://www.dsm5.org/ProposedRevisions/Pages/proposedrevision.aspx?rid=367

Baker, J., & Sedney, M. (1996). How bereaved children cope with loss: An overview. In C. Corr & D. Corr (Eds.), *Handbook of childhood death and bereavement* (pp. 109–129). New York: Springer.

Boelen, P., & Huntjens, R. (2008). Intrusive images in grief: An exploratory study. *Clinical Psychology and Psychotherapy*, *15*, 217–226.

Boelen, P., & Prigerson, H. (2007). The influence of symptoms of prolonged grief disorder, depression, and anxiety on quality of life among bereaved adults: A prospective study. *European Archives of Psychiatry and Clinical Neuroscience*, *257*, 444–452.

Boelen, P., & van den Bout, J. (2008). Complicated grief and uncomplicated grief are distinguishable constructs. *Psychiatry Research*, *157*, 311–314.

Boelen, P., van den Bout, J., & van den Hout, M. (2006). Negative cognitions and avoidance in emotional problems after bereavement: A prospective study. *Behaviour Research and Therapy*, *44*, 1657–1672.

Boelen, P., van den Hout, M., & van den Bout, J. (2006). A cognitive-behavioral conceptualization of complicated grief. *Clinical Psychology Science and Practice*, *44*, 109–128.

Bonanno, G. (2004). Loss, trauma, and human resilience: Have we underestimated the human capacity to thrive after extremely aversive events? *American Psychologist*, *59*, 20–28.

Bonanno, G., Boerner, K., & Wortman, C. (2008). Trajectories of grieving. In M. Stroebe, R. O. Hansson, H. Schut, & W. Stroebe (Eds.), *Handbook of bereavement research and practice: Advances in theory and intervention* (pp. 287–308). Washington, DC: APA Books.

Bonanno, G., Goorin, L., & Coifman, K. (2008). Sadness and grief. In M. Lewis, J. Haviland-Jones, & L. F. Barett (Eds.), *Handbook of emotion* (3rd ed., pp. 797–810). New York: Guildford.

Bonanno, G., Wortman, C., Lehman, D., Tweed, R., Haring, M., Sonnega, J., et al. (2002). Resilience to loss and chronic grief: A prospective study from pre-loss to 18 months post-loss. *Journal of Personality and Social Psychology*, *83*, 1150–1164.

Bowlby, J. (1982). *Attachment and loss. Volume 1: Attachment*. New York: Basic Books. (Original work published 1969)

Brown, E. J., Amaya-Jackson, L., Cohen, J., Handel, S., De Bocanegra, H., Zatta, E., et al. (2008). Childhood traumatic grief: A multi-site empirical examination of the construct and its correlates. *Death Studies*, *32*, 899–923.

Brown, E. J., & Goodman, R. (2005). Childhood traumatic grief: An exploration of the construct in children bereaved on September 11. *Journal of Clinical Child and Adolescent Psychology*, *34*, 248–259.

Cohen, J., Mannarino, A., Greenberg, T., Padlo, S., & Shipley, C. (2002). Childhood traumatic grief: Concepts and controversies. *Trauma, Violence & Abuse*, *3*, 307–327.

Corr, C. (2008). Children's emerging awareness of death. In K. J. Doka & A. S. Tucci (Eds.), *Living with grief: Children and adolescents* (pp. 5–17). Washington, DC: Hospice Foundation of America.

Corr, C., & Corr, D. (Eds.). (1996). *Handbook of childhood death and bereavement*. New York: Springer.

Costello, E., Foley, D., & Angold, A. (2006). 10-year research update review: The epidemiology of child and adolescent psychiatric disorders: II. Developmental epidemiology. *Journal of the American Academy of Child and Adolescent Psychiatry*, *45*, 8–25.

Crenshaw, D. (2007). An interpersonal neurobiological-informed treatment model for childhood traumatic grief. *Omega*, *54*, 319–335.

Diareme, S., Tsiantis, J., Romer, G., Tsalamanios, E., Anasontzi, S., Paliokosta, E., et al. (2007). Mental health support for children of parents with somatic illness: A review of the theory and intervention concepts. *Families, Systems, & Health*, *25*, 98–119.

Dillen, L., Fontaine, J. R. J., & Verhofstadt-Denève, L. (2008). Are normal and complicated grief different constructs? A confirmatory factor analytic test. *Clinical Psychology and Psychotherapy*, *15*, 386–395.

Dillen, L., Fontaine, J. R. J., & Verhofstadt-Denève, L. (2009). Confirming the distinctiveness of complicated grief from depression and anxiety among adolescents. *Death Studies*, *33*, 437–461.

Doka, K. (2005/2006). Fulfillment as Sanders' sixth phase of bereavement: The unfinished work of Catherine Sanders. *Omega*, *52*, 143–151.

Dominick, S., Irvine, A., Beauchamp, N., Seeley, J., Nolen-Hoeksema, S., Doka, K., et al. (2009). An Internet tool to normalize grief. *Omega*, *60*, 71–87.

Doughty, E. (2009). Investigating adaptive grieving styles. *Death Studies*, *33*, 462–480.

Dyregrov, A., Yule, W., Smith, P., Perrin, S., Gjestad, R., & Prigerson, P. (2001). *Inventory of complicated grief for children*. Unpublished measure, Center for Crisis Psychology, Bergen, Norway.

Emde, R., & Spicer, P. (2000). Experience in the midst of variation: New horizons for development and psychopathology. *Development and Psychopathology, 12*, 313–331.

Eth, S., & Pynoos, R. (1985). Interaction of trauma and grief in childhood. In S. Eth & R. Pynoos (Eds.), *Post-traumatic stress disorder in children* (pp. 171–186). Washington, DC: American Psychiatric Press.

Faschingbauer, T., Zisook, S., & Devaul, R. (1987). The Texas Revised Inventory of Grief. In S. Zisook (Ed.), *Biopsychosocial aspects of bereavement* (pp. 111–124). Washington, DC: American Psychiatric Press.

Feigelman, W., Gorman, B., & Jordan, J. (2009). Stigmatization and suicide bereavement. *Death Studies, 33*, 591–608.

Galonos, G. (2007). Helping children grieve. *Children's Voice, 16*, 26–28.

Goldsmith, B., Morrison, R., Vanderwerker, L., & Prigerson, H. (2008). Elevated levels of prolonged grief disorder in African Americans. *Death Studies, 32*, 352–365.

Goodman, R., & Brown, F. (2008). Service and science in times of crisis. Developing, planning, and implementing a clinical research program or children traumatically bereaved after 9/11. *Death Studies, 32*, 154–180.

Gray, M., Prigerson, H., & Litz, B. T. (2004). Conceptual and definitional issues in traumatic grief. In B. T. Litz (Ed.), *Early intervention for trauma and traumatic loss in children and adults: Evidence based directions* (pp. 65–84). New York: Guildford.

Hesse, E., Main, M., Abrams, K. Y., & Rifkin, A. (2003). Unresolved states regarding loss or abuse can have "second-generation" effects: Disorganization, role inversion, and frightening ideation in the offspring of traumatized, non-maltreating parents. In M. Solomon & D. J. Siegel (Eds.), *Healing trauma* (pp. 57–106). New York: Norton.

Himebauch, A., Arnold, R., & May, C. (2008). Grief in children and developmental concepts of death #138. *Journal of Palliative Medicine, 11*, 242–243.

Holland, J., Neimeyer, R., Boelen, P., & Prigerson, H. (2009). The underlying structure of grief: A taxometric investigation of prolonged and normal reactions to loss. *Journal of Psychopathology and Behavioral Assessment, 31*, 190–201.

Hunter, S., & Smith, D. (2008). Predictors of children's understandings of death: Age, cognitive ability, death experience and maternal communicative competence. *Omega, 57*, 143–162.

Hurd, R. (1999). Adults view their childhood bereavement experiences. *Death Studies, 23*, 17–41.

Jacobs, S. (1999). *Traumatic grief: Diagnosis, treatment, and prevention.* Philadelphia: Brunner/Mazel.

Kubler-Ross, E. (1969). *On death and dying*. New York: Springer.

Lannen, P., Wolfe, J., Prigerson, H., Onelove, E., & Keicbergs, U. (2008). Unresolved grief in a national sample of bereaved parents: Impaired mental and physical health 4 to 9 years later. *Journal of Clinical Oncology, 26*, 5870–5876.

Layne, C. M., Savjak, N., Saltzman, W. R., & Pynoos, R. S. (2001). *UCLA Extended Grief Inventory*. Unpublished psychological test, University of California, Los Angeles.

Lengua, L., Long, A., Smith, K., & Meltzoff, A. (2005). Pre-attack symptomatology and temperament as predictors of children's responses to the September 11 terrorist attacks. *Journal of Child Psychology and Psychiatry, 46*, 631–645.

Liotti, G. (2004). Trauma, dissociation, and disorganized attachment: Three strands of a single braid. *Psychotherapy: Theory, Research, Practice, Training, 41*, 472–486.

Luecken, L. (2008). Long-term consequences of parental death in childhood: Psychological and physiological manifestations. In M. Stroebe, R. Hansson, H. Schut, & W. Stroebe, (Eds.), *Handbook of bereavement research and practice: Advances in theory and intervention* (pp. 397–416). Washington, DC: American Psychological Association.

Martin, T. L., & Doka, K. J. (2000). *Men don't cry . . . women do: Transcending gender stereotypes of grief*. Philadelphia: Brunner Mazel.

Melham, N., Day, N., Shear, M. K., Day, R., Reynolds, C., III, & Brent, D. (2004). Traumatic grief among adolescents exposed to a peer's suicide. *American Journal of Psychiatry, 161*, 1411–1416.

Melhem, N., Moritz, G., Walker, M., & Shear, K. (2007). Phenomenology and correlates of complicated grief in children and adolescents. *Journal of the American Academy of Child and Adolescent Psychiatry*, *46*, 493–499.

Nader, K. (1997). Childhood traumatic loss: The intersection of trauma and grief. In C. R. Figley, B. E. Bride, & N. Mazza (Eds.), *Death and trauma: The traumatology of grieving* (pp. 17–41). London: Taylor & Francis.

Nader, K. (2008). *Understanding and assessing trauma in children and adolescents: Measures, methods, and youth in context*. New York: Routledge.

Nader, K., & Layne, C. (2009). Maladaptive grieving in children and adolescents: Discovering developmentally linked differences in the manifestation of grief. *Traumatic Stress Points*, *23*(5), 12–16.

Nader, K., & Prigerson, H. (2009). *Complicated Grief Assessment – Child and Adolescent Scales, Long-Form*. Austin: Two Suns.

Nader, K., Pynoos, R., Fairbanks, L., Al-Ajeel, M., & Al-Asfour, A. (1993). Acute post traumatic stress reactions among Kuwait children following the Gulf crisis. *British Journal of Clinical Psychology*, *32*, 407–416.

Nader, K., Pynoos, R., Fairbanks, L., & Frederick, C. (1990). Children's PTSD reactions one year after a sniper attack at their school. *American Journal of Psychiatry*, *147*, 1526–1530.

Oltjenbruns, K. (2007). Lifespan issues and loss, grief, and mourning: Part 1: The importance of a developmental context: Childhood and adolescence as an example. In D. Balk, C. Wogrin, G. Thornton, & D. Meagher (Eds.), *Handbook of thanatology: The essential body of knowledge for the study of death, dying, and bereavement* (pp. 143–163). New York: Routledge.

Pearlman, M., Schwartz, K., & Cloitre, M. (2010). *The varied manifestations of grief: Assisting a child and caregiver after the loss of a parent*. Washington, DC: American Psychological Association.

Pfefferbaum, B., Call, J. A., Lensgraf, S. J., Miller, P. D., Flynn, B. W., Doughty, D. E., et al. (2001). Traumatic grief in a convenience sample of victims seeking support services after a terrorist incident. *Annals of Clinical Psychiatry*, *13*, 19–24.

Pfefferbaum, B., Nixon, S. J., Tucker, P. M., Tivis, R. D., Moore, V. L., Gurwitch, R. H., et al. (1999). Posttraumatic stress responses in bereaved children after the Oklahoma City bombing. *Journal of the American Academy of Child and Adolescent Psychiatry*, *38*, 1372–1379.

Pfefferbaum, B., Scale, T., Brandt, E., Pfefferbaum, R., Doughty, D., & Rainwater, S. (2003). Media exposure in children one hundred miles from a terrorist bombing. *Annals of Clinical Psychiatry*, *15*, 1–8.

Phillips, D., Prince, S., & Scheibelhut, L. (2004). Elementary school children's responses 3 months after the September 11 terrorist attack: A study in Washington, DC. *American Journal of Orthopsychiatry*, *27*, 509–528.

Prigerson, H. (2004). Complicated grief: When the path of adjustment leads to a dead-end. *Bereavement Care*, *23*, 38–40.

Prigerson, H., Horowitz, M., Jacobs, S., Parkes, C., Aslan, M., Raphael, B., et al. (2009). Prolonged grief disorder: Psychometric validation of criteria proposed for *DSM-V* and ICD11. *PLoS Medicine*, *6*(8), 1–12.

Prigerson, H., & Jacobs, S. (2001). Traumatic grief as a distinct disorder: A rationale, consensus criteria, and a preliminary empirical test. In M. Stroebe, R. O. Hansson, W. Stroebe, & H. Schut (Eds.), *Handbook of bereavement research: Consequences, coping and care* (pp. 163–645). Washington, DC: American Psychological Association.

Prigerson, H., & Maciejewski, P. (2008). Grief and acceptance as opposite sides of the same coin: Setting a research agenda to study peaceful acceptance of loss. *British Journal of Psychiatry*, *193*, 435–437.

Prigerson, H., Maciejewski, P., Reynolds. C., Bierhals, A., Newsom J., Fasiczka, A., et al. (1995). The Inventory of Complicated Grief: A scale to measure certain maladaptive symptoms of loss. *Psychiatry Research*, *59*, 65–79.

Pynoos, R., Frederick, C., Nader, K., Arroyo, W., Eth, S., Nunez, W., et al. (1987). Life threat and posttraumatic stress in school age children. *Archives of General Psychiatry*, *44*, 1057–1063.

Pynoos, R., Nader, K., Frederick, C., Gonda, L., & Stuber, M. (1987). Grief reactions in school age children following a sniper attack at school. *Israeli Journal of Psychiatry and Related Sciences, 24*(1–2), 53–63.

Raphael, B., Martinek, N., & Wooding, S. (2004). Assessing traumatic bereavement. In J. Wilson & T. Keane (Eds.), *Assessing psychological trauma & PTSD* (2nd ed., pp. 492–510). New York: Guildford.

Saldinger, A., Porterfield, K., & Cain, A. (2004). Meeting the needs of parentally bereaved children: A framework for child-centered parenting. *Psychiatry, 67*, 331–352.

Sanders, C. M. (1989). *Grief: The mourning after—Dealing with adult bereavement*. New York: Wiley.

Sanders, C. M. (1992). *Surviving grief and learning to live again*. New York: Wiley.

Schore, A. (2003). Early relational trauma, disorganized attachment, and the development of a predisposition to violence. In M. Solomon & D. J. Siegel (Eds.), *Healing trauma* (pp. 107–167). New York: Norton.

Shapiro, E. (2008). Whose recovery of what: Relationships and environments promoting grief and growth. *Death Studies, 32*, 40–58.

Shear, K., Jackson, C., Essock, S., Donahue, S., & Felton, C. (2006). Screening for complicated grief among Project Liberty service recipients 18 months after September 11, 2001. *Psychiatric Services, 57*, 1291–1297.

Shear, K., Monk, T., Houck, P., Melhem, N., Frank, E., Reynolds, C., et al. (2007). An attachment-based model of complicated grief including the role of avoidance. *European Archives of Psychiatry and Clinical Neuroscience, 257*, 453–461.

Shear, K., & Shair, H. (2005). Attachment, loss, & complicated grief. *Developmental Psychobiology, 47*, 253–267.

Siegel, D. (2003). An interpersonal neurobiology of psychotherapy: The developing mind and the resolution of trauma. In M. Solomon & D. J. Siegel (Eds.), *Healing trauma* (pp. 1–56). New York: Norton.

Silver, R., Holman, E., McIntosh, D., Poulin, M., & Gil-Rivas, V. (2002). Nationwide longitudinal study of psychological responses to September 11. *Journal of the American Medical Association, 288*, 1235–1244.

Silverman, P. R., & Worden, W. (1992). Children's reactions in the early months after the death of a parent. *American Journal of Orthopsychiatry, 62*, 93–104.

Speece, M., & Brent, S. (1996). The development of children's understanding of death. In C. Corr & D. Corr (Eds.), *Handbook of childhood death and bereavement* (pp. 29–50). New York: Springer.

Stroebe, M., Hansson, R., Stroege, W., & Schut, H. (Eds.). (2008). *Handbook of bereavement research: Consequences, coping and care*. Washington, DC: American Psychological Association.

Stroebe, M., Schut, H., & Stroebe, W. (2007). Health outcomes of bereavement. *Lancet, 370*, 1960–1973.

Webb, N. B. (Ed.). (2002). *Helping bereaved children* (2nd ed.). New York: Guildford.

Introduction

The Assessment of Associated Features Important to Understanding Childhood Trauma

KATHLEEN NADER

Two Suns

Assessment variables are multidimensional and likely combine synergistically to influence outcomes. Failure to assess the wide range of variables proven important to posttrauma outcomes or to use appropriate variable groupings may hinder the accuracy of findings. A number of variables, such as the number and types of traumatic exposures in a lifetime or in an event, the presence of strong negative emotions (e.g., shame, guilt, or anger), children's genetic and personality traits, and measures of reactivity (e.g., cortisol levels), are important to our understanding and assessment of children's posttrauma reactions over time. Some variables previously assessed primarily in relationship to complex traumatic reactions are relevant to children's ongoing development regardless of the complexity of exposure or reactions.

In the preceding issue of this journal, Part I of this two journal series, researcher clinicians elaborated developmental issues important to the assessment and nature of childhood trauma as well as the nature of trauma-related complicated reactions (complicated trauma and grief). Part II of this special series will examine some of the variables associated with traumatic reactions, including attachment (Breidenstine, Bailey, Zeanah, & Larrieu, this issue), multiple exposures (Finkelhor, Shattuck, Turner, Ormrod, & Hamby, this issue), personality and genetics (Cisler, Amstadter, & Nugent, this issue), age and other differences in the manifestation and reporting of cortisol reactivity (Nader & Weems, this issue), and guilt, shame, and anger (Fletcher, this issue). To follow is a brief discussion of trauma's associations, the complexity of their interrelationships, and the variables elaborated in this journal issue. A brief look at choices of outcome variables is also included.

Trauma, Associated Variables, and Complexity

Studies of the associations of putative psychosocial risk factors with specific disorders have often been flawed by their failure to control for comorbidity, to examine a wide range of risk factors, and to examine gender and developmental phase effects (Shanahan, Copeland, Costello, & Angold, 2008). Among the results of these noncomprehensive research studies may be faulty assumptions that in turn influence subsequent research methods and foci. For example, some outcome disorders are routinely combined rather than treated separately in analyses because of perceptions about similarities in their associations. Contrary to common beliefs, routinely combined disorders (e.g., conduct disorder [CD] and oppositional defiant disorder [ODD]) have nonshared risk factors (e.g., loss events, parental depression associated with CD; neglect for females with CD) as well as shared risk factors (e.g., for both CD and ODD: sexual abuse, peers with behavior problems, poor sibling relationships, poor supervision, parental unemployment).

Among a wide range of variables proven to be of importance to posttrauma outcomes in youths are the following: (a) parent and family factors, such as parental mental health, parenting, and attachment styles (Chung & Steinberg, 2006; Fletcher, Steinberg, & Williams-Wheeler, 2004), family history, structure, and demographic variables (Langenkamp & Frisco, 2008; Scaramella, Sohr-Preston, Callahan, & Mirabile, 2008); (b) school and neighborhood community influences, such as peer associations and community cohesion and/or violence (Chung & Steinberg, 2006; Laird, Jordan, Dodge, Pettit, & Bates, 2001); (c) child qualities, such as genetic predispositions, personality traits, gender, coping styles, pubertal stage, functioning age, ethnicity, and intelligence (Cisler et al., this issue; Nader, 2008); and (d) child trauma history variables, such as loss, comorbidity, and the number of types of exposures in a lifetime or in an event (Finkelhor et al., this issue, 2009; Nader, 2008; Scheeringa, 2011), as well as aspects of the traumatic event (e.g., dissociative reactions, the intensity of peritraumatic emotions, exposure levels, guilt; Fletcher, this issue; Nader, 2008, 2010). Meta-analytic studies have demonstrated a number of clear predictors of posttraumatic stress disorder (PTSD) reactions, including lack of social support, family background, prior psychiatric history, and aspects of the traumatic experience itself (Bonanno, 2008). Some studies of child pathology have suggested including loneliness and theory of mind (i.e., the ability to attribute to others' mental states—beliefs, desires, emotions, intentions—and to use the information to predict and interpret behavior; Angold & Heim, 2007; Ferguson & Austin, 2010). The need to adapt for and evaluate developmental and cultural issues when assessing youths has been well demonstrated (Kerns, Abraham, Schlegelmilch, & Morgan, 2007). It is likely that children's traits and history, family variables, other environmental influences, and event variables combine synergistically to influence outcomes. Large prospective studies are needed to assess the complexity of variable interrelationships and their influence on posttrauma outcomes.

Complexity of Variable Interrelationships

People and the variables that influence their growth, adaptation, or failure of adaptation are multidimensional, and the interrelationships among variables can be complex (Angold & Heim, 2007; Nader, 2008). Gene × Environment × Development interactions (i.e., the interaction of genes, environment, and development) indicate that genetic risk and protective factors fluctuate across development and are affected by changing contexts (Dahl & Gunnar, 2009; Emde & Spicer, 2000; see Table 1). For example, early attachment and other emotional experiences are complexly influenced by qualities of the individual child in transaction with diverse aspects of the child's environment. Across life, relationship experiences are internalized according to personally meaningful contexts. In addition, there are still a multitude of unknowns in the neurobiological development of youths. Understanding trauma in youths will require an increasing understanding of issues regarding development and complexity through assessment across time of individuals as well as groups.

Table 1
Types of genetic influences on the outcomes of adversity

Relationship	Description
Gene × Environment (G × E)	G × E interactions occur when environmental experiences moderate gene expression (or conversely, when the effects of exposure to a particular environment on a person is conditional upon their genotype; Caspi et al., 2005; Costello, Foley, & Angold, 2006; Lau & Pine, 2008)
G × E × Development	G × E × D recognizes the developmental variations in genetic expression (Dahl & Gunnar, 2009)
Gene Environment Correlations (rGE)	rGE occur because parents and children share both genes and home environments (Prom-Wormley et al., 2008)
	Passive rGE refer to children receiving genotypes that are correlated with their family environment
	Evocative rGE reflect a situation in which the child's genotype and behavior elicit responses such as neglect or abuse
	Active rGE indicate individuals who seek out environments that correspond to their genetically influenced traits
Monamine Oxidaze A (MAOA)	As young as age 7 in boys, low rather than high levels of the MAOA enzyme are associated with externalizing (Kim-Cohen et al., 2006)
	Low-enzyme MAOA is not associated with internalizing
Serotonin (5-HTT)	A short allele serotonin transporter gene interaction with high environmental risks (e.g., abuse) has been linked to depression (Rutter, Moffit, & Caspi, 2006; Pauli-Pott et al., 2009)
	A short allele serotonin transporter gene interaction with high environmental risks is not linked to antisocial behavior
	For young children, social support is protective against the manifestation of the disorder
Dopamine (DA)	A relationship has been documented between PTSD symptoms, primarily arousal symptoms, and the dopamine (DA) polymorphism (DAT; Drury, Theall, Keats, & Scheeringa, 2009)
	Dopamine D4 receptor polymorphism (DRD4) 7-repeat allele has been associated with externalizing but may interact with child-rearing practices (Bakermans-Kranenburg, Van IJzendoorn, Pijlman, Mesman, & Juffer, 2008)
	Short DRD4 allele in combination with maternal behaviors is related to disorganized attachment, which in turn is associated with mental health outcomes (Gervai et al., 2007; see Bakermans-Kranenburg & Van IJzendoorn, 2010)

Complex interrelationships among variables and their developmentally diverse impacts on traumatic reactions will require extending and/or supplementing current assessment measures. Some variables previously assessed primarily in relationship to complex traumatic reactions are relevant to developing children regardless of the complexity of exposure or reactions. Their pretrauma levels may influence outcomes. Their posttrauma alteration may have a cascading effect on development. Self-regulation, for example, is an evolving process across childhood and can be measured by behavioral, neurobiological, self-report, or narrative-response measures (e.g., sentence completion, story interpretation; Bunge & Wright, 2007). It enlists multiple brain regions (e.g., those involved in memory, inhibition, and planning), and it is influenced by genetic, other biological, and environmental factors, as well as by individual child traits. Furthermore, self-regulation is needed in multiple aspects of functioning, such as communication, social functioning, work and other goal-directed activity, and self-defense (Barkley, 2001).

The ability to delay gratification or emotional response is an aspect of self-regulation. Studies have shown that the ability to delay gratification is also important to a number of skills in childhood and later in adulthood (e.g., coping and social interaction; Krueger, Caspi, Moffitt, White, & Stouthamer-Loeber, 1996; Posner & Rothbart, 2007). An early ability to delay gratification may moderate negative outcomes in adulthood for those who are sensitive to rejection (Ayduk et al., 2000). An additional variable, processing of facial expressions and other indicators of emotional states, is central to human interaction (Douglas & Porter, 2010). Following traumas, traumatic and depressive reactions may influence information processing such as emotion recognition in complex ways (Nader, 2008). For example, youths have reported increased expectations of additional victimization, personal and community-wide bad luck, and/or hostile intent from others following traumas. Expectations and interpretations of others' behaviors and emotions in turn influence a youth's behavior and emotions, which influence relationships and other life experiences. Douglas and Porter (2010) found that depressed individuals see sadness more often than others and happiness less often than others in neutral faces, and depressed individuals are also less skilled at recognizing disgust in facial expressions. Because trauma may influence variables, without pretrauma measures of the variables, findings are difficult to interpret.

Grouping or Classes of Variables

Recognizing the full range of grouping variables is essential to accurate assessment. As noted earlier, the number of types of victimizations is important to findings. Additionally, as Scheeringa (2011) has pointed out, longitudinal studies have demonstrated different trajectories of posttrauma symptoms. Bonanno and colleagues (e.g., Bonanno, Boerner, & Wortman, 2008; Bonanno, Rennicke, & Dekel, 2005), for example, have suggested four resilience-related groupings that influence outcomes. In addition, recognizing all subtypes of variables is important. For example, researchers have demonstrated the importance of including *unknown* and/or *accurate* as well as *internal* and *external* locus of control domains (Jackson, Frick, & Dravage-Bush, 2000), and including *mixed internalizing/externalizing* groups as well as *externalizing* and *internalizing* groups in studies of those variables. Studies have also suggested the importance of including groupings of comorbid disorders for accurate findings (e.g., Attention-Deficit and Hyperactivity Disorder [ADHD], ODD/CD, or ADHD + ODD/CD; Waschbusch et al., 2002). Failure to include these and other additional variable classifications may result in inaccurate findings (Waschbusch et al., 2002).

Comorbidity

Adverse experience is a major risk factor for a wide range of disorders such as depression, anxiety, substance abuse, cardiovascular disorders, immune disorders, and metabolic disorders (Angold & Heim, 2007; Kimerling, Prins, Westrup, & Lee, 2004; Nader, 2008) as well as externalizing disorders (Cicchetti, 2003; Laird et al., 2001; Nader, 2008). Comorbidity is common among stress-related disorders (Angold & Heim, 2007; Nader, 2008). Comorbid depressive, other anxiety, behavioral, and substance abuse disorders are common in association with PTSD (Carrion, Weems, Ray, & Reiss, 2002; Cicchetti, 2003; Ford, 2002; Nader, 2008; Udwin, Boyle, Yule, Bolton, & O'Ryan, 2000). Research has demonstrated that a portion of comorbid conditions predate the development of PTSD and may be vulnerability factors for PTSD (Koenen et al., 2008; Scheeringa, 2011). Evaluating comorbidity is important to assessment and treatment (Ford, Courtois, Steele, van der Hart, & Nijenhuis, 2005).

Specific Mediating and Moderating Variables

As discussed, multiple variables complexly influence outcomes. To follow is a brief discussion of specific variables elaborated in this issue: (a) polyvictimization; (b) attachment; (c) child personality and genetic traits; (d) shame, guilt, and anger; and (e) cortisol.

Polyvictimization

Early adverse experiences appear to leave "biological scars" that increase vulnerability to later stress and predisopose a person to a variety of disorders that may worsen in response to stress (Angold & Heim, 2007). Although research has demonstrated that single and chronic victimizations may have a severe impact on youths, their functioning, and their development, studies of adults (Anda et al., 2006; Nijenhuis, van der Hart, & Steele, 2002; Richmond, Elliott, Pierce, Aspelmeier, & Alexander, 2009) and children (Fergusson & Horwood, 2003; Finkelhor, Ormrod, & Turner, 2007a, 2007b; Finkelhor, Shattuck, Turner, Ormrod, & Hamby, this issue; Ford, Elhai, Connor, & Frueh, 2010) have demonstrated that experiencing multiple types of trauma or trauma plus adversities increases risk of psychopathology and higher levels of symptoms (e.g., PTSD, dissociation, substance abuse, anxiety, depression, and anger/aggression outcomes, and even the possibility of psychosis; Shevlin, Dorahy, & Adamson, 2007). Finkelhor, Ormrod, and Turner (2007a) have used the term *polyvictimization* to refer to victims with the same type of victimization (e.g., assault) who also have a number of additional kinds of victimizations (e.g., assault, as well as witnessing, theft, and bullying victimizations; see Table 2). Finkelhor and colleagues (2007a) found that polyvictims were considerably more symptomatic than children with repeated episodes of the same kind of victimization, and, when accounted for, polyvictimization greatly reduced or eliminated the association between individual types of victimizations (e.g., sexual abuse) and symptomatology. Briere, Kaltman, and Green (2008) found that even after controlling for individual traumas that also increase complexity, the total number of different types of childhood traumatic events experienced was related to symptom complexity in adulthood. Perhaps especially for violent victimizations, studies have reported the commonality of additional exposures (Finkelhor et al., 2007b; Hanson et al., 2006). These findings suggest that assessing the number of types of trauma experienced as well as the number of types of exposure within a single trauma is essential in understanding complex and other posttrauma outcomes.

Attachment

Across demographic groups (race and socioeconomic status), the combination of strong parental supervision and positive parental involvement is protective against outcomes such

Table 2
Finkelhor's victimization categories (Finkelhor et al., 2007a, this issue)

Category	Definition (have experienced)
Single victims	Only one victimization of one type (e.g., one physical assault)
Chronic victims	Multiple episodes of one type of victimization (e.g., more than one physical assault)
Low polyvictims	Four or more types of victimization
High polyvictims	Seven or more types of victimization
Developmentally Defined Polyvictimization (see Finkelhor et al., this issue)	Five or more types of victimization for 2- to 6-year-olds Six or more for 6- to 9-year-olds Seven or more for 10- to 13-year-olds Eight or more for 14- to17-year-olds

as aggression and delinquency (Chung & Steinberg, 2006). Attachment classifications, especially disorganized attachments and other insecure attachments, have been linked to a number of vulnerabilities, symptoms, and disorders (Breidenstine et al., this issue). Insecure attachments have been linked to disorders including depressive, anxiety, dissociative, somatic, personality, externalizing, internalizing, and overall psychopathology across youth groups as well as in adults maltreated as children (Lyons-Ruth, Zeanah, & Benoit, 2003; Moss, Pascuzzo, & Simard, in press; Nader, 2008). Such attachments have been associated with aggression, low self-esteem, suicidality, memory problems, higher cortisol levels in response to stressful or novel situations, negative emotionality, and poor coping skills. In adolescents specifically, insecure attachments have been associated with increased hostility, poorer social skills, more problematic romantic relationships, and ongoing problems with parents (Allen & Land, 1999; Hesse, Main, Abrams, & Rifkin, 2003; Nader, 2008; Rutter, 1997; Schore, 2003). Traumas may interfere with attachment relationships, and disorganized attachments are often linked to abuse (Breidenstine et al., this issue; Cook et al., 2005; Nader, 2008). Schore (2003) has suggested that abuse-related disorganized-disoriented insecure attachment manifests as an inability to generate a coherent coping strategy with relational stress that may make an individual vulnerable to PTSD. Whether or not traumatic reactions are complex and whether or not insecure attachments are trauma-engendered, insecure attachments suggest the need for appropriate interventions (see Moss et al., in press).

Child Qualities

Children's personality traits are among the understudied mediating and moderating variables within trauma research. Most often, personality traits have been assessed following traumas and may be influenced by the traumatic exposure and reactions (see Nader, 2008 for a summary of personality theories and traits). Strelau and Zawadzki (2005) found that *briskness* (i.e., the tendency to react quickly, maintain high tempo in carrying out activities, and shift behavior/reactions easily in response to environmental changes), *endurance* (i.e., the ability to react adequately in situations that demand long-lasting or high-stimulative activity, under intense external stimulation), and *activity* (i.e., the "tendency to undertake behaviors of high-stimulative value or to supply by means of behavior strong stimulation from the surroundings") were negatively related to PTSD severity, while *emotional reactivity* (i.e., the "tendency to react intensively to emotion-generating stimuli, expressed in high-emotional sensitivity and in low emotional endurance") and *perseveration* (i.e., the "tendency to continue and to repeat behavior or experience emotions after cessation of stimuli [situations] evoking this behavior or emotions") were positively related to PTSD severity (p. 125). Notably, *emotional reactivity* was the best predictor of intensity of PTSD, whether PTSD was assessed shortly or long after a disaster. *Neuroticism* (negative emotionality) and *introversion* have also been associated with increased trauma symptoms (Carrion et al., 2002; Nader & Weems, this issue). *Morningness/eveningness*, believed to have a genetic component, refers to individual differences in sleep-wake patterns and preferences for activity and alertness during the morning versus the evening. In a study of antisocial behavior, Susman and colleagues (2007) demonstrated the importance of morningness/eveningness to cortisol levels in children ages 8–13. Eveningness and early puberty onset were associated with girls' self-reports of relational aggression and boys' rule-breaking, attention problems, and conduct disorder symptoms. At least in some cases, the association of mental health outcomes and personality traits may be linked to shared genetic mechanisms. For example, evidence has suggested that the correlation between neuroticism and depression is attributable to a genetic factor linked to both (Cisler et al., this issue). A three-way interaction involving genotype (a 5-HTTLPR polymorphism), attachment security, and age has had a highly significant association with negative emotionality (Pauli-Pott, Friedl, Hinney, & Hebebrand, 2009).

Genetic predispositions have been implicated in postadversity outcomes (Cisler et al., this issue). Without a trigger such as trauma or other adversity, the effects of genetic factors on specific dysfunction are reduced and, in turn, the probability of developing a phenotype (i.e., the observable manifestation of a genotype in response to its interaction with the environment) is lowered (Lau & Pine, 2008). Differential vulnerabilities have been associated with a short allele serotonin (5HTT) transporter gene (Rutter, Moffit, & Caspi, 2006), low rather than high levels of the monoamine oxidase A (MAOA) enzyme (Kim-Cohen et al., 2006), and a dopamine polymorphism (Drury, Theall, Keats, & Scheeringa, 2009; see Table 1). Genetic vulnerabilities may interact with other variables such as child-rearing conditions. Bakermans-Kranenburg, Van IJzendoorn, Pijlman, Mesman, and Juffer (2008) found that toddlers with the Dopamine D4 receptor polymorphism (DRD4) 7-repeat allele were more likely than children without the allele to show decreases in externalizing behavior problems following a short-term intervention to promote positive parenting.

Genetically informed research designs control for age-specific genetic effects (Costello, Foley, & Angold, 2006). For example, heritability for depression appears to increase across adolescence (Lau & Eley, 2006). Mixed findings in the association of long versus short 5-HTTLPR allele to shyness/behavioral inhibition or neuroticism may be explained by age differences. Harro and colleagues (2009) found that adolescents, homozygous for the short 5-HTTLPR allele, were more likely to report elevated neuroticism at age 15 but not at 18 (Cisler et al., this issue). Studies of 5-HTTLPR have strongly suggested interaction effects between the genotype and environmental conditions on infant emotionality development (Pauli-Pott, Friedl, Hinney, & Hebebrand, 2009). The short allele 5-HTTLPR polymorphism has been associated with a reduced transcriptional efficiency and expression of 5-HTT in infants but not in human adults, presumably because the 5-HTTLPR genotype dependent 5-HTT expression exerts its influence predominantly in early brain development.

Shame, Guilt, and Anger

In addition to the fear, helplessness, and horror required in the diagnostic criteria for PTSD, research has suggested that whether trauma exposure is direct or indirect (e.g., via media), other strong emotions such as panic, shame, anger, or worry are also associated with trauma symptom levels (Ahern, Galea, Resnick, & Vlahov, 2004; Andrews, Brewin, Rose, & Kirk, 2000; Fletcher, this issue; Nader, 2010; Pfefferbaum, Stuber, Galea, & Fairbrother, 2006). Following traumatic events, guilt has also been associated with increased traumatic reactions (Nader, Pynoos, Fairbanks, & Frederick, 1990; Pynoos et al., 1987) and may be influenced by whether a youth is guilt-prone (Walter & LaFreniere, 2007). For a group of sexually abused adolescent girls, Daigneault, Hébert, and Tourigny (2011) found that general self-attributions of blame for negative events was the best predictor of functioning, while self-attributions of blame for the abuse did not predict additional unique variance.

Shame is among the symptoms of complicated traumatic reactions and may be important to the manifestation and reporting of complex and noncomplex traumatic reactions (Courtois & Ford, 2011; van der Kolk, 2005). Intense feelings of powerlessness or humiliation that may instigate shame and/or anger may be followed by *lashing out or in* (e.g., aggression or suicidality; Ding, Nelsen, & Lassonde, 2002; Nader, in press). As Fletcher (this issue) points out, shame may develop into "a kind of retaliatory anger that manifests as a lashing out, a humiliated rage that attempts to erase the shame by shifting the rejection from the self to the other." Such humiliated rage has been found, for example, among incarcerated violent individuals and school shooters (Nader, 2008, in press). When triggered by traumatic memories such as severe/ongoing child sexual abuse (CSA), strong emotions such as shame or anger may segue into dissociative episodes (Wagner, Rizvi, & Harned, 2007). Consequently, such youth may have difficulty reporting, discussing, or processing their experiences.

For CSA survivors, humiliation is associated with shame and is a sensitive marker of a lack of emotional coherence (Negrao, Bonanno, Noll, Putnam, & Trickett, 2005). In contrast to normal controls, CSA survivors' verbal reports and facial expressions (e.g., of shame or anger) may be incongruent (Negrao et al., 2005; Wagner, Roemer, Orsillo, & Litz, 2003); a finding that may be important to the assessment of such children in face-to-face interviews. Based on their own and related findings, Negrao et al. (2005) concluded that participants who voluntarily disclosed abuse histories tended to express shame and humiliation verbally, whereas CSA participants who did not disclose such a history tended to express shame nonverbally (i.e., facially). The tendency to evidence concordance between verbally narrated humiliation and facial shame was differentially related to symptomatic presentation. For example, concordance was unrelated to PTSD in disclosers but was associated with increased PTSD for nondisclosers. On the other hand, disclosers who evidenced facial shame without verbally narrated humiliation (i.e., lack of emotional coherence) evidenced better adjustment.

Cortisol

A number of researchers have assessed youths' posttrauma cortisol levels across time (Carrion et al., 2002; Nader & Weems, this issue; Weems & Carrion, 2007, 2009). Patterns of cortisol reactivity following traumas demonstrate one of the ways that posttrauma symptoms may change over time (Weems & Carrion, 2007). Evidence has suggested a pattern of high cortisol levels in the first two years after childhood exposure to traumas and low cortisol levels later and in adulthood. The association of low and high cortisol levels with different outcomes (e.g., externalizing versus internalizing; Nader & Weems, this issue) and the associations of specific genetic vulnerabilities with the same outcomes (Cisler et al., this issue) suggest the need for studies of both genetic factors and cortisol.

Selection of Outcome Variables

Multiple variables are linked to a single outcome, and multiple outcomes may follow a single variable (e.g., trauma exposure; Nader, 2008). The selection of outcome variables is important for understanding childhood traumatic reactions and for choosing appropriate interventions. Some variables may be either influencing variables or outcome variables. For example, resilience levels may influence symptomatic outcomes or be influenced by trauma. Personality traits, shame, or guilt may influence reactions or be a result of exposure. As noted, comorbidity may suggest more complex traumatic reactions and is important to treatment selection. It is essential to include in studies a comprehensive list of outcome variables as well as appropriate subgroups of influencing and outcome variables, as discussed earlier. In addition to an effect on the accuracy of findings, failure to assess important outcome variables or variable combinations may affect the richness of information gathered and the success of interventions. For example, variables such as sibling abuse and emotional abuse are not always assessed, perhaps because they are considered difficult to confirm or to report/measure and/or are considered a lesser victimization. Nevertheless, both emotional abuse and sibling abuse are associated with increased isolation, low self-esteem, external locus of control, depressive symptomatology, aggression, and/or increased sexual risk-taking or abuse behaviors (Caffaro & Conn-Caffaro, 1998/2007; Younge et al., 2010; Zurbriggen, Gobin, & Freyd, 2010).

Most studies of children exposed to traumatic events focus on traumatic reactions and recovery. Bonanno (2008) pointed out that resilience is common following exposure to putative traumatic events. Pathways to resilience (including resilient coping) are multiple and differ from pathways to recovery. The examination of resilience as a separate trajectory from traumatic reactions and recovery is needed. For children, traits such as trust, internal or accurate locus of control (the belief that one has control over circumstances and/or recognition when circumstances are not controllable), and positive self-esteem are among variables associated with resilience and better adjustment. Research has suggested that positive emotions are also linked to better outcomes after loss or trauma (Bonanno, 2008; Nader, 2008).

Studies of adults have suggested that, in addition to *hardiness* (i.e., commitment to finding meaningful purpose in life; beliefs in one's personal ability to influence his/her surroundings and outcomes and that one can learn and grow from experiences; and ability to use active coping and social support), *self-enhancement* (i.e., a more than average positive bias in favor of self) and *repressive coping* (i.e., a tendency to avoid unpleasant thoughts, emotions, and memories) are associated with better posttrauma outcomes (Bonanno, 2008). It will be important to examine the place of such variables in children's posttrauma resilience and to elaborate some seeming contradictions in these adult findings on posttrauma resilience. For example, although temporary escape can be protective, persistent avoidance has been demonstrated to interfere with integration and adjustment for some posttrauma outcomes (e.g., posttrauma grief; Boelen, van den Bout, & van den Hout, 2006; Nader & Salloum, 2011; traumatic reactions; Pacella et al., 2011).

Avoidant coping has been associated with negative posttrauma outcomes in a number of studies (Mello & Nader, in press; Min, Farkas, Minnes, & Singer, 2007). In contrast, although active coping has been associated with resilience and better posttrauma outcomes, active coping (e.g., memorialization, helping efforts) after some events has been associated with increased symptoms (Brown et al., 2008). Evidence suggests that the ability to flexibly employ different types of coping behaviors consistent with the varying demands of diverse situations is advantageous (Bonanno, Pat-Horenczyk, & Noll, 2011). It is possible that it is not avoidant versus active coping or problem-focused versus emotional coping that defines the nature of outcomes or pathways to resilience, but instead, that the defining elements are the youth's appropriate and timely application of specific methods to particular circumstances and the specific needs of the youth.

Conclusions

The variables and variable combinations that influence trauma reactions and their course are often complexly interrelated and likely to contribute synergistically to outcomes. Assessing a broad range of variables and outcomes is important to the richness of information gathered from an individual or group and to the effectiveness of posttrauma intervention selection. A number of variables, including specific child qualities and histories, family/environmental contexts, and traumatic event-related factors, have been indentified in association with childhood traumatic reactions. Studies have repeatedly confirmed their trauma associations or the predictive power of such variables, and they should be routinely included in assessments and analyses. Mixed findings for some of them may be related to differing variable definitions and diverse components of assessments (see previous issue), including failure to include sufficient numbers of and appropriately categorized influencing and outcome variables.

As discussed in this two-part series, a number of variables including developmental issues may influence outcomes such as PTSD, comorbidity, complex posttrauma reactions, and/or other changes in a youth's life trajectory. Among the variables and outcomes demonstrated to be of importance are those to follow in the articles of this issue. For example, repeated evidence suggests that the number of types of traumas, over a lifetime and/or during an event, clearly influence youth and their reactions to traumas. Any putative traumatic event in combination with particular child history, traits, and circumstances, including a history of adversities, may engender complicated reactions or developmental disruptions that undermine a youth's life. Personality and genetics, attachment, and peritraumatic or posttraumatic shame, guilt, and rage are also well established as influencing variables. Youths' reactions may change over time, subtly or blatantly. Neurochemical reactivity (e.g., cortisol reactivity) is one important indicator of reactions and demonstrates the changing nature of symptoms across time. More study is needed to elaborate the variable combinations that influence the intensity and complexity of traumatic reactions at different life stages.

Acknowledgment

The Editor of *JCAT,* and the guest editor of this special issue would like to acknowledge and express thanks to Teri Arnold, MSW, Assistant Editor of the *Journal of Child & Adolescent Trauma,* for providing feedback and editing for this special issue.

References

Ahern, J., Galea, S., Resnick, H., & Vlahov, D. (2004). TV images and probable posttraumatic stress disorder after September 11: The role of background characteristics, event exposures, and perievent panic. *The Journal of Nervous and Mental Disease, 192*(3), 217–226.

Allen, J. P., & Land, D. (1999). Attachment in adolescence. In J. Cassidy & P. R. Shaver (Eds.), *Handbook of attachment: Theory, research, and clinical applications* (pp. 319–335). New York: Guilford Press.

Anda, R., Felitti, V., Bremner, J., Walker, J., Whitfield, C., Perry, B. D., et al. (2006). The enduring effects of abuse and related adverseexperiences in childhood: A convergence of evidence from neurobiology and epidemiology. *European Archives of Psychiatry and Clinical Neuroscience, 256*, 174–186.

Andrews, B., Brewin, C., Rose, S., & Kirk, M. (2000). Predicting PTSD symptoms in victims of violent crime: The role of shame, anger, and childhood abuse. *Journal of Abnormal Psychology, 109*, 69–73.

Angold, A., & Heim, C. (2007). A developmental perspective, with a focus on childhood trauma. In W. Narrow, M. First, P. Sirovatka, & D. Regier (Eds.), *Age and gender considerations in psychiatric diagnosis: A research agenda for DSM-V* (pp. 81–100). Arlington, VA: American Psychiatric Publishing.

Ayduk, O., Mendoza-Denton, R., Mischel, W., Downey, G., Peake, P., & Rodriguez, M. (2000). Regulating the interpersonal self: Strategic self-regulation for coping with rejection sensitivity. *Journal of Personality and Social Psychology, 79*(5), 776–792.

Bakermans-Kranenburg, M. J., & Van IJzendoorn, M. H. (2010). Parenting matters: Family science in the genomic era. *Family Science, 1*, 26–36.

Bakermans-Kranenburg, M., Van IJzendoorn, M., Pijlman, F., Mesman, J., & Juffer, F. (2008). Experimental evidence for differential susceptibility: Dopamine D4 receptor polymorphism (DRD4 VNTR) moderates intervention effects on toddlers' externalizing behavior in a randomized controlled trial. *Developmental Psychology, 44*, 293–300.

Barkley, R. (2001). The executive functions and self-regulation: An evolutionary neuropsychological perspective. *Neuropsychology Review, 11*(1), 1–29.

Boelen, P., van den Bout, J., & van den Hout, M. (2006). Negative cognitions and avoidance in emotional problems after bereavement: A prospective study. *Behaviour, Research, and Therapy, 44*, 1657–1672.

Bonanno, G. (2008). Loss, trauma, and human resilience: Have we underestimated the human capacity to thrive after extremely aversive events? *Psychological Trauma: Theory, Research, Practice, and Policy, 5*(1), 101–113.

Bonanno, G., Boerner, K., & Wortman, C. (2008). Trajectories of grieving. In M. Stroebe, R. O. Hansson, H. Schut, & W. Stroebe (Eds.), *Handbook of bereavement research andpractice: Advances in theory and intervention* (pp. 287–308). Washington, DC: APA Books.

Bonanno, G., Pat-Horenczyk, R., & Noll, J. (2011). Coping flexibility and trauma: The Perceived Ability to Cope with Trauma (PACT) Scale. *Psychological Trauma: Theory, Research, Practice, and Policy, 3*(2), 117–129.

Bonanno, G., Rennicke, C., & Dekel, S. (2005). Self-enhancement among high-exposure survivors of the September 11th terrorist attack: Resilience or social maladjustment? *Journal of Personality and Social Psychology, 88*, 984–998.

Briere, J., Kaltman, S., & Green, B. (2008). Accumulated childhood trauma and symptom complexity. *Journal of Traumatic Stress, 21*(2), 223–226.

Brown, E., Amaya-Jackson, L., Cohen, J., Handel, S., De bocanegra, H., Zatta, E., et al. (2008). Childhood traumatic grief: A multi-site empirical examination of the construct and its correlates. *Death Studies, 32*, 899–923.

Bunge, S., & Wright, S. (2007). Neurodevelopmental changes in working memory and cognitive control. *Current Opinion in Neurobiology, 17*, 243–250.

Caffaro, J., & Conn-Caffaro, A. (2007). *Sibling abuse trauma: Assessment and intervention strategies for children, families, and adults.* New York: Routledge. (Original work published in 1998)

Carrion, V., Weems, C., Ray, R., & Reiss, A. (2002). Toward an empirical definition of pediatric PTSD: The phenomenology of PTSD symptoms in youth. *Journal of the American Academy of Child and Adolescent Psychiatry, 41*(2), 166–173.

Caspi, A., Moffitt, T., Cannon, M., McClay, J., Murray, R., Harrington, H., et al. (2005). Moderation of the effect of adolescent-onset cannabis use on adult psychosis by a functional polymorphism in the catechol-Omethyltransferase gene: Longitudinal evidence of a gene x environment interaction. *Biological Psychiatry*, *57*, 1117–1127.

Chung, H., & Steinberg, L. (2006). Relations between neighborhood factors, parenting behaviors, peer deviance, and delinquency among serious juvenile offenders. *Developmental Psychology*, *42*(2), 319–331.

Cicchetti, D. (2003). Foreword. In S. Luthar (Ed.), *Resilience and vulnerability: Adaptation in the context of childhood adversities* (pp. xix–xxxi). New York: Cambridge University Press.

Cook, A., Spinazzola, J., Ford, J., Lanktree, C., Blaustein, M., Cloitre, M., et al. (2005). Complex trauma in children and adolescents. *Psychiatric Annals*, 35, 390–398

Costello, E., Foley, D., & Angold, A. (2006). 10-year research update review: The epidemiology of child and adolescent psychiatric disorders: II. Developmental epidemiology. *Journal of the American Academy of Child and Adolescent Psychiatry*, *45*, 8–25.

Courtois, C., & Ford, J. (2011). *Clinician's guide to treatment of complex traumatic stress disorders.* New York: Guilford.

Dahl, R., & Gunnar, M. (2009). Heightened stress responsiveness and emotional reactivity during pubertal maturation: Implications for psychopathology. *Development and Psychopathology*, *21*, 1–6.

Daigneault, I., Hébert, M., & Tourigny, M. (2006). Attributions and coping in sexually abused adolescents referred for group treatment. *Journal of Child Sexual Abuse*, *15*(3), 35–59.

Ding, C., Nelsen, D., & Lassonde, C. (2002). Correlated of gun involvement and aggressiveness among adolescents. *Youth & Society, 34*, 195–213.

Douglas, K., & Porter, R. (2010). Recognition of disgusted facial expressions in severe depression. *The British Journal of Psychiatry*, *197*, 156–157.

Drury, S., Theall, K., Keats, B., & Scheeringa, M. (2009). The role of the dopamine transporter (DAT) in the development of PTSD in preschool children. *Journal of Traumatic Stress*, *22*(6), 534–539.

Emde, R., & Spicer, P. (2000). Experience in the midst of variation: New horizons for development and psychopathology. *Development and Psychopathology*, *12*, 313–331.

Ferguson, F., & Austin, E. (2010). Associations of trait and ability emotional intelligence with performance on Theory of Mind tasks in an adult sample. *Personality and Individual Differences*, *49*, 414–418.

Fergusson, D., & Horwood, L. (2003). Resilience to childhood adversity: Results of a 21-year study. In S. S. Luthar, (Ed.), *Resilience and vulnerability: Adaptation in the context of childhood adversities* (pp. 130–155). New York: Cambridge University Press.

Finkelhor, D., Ormrod, R., & Turner, H. (2007a). Poly-victimization: A neglected component in child victimization. *Child Abuse & Neglect*, *31*, 7–26.

Finkelhor, D., Ormrod, R., & Turner, H. (2007b). Re-victimization patterns in a national longitudinal sample of children and youth. *Child Abuse & Neglect*, *31*, 479–502.

Finkelhor, D., Ormrod, R., & Turner, H. (2009). Lifetime assessment of poly-victimization in a national sample of children & youth. *Child Abuse & Neglect*, *33*, 403–411.

Fletcher, A., Steinberg, L., & Williams-Wheeler, M. (2004). Parental influences on adolescent problem behavior: Revisiting Stattin and Kerr. *Child Development*, *75*(3), 781–796.

Ford, J. (2002). Traumatic victimization in childhood and persistent problems with oppositional-defiance. *Journal of Aggression, Maltreatment and Trauma*, *6*(1), 25–58.

Ford, J., Courtois, C., Steele, K., van der Hart, O., & Nijenhuis, E. (2005). Treatment of complex posttraumatic self-dysregulation. *Journal of TraumaticStress*, *18*(5), 437–447.

Ford, J., Elhai, J., Connor, D., & Frueh, B. (2010). Poly-victimization and risk of posttraumatic, depressive, and substance use disorders and involvement in delinquency in a national sample of adolescents. *Journal of Adolescent Health*, *46*, 545–552.

Gervai, J., Novak, A., Lakatos, K., Toth, I., Danis, I., Ronai, Z., et al. (2007). Infant genotype may moderate sensitivity to maternal affective communications: Attachment disorganization, quality of care, and the DRD4 polymorphism. *Social Neuroscience*, *2*(3–4), 307–319.

Hanson, R., Self-Brown, S., Fricker-Elhai, A., Kilpatrick, D., Saunders, B., & Resnick, H. (2006). The relations between family environment and violence exposure among youth: Findings from the national survey of adolescents. *Child Maltreatment*, *11*(1), 3–15.

Harro, J., Merenakk, L., Nordquist, N., Konstabel, K., Comasco, E., & Oreland, L. (2009). Personality and the serotonin transporter gene: Associations in a longitudinal population-based study. *Biological Psychiatry*, *81*, 9–13.

Hesse, E., Main, M., Abrams, K. Y., & Rifkin, A. (2003). Unresolved states regarding loss or abuse can have "second-generation" effects: Disorganization, role inversion, and frightening ideation in the offspring of traumatized, non-maltreating parents. In M. Solomon & D. J. Siegel (Eds.), *Healing trauma* (pp. 57–106). New York: W. W. Norton.

Jackson, Y., Frick, P., & Dravage-Bush, J. (2000). Perceptions of control in children with externalizing and mixed behavior disorders. *Child Psychiatry and Human Development*, *31*(1), 43–58.

Kerns, K., Abraham, M., Schlegelmilch, A., & Morgan, T. (2007). Mother-child attachment in later middle childhood: Assessment approaches and associations with mood and emotion regulation. *Attachment & Human Development*, *9*(1), 33–53.

Kim-Cohen, J., Caspi, A., Taylor, A., Williams, B., Newcombe, R., Craig, I., et al. (2006). MAOA, maltreatment, and gene-environment interaction predicting children's mental health: New evidence and a meta-analysis. *Molecular Psychiatry*, *11*, 903–913.

Kimerling, R., Prins, A., Westrup, D., & Lee, T. (2004). Gender issues in the assessment of PTSD. In J. P. Wilson & T. M. Keane (Eds.), *Assessing psychological trauma and PTSD* (2nd ed., pp. 565–599). New York: Guilford Press.

Koenen, K., Moffit, T., Caspi, A., Gregory, A., Harrington, H., & Poulton, R. (2008). The developmental mental-disorder histories of adults with posttraumatic stress disorder: A prospective longitudinal birth cohort study. *Journal of Abnormal Psychology*, *117*(2), 460–466.

Krueger, R. F., Caspi, A., Moffitt, T. E., White, J., & Stouthamer-Loeber, M. (1996). Delay of gratification, psychopathology, and personality: Is low self-control specific to externalizing problems? *Journal of Personality*, *64*, 107–129.

Laird, R., Jordan, K., Dodge, K., Pettit, G., & Bates, J. (2001). Peer rejection in childhood, involvement with antisocial peers in early adolescence, and the development of externalizing behavior problems. *Development and Psychopathology*, *13*, 337–354.

Langenkamp, A., & Frisco, M. (2008). Family transitions and adolescent severe emotional distress: The salience of family context. *Social Problems*, *55*(2), 238–253.

Lau, J., & Eley, T. (2006). Changes in genetic and environmental influences on depressive symptoms across adolescence and young adulthood. *The British Journal of Psychiatry*, *189*(5), 422–427.

Lau, J., & Pine, D. (2008). Elucidating risk mechanisms of gene-environment interactions on pediatric anxiety: Integrating findings from neuroscience. *European Archives of Psychiatry and Clinical Neuroscience*, *258*, 97–106.

Lyons-Ruth, K., Zeanah, C. H., & Benoit, D. (2003). Disorder and risk for disorder during infancy and toddlerhood. In E. J. Mash & R. A. Barkley (Eds.), *Child psychopathology* (2nd ed., pp. 589–631). New York: Guilford Press.

Mello, C., & Nader, K. (in press). Teaching coping and social skills to elementary school children. In K. Nader (Ed.), *School rampage/shootings and other youth disturbances: Early preventive interventions*. New York: Routledge.

Min, M., Farkas, K., Minnes, S., & Singer, L. (2007). Impact of childhood abuse and neglect on substance abuse and psychological distress in adulthood. *Journal of Traumatic Stress*, *20*(5), 833–844.

Moss, E., Pascuzzo, K., & Simard, V. (in press). Treating insecure and disorganized attachments in school-aged children. In K. Nader (Ed.), *School rampage/shootings and other youth disturbances: Early preventive interventions*. New York: Routledge.

Nader, K. (2008). *Understanding and assessing trauma in children and adolescents: Measures, methods, and youth in context*. New York: Routledge.

Nader, K. (2010). Children and adolescent's exposure to the mass violence of war and terrorism: Role of the media. In N. B. Webb (Ed.), *Helping bereaved children* (3rd ed., pp. 215–239). New York: Guilford.

Nader, K. (Ed.). (in press). *School rampage/shootings and other youth disturbances: Early preventive interventions*. New York: Routledge.

Nader, K., Pynoos, R., Fairbanks, L., & Frederick, C. (1990). Children's PTSD reactions one year after a sniper attack at their school. *American Journal of Psychiatry*, *147*, 1526–1530.

Nader, K., & Salloum, A. (2011). Complicated grief reactions in children and adolescents. *Journal of Child & Adolescent Trauma*, *4*(3), 233–257.

Negrao, C., II, Bonanno, G., Noll, J., Putnam, F., & Trickett, P. (2005). Shame, humiliation, and childhood sexual abuse: Distinct contributions and emotional coherence. *Child Maltreatment*, *10*, 350–363.

Nijenhuis, E., van der Hart, O., & Steele, K. (2002). The emerging psychobiology of trauma-related dissociation and dissociative disorders. In H. D'haenen, J. den Boer, & P. Willner (Eds.), *Biological psychiatry* (pp. 1079–1098). New York: John Wiley & Sons.

Pacella, M., Irish, L., Ostrowski, S., Sledjeski, E., Ciesla, J., Fallon, W., et al. (2011). Avoidant coping as a mediator between peritraumatic dissociation and posttraumatic stress disorder symptoms. *Journal of Traumatic Stress*, *24*(3), 317–325.

Pauli-Pott, U., Friedl, S., Hinney, A., & Hebebrand, J. (2009). Serotonin transporter gene polymorphism (5-HTTLPR), environmental conditions, and developing negative emotionality and fear in early childhood. *Journal of Neural Transmission*, *116*(4), 503–512.

Pfefferbaum, B., Stuber, J., Galea, S., & Fairbrother, G. (2006). Panic reactions to terrorist attacks and probable posttraumatic stress disorder in adolescents. *Journal of Traumatic Stress*, *19*(2), 217–228.

Posner, M., & Rothbart, M. (2007). *Educating the human brain*. Washington, DC: American Psychological Association.

Prom-Wormley, E., Eaves, L., Foley, D., Gardner, C., Archer, K., Wormley, B., et al. (2008). Monoamine oxidase A and childhood adversity as risk factors for conduct disorder in females. *Psychological Medicine*, *39*(4), 579–590.

Pynoos, R., Frederick, C., Nader, K., Arroyo, W., Eth, S., Nunez, W., et al. (1987). Life threat and posttraumatic stress in school age children. *Archives of General Psychiatry*, *44*, 1057–1063.

Richmond, J., Elliott, A., Pierce, T., Aspelmeier, J., & Alexander, A. (2009). Polyvictimization, childhood victimization, and psychological distress in college women. *Child Maltreatment*, *14*(2), 127–147.

Rutter, M. (1997). Clinical implications of attachment concepts: Retrospective and prospective. In L. Atkinson & K. Zucker (Eds.), *Attachment and psychopathology* (pp. 17–46). New York: Guilford Press.

Rutter, M., Moffitt, T., & Caspi, A. (2006). Gene-environment interplay and psychopathology: Multiple varieties but real effects. *Journal of Child Psychology and Psychiatry*, *47*(3/4), 226–261.

Scaramella, L., Sohr-Preston, S., Callahan, K., & Mirabile, S. (2008). A test of the family stress model on toddler-aged children's adjustment among Hurricane Katrina impacted and non-impacted low-income families. *Journal of Clinical Child & Adolescent Psychology*, *37*(3), 530–541.

Scheeringa, M. S. (2011). PTSD in children younger than the age of 13: Toward developmentally sensitive assessment and management. *Journal of Child & Adolescent Trauma*, *4*(3), 181–197.

Schore, A. N. (2003). Early relational trauma, disorganized attachment, and the development of a predisposition to violence. In M. Soloman & D. J. Siegel (Eds.), *Healing trauma* (pp. 107–167). New York: W. W. Norton.

Shanahan, L., Copeland, W., Costello, E., & Angold, A. (2008). Specificity of putative psychosocial risk factors for psychiatric disorders in children and adolescents. *Journal of Child Psychology and Psychiatry*, *49*(1), 34–42.

Shevlin, M., Dorahy, M., & Adamson, G. (2007). Trauma and psychosis: An analysis of the National Comorbidity Survey. *American Journal of Psychiatry*, *164*, 1–3.

Strelau, J., & Zawadzki, B. (2005). Trauma and temperament as predictors of intensity of posttraumatic stress disorder symptoms after disaster. *European Psychologist*, *10*(2), 124–135.

Susman, E., Dockray, S., Schiefelbein, V., Herwehe, S., Heaton, J., & Dorn, L. (2007). Morningness/eveningness, morning-to-afternoon cortisol ratio, and antisocial behavior problems during puberty. *Developmental Psychology*, *43*(4), 811–822.

Udwin, O., Boyle, S., Yule, W., Bolton, D., & O'Ryan, D. (2000). Risk factors for long-term psychological effects of a disaster experienced in adolescence: Predictors of post traumatic stress disorder. *Journal of Child Psychology and Psychiatry*, *41*(8), 969–979.

van der Kolk, B. (2005). Developmental Trauma Disorder: Toward a rational diagnosis for children with complex trauma histories. *Psychiatric Annals*, *35*(5), 401–408.

Wagner, A., Rizvi, S., & Harned, M. (2007). Applications of dialectical behavior therapy to the treatment of complex trauma-related problems: When one case formulation does not fit all. *Journal of Traumatic Stress*, *20*(4), 391–400.

Wagner, A., Roemer, L., Orsillo, S., & Litz, B. (2003). Emotional experiencing in women with posttraumatic stress disorder: Congruence between facial expressivity and self-report. *Journal of Traumatic Stress*, *16*(1), 67–75.

Walter, J., & LaFreniere, P. (2007). Preschoolers' avoidance in a mishap paradigm: Implications for emotional adjustment, guilt, and shame. *North American Journal of Psychology*, *9*(1), 111–130.

Waschbusch, D., Pelham, W., Jennings, J., Greiner, A., Tarter, R., & Moss, H. (2002). Reactive aggression in boys with disruptive behavior disorders: Behavior, physiology, and affect. *Journal of Abnormal Child Psychology*, *30*(6), 641–656.

Weems, C., & Carrion, V. (2007). The association between PTSD symptoms and salivary cortisol in youth: The role of time since the trauma. *Journal of Traumatic Stress*, *20*, 903–907.

Weems, C., & Carrion, V. (2009). Brief report: Diurnal salivary cortisol in youth — Clarifying the nature of posttraumatic stress dysregulation. *Journal of PediatricPsychology*, *34*, 389–395.

Younge, S., Salazar, L., Sales, J., DiClemente, R., Wingood, G., & Rose, E. (2010). Emotional victimization and sexual risk-taking behaviors among adolescent African American women. *Journal of Child & Adolescent Trauma*, *3*(2), 79–94.

Zurbriggen, E., Gobin, R., & Freyd, J. (2010). Childhood emotional abuse predicts late adolescent sexual aggression perpetration and victimization. *Journal of Aggression, Maltreatment & Trauma*, *19*, 204–223.

Child Exposure and Developmental Variables

Attachment and Trauma in Early Childhood: A Review

ANGELA S. BREIDENSTINE, LETIA O. BAILEY,
CHARLES H. ZEANAH, AND JULIE A. LARRIEU

Tulane University School of Medicine

Attachment relationships are critical to a young child's optimal development. Both the presence and quality of attachment matter. Experiences of trauma can affect caregiver/child attachment relationships in a variety of ways. This article explores possible associations among trauma and the presence and quality of attachment relationships between young children and their caregivers. The nature of attachment, phases in the development of attachment relationships, and classifications of the quality of attachment are presented. Possible linkages among past traumatic experiences, parental states of mind, parental interactive behaviors, and infant attachment relationships are postulated. The most severe attachment disturbance, reactive attachment disorder, is discussed, including evidence that suggests modification of the current formulation of reactive attachment disorder subtypes; namely, that the indiscriminate subtype of reactive attachment disorder may not qualify as an attachment disorder. More research is needed to better understand reactive attachment disorder and the reciprocal relationships between attachment and trauma experienced by both parents and children.

Attachment describes an emotional bond that serves to promote and preserve closeness between a young child and a small number of adult caregivers who are responsible for comforting, supporting, nurturing, and protecting the child. Under typical rearing conditions, human infants form attachments to caregivers whom they have learned through experience are available and dependable. Attachment theory and research findings regarding attachment styles, disturbances, and disorders have created a foundation for understanding this important relational context for child well-being and development. Variations in the quality of attachments, particularly whether or not they form, have important implications for development in the young child. Children who have adverse attachment experiences, such as disorganized attachment relationships, or absent attachments as in reactive attachment disorder, are seen as being at the greatest risk for concurrent and future psychopathology. It is clear that traumatic experiences can compromise attachment relationships, can occur within attachment relationships or can influence the attachment patterns of infants/children when the parent has been previously traumatized. Despite thoughtful syntheses about attachment, trauma, and brain development (e.g., Schore, 2001), there is still much to be learned about how traumatic experiences affect attachment relationships, both directly or indirectly, and how attachment relationships may moderate the effects of trauma on children.

In this review, we briefly summarize attachment theory and attachment classifications in children and adults. We then discuss relationships between trauma and attachment, including what we currently understand about how past parental trauma and attachment styles may confer risk to present parent-child attachment relationships. Many questions about the complex interrelationships between attachment and trauma remain unresearched and unanswered at this time. Finally, we provide an overview of reactive attachment disorder (RAD). This diagnosis is frequently misunderstood and is sometimes applied to children with a variety of traumatic experiences and/or externalizing behavior problems. Thus, for the interested reader, we include both a review of the current conceptualization of RAD as well as the basic principles of assessment for this disorder.

Summary of Attachment Theory and Related Findings

Development of Attachment

John Bowlby (1969/1982), a British child psychiatrist and psychoanalyst, developed attachment theory to explain young children's behaviors in ethological terms. He characterized the *attachment system* as a behavioral or motivational system with an external goal of maintaining an infant's physical proximity to the caregiver and an internal goal of achieving "felt security" (Bischof, 1975; Sroufe & Waters, 1977, p. 1186). Central to this conceptualization of attachment are observable, biologically driven behaviors, which Bowlby referred to as *attachment behaviors*. These are any behaviors of the infant or young child that serve to promote physical proximity to the caregiver, such as crying, smiling, crawling toward, or clinging to the caregiver. Infants are not born with any obvious attachment preference. Instead, attachment develops gradually over the first 3 years of life.

Table 1 summarizes various distinct phases in the development of infant attachment, which coincide with predictable *biobehavioral shifts* of early childhood (Boris, Aoki, & Zeanah, 1999). These shifts describe points in time after which qualitative changes occur rapidly and new capacities emerge in the infant that had not been present previously. As Table 1 illustrates, focused or preferred attachment emerges as a new phenomenon sometime between 7 and 9 months of age, at least under typical childrearing conditions. Separation protest from attachment figures and initial wariness with strangers are behavioral indicators that focused attachments have formed.

By 1 year of age, it is possible to observe a balance in the toddler's motivation to explore the environment and motivation to seek proximity to the adult caregiver. That is, the toddler, equipped with newfound capabilities for independent locomotion, is motivated to venture away from the caregiver and explore. Counterbalancing this desire is the motivation to seek proximity in times of fear, stress, or distress. Thus, when a toddler is in the presence of an attachment figure and feeling secure, the attachment system is relatively deactivated, and the child is motivated to explore the environment. If the toddler becomes frightened, threatened, or hurt, the attachment system is activated, and the

Table 1
Phases in the development of attachment

Phase	Characteristics
Limited Discrimination (Birth–8 weeks)	The infant's ability to discriminate among individuals is limited to olfactory and auditory stimuli.
Discrimination with Limited Preference (2–7 months)	The infant becomes increasingly social and more interactive (e.g., gazing and cooing), and, although his/her signals are directed at familiar caregivers, strong preferences are not yet expressed.
Preferred Attachment (7–12 months)	The infant becomes more discriminating, developing a clear preference for a small number of caregivers, who are hierarchically ranked. Stranger wariness and separation protest become apparent at this time.
Secure Base and Safe Haven (12–18 months)	The infant or toddler begins to use the attachment figure as a secure base from which to explore and as a safe haven to return to when frightened or distressed. The attachment-exploration balance as described by Ainsworth et al. (1971) becomes apparent.
Formation of a Goal-Corrected Partnership (18 months and beyond)	Young children and their parents learn to jointly adjust goals; the child begins to purposefully consider, to anticipate, and/or to infer the caregiver's probable actions, and accordingly to balance autonomous functioning with reliance on the caregiver.

motivation to explore diminishes or disappears. Instead, the toddler either seeks proximity to the caregiver or engages in signaling behaviors to alert the caregiver of his/her distress. This attachment/exploration balance (Ainsworth, Bell, & Stayton, 1971) can be observed readily whenever young toddlers and their attachment figures are interacting together.

Classifications of Attachment in Infants and Young Children

Ainsworth, Blehar, Waters, and Wall (1978) developed a laboratory paradigm known as the Strange Situation Procedure (SSP) to look at variations in the balance between exploratory and attachment behaviors in the context of specific caregiving relationships. This 20-minute assessment procedure involves a series of separations and reunions with the young child, an attachment figure, and an adult female stranger. The SSP reveals qualitatively different patterns of infant-to-caregiver attachment, including *secure* attachment and several forms of insecure attachment, known as *avoidant*, *resistant*, and *disorganized*. These patterns tend to be relationship specific; that is, the same infant may have a different SSP classification with different caregivers. These patterns have been described and replicated in studies conducted throughout the world (van IJzendoorn & Sagi-Schwartz, 2008).

Infants who demonstrate a balance between proximity-seeking and exploration are described as *securely attached*. Throughout the procedure, they indicate comfort with their attachment figures in comparison to relative reticence with the stranger. During separation, these infants typically decrease exploration and often show distress. On reunion with their attachment figures, securely attached infants directly express their distress and seek proximity to and comfort from the adult caregiver (Ainsworth et al., 1978). In preschool children, who are less likely than younger children to express overt distress during separations, the reconnection during reunion may be more verbal than behavioral (Cassidy, Marvin, & the MacArthur Working Group, 1992).

Infants who show little evidence of distress upon separation from their caregivers, instead turning their attention to toys or other objects, are classified as having *avoidant attachments*. During reunion, they ignore or actively avoid physical closeness with their caregivers (Ainsworth et al., 1978). In preschool children, the avoidance includes avoiding conversation, gaze that is minimal or fleeting, and neutral affect throughout the interaction. There is usually clear evidence of the child's actively inhibiting affect (Cassidy, Marvin, & the MacArthur Working Group, 1992).

Infants whose attachments are classified as *resistant* or *ambivalent* typically protest strongly at being separated from their caregivers. On reunion, however, they are unable to use the caregiver to obtain comfort for their distress. They seem alternately to seek comfort and to resist being comforted (Ainsworth et al., 1978). In the preschool years, this classification is called *dependent* to emphasize the passive, helpless, or immature behaviors these children display; although this style also includes angry and petulant behaviors directed toward the caregiver (Cassidy, Marvin, & the MacArthur Working Group, 1992).

Infants who demonstrate incomplete, confused, or contradictory behavioral strategies for using the caregiver as a source of comfort have attachments classified as *disorganized*. They may display disordered sequences of behavior (e.g., approach for comfort followed by avoidance of the caregiver), simultaneous contradictory behaviors (e.g., approach for comfort with marked gaze aversion), or repetitive, stereotyped behaviors, freezing or stilling in the presence of the caregiver, fear of the caregiver, and/or directing attachment behaviors to a stranger in the presence of the caregiver (Main & Solomon, 1990). In preschool children, behaviors may be similar to those evident in infants, or the child may show solicitous or punitive efforts to control the behavior of the caregiver (Cassidy et al., 1992).

Those infants who do not meet criteria for any other classifications are designated *cannot classify* (Hesse, 2008). They may demonstrate avoidant behavior in one reunion and resistant behavior in the other, but without disorganized behaviors as described above. This designation also may be used to describe infants who are assessed in the Strange Situation Procedure with caregivers to whom they have no attachments (see Zeanah, Smyke, Koga, Carlson, & BEIP Core Group, 2005). *Cannot classify* is used to describe either very disturbed or nonexistent attachment relationships; although, to date, this has not been well studied as a category.

There are also some preschool children who display behaviors not seen in other classifications, and they are classified *insecure other*. This classification includes children who display a combination of avoidant and dependent behaviors in sequential transitions or simultaneous display of both, children who display depressed or dissociative-like disengagement, children who appear engaged but fearful of the caregiver (includes compulsive-compliance with the caregiver's instructions or demands), and affectively dysregulated behaviors that may involve silly, hyperactive, or other poorly organized behaviors (Marvin & Brittner, 1995).

These classifications or patterns of attachment should not be confused with diagnoses or psychopathology. Rather, they are risk and protective factors that predict subsequent or concurrent psychopathology (DeKlyen & Greenberg, 2008). Secure attachment is a protective factor and insecure attachment is a risk factor for psychopathology; although these differences are most evident within the context of high-risk conditions. More recently, even stronger links have been demonstrated between disorganized attachment and psychopathology, particularly disturbances in interpersonal relatedness. Disorganized attachment has been demonstrated to predict both externalizing and internalizing problems concurrently and in later childhood and adolescence (Green & Goldwyn, 2002; Lyons-Ruth & Jacobvitz, 2008; Zeanah, Keyes, & Settles, 2003).

Classifications of Attachment in Adults

Drawing on Bowlby's (1969/1982) assertion that attachment is a lifespan construct, Main, Kaplan, and Cassidy (1985) developed a method of assessing patterns of attachment in adults: the Adult Attachment Interview (AAI). The AAI inquires about early relationship experiences and the adult's current perspective on early childhood relationships. Classifications of attachment are assigned on the basis of qualitative differences in narrative discourse and expressed attitudes about attachment. Theoretically, AAI classifications are presumed to reflect differences in internal working models of attachment, that is, those processes involved in attending to and perceiving social and emotional information and regulating responses to that information. The qualitative narrative characteristics of interview responses are believed to reflect important differences in the organization of the individual's internal experience, including defensive processes.

Adults who describe their own childhood attachment relationships in a clear and straightforward manner, who convey that relationship experiences matter and have effects, and who demonstrate emotionally well-integrated responses are deemed to have *autonomous classifications*. Adults with this classification are expected to have children who are securely attached to them because they have an attachment style that directly conveys positive and negative affects, acknowledges needs directly and is emotionally well regulated. According to a meta-analysis of 854 parent/infant dyads (van IJzendoorn, 1995), the effect size for concordance between adult autonomous and infant secure attachments was large ($d = 1.00$).

In contrast, adults who dismiss the importance of attachment relationship experiences or who assert that they had no effect or do not matter are classified as *dismissing* in the AAI (Hesse, 2008). Their style consistently minimizes any negative aspects of relationship experiences, much as infants with avoidant attachments turn their attention away from separation distress and their own need for comfort during the Strange Situation Procedure. The meta-analytic effect size of dismissing attachments in adults and avoidant attachment in infants was medium to large ($d = 0.70$; van IJzendoorn, 1995).

Adults who describe relationships incoherently, conveying intense involvement with poor emotional regulation and difficulty maintaining focus on the topic have attachments classified as *preoccupied* (Hesse, 2008). These interviews may display oscillations between contradictory appraisals as well as current internal entanglements with parent figures, often conveying a sense that the adult is angrily preoccupied or passively overwhelmed. The effect size of preoccupied adult classifications and child resistant attachment classifications was significant but small ($d = 0.30$) in the van IJzendoorn (1995) meta-analysis.

Adults who have significant lapses in coherence and monitoring when describing childhood experiences of loss or trauma, often in the form of confusion, disorientation, or affectively unregulated fear or guilt, are classified as having *unresolved* attachments

(Hesse, 2008). These interviews may have underlying features of autonomous, dismissing, or preoccupied attachments, but the significant incoherence regarding loss or trauma leads to the unresolved classification. In the van IJzendoorn (1995) meta-analysis, there was a medium effect size ($d = 0.65$) of unresolved attachment in parents predicting disorganized attachment in infants.

These AAI classifications, like infant SSP classifications, are believed to reflect differences in how internal representations are organized, and they relate to caregiving interactional behavior as well as infant and preschool attachment classifications (Hesse, 2008). Table 2 describes these associations as understood currently. As with attachment classifications, AAI classifications are not designations of psychopathology but rather represent risk and protective factors for psychopathology.

Trauma and Attachment

The reciprocal relationships between trauma and parent-child attachment relationships are incompletely understood. Any attachment relationship will likely be affected by a child and/or parent's traumatic experience. For example, experiencing violence and trauma can

Table 2

Infant and adult attachment patterns, caregiving behaviors, and associated risks

Infant attachment patterns	Adult attachment patterns	Associated adult caregiving behavior	Links to child psychopathology and social maladaptation
Secure	Autonomous	Sensitive/responsive	Protective factor in high-risk samples
Avoidant	Dismissing	Emotionally distant; encouraging independence and discouraging neediness	Modest risk factor in high-risk samples
Resistant/Dependent	Preoccupied	Inconsistent responsiveness	Modest risk factor in high-risk samples
Disorganized	Unresolved	Frightening or frightened behavior or disrupted affective communication (affective communication errors, role confusion, negative-intrusive behavior, disorientation, withdrawal)	Risk factor for externalizing disorders, dissociative disorders, internalizing disorders, social incompetence
Cannot Classify	Unknown	Unknown but substantially increased in institutions	Overlaps with emotionally withdrawn/inhibited RAD
Insecure Other	Unknown	Unknown but substantially increased in institutions	Risk factor for internalizing and externalizing disorders

stress and compromise a previously secure and organized attachment relationship or preclude the development of a secure attachment relationship (Lieberman, 2004; Schechter & Willheim, 2009). Lieberman (2004) has noted that young children's ability to recover from the damaging effect of traumatic events is deeply influenced by the quality of the child's attachments and by the parent's ability to respond sensitively to the child's traumatic responses. Although a causal mechanism is not yet clear, it has also been observed that following trauma, young children with more trauma-related symptoms have parents with more trauma-related symptoms (Scheeringa & Zeanah, 2001).

As noted previously, disorganized attachment is the pattern that carries the greatest risk for concurrent and future psychopathology. A disorganized attachment relationship may leave a child more vulnerable to the effects of new traumatic experiences and may also come about, in part, because of the influence of various past and current traumas on the parent and child. There is very little longitudinal research specifically looking at whether attachment styles affect later adjustment following traumatic experiences. A recent study examined whether disorganized attachment relationships at 12 months of age predicted level and type of posttraumatic stress disorder (PTSD) symptoms or other anxiety disorders when children were 8½ years old (MacDonald et al., 2008). In this low-income sample, early disorganized attachment status was associated with a higher rate of PTSD total symptoms, a higher rate of avoidance cluster PTSD symptoms, and a higher rate of re-experiencing cluster PTSD symptoms at 8½ but was not associated with symptoms of other anxiety disorders. The results lent support to the hypothesis that early disorganized attachment status may relate to a child's greater difficulty coping with traumatic and stressful experiences in later childhood.

Parental Characteristics, Trauma, and Attachment

There is now considerable evidence that various parental characteristics are associated with disorganized attachment in both low- and middle-income families. There is evidence that mothers with substance-use disorders, severe mood disorders, and borderline personality disorders all have children at increased risk for disorganized attachment (see Lyons-Ruth & Jacobvitz, 2008, for review). These distal risk factors for disorganized attachment often co-occur with trauma, but the relationship between trauma and attachment frequently has not been studied. Somewhat more proximal risks relevant to the question of trauma and caregiving that have been studied include parental states of mind with respect to attachment as well as parental interactional behaviors, as are outlined below.

Parental States of Mind and Infant Disorganized Attachment

Traumatic events experienced by a caregiver, even years before a child is born, may affect the child/caregiver attachment relationship. Research findings regarding narratives on the AAI indicate that parents who are classified as unresolved on the AAI have increased risk for disorganized attachment relationships with their infants. This means that when parents' childhood traumatic experiences (abuse, loss, etc.) are not successfully resolved, as evidenced by nonintegrated emotional reactions, disorientation, or dissociative-like responses, they have children whose attachments to them are more likely to be disorganized. In the van IJzendoorn (1995) meta-analysis, 53% of infants with disorganized attachment had mothers whose attachment classifications were unresolved, and 53% of mothers who were unresolved had infants whose attachments to them were disorganized.

Other aspects of parental states of mind besides being unresolved with respect to loss or trauma are also associated with disorganized attachment in infants. For example, Lyons-Ruth, Yellin, Melnick, and Atwood (2005) coded *hostile helpless* states of mind based on AAI narratives that combined positive identification and devaluing of the same person, a clinical phenomenon known as *splitting*. This splitting defense is characteristic of individuals diagnosed with borderline personality disorder, which is often associated with childhood trauma, particularly sexual abuse (Widiger & Mullins-Sweatt, 2008). The hostile subtype of this state of mind includes devaluing a caregiver as hostile or threatening while also identifying positively with the individual without awareness of the discrepancy. In the helpless subtype of this state of mind, the individual devalues but also positively identifies with an abdicating (role-reversing) parental figure.

Parental Interactive Behaviors and Disorganized Attachments

It is clear that parental behaviors affect the quality of attachment relationships. Maltreated infants, for example, had high rates of disorganized attachment in studies involving the maltreating parent (Carlson, Cicchetti, Barnett, & Braunwald, 1989; Cicchetti, Rogosch, & Toth, 2006). The original putative mechanism proposed to explain the association between a caregiver's unresolved trauma and infant disorganized attachment was offered by Main and Hesse (1990). They argued that the parent who has not resolved a trauma demonstrates lapses in monitoring of discourse, perhaps related to dissociative, quasi-dissociative, or other defensive processes. For the traumatized parent, the infant serves as a traumatic trigger, leading the parent to reenact frightening behavior that he or she had experienced in other relationships toward the child (see also Schechter et al., 2005, 2008). Because the parent's behavior derives from experiences that could not be known by the infant, it is experienced by the infant as inexplicable and unpredictable. Further, when the infant's attachment needs are activated, particularly when the parent is frightening, the infant's source of comfort is also simultaneously a source of fear (Main & Hesse, 1990). This circumstance leads to conflicted impulses within the infant about approaching or withdrawing, which corresponds with the observed infant behaviors that define disorganized attachment.

To explain the link between unresolved attachment in the AAI and infant disorganized attachment, one study demonstrated that parental frightening/frightened/dissociative behavior partially mediated the effect of unresolved adult attachment on infant disorganized attachment (Madigan et al., 2006). In addition, Lyons-Ruth, Bronfman, and Parsons (1999) expanded the focus from frightened/frightening/dissociative behavior to disrupted affective communication between parents and infants. These patterns included negative intrusive behavior, role confusion, affective communication errors (e.g., contradictory signals), and disorientation (Lyons-Ruth et al., 1999). Several studies have demonstrated an association between disrupted affective communication and infant disorganized attachment (see Lyons Ruth & Jacobvitz, 2008, for review).

The states of mind and interactive behaviors in parents that are associated with infant disorganized attachment may plausibly be linked to parental experiences of trauma. These data underscore the importance of traumatic experiences of parents on their young children.

Attachment Disorders

Although children are biologically predisposed to develop preferred attachment relationships with caregivers, there are times when developmentally expected attachment relationships do not form. Next, we review current conceptualizations of attachment disorders as recognized by existing diagnostic systems.

Reactive Attachment Disorder

It is clear that attachment relationships fail to develop in only the most maladaptive and extreme caregiving environments (Zeanah & Smyke, 2009). Beginning in the 1940s, children living in institutions were described as showing abnormal attachment behaviors or even a lack of attachment behaviors (O'Connor & Zeanah, 2003; Zeanah & Smyke, 2009). Tizard and Rees (1975) reported that a majority of children in United Kingdom residential nurseries exhibited atypical attachment behaviors at the age of 4 years, including children who were withdrawn and unresponsive, as well as children who were indiscriminately social and attention seeking. Descriptions such as these created the foundation for current conceptualizations of reactive attachment disorder (RAD).

The revised fourth edition of the *Diagnostic and Statistical Manual of Mental Disorders* (*DSM-IV-TR*; American Psychiatric Association, 2000) and the tenth revision of the *International Statistical Classification of Diseases and Related Health Problems* (*ICD-10*; World Health Organization, 1992) provide similar criteria for the diagnosis of RAD, with both describing an *emotionally withdrawn/inhibited* type and a *socially indiscriminate/disinhibited* type. Both nosologies indicate that extremely adverse caregiving experiences or pathogenic care is presumed to be an etiological factor. Children with the emotionally withdrawn/inhibited type of RAD exhibit few or no attachment behaviors even in situations that should elicit such behaviors. The disorder is characterized by the absence of organized attachment behaviors, low levels of social engagement and reciprocity, difficulties with emotional regulation, little or no comfort seeking even when distressed, and limited response to soothing by others (Zeanah & Smyke, 2009). The indiscriminately social/disinhibited type of RAD is characterized by a failure to display developmentally appropriate reticence with unfamiliar adults and a tendency to violate social boundaries. Although stranger wariness typically emerges in the second half of the first year of life, children with this type of RAD exhibit little to no wariness. This lack of reticence can be seen in children's willingness to approach and engage socially with strange adults, their tendency to wander off and to fail to check back with caregivers when in unfamiliar settings, and their willingness to go off with strangers.

There are few longitudinal studies of the signs and symptoms of RAD. Findings have indicated that there is some stability of signs in the emotionally withdrawn type of RAD during the first four to five years of life when caregiving environments remain the same. However, when children are placed in more favorable caregiving environments, such as foster care or adoptive families, signs of the disorder lessen substantially (Smyke et al., 2010; see Zeanah & Smyke, 2009). In contrast, signs of the indiscriminate type have been found to persist despite placement in more positive and appropriate caregiving environments (Chisholm, 1998; Rutter et al., 2007; Smyke et al., 2010). There has been limited research on signs or symptoms of attachment disorders in middle childhood and adolescence (Zeanah & Gleason, 2010). Tables 3 and 4 outline what we understand currently about the signs of both types of RAD in different age groups. The emotionally withdrawn/inhibited type of RAD has not been described in children older than 8 years, and it is not yet known whether the symptoms seen in earlier years persist in the same form if caregiving environments do not improve or if caregiving environments only improve when children are older. We know more about the persistence and evolution of indiscriminately social/disinhibited signs across ages, as outlined in Table 4.

Table 3

Reactive Attachment Disorder (emotionally withdrawn/inhibited) from infancy to adolescence

	9–24 months	2–4.5 years	4.5–8 years	8–11 years	11–16 years
Emotionally Withdrawn/ Inhibited RAD	1. No preferred attachment figure 2. Fails to seek or respond to comfort when distressed 3. Reduced or absent positive affect 4. Reduced social responsiveness 5. Unprovoked and poorly regulated irritability, fear, or sadness 6. Limited exploration	1. No preferred attachment figure 2. Fails to seek or respond to comfort when distressed 3. Reduced or absent positive affect 4. Reduced social responsiveness 5. Unprovoked and poorly regulated irritability, fear, or sadness 6. Limited exploration	1. No preferred attachment figure 2. Fails to seek or respond to comfort when distressed 3. Reduced or absent positive affect 4. Reduced social responsiveness 5. Unprovoked and poorly regulated irritability, fear, or sadness 6. Limited exploration	Not described	Not described

Table 4

Reactive Attachment Disorder (socially indiscriminate/disinhibited) from infancy to adolescence

	9–24 months	2–4.5 years	4.5–8 years	8–11 years	11–16 years
Socially Indiscriminate/ Disinhibited RAD	1. Actively approaches and interacts with strangers without reticence	1. Actively approaches and interacts with strangers	1. Actively approaches and interacts with strangers	1. Actively approaches and interacts with strangers	1. No best friend
	2. Fails to check back with caregiver in unfamiliar settings	2. Fails to check back with adult in unfamiliar settings	2. Fails to check back with adult in unfamiliar settings	2. Fails to check back with adult in unfamiliar settings	2. Superficial peer relationships in which mere acquaintances are described as close friends
	3. Willing to "go off" with strangers	3. Willing to "go off" with strangers	3. No hesitation in going off with strangers	3. No hesitation in going off with strangers	3. Possibly indiscriminate sexual relations
		4. Clingy and attention seeking with everyone	4. Approaches unfamiliar adults in an aggressive and intrusive way	4. Approaches unfamiliar adults in an aggressive and intrusive way	
			5. Takes unusual (nonaggressive) liberties with unfamiliar adults, such as getting too close physically or asking overly personal questions	5. Takes unusual (nonaggressive) liberties with unfamiliar adults, such as getting too close physically or asking overly personal questions	

RAD is very rare, particularly in the absence of extreme rearing conditions. There were no reported cases in a quasi-community sample of 2- to 5-year-old children recruited from pediatric clinics in North Carolina (Egger et al., 2006). In one study, few cases were identified in high-risk groups, such as impoverished or homeless young children (Boris et al., 2004). Although signs of both types of RAD have been identified in maltreated children in foster care (Oosterman & Schuengel, 2008; Zeanah et al., 2004), we have limited data on actual prevalence rates at this time. Even among young children being raised in institutions, only a minority meet categorical criteria for RAD (Gleason et al., 2011).

Current research and clinical findings support the conceptualization of the emotionally withdrawn/inhibited type of RAD as analogous to the absence or near absence of preferred attachments (Zeanah & Smyke, 2008). This type of RAD is related to the quality of the caregiving environment, and children diagnosed with this type tend to recover with appropriate caregiving (Rutter, Kreppner, & Sonuga-Barke, 2009; Zeanah & Smyke, 2009). The indiscriminate type of RAD has been identified in children with and without preferred attachment relationships, but the risk for more persistent indiscriminate behavior appears to increase the longer a child is raised in an institutional setting (Rutter et al., 2007; Zeanah & Smyke, 2009). Signs of the indiscriminate type tend to persist and are not related to the quality of the current caregiving environment. Overall, evidence suggests that these two types may not in fact reflect the same construct, and that the indiscriminate type of RAD is something other than an attachment disorder (Zeanah & Gleason, 2010; Zeanah & Smyke, 2009).

Trauma is implicit in the construct of pathogenic care, but since RAD may arise primarily in response to social neglect (Zeanah & Smyke, 2009), it is unclear how to disentangle the effects of the presence of traumatic experiences rather than the absence of normative caregiving experiences in the etiology of these disorders. An important question is whether trauma provides the correct model for the caregiving environment of children with RAD. That is, they may be suffering from an absence of normative caregiving behavior (neglect) rather than the presence of harmful behaviors. In cases in which both abuse and neglect are evident, young children may exhibit PTSD and RAD comorbidly (Hinshaw-Fusilier, Boris, & Zeanah, 1999). Much work on the delineation of what comprises pathogenic care is needed.

Assessment of Reactive Attachment Disorder

Adequate assessment of RAD requires a multimethod evaluation approach. The American Academy of Child and Adolescent Psychiatry released practice parameters for RAD in 2005. Their recommendations for assessment included the following: (a) observing the child individually with each important caregiver and with an unfamiliar adult, (b) gathering a complete history of early caregiving experiences from collateral sources, and (c) using a relatively structured observational procedure to acquire analogous sets of observations across different relationships. Boris and colleagues (2004) also recommended combining a structured observational procedure with a structured interview to assess for symptoms of RAD.

Although the assessment of RAD continues to be complicated by questions about the diagnostic criteria (see Chaffin et al., 2006), it is clear that any diagnostic decisions related to RAD need to be based on a thorough understanding of a child's history of caregiving experiences in conjunction with an understanding of their attachment behaviors in the context of current caregiving relationships. In practice, a thorough assessment for attachment disorders should thus include a combination of clinical interview with the child's caregiver(s) and relational observation methods. Through interview, it is important to obtain information about the child's current and past attachment relationships, caregiving history, specific attachment behaviors, and experiences/symptoms that would suggest other or additional diagnostic concerns (for example, pervasive developmental disorders). As noted by Zeanah and Smyke (2009), clinicians can use a comprehensive structured psychiatric interview, such as the Preschool Age Psychiatric Assessment (PAPA; Egger et al., 2006), or a semistructured interview specifically created to assess for signs of RAD, such as the Disturbances of Attachment Interview (DAI; Smyke, Dumitrescu, & Zeanah, 2002; Zeanah, Smyke, & Dumitrescu, 2002). The DAI contains questions designed to evaluate the extent to which a child has a focused attachment, and to determine whether there are symptoms of the emotionally withdrawn/inhibited or the socially indiscriminate/disinhibited types of RAD.

The observational portion of assessment should provide opportunities to see the child's interaction with each caregiver and with unfamiliar adults. Particular attention is paid to the presence or absence of expected attachment behaviors (e.g., seeking comfort when distressed or stressed, inhibition of exploration in the absence of the caregiver), as well as to the presence of characteristic symptoms (e.g., indiscriminate sociability). Although attachment behaviors can be observed in a variety of contexts, use of a fairly structured procedure allows the clinician to construct comparable observations of different caregiver-child dyads and to easily create opportunities to observe the desired behaviors in a clinic setting. One available structured dyadic procedure, known as the Clinical Observation of Attachment, was designed as a clinic-based observational measure for use in the diagnostic assessment of attachment disorders (see Boris et al., 2004, for details). This procedure, designed to elicit attachment behaviors, involves a series of interactions with the caregiver and a stranger as well as separation and reunion episodes. Other observational measures of attachment relationships are available, such as the Crowell Problem-Solving Procedure (see Miron, Lewis, & Zeanah, 2009).

The aforementioned assessment guidelines for RAD are used with children between the ages of 9 months and 6 years of age; 9 months is the point at which infants are developmentally capable of having formed a focused attachment. Thus, diagnosis of RAD prior to 9 months of age is not possible. Presumably, a similar multimethod diagnostic approach is needed to assess for RAD in older children. However, assessment for RAD in older age groups is complicated by the fact that there is still limited research on the signs and symptoms of attachment disorders in older children. In addition, there is also no gold standard for assessing attachment security in older children, which complicates the process of recognizing the presence or absence of expected attachment behaviors and cognitions (Zeanah & Gleason, 2010).

Conclusions and Directions for Future Research

It is clear that adverse and pathogenic caregiving can lead to significantly disturbed attachments in infants and young children. At the most extreme end of the caregiving spectrum, as may be seen with severe maltreatment, severe neglect, or institutional care, young children can exhibit very aberrant relational behaviors, such as emotionally withdrawn/inhibited or socially indiscriminate/disinhibited behaviors. Another relational effect of trauma includes increased risk for less adaptive attachment relationships. As we have noted, research has begun to elucidate links between parents' past experiences of trauma, parental states of mind, interactive behaviors, and the parent-child attachment relationship. If shaped by trauma, attachment relationships may lead to lasting effects on the child's emotional regulation, interpersonal style, and experience of intimate relationships.

There is much that we still do not know about the complex, reciprocal, direct, and indirect relationships that exist between trauma and attachment. It is noteworthy that our conceptualizations of the etiology of reactive attachment disorder and significantly disturbed attachment patterns such as disorganized attachment presume that the infant endures markedly atypical and severely distressing relational experiences. For an exceedingly dependent infant or young child who is biologically and psychologically primed for nurturing caregiving, severe neglect, abuse, or a lack of a reliable caregiver must indeed feel threatening and may, in many cases, be experienced as traumatic. In our clinical work with young children in foster care, we have seen children who have not been able to disclose or truly begin healing from past trauma until they form a secure or at least organized attachment relationship with a new caregiver. Although we certainly would not propose that this is the only factor in recovery from traumatic experiences, many clinicians have observed the importance of a consistent attachment relationship for children who are coping with various forms of trauma.

Increasingly, the effects of adverse early experiences on subsequent development are recognized as having potentially long-term effects on health and mental health. Specific studies are needed now to delineate more precisely the mechanisms linking traumatic experiences of caregivers and their effects on attachment relationships with their children. For example, a study with a longitudinal design that assesses trauma in caregivers, adult attachment, and infant attachment independently has not yet been conducted. A study with this design might confirm whether the initial suppositions described herein are warranted. Exploring mechanisms through which trauma and disturbed attachment exert their effects necessarily invites studies of the effects of trauma on the developing brain. Interest in epigenetics is one example of recent attempts to understand how trauma and disturbances of attachment lead to lasting maladaptation (McGowan et al., 2009).

A great deal also remains to be learned about how the quality of attachment protects or undermines a child's experience of a potentially traumatic event, a child's ability to recover from trauma, and how trauma can affect those same attachment relationships. Future research should explore the manner in which attachment relationships facilitate or complicate a child's ability to identify, to integrate, and to manage intense and distressing emotions and behavior arising from exposure to trauma, and how such experiences are incorporated into beliefs and expectations about safety relative to the self and the caregiving other. Having knowledge about the complex interplay of trauma, cognitions, expectations, emotions, memories, and behaviors can assist clinicians in promoting healthier functioning in adults and their young children.

References

Ainsworth, M., Bell, S., & Stayton, D. (1971). Individual differences in strange situation behavior of one-year-olds. In H. Schafer (Ed.), *The origins of human social relations* (pp. 17–57). London: Academic Press.

Ainsworth, M. S., Blehar, M. C., Waters, E., & Wall, S. (1978). *Patterns of attachment: A psychological study of the strange situation*. Oxford, England: Lawrence Erlbaum.

American Academy of Child and Adolescent Psychiatry. (2005). Practice parameter for the assessment and treatment of children and adolescents with reactive attachment disorder of infancy and early childhood. *Journal of the American Academy of Child and Adolescent Psychiatry*, *44*, 1206–1219.

American Psychiatric Association. (2000). *Diagnostic and statistical manual of mental disorders* (text revision). Washington, DC: Author.

Bischof, N. (1975). A systems approach toward the functional connections between fear and attachment. *Child Development*, *46*(4), 801–817.

Boris, N. W., Aoki, Y., & Zeanah, C. H. (1999). The development of infant-parent attachment: Considerations for assessment. *Infants and Young Children*, *11*, 1–10.

Boris, N. W., Hinshaw-Fuselier, S. S., Smyke, A. T., Scheeringa, M., Heller, S. S., & Zeanah, C. H., Jr. (2004). Comparing criteria for attachment disorders: Establishing reliability and validity in high-risk samples. *Journal of the American Academy of Child and Adolescent Psychiatry*, *43*(5), 568–577.

Bowlby, J. (1982). *Attachment and loss: Vol. I: Attachment* (2nd ed.). New York: Basic Books. (Original work published in 1969)

Carlson, V., Cicchetti, D., Barnett, D., & Braunwald, K. (1989). Finding order in disorganization: Lessons for research from maltreated infants' attachments to their caregivers. In D. Cicchetti & V. Carlson (Eds.), *Child maltreatment: Theory and research on the causes and consequences of child abuse and neglect* (pp. 494–528). Cambridge, MA: Cambridge University Press.

Cassidy, J., Marvin, R., & the MacArthur Working Group. (1992). *Attachment organization in preschool children: Procedures and working manual.* Unpublished manual.

Chaffin, M., Hanson, R., Saunders, B. E., Nichols, T., Barnett, D., Zeanah, C., et al. (2006). Report of the APSAC task force on attachment therapy, reactive attachment disorder, and attachment problems. *Child Maltreatment*, *11*(1), 76–89.

Chisholm, K. (1998). A three-year follow-up of attachment and indiscriminant friendliness in children adopted from Romanian orphanages. *Child Development*, *69*(4), 1092–1106.

Cicchetti, D., Rogosch, F. A., & Toth, S. L. (2006). Fostering secure attachment in infants in maltreating families through preventive interventions. *Development and Psychopathology*, *18*(3), 623–649.

DeKlyen, M., & Greenberg, M. T. (2008). Attachment and psychopathology in childhood. In J. Cassidy & P. R. Shaver (Eds.), *Handbook of attachment: Theory, research, and clinical applications* (2nd ed., pp. 637–665). New York: Guilford Press.

Egger, H. I., Erkanli, A., Keeler, G., Potts, E., Walter, B. K., & Angold, A. (2006). Test-retest of the Preschool Age Psychiatric Assessment (PAPA). *Journal of the American Academy of Child and Adolescent Psychiatry*, *45*(5), 538–549.

Gleason, M. M., Fox, N. A., Drury, S., Smyke, A., Egger, H. L., Nelson, C. A., et al. (2011). Validity of evidence-derived criteria for reactive attachment disorder: Indiscriminately social/disinhibited and emotionally withdrawn/inhibited types. *Journal of the American Academy of Child and Adolescent Psychiatry*, *50*(3), 216–231.

Green, J., & Goldwyn, R. (2002). Annotation: Attachment disorganization and psychopathology: New findings in attachment research and their potential implications for developmental psychopathology in childhood. *Journal of Child Psychology and Psychiatry*, *43*(7), 835–846.

Hesse, E. (2008). The adult attachment interview: Protocol, method of analysis, and empirical studies. In J. Cassidy & P. R. Shaver (Eds.), *Handbook of attachment: Theory, research, and clinical applications* (pp. 552–598). New York: Guilford Press.

Hinshaw-Fusilier, S., Boris, N. W., & Zeanah, C. H. (1999). Reactive attachment disorder in maltreated twins. *Infant Mental Health Journal*, *20*(1), 42–59.

Lieberman, A. (2004). Traumatic stress and quality of attachment: Reality and internalization in disorders of mental health. *Infant Mental Health Journal*, *24*(4), 336–351.

Lyons-Ruth, K., Bronfman, E., & Parsons, E. (1999). Maternal frightened, frightening, or atypical behavior and disorganized infant attachment patterns. *Monographs of the Society for Research in Child Development*, *64*(3), 67–96.

Lyons-Ruth, K., & Jacobvitz, D. (2008). Attachment disorganization: Genetic factors, parenting contexts, and developmental transformation from infancy to adulthood. In J. Cassidy & P. R. Shaver (Eds.), *Handbook of attachment: Theory, research, and clinical applications* (2nd ed., pp. 666–697). New York: Guilford Press.

Lyons-Ruth, K., Yellin, C., Melnick, S., & Atwood, G. (2005). Expanding the concept of unresolved mental states: Hostile/helpless states of mind on the adult attachment interview are associated with disrupted mother-infant communication and infant disorganization. *Development and Psychopathology*, *17*(1), 1–23.

MacDonald, H. Z., Beeghly, M., Grant-Knight, W., Augustyn, M., Woods, R. W., Cabral, H., et al. (2008). Longitudinal association between infant disorganized attachment and childhood posttraumatic stress symptoms. *Development and Psychopathology*, *20*(2), 493–508.

Madigan, S., Bakermans-Kranenburg, M. J., Van Ijzendoorn, M. H., Moran, G., Pederson, D. R., & Benoit, D. (2006). Unresolved states of mind, anomalous parental behavior, and disorganized attachment: A review and meta-analysis of a transmission gap. *Attachment & Human Development*, *8*(2), 89–111.

Main, M., & Hesse, E. (1990). Parents' unresolved traumatic experiences are related to infant disorganized attachment status: Is frightened and/or frightening parental behavior the linking mechanism? In M. Greenberg, D. Cicchetti, & E. M. Cummings (Eds.), *Attachment in the preschool years: Theory, research*, and intervention (pp. 161–184). Chicago: University of Chicago Press.

Main, M., Kaplan, N., & Cassidy, J. (1985). Security in infancy, childhood, and adulthood: A move to the level of representation. *Monographs of the Society for Research in Child Development*, *50*(1–2), 66–104.

Main, M., & Solomon, J. (1990). Procedures for identifying infants classified as disorganized/disoriented during the Ainsworth strange situation. In M. T. Greenburg, D. Ciccheti, & E. M. Cummings (Eds.), *Attachment in the preschool years: Theory, research, and interventions* (pp. 120–160). Chicago: University of Chicago Press.

Marvin, R., & Britner, P. (1995). *Classification system for parental caregiving patterns in the preschool strange situation*. Unpublished classification manual.

McGowan, P. O., Sasaki, A., D'Alessio, A. C., Dymov, S., Labonte, B., Szyf, M., et al. (2009). Epigenetic regulation of the glucocorticoid receptor in human brain associates with childhood abuse. *Nature Neuroscience*, *12*, 342–348.

Miron, D., Lewis, M. L., & Zeanah, C. H. (2009). Clinical use of observational procedures in early childhood relationship assessment. In C. H. Zeanah (Ed.), *Handbook of infant mental health* (3rd ed., pp. 252–265). New York: Guilford Press.

O'Connor, T., & Zeanah, C. H. (2003). Attachment disorders: Assessment strategies and treatment approaches. *Attachment and Human Development*, *5*(3), 223–244.

Oosterman, M., & Schuengel, C. (2008). Attachment in foster children associated with sensitivity and behavioral problems. *Infant Mental Health Journal*, *29*(6), 609–623.

Rutter, M., Colvert, E., Kreppner, J., Beckett, C., Castle, J., Groothues, C., et al. (2007). Early adolescent outcomes for institutionally-deprived and non-deprived adoptees: I. Disinhibited attachment. *Journal of Child Psychology and Psychiatry*, *48*(1), 17–30.

Rutter, M., Kreppner, J., & Sonuga-Barke, E. (2009). Emanuel Miller Lecture: Attachment insecurity, disinhibited attachment, and attachment disorders: Where do research findings leave the concepts? *Journal of Child Psychology and Psychiatry*, *50*(5), 529–543.

Schechter, D. S., Coates, S. W., Kaminer, T., Zeanah, C. H., Schonfield, I. S., Liebowitz, M. R., et al. (2008). Distorted maternal mental representations and atypical behavior in a clinical sample of violence-exposed mothers and their toddlers. *Journal of Trauma and Dissociation*, *9*(2), 123–147.

Schechter, D. S., Coots, T., Zeanah, C. H., Davies, M., Coates, S. W., Trabka, K. A., et al. (2005). Maternal mental representations of the child in an inner-city clinical sample: Violence-related posttraumatic stress and reflective functioning. *Attachment and Human Development*, *7*(3), 313–331.

Schechter, D. S., & Willheim, E. (2009). The effects of violent experiences on infants and young children. In C. Zeanah (Ed.), *Handbook of infant mental health* (3rd ed., pp. 197–213). New York: Guilford Press.

Scheeringa, M. S., & Zeanah, C. H. (2001). A relational perspective on PTSD in early childhood. *Journal of Traumatic Stress*, *14*, 799–815.

Schore, A. N. (2001). The effects of early relational trauma on right brain development, affect regulation, and infant mental health. *Infant Mental Health Journal*, *22*(1–2), 201–269.

Smyke, A. T., Dumitrescu, A., & Zeanah, C. H. (2002). Attachment disturbances in young children: I. The continuum of caretaking casualty. *Journal of the American Academy of Child & Adolescent Psychiatry*, *41*(8), 972–982.

Smyke, A. T., Zeanah, C. H., Gleason, M. M., Drury, S. S., Fox, N. A., & Nelson, C. A. (2010). *A randomized controlled trial of foster care vs. institutional care for children with signs of reactive attachment disorder*. Manuscript submitted for publication.

Sroufe, L. A., & Waters, E. (1977). Attachment as an organizational construct. *Child Development*, *48*(4), 1184–1199.

Tizard, B., & Rees, J. (1975). The effect of early institutional rearing on the behavior problems and affectional relationships of four-year-old children. *Journal of Child Psychology and Psychiatry*, *27*, 61–73.

van IJzendoorn, M. (1995). Adult attachment representations, parental responsiveness, and infant attachment: A meta-analysis on the predictive validity of the adult attachment interview. *Psychological Bulletin*, *117*(3), 387–403.

van IJzendoorn, M. H., & Sagi-Schwartz, A. (2008). Cross-cultural patterns of attachment: Universal and contextual dimensions. In J. Cassidy & P. Shaver (Eds.), *Handbook of attachment* (2nd ed., pp. 880–905). New York: Guilford.

Widiger, T. A., & Mullins-Sweatt, S. N. (2008). Personality disorders. In A. Tasman, J. Kay, J. A. Lieberman, M. B. First, & M. Maj (Eds.), *Psychiatry* (3rd ed., pp. 1718–1753). West Sussex, England: John Wiley & Sons.

World Health Organization. (1992). *The ICD-10 classification of mental and behavioral disorders: Clinical descriptions and diagnostic guidelines*. Geneva, Switzerland: Author.

Zeanah, C. H., & Gleason, M. M. (2010). *Reactive attachment disorder: A review for DSM-V*. Retrieved from http://www.dsm5.org/Proposed%20Revision%20Attachments/APA%20DSM-5%20Reactive%20Attachment%20Disorder%20Review.pdf

Zeanah, C. H., Keyes, A., & Settles, L. (2003). Attachment relationship experiences and childhood psychopathology. *Annals of the New York Academy of Sciences*, *1008*, 22–30.

Zeanah, C. H., Scheeringa, M. S., Boris, N. W., Heller, S., S., Smyke, A. T., & Trapani, J. (2004). Reactive attachment disorders in maltreated toddlers. *Child Abuse and Neglect: The International Journal*, *28*(8), 877–888.

Zeanah, C. H., & Smyke, A. T. (2008). Attachment disorders in family and social context. *Infant Mental Health Journal*, *29*(3), 219–233.

Zeanah, C. H., & Smyke, A. T. (2009). Disorders of attachment. In C. H. Zeanah (Ed.), *Handbook of infant mental health* (3rd ed., pp. 421–434). New York: Guilford Press.

Zeanah, C. H., Smyke, A. T., & Dumitrescu, A. (2002). Attachment disturbances in young children: II. Indiscriminate behavior and institutional care. *Journal of the American Academy of Child and Adolescent Psychiatry*, *41*(8), 983–989.

Zeanah, C. H., Smyke, A. T., Koga, S., Carlson, E., & BEIP Core Group. (2005). Attachment in institutionalized and community children in Romania. *Child Development*, *76*(5), 1015–1028.

Update to Chapter 7

Attachment and Trauma in Early Childhood: A Review

The upcoming fifth edition of the Diagnostic and Statistical Manual of Mental Disorders (DSM-5), which published in May of 2013, includes revisions to the definition of reactive attachment disorder. As noted in the chapter, research and clinical findings have accumulated evidence suggesting that the two subtypes of reactive attachment disorder (RAD), as described in the DSM-IV—TR, may in fact reflect different constructs. The DSM-5 will now define these subtypes as two distinct disorders: reactive attachment disorder of infancy or early childhood, and disinhibited social engagement disorder. Although both disorders presuppose a history of inadequate caregiving, they involve different core symptoms.

Reactive attachment disorder of infancy or early childhood (RAD) requires that a child exhibits a pattern of disturbed and developmentally inappropriate attachment behaviors before the age of 5 years, along with persistent social and emotional disturbance. The inappropriate attachment behaviors must involve a consistent pattern of inhibited and emotionally withdrawn behavior, manifested by the child's rare or minimal response to comfort from adult caregivers when distressed and rare or minimal seeking of comfort from caregivers when distressed. The social and emotional disturbance must be characterized by at least two behaviors, including: relative lack of social and emotional responsiveness to others, reduced or limited expression of positive affect, and episodes of unexplained irritability, sadness, or fearfulness during non-threatening interactions with caregivers. For the diagnosis, the child must have a developmental age of at least 9 months and cannot meet the criteria for an autism spectrum disorder. As mentioned, the child must have experienced severely insufficient caregiving, which can include persistent social neglect or deprivation, repeated changes in caregivers that limit opportunities to form attachment relationships, or rearing in unusual settings, such as institutions, that limit opportunities to form selective attachment relationships. It is presumed that the child's inadequate caregiving experiences are responsible for the core presenting symptoms. Essentially, this disorder describes children who lack selective attachment to anyone.

Disinhibited social engagement disorder (DSED) requires that a child demonstrates a pattern of actively approaching and interacting with unfamiliar adults, characterized by at least two behaviors, including: reduced or no reticence to approach and interact with unfamiliar adults, overly familiar behavior with others, which violates culturally sanctioned social boundaries, reduced or absent checking back with an adult caregiver, even in unfamiliar settings, and willingness to go with an unfamiliar adult with little or no hesitation. These behaviors are not limited to the impulsivity of attention deficit/hyperactivity disorder, but must include socially disinhibited behavior. As with the reactive attachment disorder of infancy or early childhood, a child must have a developmental age of at least 9 months. The child also must have experienced severely insufficient caregiving, and the core symptoms are presumed to be due to that experience of pathogenic care.

In our opinion, assessment approaches for both of these DSM-5 disorders can use methods described in our chapter to assess for the previous subtypes of RAD. However, we presume that clinicians and researchers will continue to refine assessment tools for these disorders over time. Critical in RAD assessment is observing the child with his/her putative caregiver, whereas in DSED assessment, what is critical is observing the child with an unfamiliar adult. As mentioned in our chapter, there is less clarity regarding how these symptoms present in older children or how to best assess for signs in older children, particularly RAD. Hopefully, understanding of these disorders at older ages will continue to progress, along with best practices for evaluation.

Polyvictimization in Developmental Context

DAVID FINKELHOR,[1] ANNE SHATTUCK,[1]
HEATHER A. TURNER,[1] RICHARD ORMROD,[1]
AND SHERRY L. HAMBY[2]

[1]University of New Hampshire
[2]Sewanee, the University of the South

Polyvictimization (i.e., exposure to multiple forms of victimization) appears highly correlated with indicators of traumatic stress in children. In this study, a national sample of children and youth were assessed for 36 different kinds of victimization using the Juvenile Victimization Questionnaire. Polyvictims were defined as the 10% of children experiencing the most different kinds of victimization in each of 4 developmental cohorts. The younger polyvictims had somewhat fewer victimizations overall, less sexual victimization, and more victimization at the hands of family members, particularly siblings. However, polyvictimization at every developmental level was strongly associated with distress symptoms. This study suggests the importance of assessing for and identifying polyvictims at all ages, including among preschoolers.

There is a lengthy literature on child maltreatment and trauma, much of it focused on specific categories of victimization such as sexual abuse, physical abuse, or bullying. However, many children experience several of these different victimizations (Saunders, 2003). For one thing, the sheer frequency of victimizations in childhood suggests that some of these victimizations should overlap (Nishina & Juvonen, 2005). In addition, most victimizations seem to have common correlates, like family instability or neighborhood disorder. The clustering of victimizations among some high-risk individuals is a well-established finding in victimology (Outlaw, Ruback, & Britt, 2002; Saunders, 2003).

Using an instrument designed to assess a much more comprehensive range of childhood victimizations, the Juvenile Victimization Questionnaire (JVQ), our research has shown that exposure to multiple forms of victimization is actually the norm for victimized children even over as short a period as a single year (Finkelhor, Ormrod, & Turner, 2007a). Half of a national sample of youth ages 2–17 experienced two or more different kinds of victimization in a single year, and among victims, the median number of victimizations was three.

Victimizations accumulate in childhood for a variety of reasons. There are common risk factors for different kinds of victimization, both in children's environments (families and neighborhoods) as well as in their personal and behavioral characteristics. Theory also suggests that victimizations create vulnerability for other victimizations, through mechanisms such as lowered self-esteem, learned helplessness, and distorted cognitions. These links are described by researchers such as Perry, Hodges, and Egan (2001), who have posited that cognitive schemas acquired in aggressive family interactions create a vulnerability for extrafamilial victimization.

The findings about accumulating victimizations draw attention to important conceptual and methodological problems in some of the research on child maltreatment and trauma. As mentioned, most studies in this field focus on only one kind of victimization like sexual abuse, bullying, or exposure to dating violence but then do not assess how many other kinds of victimization these narrowly categorized victims have also experienced. In efforts to look at associations between victimization and trauma, this can lead to a serious overestimation of the impact of individual victimization experiences, since the trauma may be explained by the other victimizations or the combination, rather than the individual victimization (Saunders, 2003; Turner, Finkelhor, & Ormrod, 2006, 2010).

In testing this, we reported that when other victimizations were accounted for, the effect of individual victimizations declines substantially (Finkelhor et al., 2007a). Thus, even though as in many studies, our data have shown that a sexual victimization by itself is associated with psychological symptoms, when other victimizations were controlled, there was little contribution of sexual victimization alone. This would appear to imply that the polyvictimized youth were the ones with the trauma symptoms, while youth with just a single type of victimization had much less or in some cases no measureable trauma.

For these polyvictims, victimization may be better thought of as a condition rather than an event. Much of the literature on victimization impact grows out of traumatic stress theory (Finkelhor, 1988), which began with observations of rape victims (Burgess & Holmstrom, 1975). The prototypical traumatic victimization in this literature was a terrifying, unpredictable event occurring to an otherwise unsuspecting and unafflicted person. But the situation for many victimized children is not so much an individual traumatizing event but a pattern of ongoing and multiple victimizations (Clausen & Crittenden, 1991; Duncan, 1999a, 1999b; Perry et al., 2001). For such children, victimization may be better conceptualized as a condition. Assessing polyvictimization may be important for identifying this group for whom victimization has become a condition.

We have proposed the terms *polyvictim* and *polyvictimization* to flag this multiply victimized group of youth who experience so much victimization, including much serious victimization, and who manifest substantial traumatic symptomatology. Individuals with intersecting adversities and conditions have proven important to identify in other fields, such as substance abuse and mental health, where concepts such as dual diagnosis, comorbidity (Sacks, 2003), and polydrug use (Bower, 1985; Kaufman, 1977) have helped both clinicians and researchers.

Cumulative effects are relatively common in the research on stress, adversity, and psychopathology (Rutter, 1988). That is, stresses and adversities often combine and interact in important and different ways. Several mechanisms may explain such effects. For example, self-blame seems to be one important component of victimization trauma (Mannarino & Cohen, 1996). Children have a much harder time resisting this self-blame when they experience victimization from multiple sources. Another possibility is that because victimization is so common, children do not see themselves as stigmatized on this dimension, unless they are experiencing multiple sorts of victimization (Nishina & Juvonen, 2005).

An important finding from our previous work is that polyvictimization was associated with considerably more severe symptoms than repeated or chronic victimizations of the same sort (Finkelhor et al., 2007a). One interpretation could be that the generalization of self-blame or other inadequacy may be easier for children to make when victimizations occur in more disparate contexts, in different ways and at the hands of more diverse categories of offenders.

One very widely cited example of the cumulative adversity or polyvictimization approach described here is the Adverse Childhood Experience (ACES) study (Felitti et al., 1998). This study confirmed that greater trauma is associated with greater numbers of childhood victimizations. Like a number of such approaches, however, this study cumulates victimizations from the entirety of childhood and gathers them retrospectively from adulthood recollection (or in some cases from late in adolescence). This approach has certain limitations. One is the possibility that selective recall might lead unhappy, distressed, or disadvantaged individuals to remember negative childhood experiences more readily or apply a more negative label to those experiences, creating an artificial association between distress and childhood adversity. Another limitation is the lack of perspective concerning the characteristics and mental health profiles of these individuals when assessed during childhood. Would such individuals show considerable cumulative adversity across childhood on a contemporaneous basis, or is it necessary to have the picture of their full childhood? Among other advantages, contemporary assessment would allow one to identify at-risk youth more quickly without having to wait for the completion of childhood. Such assessment might allow us to target interventions that may reduce the likelihood of long-term detrimental effects into adulthood. In the present study we look to see whether contemporary assessment of the accumulation of victimizations is effective in identifying distressed children, even at an early age.

Method

Sample

The National Survey of Children's Exposure to Violence (NatSCEV) was a telephone survey conducted from January–May 2008 on a nationally representative sample of 4,549 children ages 0–17 living in the contiguous United States. The present analysis is limited to the children ages 2 or older who comprised 4,046 participants from the entire sample. NatSCEV was designed to obtain 1-year and lifetime prevalence estimates of a wide range of childhood victimizations. Interviews with parents and youth were conducted over the phone by the employees of an experienced survey research firm.

Sample households were drawn from a nationwide sampling frame of residential telephone numbers through random digit dialing (RDD). This nationally representative cross-section yielded 3,053 of the 4,549 completed interviews. To ensure that the study included an adequate number of minority and low-income respondents for more accurate subgroup analyses, there was also an oversampling of telephone exchanges that had high concentrations of African American, Hispanic, or low-income households. This second "oversample" yielded 1,496 of the completed interviews. Sample weights were generated to correct for disproportionate sampling procedures when combining the two samples. Additional information on sampling methods and procedures has been provided elsewhere (Finkelhor, Turner, Ormrod, & Hamby, 2009).

Procedure

A short interview was conducted with an adult caregiver in each household to obtain family demographic information. One child was randomly selected from all eligible children living in a household by selecting the child with the most recent birthday. If the selected child was 10–17 years old, the main telephone interview was conducted with the child. If the selected child was under age 10, the interview was conducted with the caregiver who "is most familiar with the child's daily routine and experiences." Caregivers were interviewed as proxies for this age group because of concerns about limited language and cognitive skills of young children and their ability to be recruited and participate in phone interviews. Also, such children are still at an age when parents tend to be well informed about their day-to-day experiences.

To maximize response rate, up to 13 telephone callbacks were made initially to select and contact a respondent, and up to 25 callbacks were made to complete the interview. Respondents were promised complete confidentiality and were paid $20 for their participation. The interviews, averaging 45 minutes in length, were conducted in both English and Spanish. Two hundred seventy-nine of the interviews with the parents were conducted in Spanish. Nearly all of the adolescents from age 10–17 chose to be interviewed in English.

Respondents who disclosed a situation of serious threat or ongoing victimization were recontacted by a clinical member of the research team who was trained in telephone crisis counseling and whose responsibility it was to stay in contact with the respondent until the situation was resolved or brought to the attention of appropriate authorities. All procedures were authorized by the Institutional Review Board of the University of New Hampshire.

Response Rates and Nonresponse Analyses

The cooperation rate (number of households contacted that actually agreed to complete the survey) for the RDD cross-section portion of this survey ($n = 3{,}053$) was 71%, and the response rate based on American Association for Public Opinion Research (2004) standard guidelines was 54%. The rates associated with the oversample were somewhat lower at 63% and 43%, respectively. Given background trends in survey responses, the rates associated with this survey are quite good by current standards (Babbie, 2007; Keeter, Kennedy, Dimock, Best, & Craighill, 2006). Further, several recent studies have shown no strong association between response rates and response bias (Curtin, Presser, & Singer, 2000; Groves, 2006; Keeter, Miller, Kohut, Groves, & Presser, 2000; Merkle & Edelman, 2002). Indeed, extraordinary efforts to obtain higher response rates by persuading reluctant respondents to participate may actually add bias to survey responses (Biemer, 2001; Groves & Couper, 1998).

The weighting plan for the survey was a multistage sequential process of weighting the sample to correct for study design and demographic variations in nonresponse. Weights were applied to adjust for (a) differing probabilities of household selection, including the deliberate oversampling of Black, Hispanic, and low-income respondents, (b) variations in within-household selection probability due to differing numbers of household children, and (c) differences in sample proportions by gender, age, race/ethnicity, and income relative to Census Population Projections for 2008 of each strata (United States Census Bureau, 2008).

Measurement

Polyvictimization. The NatSCEV survey utilized an enhanced version of the Juvenile Victimization Questionnaire (JVQ), an inventory of childhood victimization (Finkelhor, Hamby, Ormrod, & Turner, 2005; Finkelhor, Ormrod, Turner, & Hamby, 2005a; Hamby, Finkelhor, Ormrod, & Turner, 2004). The enhanced JVQ obtains reports on 48 specific forms of youth victimization covering five general areas of interest: (a) conventional crime, (b) maltreatment, (c) victimization by peer and siblings, (d) sexual victimization, and

(e) witnessing and exposure to violence (Finkelhor, Ormrod, Turner, & Hamby, 2005b). A measure of past-year victimizations was constructed for each child using a subset of 36 out of the 48 victimization items by summing the number of different types of victimizations in this subset that the child had been exposed to in the previous year.

Examples of individual items include robbery, assault with a weapon, peer or sibling assault, neglect by caregiver, bullying, sexual assault, sexual harassment, living in an area with shooting or other violence, and witnessing or exposure to family violence, among others. Specific wording for all of the JVQ victimization screeners is available elsewhere (Finkelhor et al., 2009, Appendix 1).

The present analysis was limited to victimizations that occurred in the past year. A measure of past-year victimizations was constructed for each child by summing the number of different types of victimizations that the child had been exposed to in the previous year out of a total of 36 possible types. Children who had been exposed to particularly large numbers of different kinds of victimizations were designated as polyvictims. These polyvictims comprised the approximately 10% of children in each of the four age groups who had experienced the highest numbers of victimizations. Since the total number of victimization types that children are exposed to tends to increase with age, the threshold for polyvictimization varied by age group. For 2- to 5-year-olds, polyvictims had experienced five or more kinds of victimizations in the past year. Among 6- to 9-year-olds, the number was six or more; 10- to 13-year-olds, seven or more; and 14- to 17-year-olds, eight or more.

Aggregate Victimization Types. Individual victimization screeners in NatSCEV represent variations on several general classes of victimizations. For this study, screeners were grouped into seven general classes in order to assess the mix of victimization types experienced by developmental stage. The seven aggregate victimization types were: (a) physical assault, (b) property crime, (c) maltreatment, (d) bullying, (e) sexual victimization, (f) witnessing family violence, and (g) exposure to community violence.

Demographics. Child and household characteristics were collected during the initial parent interview. Measures used in this study included the child's sex, age (four groups: 2–5, 6–9, 10–13, or 14–17), race and Hispanic ethnicity (four groups: White, non-Hispanic; Black, non-Hispanic; other race, non-Hispanic; and Hispanic, any race), and socioeconomic status (SES) based on household income and parent education. Also used was a measure of the child's family structure, which assigned the child to one of four categories based on the relationship of adults with whom he or she lived: (a) two biological or adoptive parents, (b) one parent and a stepparent or unmarried partner, (c) one single parent, or (d) another adult including foster parents.

Family Adversity. Respondents were asked a series of questions to determine whether they or their families had experienced certain adverse life events in the past year. "Yes" responses to any of the 15 adversity items were summed to obtain a total score of past-year adversity for each child. Some examples of adversity items include serious illness of the child or his or her parent, experiencing a natural disaster, being homeless, or having a parent lose a job.

Trauma Symptoms. The NatSCEV survey includes shortened versions of the anger, depression, anxiety, and dissociation scales of two closely related measures: the Trauma Symptoms Checklist for Children (TSCC; Briere, 1996), which was used in the self-report interviews of 10- to 17-year-olds, and the Trauma Symptom Checklist for Young

Children (TSCYC; Briere et al., 2001), which was used in the caregiver interviews for 2- to 9-year-olds. Respondents were asked to indicate how often they (or their children) had experienced each symptom within the past month. An aggregate trauma symptom score for each age group (2- to 9-year-olds and 10- to 17-year-olds) was created by summing all item responses for the three scales. A unified trauma symptom score for all children in the sample was then constructed by merging the standardized trauma scores for each age group. The TSCC and TSCYC have shown very good reliability and validity in both population-based and clinical samples (Briere, 1996; Briere et al., 2001). In this study, the alpha coefficient was .93 for the TSCC and .86 for the TSCYC.

Data Analysis

The goals of this analysis were to assess the characteristics of past-year polyvictims by developmental stage and to determine if the victimization profiles of polyvictims differed by developmental stage. Chi-square tests, one-way analysis of variance, and t tests were used to compare developmental groups on demographic characteristics, trauma symptom scores, rates of polyvictimization by demographic group, and the mix of aggregate victimization types by age group. Analysis of covariance and ordinary least squares regression were used to evaluate the relationship between number of victimizations, past-year adversity, and demographic characteristics and the dependent variable of trauma symptom scores.

Results

We identified the most victimized children (the polyvictims) in each of four developmental groups (2–5, 6–9, 10–13, and 14–17) as the top 10% of the distribution in each group with the most different kinds of victimization in the past year. Because older children have somewhat more victimizations, this meant that the threshold for polyvictims was five or more for the 2- to 5-year-olds, six or more for 6- to 9-year-olds, seven or more for 10- to 13-year-olds, and eight or more for 14- to 17-year-olds.

The polyvictimization profiles for the four developmental groups differed somewhat (see Table 1). A substantially larger portion of the victimizations for the 2- to 5-year-olds (73%) and 6- to 9-year-olds (55%) was comprised of family member perpetrators, compared to 10- to 13-year-olds (32%) or 14- to 17-year-olds (30%). Somewhat more of the perpetrators against both the youngest and oldest groups were adults compared to the 6- to 9-year-olds. Older polyvictims had more physical assaults, sexual victimizations, and exposure to community violence. However, 14- to 17-year-old polyvictims had less bullying.

There were also some demographic differences among the polyvictims from the different age groups (see Table 2). The gender proportions were similar across all age groups; however, Black 10- to 13-year-olds had particularly elevated rates, and 14- to 17-year-old polyvictims had significantly lower SES. Polyvictim rates were generally lowest for children living with two biological parents. This was true for all age groups, and none of the differences between groups were significant.

Polyvictim children in all four age groups had high levels of other adversities such as illnesses, accidents, and family problems. The absolute level of additional adversities in the past year, however, was higher for the older two groups (2.46 and 2.57 for 10- to 13-year-olds and 14- to 17-year-olds, respectively) than the younger two groups (1.58 and 1.49 for the 2- to 5-year-olds and 6- to 9-year-olds). The association of polyvictimization

Table 1
Victimization profile of past-year polyvictims by age group

	2 to 5	6 to 9	10 to 13	14 to 17
(*n*)	(93)	(71)	(85)	(119)
Polyvictim threshold (# past-year screeners)	5	6	7	8
Mean percentage of past-year victimizations by family perpetrator	$73^{b,c,d}$	$55^{c,d}$	32	30
Mean percentage of past-year victimizations by adult perpetrator	31^{b}	19^{d}	24	35
Percent of polyvictims experiencing any victimization type in past year:				
Any physical assault	$54^{c,d}$	$66^{c,d}$	85	86
Any property crime	77	90	85	90
Any maltreatment	43	34	52	55
Any bullying	74	88^{d}	77^{d}	57
Any sexual victimization	$5^{c,d}$	$12^{c,d}$	41	55
Any witnessing family violence	47	42	45	52
Any exposure to community violence	$64^{c,d}$	$62^{c,d}$	90	85

Note. Group differences, $p < .05$.
[a]Differs from 2–5. [b]Differs from 6–9. [c]Differs from 10–13. [d]Differs from 14–17.

with trauma symptoms was strong for all four groups in bivariate as well as in multivariate analyses, controlling for gender, ethnicity, family structure, SES, and other adversities. The standardized betas for polyvictimization were .48 for 2- to 5-year-olds, .40 for the 6- to 9-year-olds, .48 for the 10- to 13-year-olds, and .43 for the 14- to 17-year-olds (all significant $p < .001$).

Discussion

The results of this study suggest that groups of children with high-victimization rates can be identified across the spectrum of childhood from age 2 to age 17, and that, although the numbers are lower and the assortment of victimization types is somewhat different for younger children, the key dynamics are similar for all age groups. The highly victimized children in each age group are considerably more likely to be distressed and have higher levels of other adversities.

Older polyvictim children are exposed to more victimizations overall, more sexual victimizations, and more victimizations at the hands of nonfamily members as they move out into the world. However, younger polyvictim children or those in the equivalent upper range of the victimization distribution for their age group are just as distressed. High levels of victimization predict distress for all age groups.

Some might have predicted that younger children would be less affected by victimization, because more of their victimizations include bullying and sibling assaults at the hands of equivalently young children, episodes that parents and school officials tend to view as less serious. But the findings here are not consistent with such a supposition. A question we cannot answer in this study, however, is whether younger children may be better able to escape continuing high levels of victimization. In earlier studies, polyvictimization was shown to have considerable stability, with over half of polyvictims in one year continuing

Table 2
Past-Year polyvictimization by demographic characteristics by age group

	% Polyvictims			
(*n*)	2 to 5 (1047)	6 to 9 (904)	10 to 13 (920)	14 to 17 1175)
Percent of all children in each group who are polyvictims				
Male	11	8	10	10
Female	10	8	9	9
Race and ethnicity				
White, non-Hispanic	12	10	8	8
Black, non-Hispanic	14	7	19[a]	15
Other race, non-Hispanic	10	5	13	10
Hispanic, any race	5	5	4	10
Socioeconomic status*				
Low	12	7	9	10
Average	11	8	11	11
High	8	9	3	4
Household parent structure				
Two parents	7	7	7	6
Parent and stepparent or unmarried partner	17	11	10	16
Single parent	17	9	13	14
Other adult	24	13	16	13

*Low: 1 or more standard deviation below sample mean SES; Average: within 1 standard deviation of mean SES; High: 1 or more standard deviation above mean.
[a]Differs from 6–9, $p < .05$.

to polyvictimization in a second or third year (Finkelhor, Ormrod, & Turner, 2007b). This would suggest that a considerable portion of the younger polyvictims will continue to be polyvictims as they get older. This is likely to be true even if it is easier for younger polyvictims to escape from this condition.

Whatever the trajectory, however, there is good justification based on these data to identify and intervene with polyvictims at a young age. This highly victimized group has both substantial distress and higher levels of other adversity. They would appear to be in need of mental health services to deal with distress as well as to help develop skills to protect themselves from additional victimization. If early polyvictimization does tend to persist across developmental stages, intervention at this early stage may be a good strategy for protecting children from later victimization as well.

Acknowledgment

For the purposes of compliance with Section 507 of PL 104-208 (the "Stevens Amendment"), readers are advised that 100% of the funds for this program are derived from federal sources (this project was supported by Grant Nos. 2006-JW-BX-0003 and 2009-JW-BX-0018 awarded by the Office of Juvenile Justice and Delinquency Prevention, Office of Justice Programs, U.S. Department of

Justice). The total amount of federal funding involved is $2,848,809. Points of view or opinions in this document are those of the author and do not necessarily represent the official position or policies of the U.S. Department of Justice.

References

American Association for Public Opinion Research. (2004). *Standard definitions: Final dispositions of case codes and outcome rates for surveys* (3rd ed.). Lenexa, KS: Author.

Babbie, E. (2007). *The practice of social research* (11th ed.). Belmont: CA: Wadsworth.

Biemer, P. P. (2001). Nonresponse bias and measurement bias in a comparison of face to face and telephone interviewing. *Journal of Official Statistics*, *17*, 295–320.

Bower, B. (1985). Multiple drug use: A dangerous trend. *Science News*, *128*(1), 6.

Briere, J. (1996). *Trauma Symptoms Checklist for Children (TSCC): Professional manual.* Odessa, FL: Psychological Assessment Resources.

Briere, J., Johnson, K., Bissada, A., Damon, L., Crouch, J., Gil, E., et al. (2001). The Trauma Symptom Checklist for Young Children (TSCYC): Reliability and association with abuse exposure in a multi-site study. *Child Abuse & Neglect*, *25*, 1001–1014.

Burgess, A. W., & Holmstrom, L. L. (1975). *Rape: Victims of crisis*. Bowie, MD: R. J. Brady.

Clausen, A. H., & Crittenden, P. M. (1991). Physical and psychological maltreatment: Relations among types of maltreatment. *Child Abuse & Neglect*, *15*, 5–18.

Curtin, R., Presser, S., & Singer, E. (2000). The effects of response rate changes on the index of consumer sentiment. *Public Opinion Quarterly*, *64*, 413–428.

Duncan, R. D. (1999a). Maltreatment by parents and peers: The relationship between child abuse, bully victimization, and psychological distress. *Child Maltreatment*, *4*, 45–55.

Duncan, R. D. (1999b). Peer and sibling aggression: An investigation of intra- and extra-familial bullying. *Journal of Interpersonal Violence*, *14*, 871–886.

Felitti, V. J., Anda, R. F., Nordenberg, D., Williamson, D. F., Spitz, A. M., Edwards, V., et al. (1998). Relationship of childhood abuse and household dysfunction to many of the leading causes of death in adults: The Adverse Childhood Experiences (ACE) Study. *American Journal of Preventative Medicine*, *14*(4), 245–258.

Finkelhor, D. (1988). The trauma of child sexual abuse: Two models. In G. Wyatt & G. J. Powell (Eds.), *The lasting effects of child sexual abuse* (pp. 61–82). Newbury Park, CA: Sage Publications.

Finkelhor, D., Hamby, S. L., Ormrod, R. K., & Turner, H. A. (2005). The JVQ: Reliability, validity, and national norms. *Child Abuse & Neglect*, *29*(4), 383–412.

Finkelhor, D., Ormrod, R. K., & Turner, H. A. (2007a). Polyvictimization: A neglected component in child victimization trauma. *Child Abuse & Neglect*, *31*, 7–26.

Finkelhor, D., Ormrod, R. K., & Turner, H. A. (2007b). Revictimization patterns in a national longitudinal sample of children and youth. *Child Abuse & Neglect*, *31*(5), 479–502.

Finkelhor, D., Ormrod, R. K., Turner, H. A., & Hamby, S. L. (2005a). Measuring polyvictimization using the JVQ. *Child Abuse & Neglect*, *29*(11), 1297–1312.

Finkelhor, D., Ormrod, R. K., Turner, H. A., & Hamby, S. L. (2005b). The victimization of children and youth: A comprehensive, national survey. *Child Maltreatment*, *10*(1), 5–25.

Finkelhor, D., Turner, H. A., Ormrod, R., & Hamby, S. L. (2009). Violence, abuse, and crime exposure in a national sample of children and youth. *Pediatrics*, *124*(5), 1–13.

Groves, R. M. (2006). Nonresponse rates and nonresponse bias in household surveys. *Public Opinion Quarterly*, *70*(5), 646–675.

Groves, R. M., & Couper, M. P. (1998). *Nonresponse in household surveys*. New York: John Wiley and Sons.

Hamby, S. L., Finkelhor, D., Ormrod, R. K., & Turner, H. A. (2004). *The Juvenile Victimization Questionnaire (JVQ): Administration and scoring manual.* Durham, NH: Crimes Against Children Research Center.

Kaufman, E. (1977). Polydrug abuse or multidrug misuse: It's here to stay. *British Journal of Addiction*, *72*(4), 339–348.

Keeter, S., Kennedy, C., Dimock, M., Best, J., & Craighill, P. (2006). Gauging the impact of growing nonresponse on estimates from a national RDD telephone survey. *Public Opinion Quarterly*, *70*(5), 759–779.

Keeter, S., Miller, C., Kohut, A., Groves, R. M., & Presser, S. (2000). Consequences of reducing nonresponse in a national telephone survey. *Public Opinion Quarterly*, *64*, 125–148.

Mannarino, A. P., & Cohen, J. A. (1996). Abuse-related attributions and perceptions, general attributions, and locus of control in sexually abused girls. *Journal of Interpersonal Violence*, *11*(2), 162–180.

Merkle, D., & Edelman, M. (2002). Nonresponse in exit polls: A comprehensive analysis. In R. M. Groves, D. A. Dillman, J. L. Eltinge, & R. J. A. Little (Eds.), *Survey nonresponse* (pp. 343–358). New York: Wiley.

Nishina, A., & Juvonen, J. (2005). Daily reports of witnessing and experiencing peer harassment in middle school. *Child Development*, *76*(2), 435–450.

Outlaw, M., Ruback, B., & Britt, C. (2002). Repeat and multiple victimizations: The role of individual and contextual factors. *Violence and Victims*, *17*(2), 187–204.

Perry, D. G., Hodges, E. V. E., & Egan, S. K. (2001). Determinants of chronic victimization by peers: A review and new model of family influence. In J. Juvonen & S. Graham (Eds.), *Peer harassment in school: The plight of the vulnerable and victimized* (pp. 73–104). New York: Guilford Press.

Rutter, M. (1988). Epidemiological approaches to developmental psychopathology. *Archives of General Psychiatry*, *45*, 486–495.

Sacks, S. (2003). Co-occurring substance use and mental disorders in offenders: Approaches, findings, and recommendations. *Federal Probation*, *67*(2), 32–40.

Saunders, B. E. (2003). Understanding children exposed to violence: Toward an integration of overlapping fields. *Journal of Interpersonal Violence*, *18*(4), 356–376.

Turner, H. A., Finkelhor, D., & Ormrod, R. K. (2006). The effects of lifetime victimization on the mental health of children & adolescents. *Social Science & Medicine*, *62*(1), 13–27.

Turner, H. A., Finkelhor, D., & Ormrod, R. K. (2010). Poly-victimization in a national sample of children & youth. *American Journal of Preventive Medicine*, *38*(3), 323–330.

United States Census Bureau. (2008). *2008 national population projections*. Retrieved from http://www.census.gov/population/www/projections/2008projections.html

Genetic and Environmental Influences on Posttrauma Adjustment in Children and Adolescents: The Role of Personality Constructs

JOSH M. CISLER,[1] ANANDA B. AMSTADTER,[2] AND NICOLE R. NUGENT[3]

[1]University of Arkansas for Medical Sciences
[2]Virginia Commonwealth University
[3]Bradley Hasbro Children's Research Center

The prevalence of exposure to traumatic events in childhood and adolescence is high and is associated with a host of mental health difficulties. However, not all trauma-exposed youth develop mental health difficulties in the wake of trauma, suggesting that other factors, such as personality and genetic influences, may play a role in posttrauma adjustment. In the present article, we provide an overview of how personality factors influence posttrauma trajectories and how both personality and posttrauma adjustment may be influenced by genetic factors. We first review major personality constructs, with a focus on developmental and assessment considerations in trauma–exposed youth. Next, we provide a discussion of genetic influences on personality, exposure to traumatic events, and the development of mental health disorders following traumatic event exposure. Lastly, recommendations for future research are provided.

Trauma exposure during childhood and adolescence has been associated with a host of negative outcomes spanning emotional, behavioral, and physical health domains (Fairbank & Fairbank, 2009). For many youth, early trauma may result in a range of psychiatric concerns including posttraumatic stress disorder (PTSD), depression, substance use disorders, and personality disorders (Copeland, Keeler, Angold, & Costello, 2007; Fairbank & Fairbank, 2009; Fergusson, Horwood, & Lynskey, 1996). However, not all trauma-exposed youth develop psychiatric concerns. Genetic differences may partly account for this variability, possibly through their influence on personality constructs (e.g., temperament, personality traits), and particularly to the degree that these personality constructs represent biologically driven constitutional differences among individuals. Indeed, personality has been found to predict psychiatric morbidity (Clark, 2005; Gerra et al., 2004) and to be influenced by genetic factors (Jang, Stein, Taylor, Asmundson, & Livesley, 2003; Kendler & Baker, 2007; Kendler, Gardner, & Prescott, 2003). The influence of personality has been neglected in trauma and posttraumatic stress disorder (PTSD) research.

The present article provides an overview of the influences of genes on personality and posttraumatic adjustment in trauma-exposed youth. First, we review major personality constructs relevant for understanding: (a) risk for traumatic event exposure and (b) the development of psychopathology following traumatic event exposure in children and adolescents. Second, evidence for genetic influences on personality, traumatic event exposure, and psychopathology following traumatic event exposure are highlighted, focusing on studies of trauma-exposed youth when possible. Finally, we provide recommendations for researchers interested in incorporating personality in child and adolescent trauma research.

Genetically Informed Assessment of Personality in Children and Adolescents

The term *personality* is used here to reference temperament, personality, and traits, but it is important to acknowledge that these constructs have distinct definitions and theoretical underpinnings. Personality constructs, particularly superordinate personality constructs such as neuroticism (reviewed below in detail), are believed to represent stable constitutional differences and are therefore well suited to research with children and adolescents. The overarching concept is that the pathway from genes to psychopathology is not likely to be direct. Rather, genes likely affect the development of other mediating processes, such as temperament/personality, which may influence both (a) the selection into environments with higher or lower rates of trauma exposure and (b) the likelihood of developing psychopathology following trauma exposure.

From a developmental perspective, temperament has been regarded as the foundation of personality (Buss & Plomin, 1975; Goldsmith & Rothbart, 1991). Temperament is believed to be a stable, biologically and genetically determined construct that is shaped over the course of development by environmental influences (i.e., culture, family, key life events such as trauma) into personality and traits (Eysenck, 1981; Gray, 1982). Structurally, temperament represents a "rubric for a group of related traits and not a trait itself" (Goldsmith et al., 1987, p. 506). The present section provides an overview of personality constructs implicated in trauma exposure and posttraumatic adjustment in youth. As is discussed below, these constructs involve considerable conceptual and developmental overlap. As a detailed exploration of these constructs is outside of the present scope, interested readers are directed to more comprehensive papers and books on personality constructs (e.g., Goldsmith et al., 1987; Lemery, Goldsmith, Klinnert, & Mrazek, 1999; McCrae et al., 2000; Nader, 2008).

Weems and Stickle (2005) provided an integrative framework for childhood anxiety disorders, highlighting both the role of trauma and of personality constructs in the etiology of clinical anxiety. Weems and Stickle proposed that our understanding of PTSD and other anxiety disorders is best facilitated through the study of diagnostic symptoms in combination with the *mechanisms* underlying the disorder. Genetic research paradigms also include mechanisms (referred to as *intermediary phenotypes*) proposed to mediate the effects of genotype on observed phenotypes such as PTSD or depression; temperament and personality constructs are examples of possible intermediary phenotypes for key trauma-related phenotypes. These biologically driven intermediary phenotypes are believed to be more proximal to genotype than more distal outcomes that may be influenced by a host of moderating environmental or even intraindividual factors. For example, genetic vulnerability towards the development of PTSD (i.e., the distal phenotype) following trauma exposure may be mediated by more direct genetic influences on neuroticism (i.e., the intermediary phenotype).

The Importance of Personality Factors in Understanding Posttrauma Adjustment

One of the most widely used personality models, the five-factor model (FFM), defines personality using five broad traits: (a) neuroticism, (b) extraversion, (c) agreeableness, (d) conscientiousness, and (e) openness to experience (Goldberg, 1993). Most of these personality constructs, as well as the construct of *externalizing*, have been examined in investigations of personality and posttrauma psychopathology. Of the FFM components, *neuroticism*, defined as a stable tendency to experience negative emotional states, has received the most empirical attention in the trauma field. Neuroticism has been tied to anxiety and mood disorders in general and to PTSD in particular (Hettema, Neale, Myers, Prescott, & Kendler, 2006; Hettema, Prescott, & Kendler, 2004; Jardine, Martin, & Henderson, 1984; Kirk et al., 2000). In a related vein, difficult temperament is a broad construct that consists of difficulties across multiple traits; difficult temperament children show high activity, difficulties with adaptability, low levels of approach to novelty, high levels of distractibility, high-intensity response to stimuli, negative mood, low levels of persistence with rapid frustration, irregularity in rhythmicity of biological functions such as sleeping and eating, and a low threshold for sensory stimuli (Goldsmith et al., 1987; Thomas & Chess, 1977). Genetically driven levels of neuroticism/negative affectivity in infancy and early childhood are believed to develop into levels of neuroticism in adolescence and adulthood, with these constructs influencing the likelihood that individuals will evidence symptoms of depression and/or anxiety under conditions of environmental risk.

Numerous other personality constructs, some of which may arguably represent lower order facets of neuroticism/negative affectivity, may be associated with trauma exposure or posttrauma response in children and adolescents. For example, *behavioral inhibition*, or withdrawal from novelty (Kagan, Reznick, & Gibbons, 1989), has been characterized as a behavioral expression of neuroticism (Turner, Bieidel, & Wolff, 1996). Behavioral inhibition is one candidate for research involving child response to trauma, as it has been shown to be a developmental risk factor for anxiety disorders (Battaglia et al., 1997; Biederman et al., 2001; Mannasis, Bradley, Goldberg, Hood, & Swinson, 1995; Rosenbaum et al., 2000; Schwartz, Snidman, & Kagan, 1999). Similarly, broad constructs that likely reflect superordinate neuroticism/negative affectivity are *trait anxiety*, defined as a general tendency to perceive anticipated and experienced situations as threatening, and *anxiety sensitivity*, defined as sensitivity to interoceptive manifestations of anxiety.

Research has demonstrated that these constructs are relevant for understanding posttrauma adjustment. For example, research has demonstrated an association between pretrauma neuroticism and PTSD symptoms in adolescent survivors of a serious fire (Dekovic, Koning, Jan Stams, & Buist, 2008). Narrowing to anxiety-specific constructs, both trait anxiety and anxiety sensitivity have been associated with PTSD in children and adolescents (Kilic, Kilic, & Yilmaz, 2008). One prospective study of children found that predisaster measures of trait anxiety and negative affect predicted PTSD and generalized anxiety disorder symptoms 6–7 months after Hurricane Katrina, even after controlling for key aspects of the hurricane exposure (Weems et al., 2007). Another investigation of sixth and seventh graders in New Orleans found that both trait anxiety and anxiety sensitivity were associated with PTSD symptoms, with anxiety sensitivity explaining an additional 6% of the variance associated with PTSD after adjusting for trait anxiety (Hensley & Varela, 2008). Finally, personality factors may provide markers for alternative pathways for developing psychopathology such as PTSD (i.e., equifinality). For example, whereas neurotic or internalizing individuals may be more sensitive to the effects of trauma once experienced, externalizing/difficult temperament individuals may develop PTSD partly as a function of their increased exposure to trauma. In other words, there may be multiple pathways by which disparate personality factors confer risk for both trauma exposure and posttrauma trajectory. Explicating these pathways is a key future research direction.

Developmental Challenges in Assessment of Children and Adolescents

Assessment challenges in trauma-exposed youth are substantial, with psychiatric diagnosis necessitating unique considerations (Cohen & Scheeringa, 2009; Scheeringa, 2008). For example, Meiser-Stedman and colleagues (2008) recently proposed an alternative algorithm for PTSD in children 2–10 years of age. Similarly, Scheeringa, Wright, Hunt, and Zeanah (2006) concluded that Criterion C (persistent avoidance of trauma-related cues, emotional numbing, and social detachment) is inappropriate for preschool children and that "findings were mixed as to whether the three-symptom threshold is appropriate for 7–11-year-old-children" (p. 649). Difficulties in measurement of any psychological construct over the course of development, including psychopathology and personality constructs, are likely attributable to both actual change in the constructs as well as the method of assessment and inherent error therein. As younger children have limited capacity to report on their internal experiences, assessment of many constructs such as internalizing symptoms is particularly challenging in young children (Cohen & Scheeringa, 2009). Finally, research is limited to the extent that measures themselves are developmentally anchored as well as culturally sensitive. Questions about work interests or romantic relationships would be irrelevant to a toddler. Sufficient differentiation to approximate adult construals of personality may not occur until 14–15 years of age (Allik, Laidra, Realo, & Pullmann, 2004). Accordingly, although our understanding of personality development is clearly enriched greatly by longitudinal research, such science is limited by the availability of developmentally sensitive yet theoretically consistent measures.

In addition to the challenges inherent in any research involving child and adolescent assessment, efforts to examine the dynamic interplay of genetic and environmental influences in trauma-exposed youth are further complicated by the age and developmental stage at the time of trauma, developmental stages negotiated since the trauma, and age/stage at follow-up assessments. The influence of genetics as well as stressful/traumatic life events has been shown to exert differential effects on psychopathology over the course of development (Rice, Harold, & Thapar, 2003; Silberg et al., 1999). Given developmental differences across neurobiological development, social development, and cognitive development, children may be more or less vulnerable to the effects of trauma at certain developmental stages, or the exact outcomes (e.g., depression vs. PTSD) of trauma may differ partly as a function of age (i.e., multifinality).

Normative pubertal biologic changes may play an important role in understanding the effects of trauma during adolescence (Olff, Langeland, Draijer, & Gersons, 2007). For example, research with normative samples has suggested that baseline and reactivity cortisol levels, which have been implicated in the development of PTSD in trauma-exposed youth, differ by age and gender (Gunnar, Wewerka, Frenn, Long, & Griggs, 2009). We have found that these gender and age effects of trauma are even further complicated when youth have experienced a prior traumatic event (Delahanty & Nugent, 2006), demonstrating a need for assessing key developmental characteristics.

Summary

The pathway from gene to posttrauma psychopathology likely involves genetic influences on temperament and personality, which influences both environment selection and psychopathology. Temperament is considered a genetically influenced foundation for personality development, and there are several key personality constructs relevant for understanding risk of anxiety disorders in general and posttrauma psychopathology in particular; these include neuroticism, behavioral inhibition, and anxiety sensitivity. Assessment of personality and psychopathology in youth is complicated by developmental differences, which need to be considered in future investigations of genes, personality, and posttrauma psychopathology.

Genetics, Trauma, and Personality in Children and Adolescents

A wealth of evidence supports contributions of both environment and genetics in shaping personality development over the course of childhood and adolescence. Although environmental influences are numerous, we focus on the environmental agent of traumatic life events with additional attention to developmentally salient environmental variables that may influence the interplay of genes, trauma, and personality in trauma-exposed children and adolescents. For further information, the interested reader is referred to extant reviews (Amstadter, Nugent, & Koenen, 2009; Koenen, Nugent, & Amstadter, 2008; Nader, 2008).

Genes, Personality, and Risk for Trauma Exposure

Our understanding of the relationship between personality and trauma exposure has been greatly informed by studies of heritability. *Heritability* is the proportion of a specific phenotype or observed outcome that can be attributed to genetics. Exposure to traumatic events is not a heritable trait per se; however, genetic factors may influence the likelihood of exposure to traumatic events. This is referred to as *gene-environment correlation* (rGE), whereby selection of environment is partly determined by genetic factors (Kendler & Eaves, 1986). A review of genetic influences on environmental measures, including stressful life events, parenting, and social support, found that heritability estimates fell between 7% and 39% with a weighted heritability estimate for all environmental measures of 27% (Kendler & Baker, 2006).

Plomin, DeFries, and Loehlin (1977) theorized that three forms of rGEs play a role in the expression of phenotypes and environments over the course of development that is relevant to personality and trauma exposure. First, *passive rGE* is due to families sharing both genetic and environmental influences. Nonadopted children are passively exposed to (i.e., they inherit) environments that are related to the shared genetic influences. Second, *reactive rGE* refers to the environment the child experiences as a function of others' reactions to the child's genetically influenced behavior. For example, adolescent personality has been found to moderate both genetic and environmental influences on the parent-adolescent relationship (South, Krueger, Johnson, & Iacono, 2008). Lastly and perhaps most related to personality factors is *active rGE*, which is when one actively seeks out or creates environments that are driven by their genetic factors.

Investigations of rGE have demonstrated that genetic factors influence exposure to potentially traumatic events (Lyons et al., 1993; Stein, Jang, Taylor, Vernon, & Livesley, 2002). Heritability estimates from a community twin sample ranged from 0% for nonassaultive violence events to 20% for assaultive violence events (Stein et al., 2002). These findings suggest that associations between genes and posttrauma psychopathology may not be fully attributable to genetic influences on posttrauma recovery. Rather, genes may influence the probability that an individual will be exposed to traumatic events, particularly assaultive traumatic events. Given that the number of prior traumatic events predicts probability of PTSD onset (Copeland et al., 2007), the influence of genes on trauma exposure itself would then necessarily confer risk for PTSD.

Gene-environment correlations related to likelihood of trauma exposure are likely partly secondary to individual differences in personality (Saudino, Pedersen, Lichtenstein, McClearn, & Plomin, 1997). As stated above, personality characteristics are moderately heritable and influence the tendency for individuals to select themselves into potentially harmful environments. For instance, difficult temperament prospectively predicts trauma exposure (Bagley & Mallick, 2000). Childhood externalizing was also found to predict both trauma exposure and PTSD in a longitudinal birth cohort (Koenen, Moffitt, Poulton, Martin, & Caspi, 2007). Further, longitudinal investigations have found that childhood adjustment and neuroticism predicted subsequent stressful life events in adulthood (Van Os & Jones, 1999). In adults, neuroticism predicts exposure to stressful life events (Kendler et al., 2003) and objective negative life events (Magnus, Diener, Frjita, & Pavot, 1993).

Although personality tends to be relatively stable over time, environmental influences, such as exposure to trauma, can also increase behaviors that seemingly enhance these genetic effects. For example, trauma exposure in childhood has been found to increase externalizing behaviors (Schwab-Stone et al., 1999), which as described above, may in turn increase exposure to negative life events. The incorporation of genetic samples and personality assessment in studies of youth trauma is needed to further elucidate these findings.

Genetic Influences on Personality

This section focuses on evidence of genetic influences on neuroticism, behavioral inhibition, and anxiety sensitivity. Discussion is limited to these constructs because of their strong link with vulnerability to anxiety disorders in general and PTSD specifically (Barlow, 2002; Hensley & Varela, 2008; Parslow, Jorm, & Chrstensen, 2006; Weems & Stickle, 2005).

Family Studies. One method of assessing genetic influences on personality is to examine the correlations between personality traits among family members. Consistent with hypotheses that neuroticism has a strong genetic component, Lake and colleagues (2000) found that the correlation of neuroticism scores between fathers and sons was .13, the correlation between uncles and nephews was .07, and the correlation between fathers and their daughters' husbands was .002. Family association studies have also supported a genetic contribution to anxiety sensitivity, with relatives of individuals with high-anxiety sensitivity evidencing increased anxiety relative to normal comparisons (van Beek & Griez, 2003). Although higher heritability has been reported in twin studies (discussed in the next section), family estimates of trait anxiety heritability have been remarkably low, estimated to be between 0 and .20 (Tambs & Mourn, 1993).

Twin Studies. Twin studies (e.g., Kendler, 2001) allow for more nuanced distinctions between genetic and environmental effects. As monozygotic and dizygotic twins typically share environments, greater concordance in a trait among monozygotic compared to dizygotic twins suggests genetic influences on the trait. The twin design has been used to calculate the proportion of the variance in a trait or disorder explained by genetic factors (i.e., heritability).

Moderate levels of heritability have been demonstrated for most personality constructs in children and adolescents. Observed measures of temperament in 14-month-olds in the

MacArthur Longitudinal Twin Study evidenced moderate heritability, ranging from .49 for shyness to .56 for behavioral inhibition (Emde et al., 1992). Behavioral genetic studies have suggested that all of the FFM factors have a substantial genetic component (Jang, McCrae, Angleitner, Riemann, & Livesley, 1998; Loehlin, 1992). Focusing on neuroticism, twin studies have demonstrated a strong genetic influence (Heath, Neale, Kessler, Eaves, & Kendler, 1992; Kendler et al., 2006). Lake and colleagues (2000) found that the correlation between neuroticism scores of monozygotic female twins was .41, compared to a correlation of .22 between dizygotic female twins.

Behavioral inhibition has evidenced strong heritability, with estimates as high as 90% (DiLalla, Kagan, & Reznick, 1994; Eley et al., 2003; Goldsmith & Lemery, 2000; Plomin et al., 1993; Robinson, Kagan, Reznick, & Corley, 1992). Heritability of trait anxiety in children and adolescents has been found to range from .23 to .57 (Legrand, McGue, & Iacono, 1999; Topolski et al., 1997), with some research supporting higher heritability in girls (Topolski et al., 1997). Heritability of anxiety sensitivity has been estimated at 45% (Stein, Jang, & Livesley, 1999).

Molecular Genetics. Molecular genetic studies examine the association between genetic polymorphisms and an outcome, such as a personality trait or psychiatric diagnosis. Molecular genetic studies of neuroticism and PTSD (see Canli, 2008, for a recent review) have most commonly demonstrated an association with the serotonin transporter (5-HTT) promoter polymorphism (commonly referred to as the 5-HTTLPR), a putatively functional variant associated with differences in transcription. Lesch and colleagues (1996) found that adults with one or two copies of the short allele of the 5-HTTLPR had higher neuroticism scores than individuals with two copies of the long allele. Meta-analyses have since demonstrated the robustness of this effect (Munafo et al., 2009; Schinka, Busch, & Robichaux-Keene, 2004); however, some inconsistencies are notable. For example, a recent study by Middeldorp and colleagues (2007) reported no association between 5-HTTLPR and neuroticism in a large sample of twins, parents, and siblings. Further, whether the 5-HTTLPR correlates with self-reported neuroticism appears to depend upon the measure of neuroticism used (Munafo et al., 2009; Schinka et al., 2004). Interestingly, studies of childhood and early adolescent shyness/behavioral inhibition have been associated with the long variant of the 5-HTTLPR (Arbelle et al., 2003; Jorm et al., 2000). One possible explanation for these apparent inconsistencies may be the timing of assessment. A recent longitudinal population-based study found that adolescents who were homozygous for the short 5-HTTLPR allele were more likely to report elevated neuroticism at age 15 but not at age 18 (Harro et al., 2009). The study revealed another potential explanation for inconsistencies in the literature, with parent reports showing cohort effects and failing to mirror the associations identified by youth self-reports. Additionally, most of these studies failed to examine the potential influence of key environmental influences such as trauma exposure or family environment. While other genes (e.g., *CRH, GABA, PDE4D, DRD4, DRD2, COMT*) relevant to other neurobiological systems (e.g., dopaminergic system, hypothalamic pituitary adrenal axis, GABA synthesis) have been studied, no consistent associations with neuroticism have been found (Canli, 2008).

Summary

Genetic influences on personality are substantial. Overall, family and twin studies support moderate-to-strong heritability across most personality constructs. Additionally, molecular genetic studies provide early support for potential associations between candidate genes and personality constructs. In particular, research appears to support an association between neuroticism and genetic variation in the promoter region of the serotonin transporter gene (i.e., 5-HTTLPR). Although mediation through personality has not been tested using candidate gene studies, many of the candidate genes found to be associated with personality constructs have also been associated with PTSD or depression.

Genetic Influences on Posttrauma Psychopathology

Although a range of mental health sequelae are common following trauma exposure, we focus here on PTSD and depression, as these are among the most investigated posttrauma disorders in children and adolescents (Kilpatrick et al., 2000, 2003). Since only a minority of individuals exposed to trauma evidence posttraumatic symptomatology (Kessler, 2000; Kilpatrick et al., 2003; Resnick, Kilpatrick, Dansky, Saunders, & Best, 1993), research that explains variability in response to trauma is critical to our understanding of posttraumatic adjustment.

Family Studies. Children of Holocaust survivors with PTSD were found to have a higher risk of PTSD following trauma compared to children of Holocaust survivors without PTSD (Yehuda, Halligan, & Grossman, 2001). Data also support familial aggregation for depression (Weissman, Warner, Wickramaratne, Moreau, & Olfson, 1987). Family studies such as these, however, have a limited ability to model the complex interplay of genes and environment (e.g., rGE). Accordingly, data from family studies can at best only broadly implicate the influence of genes.

Twin Studies. Twin studies have demonstrated strong genetic influences on PTSD symptoms (Stein et al., 2002; True et al., 1993; True & Lyons, 1999) and depression symptoms (heritability ranging from 31%–50%; Kendler, 1993, 2001; McGuffin, Katz, & Rutherford, 1991; McGuffin, Katz, Watkins, & Rutherford, 1996; Sullivan, Neale, & Kendler, 2000). Also notably, heritability for depression appears to increase over the course of adolescence (Lau & Eley, 2006). Studies have pointed to a key role for gene and stressful environment interactions (G×E) in the etiology of depression. Genetic factors were more strongly predictive of depression when family conflict levels were high (Rice, Harold, Shelton, & Thapar, 2006), and negative life events predicted adolescent female depression only when there was a history of parental emotional disorders (Silberg, Rutter, Neale, & Eaves, 2001). Adolescent twin and sibling research found genetic effects on both negative life events and maternal putative discipline that contributed to depression (i.e., rGE), with genetic risks found to vary across levels of negative life events and putative parenting (i.e., G×E; Lau & Ely, 2008). These findings continue to highlight the importance of family context in trauma-exposed youth.

Molecular Genetics. Many of the molecular genetic studies of posttrauma psychopathology have focused on the dopamine (DA) and serotonin (5-HT) systems, and most of these studies have been conducted using adult populations. A handful of adult studies have found an association between the D2 DA receptor gene (*DRD2*) and PTSD diagnosis (Comings et al., 1991; Comings, Muhleman, & Gysin, 1996; Voisey et al., 2009; Young et al., 2002), with one failure to replicate (Gelernter, Southwick, Goodson, Nagy, & Charney, 1999). A recent study in preschool children exposed to Hurricane Katrina also found a relation between PTSD symptoms, primarily the arousal symptoms, and the *DAT* polymorphism (Drury, Theall, Keats, & Scheeringa, 2009). Associations have also been found between PTSD diagnosis and the 5-HTTLPR polymorphism (Grabe et al., 2009; Kilpatrick et al., 2007; Lee et al., 2005), but this effect was potentiated by environmental influences such as the level of social support (Kilpatrick et al., 2007; Xie et al., 2009) and number of traumatic event exposures (Grabe et al., 2009). Similarly, there are many other molecular genetic studies of depression among maltreated children that suggest more sophisticated G×E interactions; these are described in the next section.

Gene by Environment (G×E) Interactions. Another molecular genetics methodology examines interactions between genetic and environmental influences in phenotype expression (Moffitt, Caspi, & Rutter, 2005), which is highly fitting for trauma research. Recent G×E molecular genetic studies of adults demonstrated that the 5-HTTLPR (Kilpatrick et al., 2007; Koenen et al., 2009; Xie et al., 2009) and a variant in the regulator of G protein signaling 2 gene (*RGS2*; Amstadter, Koenen, et al., 2009) interact with established environmental risk factors (e.g., number of prior trauma exposures, severity of trauma exposure, social support; Ozer, Best, Lipsey, & Weiss, 2003) to increase risk for depression and PTSD onset (Amstadter, Koenen, et al., 2009; Koenen et al., 2008). These data suggest that whether environmental factors increase risk for PTSD onset following trauma may partly depend on genetic influences. It will be a necessary next step to determine whether these effects generalize to child and adolescent samples.

An early demonstration of G×E involving the 5-HTTLPR polymorphism and stressful life events in the prediction of depression (Caspi et al., 2003) sparked numerous replication attempts. However, one large meta-analysis found a null overall effect size for the interaction (Risch et al., 2009), whereas another comprehensive qualitative review suggested a significant overall effect (Uher & McGuffin, 2010). Although many of the studies have been conducted with adult samples, the most often used "E" variable is retrospectively reported childhood adversary or maltreatment (e.g., Aguilera et al., 2009; Åslund et al., 2009), underscoring the need for careful study of this area in youth. There have been a small number of youth studies that have replicated the GxE interaction between stressful life events, the 5-HTTLPR, and depression in young adults (e.g., Eley et al., 2004; Veletza et al., 2009). Clearly, more research is needed to firmly establish the methodological characteristics moderating this effect. Other "E" variables have also been examined. Kaufman and colleagues (2004) found that risk of depression among maltreated children was greatest in children with low social support and at least one copy of the short allele of the 5-HTTLPR, demonstrating the importance of both social support and genotype. A later study found that a variant in the brain-derived neurotrophic factor gene (*BDNF*) further moderated these results, demonstrating a G×G×E interaction to increase risk of depression among maltreated children (Kaufman et al., 2006). Other research has suggested that polymorphisms of the monoamine oxidase A (MOA) gene moderate the impact of childhood abuse on depression, and this effect may be particularly pronounced among males (Kim-Cohen et al., 2006).

Summary

Traumatic event exposure increases risk for PTSD and depression, and personality constructs (e.g., neuroticism, anxiety sensitivity, behavioral inhibition) may confer risk for the development of posttrauma psychopathology. As such, there are several pathways by which genes may influence posttrauma psychopathology. First, research reviewed above demonstrates that traumatic event exposure is moderately heritable. Genetic influences may therefore confer risk for posttrauma psychopathology by merely increasing the likelihood of and frequency with which one is exposed to traumatic events. However, this effect is likely mediated by personality constructs (e.g., risk-taking behavior), and molecular genetic studies are still needed to clarify which specific genes confer vulnerability towards traumatic event exposure. Second, research reviewed above demonstrates that key personality constructs relevant for understanding anxiety disorders and predicting the onset of posttrauma psychopathology are also heritable. Family and twin studies demonstrate that genetic influences explain a meaningful portion of variance in these constructs, and molecular genetic studies are beginning to clarify specific genes and the neurobiological consequences that mediate expression of these phenotypes. Genetic influences may therefore confer risk for posttrauma psychopathology by mediating the expression of these personality constructs, which in turn mediate vulnerability for posttrauma psychopathology. Third, the overlapping genetic influences on the expression of neuroticism and risk of PTSD/depression following traumatic and or stressful events (i.e., the 5-HTT promoter gene) could alternatively be due to separate genetic influences on the expression of neuroticism and PTSD/depression (e.g., through altered 5-HT transmission). In this case, neuroticism and PTSD or depression would be related only because they share alterations in 5-HT transmission and not because of causal functional relationships (i.e., an epiphenomenal model). Research also demonstrates specificity in genetic influences on personality constructs and risk for PTSD and/or depression: genes affecting other neurobiological systems (e.g., DA, GABA) have been found to increase risk for PTSD but do not appear to be associated with neuroticism. Further research is needed to more carefully elucidate the complex pathways linking genes, traumatic event exposure, personality, and posttrauma psychopathology.

Conclusions

Personality constructs, particularly superordinate personality constructs such as neuroticism, are believed to represent stable constitutional differences and are therefore well suited for research with children and adolescents. Indeed, to the degree that they represent constitutional differences, personality constructs may be more proximal to genetic influences than psychopathology, reinforcing the utility of measuring personality in genetically informed research. There is evidence that traumatic event exposure is heritable, but this is likely influenced by personality characteristics, and no specific genes have been linked to traumatic event exposure. Several candidate genes have been linked with PTSD, depression, and antisocial behavior following traumatic event exposure, and these genes have also been found to interact with specific environmental characteristics (e.g., social support, degree of trauma exposure or number of traumatic life events experienced, childhood maltreatment) to increase risk of psychopathology following trauma. While clear progress has been made in elucidating genetic, personality, and environmental factors in traumatic event exposure and subsequent psychopathology onset, there are several limitations that may be addressed by future research.

Future Directions

Based on the current review of the literature, several recommendations for future research are warranted. First, longitudinal research designs among children and adolescents in which genetic samples are collected and key personality variables and environmental characteristics are assessed repeatedly over time would allow for greater insights into the relationship between genes, personality, trauma, and psychopathology. Second, perhaps the most important design consideration for future research with trauma-exposed youth involves sensitivity to the developmental stage of the youth. Developmentally tailored research questions and developmentally appropriate assessments are critical components of research with trauma-exposed youth (Salmon & Bryant, 2002; Scheeringa, 2008; Scheeringa et al., 2006). Emerging research has begun to prospectively characterize the course of neurobiologic alterations in trauma-exposed children and adolescents (Delahanty, Nugent, Christopher, & Walsh, 2005; Nugent, Christopher, & Delahanty, 2006), which is a vital area of research in need of further development. Third, developmentally sensitive research necessarily includes attention to environmental context such as family and peer relationships, which have been found to moderate the effects of trauma in youth (Green et al., 1991; Nugent, Ostrowski, Christopher, & Delahanty, 2007).

Acknowledgments

Support for this manuscript preparation was provided by MH018869-22 and DA022981-02 (JC), US-NICHD HD0558 85 (AA), and MH087240 (NN).

References

Aguilera, M., Arias, B., Wichers, M., Barrantes-Vidal, N., Moya, J., Villa, H., et al. (2009). Early adversity and 5-HTT/BDNF genes: New evidence of gene-environment interactions on depressive symptoms in a general population. *Psychological Medicine*, *39*(9), 1425–1432.

Allik, J., Laidra, K., Realo, A., & Pullmann, H. (2004). Personality development from 12 to 18 years of age: Changes in mean levels and structure of traits. *European Journal of Personality*, *18*, 445–462.

Amstadter, A. B., Koenen, K. C., Ruggiero, K. J., Acierno, R., Galea, S., Kilpatrick, D. G., et al. (2009). Variant in RGS2 moderates posttraumatic stress symptoms following potentially traumatic event exposure. *Journal of Anxiety Disorders*, *23*(3), 369–373.

Amstadter, A. B., Nugent, N. R., & Koenen, K. C. (2009). Genetics of PTSD: Fear conditioning as a model for future research. *Psychiatric Annals*, *39*(6), 358–367.

Arbelle, S., Benjamin, J., Golin, M., Kremer, I., Belmaker, R. H., & Ebstein, R. P. (2003). Relation of shyness in grade school children to the genotype for the long form of the serotonin transporter promoter region polymorphism. *American Journal of Psychiatry*, *160*, 671–676.

Åslund, C., Leppert, J., Comasco, E., Nordquist, N., Oreland, L., & Nilsson, K. (2009). Impact of the interaction between the 5HTTLPR polymorphism and maltreatment on adolescent depression: A population-based study. *Behavior Genetics*, *39*(5), 524–531.

Bagley, C., & Mallick, K. (2000). Prediction of sexual, emotional, and physical maltreatment and mental health outcomes in a longitudinal cohort of 290 adolescent women. *Child Maltreatment*, *5*(3), 218–226.

Barlow, D. H. (2002). *Anxiety and its disorders: The nature and treatment of anxiety and panic*. New York: Guilford Press.

Battaglia, M., Bajo, S., Strambi, L. F., Brambilla, F., Castronovo, C., Vanni, G., & et al. (1997). Physiological and behavioral responses to minor stressors in offspring of patients with panic disorder. *Journal of Psychiatric Research*, *31*, 365–376.

Biederman, J., Hirshfeld-Becker, D. R., Rosenbaum, J. F., Herot, C., Friedman, D., Snidman N., et al. (2001). Further evidence of association between behavioral inhibition and social anxiety in children. *American Journal of Psychiatry*, *158*, 1673–1679.

Buss, A. H., & Plomin, R. (1975). *A temperament theory of personality development*. Oxford, England: Wiley-Interscience.

Canli, T. (2008). Toward a neurogenetic theory of neuroticism. *Annals of the New York Academy of Sciences*, *1129*, 153–174.

Caspi, A., Sugden, K., Moffitt, T. E., Taylor, A., Craig, I., Harrington, H., et al. (2003). Influence of life stress on depression: Moderation by a polymorphism in the 5- HTT gene. *Science*, *301*, 386–389.

Clark, L. A. (2005). Temperament as a unifying basis for personality and psychopathology. *Journal of Abnormal Psychology*, *114*(4), 505–521.

Cohen, J. A., & Scheeringa, M. S. (2009). Post-traumatic stress disorder diagnosis in children: Challenges and promises. *Dialogues in Clinical Neuroscience*, *11*(1), 91–99.

Comings, D. E., Comings, B. G., Muhleman, D., Dietz, G., Shabbahrami, B., & Tast, D. (1991). The dopamine D2 receptor locus as a modifying gene in neuropsychiatric disorder. *Journal of the American Medical Association*, *266*(13), 1793–1800.

Comings, D. E., Muhleman, D., & Gysin, R. (1996). Dopamine D2 receptor (DRD2) gene and susceptibility to posttraumatic stress disorder: A study and replication. *Biological Psychiatry*, *40*(5), 368–372.

Copeland, W. E., Keeler, G., Angold, A., & Costello, E. J. (2007). Traumatic events and posttraumatic stress in childhood. *Archives of General Psychiatry*, *64*(5), 577–584.

Dekovic, M., Koning, I. M., Jan Stams, G., & Buist, K. L. (2008). Factors associated with traumatic symptoms and internalizing problems among adolescents who experienced a traumatic event. *Anxiety, Stress & Coping: An International Journal*, *21*(4), 377–386.

Delahanty, D. L., & Nugent, N. R. (2006). Predicting PTSD prospectively based on prior trauma history, trauma severity, and immediate biologic responses. *Annals of the New York Academy of Sciences*, *1071*, 27–40.

Delahanty, D. L., Nugent, N. R., Christopher, N. C., & Walsh, M. (2005). Initial urinary epinephrine and cortisol levels predict acute PTSD symptoms in child trauma victims. *Journal of Psychoneuroendocrinology*, *30*(2), 121–128.

DiLalla, L., Kagan, J., & Reznick, J. (1994). Genetic etiology of behavioral inhibition among 2-year-old children. *Infant Behavior Development*, *17*, 405–412.

Drury, S. S., Theall, K. P., Keats, B. J. B., & Scheeringa, M. (2009). The role of the dopamine transporter (DAT) in the development of PTSD in preschool children. *Journal of Traumatic Stress*, *22*(6), 534–539.

Eley, T. C., Bolton, D., O'Connor, T.G., Perrin, S., Smith, P., & Plomin, R. (2003). A twin study of anxiety-related behaviors in preschool children. *Journal of Child Psychology and Psychiatry*, *44*, 945–960.

Eley, T. C., Sugden, K., Corsico, A., Gregory, A. M., Sham, P., McGuffin, P., et al. (2004). Gene-environment interaction analysis of serotonin system markers with adolescent depression. *Molecular Psychiatry*, *9*(10), 908–915.

Emde, R., Plomin, R., Robinson, J., Corley, R., DeFries, J. C., Fulker, D., et al. (1992). Temperament, emotion, and cognition at fourteen months: The MacArthur Longitudinal Twin Study. *Child Development*, *63*, 1437–1455.

Eysenck, H. (1981). *A model for personality*. Berlin: Springer-Verlag.

Fairbank, J., & Fairbank, D. (2009). Epidemiology of child traumatic stress. *Current Psychiatry Reports*, *11*(4), 289–295.

Fergusson, D. M., Horwood, L. J., & Lynskey, M. T. (1996). Childhood sexual abuse and psychiatric disorder in young adulthood: II. Psychiatric outcomes of childhood sexual abuse. *Journal of the American Academy of Child and Adolescent Psychiatry*, *35*(10), 1365–1374.

Gelernter, J., Southwick, S., Goodson, S., Morgan, A., Nagy, L., & Charney, D. S. (1999). No association between D2 dopamine receptor (DRD2) 'A' system alleles, or DRD2 haplotypes, and posttraumatic stress disorder. *Biological Psychiatry*, *45*(5), 620–625.

Gerra, G., Angioni, L., Zaimovic, A., Moi, G., Bussandri, M., Bertacca, S., et al. (2004). Substance use among high-school students: Relationships with temperament, personality traits, and parental care perception. *Substance Use & Misuse*, *39*(2), 345–367.

Goldberg, L. R. (1993). The structure of phenotypic personality traits. *American Psychologist*, *48*, 26–34.

Goldsmith, H., Buss, A., Plomin, R., Rothbart, M., Thomas, A., Chess, S., et al. (1987). Roundtable: What is temperament? Four approaches. *Child Development*, *58*, 505–529.

Goldsmith, H., & Lemery, K. (2000). Linking temperamental anxiety symptoms: A behavior-genetic perspective. *Biological Psychiatry*, *48*, 1199–1209.

Goldsmith, H. H., & Rothbart, M. K. (1991). Contemporary instruments for assessing early temperament by questionnaire and in the laboratory. In J. Strelau & A. Angleitner (Eds.), *Explorations in temperament: International perspectives on theory and measurement* (pp. 249–272). New York: Plenum.

Grabe, H. J., Spitzer, C., Schwahn, C., Marcinek, A., Frahnow, A., Barnow, S., et al. (2009). Serotonin transporter gene (SLC6A4) promoter polymorphisms and the susceptibility to posttraumatic stress disorder in the general population. *American Journal of Psychiatry*, *166*, 926–933.

Gray, J. A. (1982). *The neuropsychology of anxiety*. New York: McGraw-Hill.

Green, B. L., Korol, M., Grace, M. C., Vary, M. G., Leonard, A. C., Gleser, G. C., et al. (1991). Children and disaster: Age, gender, and parental effects on PTSD symptoms. *Journal of the American Academy of Child and Adolescent Psychiatry*, *30*, 945–951.

Gunnar, M., Wewerka, S., Frenn, K., Long, J. D., & Griggs, C. (2009). Developmental changes in hypothalamus-pituitary-adrenal activity over the transition to adolescence: Normative changes and associations with puberty. *Development and Psychopathology*, *21*, 69–85.

Harro, J., Merenakk, L., Nordquist, N., Konstabel, K., Comasco, E., & Oreland, L. (2009). Personality and the serotonin transporter gene: Associations in a longitudinal population-based study. *Biological Psychiatry*, *81*, 9–13.

Heath, A. C., Neale, M. C., Kessler, R. C., Eaves, L. J., & Kendler, K. S. (1992). Evidence for genetic influences on personality from self-reports and informant ratings. *Journal of Personality and Social Psychology*, *63*, 85–96.

Hensley, L., & Varela, R. E. (2008). PTSD symptoms and somatic complaints following Hurricane Katrina: The roles of trait anxiety and anxiety sensitivity. *Journal of Clinical Child & Adolescent Psychology*, *37*(3), 542–552.

Hettema, J. M., Neale, M. C., Myers, J. M., Prescott, C. A., & Kendler, K. S. (2006). A population-based twin study of the relationship between neuroticism and internalizing disorders. *American Journal of Psychiatry*, *163*(5), 857–864.

Hettema, J. M., Prescott, C. A., & Kendler, K. S. (2004). Genetic and environmental sources of covariation between generalized anxiety disorder and neuroticism. *American Journal of Psychiatry*, *161*, 1581–1587.

Jang, K. L., McCrae, R. R., Angleitner, A., Riemann, R., & Livesley, W. J. (1998). Heritability of facet-level traits in a cross-cultural twin sample: Support for a hierarchical model of personality. *Journal of Personality and Social Psychology*, *74*(6), 1556–1565.

Jang, K., Stein, M. B., Taylor, S., Asmundson, G. J. G., & Livesley, W. J. (2003). Exposure to traumatic events and experiences: Aetiological relationships with personality function. *Psychiatry Research*, *120*, 61–69.

Jardine, R., Martin, N. G., & Henderson, A. S. (1984). Genetic covariation between neuroticism and the symptoms of anxiety and depression. *Genetic Epidemiology*, *1*(2), 89–107.

Jorm, A., Prior, M., Sanson, A., Smart, D., Zhang, Y., & Easteal, S. (2000). Association of a functional polymorphism of the serotonin transporter gene with anxiety-related temperament and behavior problems in children: A longitudinal study from infancy to the mid-teens. *Molecular Psychiatry*, *5*, 542–547.

Kagan, J., Reznick, J., & Gibbons, J. (1989). Inhibited and uninhibited types of children. *Child Development*, *60*, 838–845.

Kaufman, J., Yang, B., Douglas-Palumberi, H., Grasso, D., Lipschitz, D., Houshyar, S., et al. (2006). Brain-derived neurotrophic factor-5-HTTLPR gene interactions and environmental modifiers of depression in children. *Biological Psychiatry*, *59*, 673–680.

Kaufman, J., Yang, B., Douglas-Palumberi, H., Houshyar, S., Lipschitz, D., Krystal, J. H., et al. (2004). Social supports and serotonin transporter gene moderate depression in maltreated children. *Proceedings of the National Academy of Sciences*, *101*, 17316–17321.

Kendler, K. S. (1993). Twin studies of psychiatric illness: Current status and future directions. *Archives of General Psychiatry*, *50*(11), 905–915.

Kendler, K. S. (2001). Twin studies of psychiatric illness. *Archives of General Psychiatry*, *58*, 1005–1014.

Kendler, K. S., & Baker, J. S. (2007). Genetic influences on measures of the environment: A systematic review. *Psychological Medicine*, *37*(5), 615–626.

Kendler, K. S., Czajkowski, N., Tambs, K., Torgersen, S., Aggen, S. H., Neale, M. C., et al. (2006). Dimensional representations of DSM-IV cluster A personality disorders in a population-based sample of Norwegian twins: A multivariate study. *Psychological Medicine*, *36*(11), 1583–1591.

Kendler, K. S., & Eaves, L. J. (1986). Models for the joint effects of genotype and environment on liability to psychiatric illness. *American Journal of Psychiatry*, *143*(33), 279–289.

Kendler, K. S., Gardner, C. O., & Prescott, C. A. (2003). Personality and the experience of environmental adversity. *Psychological Medicine*, *33*(7), 1193–1202.

Kessler, R. C. (2000). Posttraumatic stress disorder: The burden to the individual and to society. *Journal of Clinical Psychiatry*, *61*, 4–14.

Kilic, E. Z., Kilic, C., & Yilmaz, S. (2008). Is anxiety sensitivity a predictor of PTSD in children and adolescents? *Journal of Psychosomatic Research*, *65*, 81–86.

Kilpatrick, D. G., Acierno, R., Schnurr, P. P., Saunders, B., Resnick, H. S., & Best, C. L. (2000). Risk factors for adolescent substance abuse and dependence: Data from a national sample. *Journal of Consulting and Clinical Psychology*, *68*, 19–30.

Kilpatrick, D. G., Koenen, K. C., Ruggiero, K. J., Acierno, R., Galea, S., Resnick, H. S., et al. (2007). The serotonin transporter genotype and social support and moderation of posttraumatic stress disorder and depression in hurricane-exposed adults. *American Journal of Psychiatry*, *164*(11), 1693–1699.

Kilpatrick, D. G., Ruggiero, K. J., Acierno, R., Saunders, B. E., Resnick, H. S., & Best, C. L. (2003). Violence and risk of PTSD, major depression, substance abuse/dependence, and comorbidity: Results from the National Survey of Adolescents. *Journal of Consulting and Clinical Psychology*, *71*(4), 692–700.

Kim-Cohen, J., Caspi, A., Taylor, A., Williams, B., Newcombe, R., & Craig, I. W. (2006). MAOA, maltreatment, and gene-environment interaction predicting children's mental health: New evidence and a meta-analysis. *Molecular Psychiatry*, *11*, 903–913.

Kirk, K., Birley, A., Statham, D., Haddon, B., Lake, R., Andrews, J., et al. (2000). Anxiety and depression in twin and sib pairs extremely discordant and concordant for neuroticism: Prodromus to a linkage study. *Twin Research and Human Genetics*, *3*, 299–309.

Koenen, K. C., Aiello, A., Bakshis, E., Amstadter, A. B., Ruggiero, K. J., Acierno, R., et al. (2009). Modification of the association between serotonin transporter genotype and risk of posttraumatic stress disorder in adults by county-level social environment. *American Journal of Epidemiology*, *169*(6), 704–711.

Koenen, K. C., Moffitt, T. E., Poulton, R., Martin, J., & Caspi, A. (2007). Early childhood factors associated with posttraumatic stress disorder: Results from a longitudinal birth cohort. *Psychological Medicine*, 37, 181–192.

Koenen, K. C., Nugent, N. R., & Amstadter, A. B. (2008). Posttraumatic stress disorder: A review and agenda for gene-environment interaction research in trauma. *European Archives of Psychiatry and Clinical Neuroscience*, *258*(2), 82–96.

Lake, R. I. E., Eaves, L. J., Maes, H. H. M., Heath, A. C., & Martin, N. G. (2000). Further evidence against the environmental transmission of individual differences in neuroticism from a collaborative study of 45,850 twins and relatives on two continents. *Behavior Genetics*, *30*, 223–233.

Lau, J. Y. F., & Eley, T. C. (2006). Changes in genetic and environmental influences on depressive symptoms across adolescence and young adulthood. *The British Journal of Psychiatry*, *189*(5), 422–427.

Lau, J. Y. F., & Eley, T. C. (2008). Disentangling gene-environment correlations and interactions on adolescent depressive symptoms. *Journal of Child Psychology and Psychiatry*, *49*(2), 142–150.

Lee, H. J., Lee, M. S., Kang, R. H., Kim, H., Kim, S. D., Kee, B. S., et al. (2005). Influence of the serotonin transporter promoter gene polymorphism on susceptibility to posttraumatic stress disorder. *Depression and Anxiety*, *21*(3), 135–139.

Legrand, L. N., McGue, M., & Iacono, W. G. (1999). A twin study of state and trait anxiety in childhood and adolescence. *Journal of Child Psychology and Psychiatry*, *40*(6), 953–958.

Lemery, K. S., Goldsmith, H. H., Klinnert, M. D., & Mrazek, D. A. (1999). Developmental models of infant and childhood temperament. *Developmental Psychology*, *35*(1), 189–204.

Lesch, K. P., Bengel, D., Heils, A., Sabol, S. Z., Greenberg, B. D., Petri, S., et al. (1996). Association of anxiety-related traits with a polymorphism in the serotonin transporter gene regulatory region. *Science*, *274*(5292), 1527–1531.

Loehlin, J. C. (1992). *Genes and environment in personality development*. Newbury Park, CA: Sage.

Lyons, M. J., Goldberg, J., Eisen, S. A., True, W., Tsuang, M. T., & Meyer, J. M. (1993). Do genes influence exposure to trauma? A twin study of combat. *American Journal of Medical Genetics*, *48*(1), 22–27.

Magnus, K., Diener, E., Frjita, F., & Pavot, W. (1993). Extraversion and neuroticism as predictors of objective life events: A longitudinal analysis. *Journal of Personality and Social Psychology*, *65*(5), 1046–1053.

Mannasis, K., Bradley, S., Goldberg, S., Hood, J., & Swinson, R. (1995). Behavioural inhibition, attachment and anxiety in children of mothers with anxiety disorders. *Canadian Journal of Psychiatry*, *40*, 87–92.

McCrae, R. R., Costa, P. T., Ostendorf, F., Angleitner, A., Hrebickova, M., Avia, M. D., et al. (2000). Nature over nurture: Temperament, personality, and life span development. *Journal of Personality and Social Psychology*, *78*, 173–186.

McGuffin, P., Katz, R., & Rutherford, J. (1991). Nature, nurture and depression: A twin study. *Psychological Medicine*, *21*, 329–335.

McGuffin, P., Katz, R., Watkins, S., & Rutherford, J. (1996). Hospital-based twin registery study of the heritability of DSM-IV unipolar depression. *Archives of General Psychiatry*, *53*, 129–136.

Middeldorp, C. M., de Geus, E. J., Beem, A. L., Lakenberg, N., Hottenga, J. J., Slagboom, P. E., et al. (2007). Family-based association analyses between the serotonin transporter gene polymorphism (5-HTTLPR) and neuroticism, anxiety, and depression. *Behavior Genetics*, *37*, 294–301.

Moffitt, T. E., Caspi, A., & Rutter, M. (2005). Strategy for investigating interactions between measured genes and measured environments. *Archives of General Psychiatry*, *62*(5), 473–481.

Munafo, M. R., Freimer, N. B., Ng, W., Ophoff, R., Veijola, J., Miettunen, J., et al. (2009). 5-HTTLPR genotype and anxiety-related personality traits: A meta-analysis and new data. *American Journal of Medical Genetics, Part B Neuropsychiatric Genetics*, *150*, 271–281.

Nader, K. (2008). The nature of the child. In K. Nader (Ed.), *Understanding and assessing trauma in children and adolescents: Measures, methods, and youth in context* (pp. 139–168). New York: Routledge.

Nugent, N. R., Christopher, N. C., & Delahanty, D. L. (2006). Initial physiological responses and perceived hyperarousal predicts subsequent emotional numbing in child trauma victims. *Journal of Traumatic Stress*, *19*, 349–359.

Nugent, N. R., Ostrowski, S., Christopher, N. C., & Delahanty, D. L. (2007). Parental symptoms of PTSD as a moderator of child's acute biological response and subsequent symptoms of PTSD in pediatric trauma patients. *Journal of Pediatric Psychology*, *32*, 309–318.

Olff, M., Langeland, W., Draijer, N., & Gersons, B. P. R. (2007). Gender differences in posttraumatic stress disorder. *Psychological Bulletin*, *133*(2), 183–204.

Ozer, E. J., Best, S. R., Lipsey, T. L., & Weiss, D. S. (2003). Predictors of posttraumatic stress disorder and symptoms in adults: A meta-analysis. *Psychological Bulletin*, *129*, 52–73.

Parslow, R. A., Jorm, A. F., & Christensen, H. (2006). Associations of pre-trauma attributes and trauma exposure with screening positive for PTSD: Analysis of a community-based study of 2085 young adults. *Psychological Medicine*, *36*, 387–395.

Plomin, R., Emde, R., Bruaungart, J., Campos, J., Corley, R., Fulker, D., et al. (1993). Genetic change and continuity from fourteen to twenty months: The MacArthur Longitudinal Twin Study. *Child Development*, *64*, 1354–1376.

Plomin, R., DeFries, J. C., & Loehlin, J. C. (1977). Genotype-environment interaction and correlation in the analysis of human behavior. *Psychological Bulletin*, *84*, 309–322.

Resnick, H. S., Kilpatrick, D. G., Dansky, B. S., Saunders, B. E., & Best, C., L. (1993). Prevalence of civilian trauma and posttraumatic stress disorder in a representative national sample of women. *Journal of Consulting and Clinical Psychology*, *61*, 984–991.

Rice, F., Harold, G. T., Shelton, K. H., & Thapar, A. (2006). Family conflict interacts with genetic liability in predicting childhood and adolescent depression. *Journal of the American Academy of Child & Adolescent Psychiatry*, *45*(7), 841–848.

Rice, F., Harold, G. T., & Thapar, A. (2003). Negative life events as an account of age-related differences in the genetic etiology of depression in childhood and adolescence. *Journal of Child Psychology and Psychiatry and Allied Disciplines*, *44*, 977–987.

Risch, N., Herrell, R., Lehner, T., Liang, K. Y., Eaves, L., Hoh, J., et al. (2009). Interaction between the serotonin transporter gene (5-HTTLPR), stressful life events, and risk of depression: A meta-analysis. *Journal of the American Medical Association*, *301*, 2462–2471.

Robinson, J. L., Kagan, J., Reznick, J. S., & Corley, R. (1992). The heritability of inhibited and uninhibited behavior: A twin study. *Developmental Psychology*, *28*(6), 1030–1037.

Rosenbaum, J. F., Biederman, J., Hirshfeld-Becker, D. R., Kagan, J., Snidman, N., Friedman, D., et al. (2000). A controlled study of behavioral inhibition in children of parents with panic disorder and depression. *American Journal of Psychiatry*, *157*(12), 2002–2010.

Salmon, K., & Bryant, R. A. (2002). Posttraumatic stress disorder in children: The influence of developmental factors. *Clinical Psychology Review*, *22*, 163–188.

Saudino, K. J., Pedersen, N. L., Lichtenstein, P., McClearn, G. E., & Plomin, R. (1997). Can personality explain genetic influences on life events? *Journal of Personality and Social Psychology*, *72*(1), 196–206.

Scheeringa, M. S. (2008). Developmental considerations for diagnosing PTSD and acute stress disorder in preschool and school-age children. *American Journal of Psychiatry*, *165*(10), 1237–1239.

Scheeringa, M. S., Wright, M. J., Hunt, J. P., & Zeanah, C. H. (2006). Factors affecting the diagnosis and prediction of PTSD symptomatology in children and adolescents. *American Journal of Psychiatry*, *163*, 644–651.

Schinka, J. A., Busch, R. M., & Robichaux-Keene, N. (2004). A meta-analysis of the association between the serotonin transporter gene polymorphism (5-HTTLPR) and trait anxiety. *Molecular Psychiatry*, *9*, 197–202.

Schwab-Stone, M., Chen, C. S., Greenberger, E., Silver, D., Lichtman, J., & Voyce, C. (1999). No safe haven: II. The effects of violence exposure on urban youth. *Journal of the American Academy of Child and Adolescent Psychiatry*, *38*, 359–367.

Schwartz, C. E., Snidman, N., & Kagan, J. (1999). Adolescent social anxiety as an outcome of inhibited temperament in childhood. *Journal of the American Academy of Child and Adolescent Psychiatry*, *38*(8), 1008–1015.

Silberg, J., Pickles, A., Rutter, M., Hewitt, J., Simonoff, E., Maes, H., et al. (1999). The influence of genetic factors and life stress on depression among adolescent girls. *Archives of General Psychiatry*, *56*, 225–232.

Silberg, J., Rutter, M., Neale, M., & Eaves, L. (2001). Genetic moderation of environmental risk for depression and anxiety in adolescent girls. *British Journal of Psychiatry*, *179*, 116–121.

South, S. C., Kruger, R. F., Johnson, W., & Iacono, W. G. (2008). Adolescent personality moderates genetic and environmental influences on relationships with parents. *Journal of Personality and Social Psychology*, *94*(5), 899–912.

Stein, M. B., Jang, K. L., & Livesley, W. J. (1999). Heritability of anxiety sensitivity: A twin study. *American Journal of Psychiatry*, *156*(2), 246–251.

Stein, M. B., Jang, K. L., Taylor, S., Vernon, P. A., & Livesley, W. J. (2002). Genetic and environmental influences on trauma exposure and posttraumatic stress disorder: A twin study. *American Journal of Psychiatry*, *159*(10), 1675–1681.

Sullivan, P. F., Neale, M. C., & Kendler, K. S. (2000). Genetic epidemiology of major depression: Review and meta-analysis. *American Journal of Psychiatry*, *157*, 1552–1562.

Tambs, K., & Mourn, T. (1993). Low genetic effect and age-specific family effect for symptoms of anxiety and depression in nuclear families, half sibs and twins. *Journal of Affect Disorders*, *27*(3), 183–195.

Thomas, A., & Chess, S. (1977). *Temperament and development*. New York: Brunner-Mazel.

Topolski, T. D., Hewitt, J. K., Eaves, L. J., Silberg, J. L., Meyer, J. M., Rutter, M., et al. (1997). Genetic and environmental influences on child reports of manifest anxiety and symptoms of separation anxiety and overanxious disorders: A community-based twin study. *Behavior Genetics*, *27*(1), 15–28.

True, W. R., & Lyons, M. J. (1999). Genetic risk factors for PTSD: A twin study. In R. Yehuda (Ed.), *Risk factors for posttraumatic stress disorder* (pp. 61–78). Washington, DC: American Psychiatric Association.

True, W. R., Rice, J., Eisen, S. A., Heath, A. C., Goldberg, J., Lyons, M. J., et al. (1993). A twin study of genetic and environmental contributions to liability for posttraumatic stress symptoms. *Archives of General Psychiatry*, *50*(4), 257–264.

Turner, S., Bieidel, D., & Wolff, P. (1996). Is behavioral inhibition related to the anxiety disorders? *Clinical Psychology Review*, *16*(2), 157–172.

Uher, R., & McGuffin, P. (2010). The moderation by the serotonin transporter gene of environmental adversity in the etiology of depression: 2009 update. *Molecular Psychiatry*, *15*, 18–22.

van Beek, N., & Griez, E. (2003). Anxiety sensitivity in first-degree relatives of patients with panic disorder. *Behavior Research and Therapy*, *41*, 949–957.

Van Os, J., & Jones, P. B. (1999). Early risk factors and adult person-environment relationships in affective disorder. *Psychological Medicine*, *29*, 1055–1067.

Veletza, S., Samakouri, M., Emmanouil, G., Trypsianis, G., Kourmouli, N., & Livaditis, M. (2009). Psychological vulnerability differences in students—Carriers or not of the serotonin transporter promoter allele S: Effect of adverse experiences. *Synapse*, *63*(3), 193–200.

Voisey, J., Swagell, C. D., Hughes, I. P., Morris, P., van Daal, A., Nobel, E. P., et al. (2009). The DRD2 gene 957C>T polymorphism is associated with posttraumatic stress disorder in war veterans. *Depression and Anxiety*, *26*(1), 28–33.

Weems, C. F., Pina, A. A., Costa, N. M., Watts, S. E., Taylor, L. K., & Cannon, M. F. (2007). Predisaster trait anxiety and negative affect predict posttraumatic stress in youths after Hurricane Katrina. *Journal of Consulting and Clinical Psychology*, *75*(1), 154–159.

Weems, C., & Stickle, T. R. (2005). Anxiety disorders in childhood: Casting a nomological net. *Clinical Child & Family Psychology Review*, *8*(2), 107–134.

Weissman, M. M., Warner, V., Wickramaratne, P., Moreau, D., & Olfson, M. (1987). Offspring of depressed parents: 10 years later. *Archives of General Psychiatry*, *54*, 932–940.

Xie, P., Kranzler, H. R., Poling, J., Stein, M. B., Anton, R. F., Brady, K., et al. (2009). Interactive effect of stressful life events and the serotonin transporter 5-HTTLPR genotype on posttraumatic stress disorder diagnosis in 2 independent populations. *Archives of General Psychiatry*, *66*, 1201–1209.

Yehuda, R., Halligan, S. L., & Grossman, R. (2001). Childhood trauma and risk for PTSD: Relationship to intergenerational effects of trauma, parental PTSD and cortisol excretion. *Development & Psychopathology*, *13*(3), 733–753.

Young, B. R., Lawford, B. R., Noble, E. P., Kanin, B., Wilkie, A., Ritchie, T., et al. (2002). Harmful drinking in military veterans with posttraumatic stress disorder: Association with the D2 dopamine receptor A1 allele. *Alcohol & Alcoholism*, *37*(5), 451–456.

Child Exposure and Response Variables

Understanding and Assessing Cortisol Levels in Children and Adolescents

KATHLEEN NADER[1] AND CARL F. WEEMS[2]

[1]Two Suns
[2]University of New Orleans

Trauma is associated with alterations in cortisol activity and reactivity that may vary in relationship to development, time, predisposition, personality, the nature of a traumatic event, and other circumstances. This article reviews existing research findings related to cortisol in laboratory, general stress, and traumatic conditions. We discuss variables that may influence cortisol activity and reactivity in an effort to discover what is known and what still needs to be learned about cortisol levels in youth exposed to traumas. The extant literature points to a number of potentially negative physical, emotional, and behavioral outcomes of altered cortisol reactivity, which suggests a clear need for early and effective interventions. Furthermore, research has often provided mixed findings from relatively small samples of youth. Improving the understanding of cortisol activity and reactivity in children and adolescents will necessitate examining large samples of different developmental age groups across time.

Trauma's effects on cortisol activity and reactivity are important in understanding children's acute and long-term reactions to trauma. Fear and stress reactions are associated with elevations in the secretion of cortisol, a stress hormone (Weems & Carrion, 2009). Physiological reactions to threat are coordinated by the sympathetic nervous system's rapid response and by the slower, longer response of the hypothalamus, pituitary gland, and outer cortex of the adrenal glands (McBurnett, King, & Scarpa, 2003; Nader, 2008; Sapolsky, 1998). Cortisol's role is part of the hypothalamic-pituitary-adrenal (HPA) axis activation in response to threat. HPA axis activation leads to secretion of various hormones by the brain's anterior pituitary (adrenocorticotropic hormone), adrenal medulla (cortisol), and other endocrine organs. Cortisol converts fats to glucose, inhibits the immune response, suppresses inflammation and assists the body in returning to a calm state after threat, as part of a negative feedback loop in the HPA axis (Lipschitz, Morgan, & Southwick, 2002; Stein & Kendall, 2004). Brain regions and neurochemicals act in concert. Serotonin, for example, appears to inhibit or regulate activation of the HPA system (Sapolsky, 1998). Insufficient serotonin may result in the overactivation of the HPA system and the release of increased cortisol. Like a thermostat, the HPA axis acts to release cortisol until levels rise and then shuts off until circulating levels fall off. Prolonged activation may lead to sensitization or desensitization. That is, disturbances in reactivity may be upward or downward (i.e., *hypercortisolism* or *hypocortisolism*; McCleery & Harvey, 2004).

Trauma is linked to altered cortisol reactivity, and altered cortisol reactivity is associated with physical, emotional, and behavioral disturbances. Chronic HPA hypo- or hyperactivity may be harmful (Sapolsky, 1998; Weems & Carrion, 2009). For example, chronic cortisol activation may alter brain structure and function in permanent ways (Cicchetti, 2003; see next section). Both excessive and dampened cortisol reactivity to acute stress or neuroendocrine challenge have been associated with disease in humans (Carpenter et al., 2009). Recurrent depression and Type 2 diabetes mellitus have been associated with cortisol hyperresponsivity. Hyporesponsivity has been associated with atypical depression, chronic stress/burnout, chronic fatigue syndrome, fibromyalgia, and brain lesions in multiple sclerosis. Alterations in reactivity persist after remission of illness. Carrion, Weems, and Reiss (2007) pointed out that the putative neurotoxic effects of cortisol may depend on at least three factors: (a) the developmental stage of the related brain structure such as the frontal lobe or hippocampus (e.g., hippocampus glucocorticoid receptor density may change throughout development), (b) the level and sustainability of cortisol released, and (c) the severity and/or chronicity of the stressful events.

Research on youth who have been exposed to traumatic events and who have posttraumatic stress disorder (PTSD) symptoms have found both relatively increased and relatively decreased cortisol levels when comparing them to nontraumatized youth (Carpenter et al., 2009; Carrion, Weems, Ray, & Reiss, 2002; De Bellis, 2001; De Bellis et al., 1999; Goenjian et al., 1996; Weems & Carrion, 2007, 2009). Some findings suggest that variations in reactivity are related to the type or nature of the trauma. Others suggest variation by age, time since the trauma, emotions elicited during the stressor, or controllability of the stress (see De Bellis, 2001). Time of day (Bevans, Cerbone, & Overstreet, 2008) and the daily trajectory of cortisol secretion (Weems & Carrion, 2009) also play a role in finding relatively increased or decreased levels (see later section, Assessing Cortisol Levels).

Assessing and interpreting cortisol-related findings necessitate examining a number of relevant variables. For example, child and adolescent researchers and clinicians have recognized the importance of Gene × Environment × Development interactions (Dahl & Gunnar, 2009). Adversity (environment), including traumatic stressors, is a key element in the expression of vulnerability factors. Ultimately, in order to fully understand the nature of posttrauma cortisol activity and the variables that influence it, research is needed that utilizes large samples of youth across diverse developmental periods and follows these participants long into adulthood. Moreover, examining the variables that influence normal children's cortisol levels under laboratory or normal conditions of distress may also assist in clarifying posttrauma activity and reactivity. The purpose of this article is to discover what is known and still needs to be learned about cortisol levels in children and adolescents exposed to trauma. We review existing research findings related to cortisol in laboratory settings and in relation to general stressful conditions as well as in response to traumatic stress. We also identify variables that may influence cortisol activity and reactivity in response to trauma in youth.

Age, Cortisol, and Stress

Developmental Differences in Cortisol Levels

Basal cortisol levels and the conditions that evoke cortisol response vary by developmental age. Findings for normal children and for stress inoculation might suggest that prolonged or ongoing separations (e.g., the death of a parent) may be traumatic for children under the age of 5, whereas intense shame and humiliation stressors may be more potent for older children and adults. For adults, Brewin, Andrews, and Rose (2000) found an association between shame, anger, and PTSD and found that shame and anger had effects on later PTSD independent from those of intense peritraumatic fear, helplessness, or horror.

For normal children, both mild laboratory stressors and normal situational stressors have been studied for their effects on cortisol levels. For normal children, the tasks used effectively to elicit cortisol elevations change across developmental age groups (see Gunnar, Talge, & Herrera, 2009, for a summary). As indicated in Table 1, being handled (up to age 3 months) and blood draws and inoculations (up to 6 months) are linked to cortisol increases in infants. In such cases, parental sensitivity serves as a moderator for cortisol levels. Studies of laboratory separations (mildly stressful situations) have found cortisol elevations for infants from 6 months to 1 year old. Stress evoked by separations from caregivers for childcare has evidenced cortisol elevations for children up to age 4.

Dickerson and Kemeny (2004) identified elements critical to evoking cortisol elevations in adults (Gunnar, Talge, & Herrera, 2009). These are unpredictability, uncontrollability (i.e., inability to control a situation or outcome), and social-evaluative threat (i.e., potential negative appraisal by others). Notably, conditions of unpredictability and uncontrollability under social evaluation amplify threat and hence increase the HPA response. Similarly, for children over the age of 4, stressor paradigms designed to evoke strong emotions are ineffective in elevating cortisol unless the task also evokes negative self-referent emotions such as shame or embarrassment. HPA axis activity occurs in response to stressors that threaten the integrity of self. From childhood to adolescence, self-processes are continually changing. As Gunnar, Talge, and Herrera pointed out, across time, a differentiated sense of self and self-referent emotions, social comparison processes, attention, and emotion-regulation develop. During adolescence, locus of security shifts from the parent-child attachment relationship to greater self-reliance and the increasing importance of peer-group relationships.

Research has suggested a natural period of hyporesponsivity in the early stages of puberty, and HPA axis activity increases with age and sexual maturation (Adam, 2006; Gunnar, Wewerka, Frenn, Long, & Griggs, 2009). Findings have demonstrated that many normally developing low-risk, periadolescent children are relatively cortisol hyporesponsive to a variety of laboratory stressor tasks (Gunnar, Frenn, Wewerka, & Ryzin, 2009). Gunnar and colleagues found that few 10- to 12-year-old children, with a range of normal to severe early life stress, showed cortisol elevations to a social stress test. Older children were more likely to be reactive to the test, and higher family income seemed to predict lower reactivity.

Although most research has suggested that cortisol increases in children ages 13 and older (Jansen et al., 2000; Klimes-Dougan, Hastings, Granger, Usher, & Zahn-Waxler, 2001; Stroud et al., 2009), gender variations have been observed. Differences in puberty onset (on average ages 10–11 for girls and 11–12 for boys; Giedd et al., 1999) may explain differences in cortisol stress-reactivity by gender. Gunnar, Wewerka, et al. (2009) reported that baseline at-home cortisol levels increased with age, from ages 9 to 15. In a Trier Social Stress Test for Children task (see Table 2), they found blunted cortisol reactivity in

Table 1
Age and cortisol activity in normal infants and toddlers

Variable	Age group	Evokes cortisol elevations
• Handling	0 to 3 months	• Handling (e.g., taken from bath or diaper change)
• Parent insensitivity	3 months olds (not 6 or 9 mo.)	• Playing with an insensitive parent for 15 minutes
• Blood draws and inoculations	0 to 6 months	• Blood draws and inoculations(less reliable stressor after 1 year; parental comfort is a moderator)
• Maternal separations	6 to 12 months	• Brief laboratory separations
	12 to 18 months	• Longer separations for insecurely attached infants
	To age 4	• Child care for securely and insecurely attached infants and toddlers
• Fear-eliciting task	2 years old	• For fearful toddlers (higher baseline cortisol levels and heart rates than extremely uninhibited)
• Child new to class	3 but not 4 years olds	• Peer social stress (e.g., unintroduced child enters new preschool class while class is working on a group project)
• Novel situations	3–5 years old	• For shy children
• Tasks to elicit negative emotions (Color matching under pressure)	4 years old	• For children who expressed high levels of anger, shame, and embarrassment
• Parent gets child to label emotion and tells of a time he or she had the emotion	5 year olds	• For children whose mother was negative toward the child during the task, if the child was rated by teacher as low in ego-resilience

Note. Sources: Ahnert et al., 2004; de Haan, Gunnar, Tout, Hart, & Stansbury, 1998; Gunnar, Talge, & Herrera, 2009; Kagan, Reznick, & Snidman, 1987; Larson et al., 1998; Lewis & Ramsay, 2002; Schmidt et al., 1997; Smeekens, Riksen-Walraven, & van Bakel, 2007; Spangler & Schieche, 1994; Stroud et al., 2009; Talge, Donzella, & Gunnar, 2008.

children age 11 and boys age 13. They found increased cortisol reactions for children ages 9, for 13-year-old girls, and for 15-years-olds of both genders. Puberty scores of 3 (on a 4-point scale) were associated with increasing basal cortisol levels. Even though the task was less threatening and less challenging for older youth, basal HPA activity and reactivity increased with age and pubertal maturation.

Stress Inoculation Versus Stress Vulnerability

The ongoing study of trauma has demonstrated that levels of stress/distress are important to the immediate and long-term outcomes of exposure. The same is true for levels of

Table 2
Age and cortisol activity in normal children and adolescents

Age group	Task/situation	Evokes increased cortisol
7–9 years old	• Trier Social Stress Test for Children (TSST-C; Buske-Kirschbaum et al., 1997)	• Public speaking
8–12 years old	• Tasks to elicit negative emotions	• Computer task with derogatory remarks from the computer (between 20 and 30 min. into the time-pressured task)
10–13 years old	• Trier Social Stress Test for Children	• Public speaking (mixed findings perhaps related to pubertal and gender differences)
	• Tasks to elicit negative emotions	• Computer task with derogatory remarks from the computer (20 to 30 min. into the time-pressured task)
13 years old and older	• Trier Social Stress Test for Children	• Public speaking tasks
	• Peer Social Stress - exclusion	• More sympathetic responses to rejection than for children (7–13), but the paradigm did not produce cortisol increases

Note. Sources: Gunnar et al., 2009; Jansen et al., 2000; Jones et al., 2006; Klimes-Dougan et al., 2001; Stroud et al., 2009; van Goozen et al., 1998, 2000; (ages 10–13 — increases: Buske-Kirschbaum et al., 1997, 2003; Gordis, Granger, Susman, & Trickett, 2006; Klimes-Dougan et al., 2001; no increase: Dorn et al., 2003; Gunnar et al., 2009; Stroud et al., 2009).

cortisol. Early cortisol exposure is associated with stress inoculation or problematic outcomes, depending on the level of stress, timing, the child's coping, parenting, and the time available for recovery. As will be shown, evidence suggests age variations in vulnerability to cortisol exposure.

Stress Inoculation

Animal studies have suggested that early life stress can result in stress vulnerability or stress resilience (Gunnar, Frenn, et al., 2009; Levine, 2005). Notably, early life stress may increase risk for the development of mood, anger, anxiety, and substance abuse disorders. In contrast, as Lyons and Parker (2007) suggested, early life stress may foster adaptations that enhance interrelated aspects of emotion regulation, cognitive control, curiosity, and diminished HPA axis activation induced by exposure to stress. The latter is more likely when the stressor is challenging enough to activate physiological and emotional coping processes, but the stress is not overwhelming (i.e., is within an infant's coping capacity). Recent animal studies have demonstrated that coping with early life stress increases prefrontal myelination and expands a region of the cortex that broadly controls arousal regulation and resilience (Katz et al., 2009). For human children, in accordance with this theory of stress inoculation is the finding that, although going to childcare activates the HPA axis (Ahnert, Gunnar, Lamb, & Barthel, 2004), in the absence of factors that may maintain fearfulness (e.g., overprotective parenting; Gunnar, Frenn, et al., 2009; Rubin, 2002), daycare also reduces fearfulness in extremely fearful children (Fox, Henderson, Rubin, Calkins, & Schmidt, 2001).

Early Cortisol Exposure

Early cortisol exposure may create vulnerability to a variety of problems. After birth, exposure to cortisol in breast milk has been shown to influence infant temperament toward behavioral inhibition (Glynn et al., 2007, as cited in Tyrka, Wier, et al., 2008). In humans and animal primates, prenatal stress has been linked to dysregulation of the HPA axis (Schneider, Moore & Kraemer, 2003). Prenatally distressed monkeys have shown decreased exploration and locomotion, increased freezing behavior, and increased adrenal hormone and cortisol reactivity to stress. Prenatal stress has been linked to increased fearfulness, irritability, sleep disturbances, aggressiveness, neuromotor difficulties, attention problems, diminished cognitive abilities, reduced interest in play, and a reduced ability to regulate stress response (Maestripieri & Wallen, 2003; Schneider et al., 2003; Stein & Kendall, 2004). In retrospective studies of humans, prenatal stress has been linked to attention-deficit/hyperactivity disorder (ADHD), severe emotional disturbances, anxiety, social withdrawal, schizophrenia, and criminality. Marked individual differences in cortisol activity among severely stressed children suggest that child factors modify the impact of severe early life stress (Gunnar, Frenn, et al., 2009). Long-lasting effects of earlier exposures to stress may become evident in adolescence (Lupien, McEwen, Gunnar, & Heim, 2009). Poor economic conditions in early life or having a depressed mother in infancy correspond to higher baseline glucocorticoid levels in adolescence (Halligan, Herbert, Goodyer, & Murray, 2007; Lupien et al., 2009).

Childhood Trauma and Adult Cortisol

For adults with trauma histories, variables such as age, traits, current stress level, and number of victimizations may influence cortisol levels. Some studies have suggested that even with genetic similarities, adults' and children's cortisol findings are the opposite (Ostrowski, Christopher, van Dulmen, & Delahanty, 2007). In a study where initial posttrauma higher cortisol levels predicted posttrauma stress symptoms in youth, mothers' low cortisol levels predicted their posttrauma stress at 7 months (high levels predicted mothers' depression at 7 months). Trauma histories are often found in incarcerated adolescents and adults (Greenwald, 2002; Nader, 2008). A study in the Netherlands (Cima, Smeets, & Jelicic, 2008) found higher levels of childhood traumas in both psychopathic and nonpsychopathic criminals than in controls. Psychopaths had the lowest diurnal cortisol concentrations, and nonpsychopaths had the highest daily average cortisol. Highest levels of aggression were related to childhood traumatic experiences in controls and nonpsychopaths, but not in psychopaths.

Although baseline cortisol levels may not differ between adults with and without childhood maltreatment, previously maltreated adults have had significantly lower cortisol concentrations in response to a stress challenge (Carpenter et al., 2007, 2009). The likelihood of multiple forms of victimization may be a factor in findings. Some of the adults studied have experienced multiple forms of maltreatment (emotional abuse, physical abuse, sexual abuse, physical neglect, and emotional neglect). Polyvictimization has been found to explain much of the variance in anxiety, depression, and aggression symptoms for youth exposed to more than one type of trauma (Finkelhor, Ormrod, & Turner, 2007, 2009).

Trauma, Cortisol, and the Brain

Emotional arousal and elevated stress hormones such as plasma cortisol enhance declarative memory (McCleery & Harvey, 2004), such that memories for highly emotional episodes contain information not found in other recall narratives (Howe, 1997; Stein,

Wade, & Liwag, 1996). On the other hand, these increased neurochemicals may adversely affect brain development and brain regions related to memory (Carrion, Weems, & Reiss, 2007). Future data may confirm differences in vulnerability at different ages and with different genetic vulnerabilities. Notably, the brain regions that are at risk may vary by age, and exposure to stress may interact with a genetic vulnerability to foster brain volume differences. Importantly, the data suggesting that cortisol may effect brain development highlights the need for early intervention with exposed youth. In the following section, research on brain regions that may be related to traumatic stress reactions in youth is reviewed.

Cortisol Exposure and Brain Volume

Hippocampus volume differences have been found in several adult studies. Compared to controls, smaller right hippocampal volumes were found in Vietnam combat veterans with PTSD (Bremner et al., 1995), smaller left hippocampal volumes were found in PTSD patients with histories of interpersonal trauma (Bremner et al., 1997), and reduced hippocampal volumes were found in Vietnam veterans (Gurvits et al., 1997) as well as adults abused as children with posttraumatic stress (Stein et al., 1997). In a monozygotic twin study (Gilbertson et al., 2002), when one twin had chronic trauma exposure (Vietnam combat) and the other did not, the unexposed co-twins of those with PTSD also had smaller hippocampi, suggesting that smaller hippocampal volume may be a preexisting familial vulnerability factor. While this twin study suggested that smaller hippocampus volumes may be a risk factor in adults, it does not rule out the possibility of shared environmental effects on hippocampus development in childhood. Research with children has suggested that hippocampus volume development may be affected by cortisol exposure and levels (Carrion et al., 2007).

With children, De Bellis, Baum, et al. (1999) found that duration of maltreatment correlated significantly with urinary free cortisol and catecholamine concentrations. Hormones such as glucocorticoids require a great deal of oxygen and energy (Sapolsky, 1998). When there is a lack of oxygen to brain regions due to such experiences as seizures, strokes, or long-term exposure to glucocorticoids, the hippocampal neurons are among the first to die. All conscious memories are processed in the hippocampus (Stein & Kendall, 2004). Decreases in hippocampal volume and explicit memory deficits have been demonstrated for Cushing's syndrome, depression, and PTSD (Bremner, 2003; Sapolsky, 2000). Hyperarousal symptoms in children with PTSD also predict the development of emotional numbing and are associated with cognitive difficulties (Saltzman, Weems, & Carrion, 2006; Weems, Saltzman, Reiss, & Carrion, 2003). Some investigators have suggested a lateralization of effects—right hippocampal atrophy predominates from adult PTSD, and left hippocampal atrophy predominates from childhood PTSD. When they controlled for pubertal maturation and gender in traumatized youth, however, Carrion et al. (2007) found that the severity of trauma (especially hyperarousal) and cortisol levels significantly predicted a reduction in right hippocampal brain volume. A reduction in cortisol has reversed atrophy in adult patients with hippocampal disorders (Byrnes, 2001; Starkman et al., 1999). Although there have been some mixed findings for trauma and hippocampal damage, it appears that the damage is related to chronic trauma or symptoms and that the plasticity of the hippocampus (its ability to recover) may blur effects if volume is measured too long after the trauma (Carrion et al., 2007).

Brain regions that regulate cognitive and emotional processes might be sensitive to glucocorticoids in an age-dependent manner (Carrion et al., 2007; Lupien et al., 2009). The frontal cortex, which continues to develop during adolescence, might be particularly vulnerable to the effects of stress during that period. Indeed, studies have shown differences in frontal lobe structure and function in youth with trauma histories and PTSD symptoms using structural and functional magnetic resonance imagery (sMRI and fMRI; see Carrion et al., 2001, 2008, 2009). Recent evidence has shown a link between elevated cortisol levels and smaller prefrontal cortex (PFC) regions in trauma-exposed youth (Carrion et al., 2010). Specifically, Carrion et al. (2010) found that youth exposed to an interpersonal traumatic stressor and having PTSD symptoms had significantly decreased total cerebral gray volumes as decreased left ventral and left inferior prefrontal gray volumes (while controlling for total gray). Moreover, a significant negative association was found between prebedtime cortisol levels and left ventral PFC gray volumes for the full sample.

In contrast, the brain's hippocampus develops mainly in the first years of life and may be less affected by adversity in adolescence than by adversity in early life (Lupien et al., 2009). Although adults with histories of childhood physical or sexual abuse have had reduced hippocampal volume (Sapolsky, 2000), adolescents exposed to early and continued adversity have shown other brain alterations. For youth ages 6.7 to 17 years with PTSD compared to matched controls, De Bellis, Keshavan, et al. (1999) showed smaller intracranial and cerebral volumes; that is, smaller cerebral and prefrontal cortex (PFC) gray matter and PFC white matter, right and left amygdala and gray matter, right and left temporal lobes, and corpus callosum Regions 4 through 7. Anderson and Teicher (2008) demonstrated changes in adolescent gray matter volume and the neuronal integrity of the frontal cortex, as well as reduced size of the anterior cingulate cortex. Adolescent twins with a history of moderate-to-severe major depression have also had reduced PFC volume compared to controls (Garber & Flynn, 2001).

Mediating and Moderating Variables and Differential Outcomes

In order to accurately assess and clearly understand the relationship of trauma and cortisol, it is essential to understand cortisol's relationship to other variables. Cortisol levels have been linked to differences in age/pubertal stage, psychopathology, personality, and attachment, among other variables. Some contrary findings have been demonstrated for most relevant variables. The complexity of the interrelationships among variables and inconsistent findings make larger samples and the testing of additional relevant variables important.

Time Since the Trauma

Some evidence suggests that within 1–2 years of a trauma, youth have had high cortisol levels (DeBellis, 2001; Ostrowski et al., 2007; Weems & Carrion, 2007). After longer duration (e.g., 5 years), youth have had lower levels of cortisol associated with posttraumatic stress (PTS; Goenjian et al., 1996; Ostrowski et al., 2007). For example, Weems and Carrion (2007) found that youth with traumas within the last year showed a positive correlation with aggregated diurnal cortisol levels, whereas those with older traumas showed a negative association. Failure to account for time since a trauma may result in faulty findings. Ostrowski et al. (2007) discovered that there were no effects when children with past traumas were included in a study of cortisol levels. When children with past traumas were excluded, initial posttrauma higher cortisol levels predicted six-week PTS symptoms for both genders and seven-month PTS for boys. In contrast, Kertes, Gunnar, Madsen, and Long (2008) found that six to seven years after adoption, it was the internationally adopted children who were more severely affected by adoption (exhibited physical growth delays) and who had higher cortisol levels, suggesting that other variables contribute to the "time since" association.

Trauma, Cortisol, and Psychopathology

A number of disorders are among the possible immediate and long-term outcomes of childhood traumas, including both internalizing and externalizing disorders. Cortisol levels are associated with psychopathology differentially (see Table 3). A number of variables (discussed earlier and to follow) are important to disorders and their associated cortisol levels. With some variations related to moderating variables (e.g., comorbidity), lower levels of cortisol are generally associated with externalizing disorders and higher levels are generally associated with internalizing disorders. Research has suggested the possibility of a genetic predisposition to internalizing or externalizing (Kim-Cohen et al., 2006; Rutter, Moffit, & Caspi, 2006).

Age and Gender

Vulnerability to disorders varies in different age groups. Disorders that are primarily childhood onset include ADHD, autism and nonautistic pervasive developmental disorder, separation anxiety, specific phobia, and oppositional defiant disorder (Costello, Foley, & Angold, 2006). Disorders that are primarily adolescent onset disorders include social phobia, panic, substance abuse, depression, anorexia nervosa, and bulimia nervosa disorders. For boys (possibly more likely when conduct disturbances lead to arrest and conviction), some studies have suggested that childhood-onset antisocial behavior has antecedents and a course different from those of adolescent-onset deviance (Costello et al., 2006; McBurnett et al., 2003; Moffitt, Caspi, Harrington, & Milne, 2002). Most childhood-onset disorders have more male than female cases, whereas most of the adolescent disorders have more female than male cases (Costello et al., 2006). Various forms of psychopathology (e.g., depression and anxiety) increase in prevalence in adolescence (Lupien et al., 2009). Some studies of PTS and cortisol have shown no age differences in cortisol levels for children ages 10–16 (Carrion et al., 2002; Weems & Carrion, 2009). Periods of heightened stress often precede the first episodes of depressive and anxiety disorders, suggesting the possibility that heightened HPA reactivity during adolescence increases sensitivity to the onset of stress-related mental disorders.

A few studies have found gender differences in the relationship of cortisol levels and youths' psychopathology. Studies have shown relatively higher cortisol levels in girls with PTSD (ages 7–14; Carrion et al., 2002), in girls with more subthreshold depressive symptoms (in response to TSST-C; Gunnar, Wewerka, et al., 2009), and for adolescent girls but not boys with general or social anxiety (Schiefelbein & Susman, 2006). Some gender differences may reflect girls' earlier onset of puberty, other physiological differences, differences in reporting style (e.g., boys' tend to report fewer anxiety symptoms than girls), or problems related to sample size (Schiefelbein & Susman, 2006).

Externalizing Disorders

Specific variables moderate or mediate the relationship between externalizing disorders and lower cortisol levels (Shirtcliff, Granger, Booth, & Johnson, 2005; Tyrka et al., 2006). For example, low cortisol has been found in childhood-onset aggressive conduct disorder (CD) rather than later-onset CD (McBurnett et al., 2003). Anxiety moderates the relationship between conduct disturbance and cortisol. Notably, youth with CD and a comorbid anxiety disorder have had higher cortisol levels. The link between cortisol and a disorder (e.g., externalizing) may be indirect. McBurnett et al. (2003) suggested that the link

Table 3
High versus low cortisol levels and their associations

Factor	Low cortisol	High cortisol
Personality and temperament	• Low harm avoidance • Low self-control • High NE • Impulsivity • Insensitivity to punishment • Carelessness • Aggression • Novelty seeking	• Eysenck: Introverted • Kagan: Inhibited • Inhibited with insecure attachments • College students' anxiety & openness to ideas • Harm-avoidance • Self-control • Reflectiveness • Caution • Low novelty-seeking
ADHD	• Persistent ADHD	
Aggression	• Childhood onset-CD (not later onset) • Childhood onset aggression that persists into adulthood	• CD + comorbid anxiety
Depression		• Elevations at sleep onset for severely depressed and suicidal adolescents • Children with PTSD & MDD (not just MDD) • Adults with childhood abuse • Maltreated youths with internalizing problems
Dominance	• Animals	
Hippocampal Damage		• Childhood PTSD • Chronic trauma, measured before repair
Internalizing	• In preschoolers	• Maltreated youths
Irritability	• In adolescents	
Psychopathy	• Prison inmates	
PTSD	• Long after a trauma	• Chronic symptoms especially hyperarousal • Within the first two years after a trauma

(*Continued*)

Table 3
(Continued)

Factor	Low cortisol	High cortisol
Shyness	• In preschoolers	
Social Competence		• In preschoolers
Attachment Disturbances		• Fearful attachments to mothers • Insecure attachments in response to novel and stressful situations • Disorganized infants
Maltreatment	• Adults with history of emotional and other forms of abuse • Nondisordered adults, maltreated as children	• Physical, emotional, & neglect but not sexual abuse
Prenatal Distress		• Animals

Note. MDD = Major Depressive Disorder. Sources: Carpenter et al., 2009; Carrion, Weems, & Reiss, 2007; Cicchetti, 2003; Cima et al., 2008; De Bellis, Baum, et al., 1999; Eysenck, 1967; Garber & Flynn, 2001; Goenjian et al., 1996; Gunnar, Brodersen, Krueger, & Rigatuso, 1996; Kagan, Snidman, & Arcus, 1995; Lipschitz et al., 2002; McBurnett et al., 2003; Nachmias & Gunnar, 1996; Nader, 2008; Rothbart & Bates, 1998; Schore, 2003; Shoal et al., 2003; Stein & Kendall, 2004; Tyrka et al., 2006, 2008; Weems & Carrion, 2007.

between cortisol and CD or hyperactivity is due to a strong association between aggression and cortisol rather than a direct association between the two disorders and cortisol.

Internalizing Disorders

Anxiety and depressive disorders are generally associated with higher cortisol levels. Raised plasma cortisol level is a consistently demonstrated biological abnormality in primary depressive disorder, for example (Costello et al. 2006; Lopez, Chalmers, Little, Watson, & AE Bennett Research Award, 1998; Nemeroff et al., 1984). Studies have shown exaggerated adrenocorticotropic hormone (ACTH) and cortisol responses to the dexamethasone/corticotropin-releasing hormone (Dex/CRH) stress test (a provocative challenge of HPA axis function that includes Dex pretreatment and next-day administration of CRH) in depressed adults and elevated cortisol concentrations in nondepressed individuals with a strong family history of mood disorders (Tyrka et al., 2006). Greater cortisol increases across a year predicted higher levels of general and social anxiety in girls aged 9 to 14 (Schiefelbein & Susman, 2006).

Attachment and Cortisol

Research has suggested that attachment security moderates cortisol levels in response to nontraumatic stressors. For example, in contrast to toddlers with secure attachments, toddlers with insecure attachments have higher cortisol levels in response to stressful or novel situations (Gunnar, Brodersen, Krueger, & Rigatuso, 1996; Nachmias & Gunnar, 1996). A post-Strange Situation (a situational assessment of caregiver-infant attachment) rise in salivary adrenocortisal has been documented in infants with disorganized attachments as well (Hesse, Main, Abrams, & Rifkin, 2003). In a study of 15-month-olds' transitions to childcare (Ahnert et al., 2004), in the first hour following the mothers' departures, salivary cortisol levels were 75%–100% higher than at home. Securely attached infants had markedly lower cortisol levels during the adaptation phase than insecure infants. Higher fuss and cry levels significantly correlated with cortisol levels. Responsive mothering facilitated adaptation and attachment security.

Personality/Temperament and Cortisol

Theorists have combined personality and temperament traits into subtypes, and many of these subtypes share commonalities (see Nader, 2008 for a summary of theories). Gray's (1972) *behavioral inhibition system* (BIS), Kagan's (1997) *inhibited* type, Chess and Thomas' (1977) *slow to warm* type, Block's (1971) *overcontrollers*, and the Big Five classification of *negative emotionality* (John, Caspi, Robins, Moffitt, & Stouthamer-Loeber, 1994) all have aspects of Jung's (1971) and Eysenck's (1967) introversion function, for example. Research evidence has suggested that personality or temperament traits are associated with differences in cortisol activity and reactivity. Notably, *introverts* are more physiologically reactive than *extraverts* (Eysenck, 1967). Accordingly, in studies of veterans (Dalton, Aubuchon, Tom, Pederson, & McFarland, 1993; Otis & Louks, 1997), introversion was prominent among PTSD samples. Cortisol levels generally have been higher for introversion, inhibition, internalizing, and fear-related problems, and levels have been lower for extraversion, novelty-seeking, and externalizing problems.

Introverted traits. Infants with *inhibited* temperaments are more reactive to stress than other infants (Kagan, Snidman, & Arcus, 1995; Lipschitz et al., 2002; Stein & Kendall, 2004). Research has suggested that inhibited children have higher home baseline cortisol levels compared with extremely uninhibited children (de Haan, Gunnar, Tout, Hart, & Stansbury, 1998; Kagan, Reznick, & Snidman, 1987; Schmidt, Fox, Rubin, Sternberg, & Gold, 1997; Talge, Donzella, & Gunnar, 2008). As noted, Nachmias and Gunnar (1996) found that attachment security moderated cortisol levels for inhibited infants. Although a number of studies have found an association between fearful temperament and cortisol reactivity, for children ages 9–15, Gunnar, Wewerka, et al. (2009) found no such association for girls and found an anomalous negative association for boys.

Notably, high cortisol is associated with a behavioral inhibition (BI) phenotype, a temperament factor demonstrated in both nonhuman primates and human children to be predictive of anxiety and depressive disorders and to include the tendency to withdraw and avoid novel situations (Fox, Henderson, Marshall, Nichols, & Ghera, 2005; Tyrka et al., 2006). The Virginia Tech shooter was described as exhibiting BI from elementary school onward. BI is characterized by excessively inhibited responses to strangers or novel situations and a dispositional tendency to activate increased pituitary-adrenal and autonomic activity (Fox et al., 2008). Cortisol has correlated with similar aspects of negative emotionality (NE; a continuum of the predisposition to states of distress, fear, anger, and hostility; Caspi et al., 1997). Low novelty-seeking and high harm avoidance are related to BI (Tyrka et al., 2006); harm avoidance has positively correlated with NE and negatively correlated with novelty-seeking. Tyrka et al. (2008) found that the combination of high harm avoidance and low novelty-seeking was linked to the highest levels of cortisol in response to the

Dex/CRH (compared to low harm avoidance/high novelty-seeking and either low harm avoidance or high novelty-seeking).

Trauma and other mental health variables have explained mixed findings for NE's association with cortisol. In healthy adults, NE and depressive temperament have made independent contributions to higher cortisol response (Zobel et al., 2004). Evidence has suggested that the correlation between NE and depression is attributable to a genetic factor linked to both depression and NE (Kendler, Health, Kessler, Heath, & Eaves, 1993; Shiner & Caspi, 2003). For adults with histories of traumatic experiences and psychiatric disorders, higher NE has predicted lower cortisol levels (McCleery & Goodwin, 2001). As noted earlier, a history of childhood trauma itself has been associated with low cortisol. Adults maltreated as children have exhibited a pattern of hyporeactive HPA response to a lab stressor that was not explained by trait anxiety, inhibited personality, perceived stress, or subthreshold anxiety and depressive symptoms (Carpenter, Carvalho, et al., 2007). Although traits associated with NE can be a set of preexisting traits or can be symptoms of trauma, most studies of trauma and personality have assessed traits only after traumas. A recent study examined youth (ages 9–19) before and after Hurricane Katrina for their PTSD, generalized anxiety disorder, major depression, and NE scores (Weems et al., 2007). Trait anxiety predicted PTSD responses in the wake of Hurricane Katrina. Although predisaster elevated NE was also linked to risk for the development of PTSD symptoms, it may have been because of shared variance.

Shoal, Giancola, and Kirillova (2003) suggested that personality traits may mediate the relation between low cortisol levels and outcomes such as self-regulation versus increased aggressive behavior. Low cortisol in preadolescents was predictive of aggressive behavior 5 years later. Of traits measured, only self-control accounted for significant amounts of variance in aggressive behavior. High resting cortisol levels predicted later reflectiveness and caution, whereas low levels predicted impulsiveness, carelessness, and the aggressive behavior associated with them. Shoal and colleagues suggested that cortisol's link to physically and verbally aggressive behaviors may be through its associations with these personality traits. Rothbart and Bates (1998) found that lower resting cortisol in preadolescents was not linked to an adolescent aggressive disposition but rather to more aggressive behavior through increased impulsivity and general behavioral dysregulation.

Extraverted traits. Outgoing and approach-related traits have been associated with low cortisol levels. As noted earlier, in healthy adults, an inverse relationship exists between novelty-seeking and cortisol levels (Tyrka et al., 2006, 2007, 2008). Extraversion is associated with low cortisol except in the context of a social stressor. With the presence of social stress, extraversion is associated with higher cortisol instead (Gunnar, Sebanc, Tout, Donzella, & van Dulmen, 2003; Tyrka et al., 2006).

Methodological Issues in Assessing Cortisol Levels

A number of factors are important in the assessment of cortisol (Nader, 2008), and there are wide individual differences in normal cortisol levels in youth. What is elevated for one person may not be so for another, and optimal levels of cortisol have not been established (Weems & Carrion, 2007). Youths' cortisol levels may be influenced by heritage, temperament, personality, pubertal status, gender, age, comorbidity, and behavior problems, as well as by the personal, social, and situational resources that influence their ability to cope with stressors (Carpenter, Carvalho, et al., 2007; Gunnar, Talge, & Herrera, 2009; Suomi, 1995; Suomi & Levine, 1998). Conditions such as dietary intake, anticipation of a stressful event, exposure to a pathogen, methodology, and time of collection can affect levels as well (McBurnett et al., 2003). Susman et al. (2007) found that adolescent youths' preference for morning versus evening activities, alertness, timing of pubertal onset (e.g., early puberty onset), and ratio of morning- to-evening cortisol were important in some outcomes.

Diurnal Cortisol Patterns

Although variable, the classic diurnal rhythm includes a rise in early morning cortisol, a steady decline throughout the day, and a nadir before sleep (Cicchetti, 2003; McBurnett et al., 2003; Susman et al., 2007). Consequently, it is essential to hold the hour of collection constant across subjects and comparisons. Morning is the best time of collection to test for low cortisol levels, and afternoon best for capturing high reactivity.

Researchers have demonstrated differences in cortisol levels related to time of day for traumatized youth compared to nontraumatized youth (Cicchetti, 2003; De Bellis, Baum, et al., 1999; Weems & Carrion, 2009). De Bellis, Baum, et al. (1999) found relatively elevated cortisol levels when averaged over 24 hours. Weems and Carrion (2009) found that compared to normal youth, those with PTS had sharper morning declines and relatively higher evening levels (an increase from before dinner to prebedtime). Bevans et al. (2008) found that exposure to trauma combined with a history of trauma earlier in life was related to relatively lower morning cortisol levels but higher afternoon cortisol levels. Although elevated cortisol levels among youth who have experienced trauma and have PTSD symptoms may exhibit larger differences around bedtime (Carrion et al., 2002; Weems & Carrion, 2009), differences between children with PTS versus nonexposed youth may be more clearly (and consistently) evident in the daily trajectories of cortisol secretion than in mean differences (Weems & Carrion, 2009). Some studies have also found cortisol elevations near sleep onset for severely depressed and suicidal adolescents (Garber & Flynn, 2001). At the transition to adolescence, high early-morning glucocorticoid levels that vary markedly from day to day predict increased risk for depression by age 16 (Lupien et al., 2009).

Collection Methodology

Cortisol levels have been assessed in the blood, urine, or saliva (Dahl, Dorn, & Ryan, 1999; Nader, 2008). Methodological differences, such as variations in the situation or length of a stressor paradigm, can alter outcomes. For example, findings were different when a preschool peer social stressor included entry into a class without introduction during a task in progress versus entry during playtime (Gunnar, Talge, & Herrera, 2009). Developmentally, the impact of separations that last a few minutes contrasts with those that last for hours (e.g., Strange Situation paradigm versus daycare). Salivary assay results for testosterone, progesterone, and other hormones may be artificially elevated when samples are collected using cotton. However, salivary cortisol levels do not appear to be affected by the use of cotton collection methods (see Shirtcliff, Granger, Schwartz, & Curran, 2001).

Conclusions

Differences have been found in the normal cortisol activity and reactivity of children based on developmental phase and the nature of stress exposures. With variations related to comorbidity, attachment, personality/temperament, or other variables, lower cortisol levels are generally associated with externalizing disorders, extraverted traits (in the absence of social stress), and years since trauma exposure. Higher cortisol levels have been associated with internalizing disorders or problems, inhibited or introverted traits or types, and recent stress exposure. Accurate assessment of cortisol requires an understanding of normal daily rhythms and the changes associated with pathology as well as the inclusion of appropriate variables in assessment. Larger studies of different age and pubertal stage groups followed from childhood well into adulthood are needed in order to discover the true nature of cortisol response across developmental levels and in response to trauma. Clarifying the role of the amount of time since the trauma may also prove to be important in understanding the linkage between trauma and cortisol. Understanding HPA reactivity may add to the discussion of PTSD diagnostic criteria (i.e., Criterion A) and the need for diagnostic differences by age group.

An understanding of developmental differences in cortisol levels and the manner of change in reactivity over time is essential to testing whether treatment methods affect altered reactivity patterns over time. For example, rhythmic massage has at least temporarily reduced cortisol levels (Field, Seligman, Scafidi, & Schanberg, 1996) and the administration of low-dose cortisol immediately after trauma has been proposed as a preventative method for PTSD (Pomerantz, 2006). Studies are needed to determine whether these or other posttrauma interventions provide ongoing repair for alterations in reactivity. The potential outcomes associated with alterations in cortisol reactivity underscore the need for early and effective interventions.

References

Adams, E. (2006). Transactions among trait and state emotion and adolescent diurnal and momentary cortisol activity in naturalistic settings. *Psychoneuroendocrinology*, *31*, 664–679.

Ahnert, L., Gunnar, M., Lamb, M., & Barthel, M. (2004). Transition to child care: Associations with infant-mother attachment, infant negative emotion, and cortisol elevations. *Child Development*, *75*, 639–650.

Andersen, S., & Teicher, M. (2008). Stress, sensitive periods and maturational events in adolescent depression. *Trends in Neuroscience*, *31*, 183–191.

Bevans, K., Cerbone, A., & Overstreet, S. (2008). Relations between recurrent trauma exposure and recent life stress and salivary cortisol among children. *Development and Psychopathology*, *20*, 257–272.

Block, J. (1971). *Lives through time*. Berkeley, CA: Bancroft.

Bremner, J. (2003). The effects of stress on the brain. *Psychiatric Times*, *20*(7), 18–22.

Bremner, J., Randall, P., Scott, T., Bronen, R., Delaney, R., Seibyl, J., et al. (1995). MRI-based measurement of hippocampal volume in patients with combat-related posttraumatic stress disorder. *American Journal of Psychiatry*, *152*, 973–981.

Bremner, J., Randall, P., Vermetten, E., Staib, L., Bronen, R., Mazure, C., et al. (1997). Magnetic resonance imaging-based measurement of hippocampal volume in posttraumatic stress disorder related to childhood physical and sexual abuse—A preliminary report. *Biological Psychiatry*, *41*, 23–32.

Brewin, C., Andrews, B., & Rose, S. (2000). Fear, helplessness, and horror in posttraumatic stress disorder: Investigating DSM-IV criterion A2 in victims of violent crime. *Journal of Traumatic Stress*, *13*, 499–509.

Buske-Kirschbaum, A., Jobst, S., Psych, D., Wustmans, A., Kirschbaum, C., Rauh, W., et al. (1997). Attenuated free cortisol response to psychosocial stress in children with atopic dermatitis. *Psychosomatic. Medicine*, *59*(4), 419–426.

Buske-Kirschbaum, A., von Auer, K., Krieger, S., Weis, S., Rauh, W., & Hellhammer, D. (2003). Blunted cortisol responses to psychosocial stress in asthmatic children: a general feature of atopic disease? *Psychosomatic Medicine*, *65*, 806–810.

Byrnes, J. P. (2001). *Minds, brains, and learning*. New York: Guilford Press.

Carpenter, L., Carvalho, J., Tyrka, A., Wier, L., Mello, A., Mello, M., et al. (2007). Decreased ACTH and cortisol responses to stress in healthy adults reporting significant childhood maltreatment. *Biological Psychiatry*, *62*(10), 1080–1087.

Carpenter, L., Tyrka, A., Ross, L., Khoury, Anderson, G., & Price, L. (2009). Effect of childhood emotional abuse and age on cortisol responsivity in adulthood. *Biological Psychiatry*, *66*, 69–75.

Carrion, V. G., Garrett, A., Menon, V., Weems, C. F., & Reiss, A. L. (2008). Posttraumatic stress symptoms and brain function during a response-inhibition task: An fMRI study in youth. *Depression and Anxiety*, *25*, 514–526.

Carrion, V., Weems, C., Eliez, S., Patwardhan, A., Brown, W., Ray R., et al. (2001). Attenuation of frontal lobe asymmetry in pediatric PTSD. *Biological Psychiatry*, *50*, 943–951.

Carrion, V., Weems, C., Ray, R., & Reiss, A. (2002). Toward an empirical definition of pediatric PTSD: The phenomenology of PTSD symptoms in youth. *Journal of the American Academy of Child and Adolescent Psychiatry*, *41*(2), 166–173.

Carrion, V., Weems, C., & Reiss, A. (2007). Stress predicts brain changes in children: A pilot longitudinal study on youth stress, posttraumatic stress disorder, and the hippocampus. *Pediatrics*, *119*, 509–516.

Carrion, V., Weems, C., Richert, K., Hoffman, B., & Reiss, A. L. (2010). Decreased prefrontal cortical volume associated with increased bedtime cortisol in traumatized youth. *Biological Psychiatry*, *68*, 491–493.

Carrion, V., Weems, C., Watson, C., Eliez, S., Menon, V., & Reiss, A. (2009). Converging evidence for morphological abnormalities of the prefrontal cortex and evaluation of midsagittal structures in pediatric posttraumatic stress disorder: An MRI study. *Psychiatry Research: Neuroimaging*, *172*, 226–234.

Caspi, A., Begg, D., Dickson, N., Harrington, H., Langley, J., Moffitt, T., et al. (1997). Personality differences predict health-risk behaviors in young adulthood: Evidence from a longitudinal study. *Journal of Personality and Social Psychology*, *73*, 1052–1063.

Chess, S., & Thomas, A. (1977). Temperamental individuality from childhood to adolescence. *Journal of the American Academy of Child Psychiatry*, *16*(2), 218–226.

Cicchetti, D. V. (2003). Neuroendocrine functioning in maltreated children. In D. Cicchetti & E. Walker (Eds.), *Neurodevelopmental mechanisms in psychopathology* (pp. 345–365). Cambridge, England: Cambridge University Press.

Cima, M., Smeets, T., & Jelicic, M. (2008). Self-reported trauma, cortisol levels, and aggression in psychopathic and non-psychopathic prison inmates. *Biological Psychology*, *78*(1), 75–86.

Costello, E., Foley, D., & Angold, A. (2006). 10-year research update review: The epidemiology of child and adolescent psychiatric disorders: II: Developmental epidemiology. *Journal of the American Academy of child and Adolescent Psychiatry*, *45*, 8–25.

Dahl, R., Dorn, L., & Ryan, N. (1999). Sleep and neuroendocrine measures. In D. Shaffer, C. Lucas, & J. Richters (Eds.), *Diagnostic assessment in child and adolescent psychopathology* (pp. 321–334). New York: Guilford Press.

Dahl, R., & Gunnar, M. (2009). Heightened stress responsiveness and emotional reactivity during pubertal maturation: Implications for psychopathology. *Development and Psychopathology*, *21*, 1–6.

Dalton, J., Aubuchon, I., Tom, A., Pederson, S., & McFarland, R. (1993). MBTI profiles of Vietnam veterans with Post-Traumatic Stress Disorder. *Journal of Psychological Type*, *26*, 3–8.

Dorn, L. Campo, J., Thato, S., Dahl, R., Lewin, D., Chandra, R., et al. (2003). Psychological cormorbidity and stress reactivity in children and adolescents with recurrent abdominal pain and anxiety disorders. *Journal of the American Academy of Child Psychiatry*, *42*(1), 66–75.

De Bellis, M. D. (2001). Developmental traumatology: The psychobiological development of maltreated children and its implications for research, treatment, and policy. *Development and Psychopathology*, *13*, 539–564.

De Bellis, M., Baum, A., Birmaher, B., Keshavan, M., Eccard, C., Boring, A., et al. (1999). Developmental traumatology part I: Biological stress systems. *Biological Psychiatry*, *45*, 1259–1270.

De Bellis, M., Keshavan, M., Clark, D., Casey, B., Giedd, H., Boring, A., et al. (1999). Developmental traumatology part II: Brain development. *Biological Psychiatry*, *45*, 1271–1284.

de Haan, M., Gunnar, M. R., Tout, K., Hart, J., & Stansbury, K. (1998). Familiar and novel contexts yield different associations between cortisol and behavior among 2-year-olds. *Developmental Psychobiology*, *33*(1), 93–101.

Dickerson, S., & Kemeny, M. (2004). Acute stressors and cortisol responses: A theoretical integration and synthesis of laboratory research. *Psychological Bulletin*, *130*(3), 355–391.

Eysenck, H. J. (1967). *The biological basis of personality*. Springfield, IL: Charles C. Thomas.

Field, T., Seligman, S., Scafidi, F., & Schanberg, S. (1996). Alleviating posttraumatic stress in children following Hurricane Andrew. *Journal of Applied Developmental Psychology*, *17*, 37–50.

Finkelhor, D., Ormrod, R., & Turner, H. (2007). Poly-victimization: A neglected component in child victimization. *Child Abuse & Neglect*, *31*, 7–26.

Finkelhor, D., Ormrod, R., & Turner, H. (2009). Lifetime assessment of poly-victimization in a national sample of children & youth. *Child Abuse & Neglect*, *33*, 403–411.

Fox, N., Henderson, H., Marshall, P., Nichols, K., & Ghera, M. (2005). Behavioral inhibition: Linking biology and behavior within a developmental framework. *Annual Review of Psychology*, *56*, 235–262.

Fox, N., Henderson, H., Rubin, K., Calkins, S., & Schmidt, L. (2001). Continuity and discontinuity of behavioral inhibition and exuberance: Psychophysiological and behavioral influences across the first four years of life. *Child Development*, *72*, 1–21.

Garber, J., & Flynn, C. (2001). Vulnerability to depression in childhood and adolescence. In R. E. Ingram & J. M. Price (Eds.), *Vulnerability to psychopathology: Risk across the lifespan* (pp. 175–225). New York: Guilford Press.

Giedd, J., Blumenthal, J., Jeffries, N., Castellanos, F., Liu, H., Zijdenbos, A., et al. (1999). Brain development during childhood and adolescence: A longitudinal MRI study. *Neuroscience*, *2*(10), 861–863.

Gilbertson, M., Shenton, M., Ciszewski, A., Kasai, K., Lasko, N., Orr, S., et al. (2002). Smaller hippocampal volume predicts pathologic vulnerability to psychological trauma. *Nature Neuroscience*, *5*(11), 1242–1247.

Glynn, L., Davis, E., Schetter, C., Chicz-Demet, A., Hobel, C., & Sandman, C. (2007). Postnatal maternal cortisol levels predict temperament in healthy breastfed infants. *Early Human Development*, *83*(10), 675–681.

Goenjian, A., Yehuda, R., Pynoos, R., Steinberg, A., Tashjian, M., Yang, R., et al. (1996). Basal cortisol, dexamethasone suppression of cortisol, and MHPG in adolescents after the 1988 earthquake in Armenia. *American Journal of Psychiatry*, *153*, 929–934.

Gordis, E., Granger, D., Susman, E., & Trickett, P. (2006). Asymmetry between salivary cortisol and alpha-amylase reactivity to stress: relation to aggressive behavior in adolescents. *Psychoneuoendocrinology*, *31*, 976–987.

Gray, J. (1972). The psychophysiological nature of introversion-extraversion: A modification of Eysenck's theory. In V. D. Nebylisyn & J. A. Gray (Eds.), *Biological bases of individual behavior* (pp. 182–206). New York: Academic Press.

Greenwald, R. (Ed.). (2002). *Trauma and juvenile delinquency: Theory, research, and interventions*. New York: Haworth Press.

Gunnar, M., Brodersen, L., Krueger, K., & Rigatuso, J. (1996). Dampening of adrenocortical responses during infancy: Normative changes and individual differences. *Child Development*, *67*, 877–889.

Gunnar, M., Frenn, K., Wewerka, S., & Ryzin, M. (2009). Moderate versus severe early life stress: Associations with stress reactivity and regulation in 10–12-year-old children. *Psychoneuroendocrinology*, *34*(1), 62–75.

Gunnar, M., Sebanc, A., Tout, K., Donzella, B., & van Dulmen, M. (2003). Peer rejection, temperament, and cortisol activity in preschoolers. *Developmental Psychobiology*, *43*, 346–358.

Gunnar, M., Talge, N., & Herrera, A. (2009). Stressor paradigms in developmental studies: What does and does not work to produce mean increases in salivary cortisol. *Psychoneuroendocrinology*, *34*, 953–967.

Gunnar, M., Wewerka, S., Frenn, K., Long, J., & Griggs, C., (2009). Developmental changes in HPA activity over the transition to adolescence: Normative changes and associations with puberty. *Development and Psychopathology*, *21*, 69–85.

Gurvits, T., Shenton, M., Hokama, H., Ohta, H., Lasko, N., Gilbertson, M., et al. (1997). Magnetic resonance imaging study of hippocampal volume in chronic combat-related posttraumatic stress disorder. *Biological Psychiatry*, *4*, 192–199.

Halligan, S., Herbert, J., Goodyer, I., & Murray, L. (2007). Disturbances in morning cortisol secretion in association with maternal postnatal depression predict subsequent depressive symptomatology in adolescents. *Biological Psychiatry*, *62*, 40–46.

Hesse, E., Main, M., Abrams, K. Y., & Rifkin, A. (2003). Unresolved states regarding loss or abuse can have "second-generation" effects: Disorganization, role inversion, and frightening ideation in the offspring of traumatized, nonmaltreating parents. In M. Solomon & D. J. Siegel (Eds.), *Healing trauma* (pp. 57–106). New York: W. W. Norton.

Howe, M. L. (1997). Children's memory for traumatic experiences. *Learning and Individual Differences*, *9*, 153–174.

Jansen, L. M. C., Gispen-de Wied, C. C., Van der Gaag, R. J., ten Hove, F., Willemsen-Swinkels, S. W. M., Harteveld, E., et al. (2000). Unresponsiveness to psychosocial stress in a subgroup of autistic-like children, multiple complex developmental disorder. *Psychoneuroendocrinology*, *25*, 753–764.

John, O., Caspi, A., Robins, R., Moffitt, T., & Stouthamer-Loeher, M. (1994). The "little five": Exploring the nomological network of the five-factor model of personality in adolescent boys. *Child Development*, *65*,160–178.

Jones, A., Godfrey, K., Wood, P., Osmond, C., Goulden, P., & Phillips, D. (2006). Fetal growth and the adrenocortical response to psychological stress. *Journal of Clinical. Endocrinology & Metabolism*, *91*, 1868–1871.

Jung, C. G. (1971). *Psychological types: The collected works of C. G. Jung* (Vol. 6). Princeton, NJ: Princeton University Press.

Kagan, J. (1997). Temperament and the reactions to unfamiliarity. *Child Development*, *68*(1), 139–143.

Kagan, J., Reznick, J. S., & Snidman, N. (1987). The physiology and psychology of behavioral inhibition in children. *Child Development*, *58*(6), 1459–1473.

Kagan, J., Snidman, N., & Arcus, D. (1995). The role of temperament in social development. *Annals of the New York Academy of Sciences*, *771*, 485–490.

Katz, M., Liu, C., Schaer, M., Parker, K., Ottet, M., Epps, A., et al. (2009). Prefrontal plasticity and stress inoculation-induced resilience. *Developmental Neuroscience*, *31*(4), 293–299.

Kendler, K., Health, M., Kessler, R., Heath, A., & Eaves, L., (1993). A longitudinal twin study of personality and major depression in women. *Archives of General Psychiatry*, *50*, 853–862.

Kertes, D., Gunnar, M., Madsen, N., & Long, J. (2008). Early deprivation and home basal cortisol levels: A study of internationally-adopted children. *Development & Psychopathology*, *20*, 473–491.

Kim-Cohen, J., Caspi, A., Taylor, A., Williams, B., Newcombe, R., Craig, I., et al. (2006). MAOA, maltreatment, and gene-environment interaction predicting children's mental health: New evidence and a meta-analysis. *Molecular Psychiatry*, *11*, 903–913.

Klimes-Dougan, B., Hastings, P., Granger, D., Usher, B., & Zahn-Waxler, C. (2001). Adrenocortical activity in at-risk and normally developing adolescents: Individual differences in salivary cortisol basal levels, diurnal variation, and responses to social challenges. *Developmental Psychology*, *13*, 695–719.

Larson, M., White, B., Cochran, A., Donzella, B., & Gunnar, M. (1998). Dampening of the cortisol response to handling at 3-months in human infants and its relation to sleep, circadian cortisol activity, and behavioral distress. *Developmental Psychobiology*, *33*(4), 327–337.

Levine, S. (2005). Developmental determinants of sensitivity and resistance to stress. *Psychoneuroendocrinology*, *30*, 939–946.

Lewis, M., & Ramsay, D. (2002). Cortisol response to embarrassment and shame. *Child Development*, *73*, 1034–1045.

Lipschitz, D., Morgan, C., & Southwick, S. (2002). Neurobiological disturbances in youth with childhood trauma and in youth with conduct disorder. *Journal of Aggression, Maltreatment and Trauma, 6*(1), 149–174.

Lopez, J., Chalmers, D., Little, K., Watson, S., & AE Bennett Research Award. (1998). Regulation of serotonin1A, glucocorticoid, and mineralocorticoid receptor in rat and human hippocampus: Implications for the neurobiology of depression. *Biological Psychiatry, 43*, 547–573.

Lupien, S., McEwen, B., Gunnar, M., & Heim, C. (2009). Effects of stress throughout the lifespan on the brain, behaviour and cognition. *Nature Reviews Neuroscience, 10*(1), 434–445.

Lyons, D., & Parker, K. (2007). Stress inoculation-induced indications of resilience in monkeys. *Journal of Traumatic Stress, 20*, 423–433.

Maestripieri, D., & Wallen, K. (2003). Nonhuman primate models of developmental psychopathology. In D. Cicchetti & E. Walker (Eds.), *Neurodevelopmental mechanisms in psychopathology* (pp. 187–214). Cambridge, England: Cambridge University Press.

McBurnett, K., King, J., & Scarpa, A. (2003). The hypothalamic-pituitary-adrenal system (HPA) and the development of aggressive, antisocial, and substance abuse disorders. In D. Cicchetti & E. Walker (Eds.), *Neurodevelopmental mechanisms in psychopathology* (pp. 324–344). Cambridge, England: Cambridge University Press.

McCleery, J., & Goodwin, G. (2001). High and low neuroticism predict different cortisol responses to the combined dexamethasone-CRH test. *Biological Psychiatry, 49*, 410–415.

McCleery, J., & Harvey, A. (2004). Integration of psychological and biological approaches to trauma memory: Implications for pharmacological prevention of PTSD. *Journal of Traumatic Stress, 17*(6), 485–496.

Moffitt, T., Caspi, A., Harrington, H., & Milne, B. (2002). Males on the lifecourse persistent and adolescence-limited antisocial pathways: Follow-up at age 26. *Developmental Psychopathology, 14*, 179–207.

Nachmias, M., & Gunnar, M. (1996). Behavioral inhibition and stress reactivity: The moderating role of attachment security. *Child Development, 67*(2), 508–522.

Nader, K. (2008). *Understanding and assessing trauma in children and adolescents: Measures, methods, and youth in context*. New York: Routledge.

Nemeroff, C., Widerlov, E., Bissette, G., Walleus, H., Karlsson, I., Eklund, K., et al. (1984). Elevated concentrations of CSF corticotropin-releasing factor-like immunoreactivity in depressed patients. *Science, 226*, 1342–1344.

Ostrowski, S., Christopher, N., van Dulmen, M., & Delahanty, D. (2007). Acute child and mother psychophysiological responses and subsequent PTSD symptoms following a child's traumatic event. *Journal of Traumatic Stress, 20*(5), 677–687.

Otis, G. D., & Louks, J. L. (1997). Rebelliousness and psychological distress in a sample of introverted veterans. *Journal of Psychological Type, 40*, 20–30.

Pomerantz, J. (2006). Can Posttraumatic Stress Disorder be prevented? *Psychiatric Times, 23*(4), 10–15.

Rothbart, M. K., & Bates, J. E. (1998). Temperament. In W. Damon (Series Ed.) & N. Eisenberg (Vol. Ed.), *Handbook of child psychology: Vol. 3. Social, emotional, and personality development* (5th ed., pp. 105–176). New York: Wiley.

Rubin, K. (2002). Peer relationships and socioemotional regulation. In B. S. Zuckerman, A. F. Lieberman, & N. A. Fox (Eds.), *Emotional regulation and developmental health: Infancy and early childhood* (pp. 81–99). New Brunswick, NJ: Johnson and Johnson.

Rutter, M., Moffitt, T., & Caspi, A. (2006). Gene–environment interplay and psychopathology: Multiple varieties but real effects. *Journal of Child Psychology and Psychiatry, 47*(3/4), 226–261.

Saltzman, K., Weems, C. F., & Carrion, V. G. (2006). IQ and posttraumatic stress symptoms in children exposed to interpersonal violence. *Child Psychiatry & Human Development, 36*, 261–272.

Sapolsky, R. M. (1998). *Biology and human behavior: The neurological origins of individuality* [Videotape series]. Chantilly, VA: The Teaching Company.

Sapolsky, R. M. (2000). Glucocorticoids and hippocampal atrophy in neuropsychiatric disorders. *Archives of General Psychiatry, 57*, 925–935.

Schiefelbein, V. & Susman, E. (2006). Cortisol levels and longitudinal cortisol change as predictors of anxiety in adolescents. *The Journal of Early Adolescence*, *26*, 397–413.

Schmidt, L. A., Fox, N. A., Rubin, K. H., Sternberg, E. M., & Gold, P. W. (1997). Behavioral and neuroendocrine responses in shy children. *Developmental Psychobiology*, *30*(2), 127–140.

Schneider, M. L., Moore, C. F., & Kraemer, G. W. (2003). On the relevance of prenatal stress to developmental psychopathology. In D. Cicchetti & E. Walker (Eds.), *Neurodevelopmental mechanisms in psychopathology* (pp. 155–186). New York: Cambridge University Press.

Schore, A. (2003). Early relational trauma, disorganized attachment, and the development of a predisposition to violence. In M. Solomon & D. J. Siegel (Eds.), *Healing trauma* (pp. 107–167). New York: W. W. Norton.

Shiner, R., & Caspi, A. (2003). Personality differences in childhood and adolescence: Measurement, development, and consequences. *Journal of Child Psychology and Psychiatry*, *44*(1), 2–32.

Shirtcliff, E. A., Granger, D. A., Booth, A., & Johnson, D. (2005). Low salivary cortisol levels and externalizing behavior problems in youth. *Development and Psychopathology*, *17*, 167–184.

Shirtcliff, E., Granger, D., Schwartz, E., & Curran, J. (2001). Use of salivary biomarkers in biobehavioral research: Cotton-based sample collection methods can interfere with salivary immunoassay results. *Psychoneuroendocrinology*, *26*(2), 165–173.

Shoal, G. D., Giancola, P. R., & Kirillova, G. P. (2003). Salivary cortisol, personality, and aggressive behavior in adolescent boys: A 5-year longitudinal study. *Journal of the American Academy of Child and Adolescent Psychiatry*, *42*(9), 1101–1107.

Smeekens, S., Riksen-Walraven, M., & van Bakel, H. (2007). Cortisol reactions in five-year-olds to parent—child interaction: the moderating role of ego-resiliency. *Journal of Child Psychology & Psychiatry*, *48*, 649–656.

Spangler, G., & Schieche, M. (1994). Biobehavioral organization in one-year-olds: Quality of mother-infant attachment and immunological and adrenocorticol regulation. *Psychologische Beitrage*, *36*(1–2), 30–35.

Starkman, M. N., Giodani, B., Gebarski, S. S., Berent, S., Schork, M. A., & Schteingart, D. E. (1999). Decrease in cortisol reverses human hippocampal atrophy following treatment of Cushing's disease. *Biological Psychiatry*, *46*, 1595–1602.

Stein, M., Koverola, C., Hanna, C., Torchia, M., & McClarty, B. (1997). Hippocampal volume in women victimized by childhood sexual abuse. *Psychological Medicine*, *27*, 951–959.

Stein, N., Wade, E., & Liwag, M. D. (1996). A theoretical approach to understanding and remembering harmful events. In M. Stein, P. A. Ornstein, B. Tversky, & C. Brainerd (Eds.), *Memory for everyday and emotional events* (pp. 15–48). Hillsdale, NJ: Erlbaum.

Stein, P. T., & Kendall, J. (2004). *Psychological trauma and the developing brain: Neurologically based interventions for troubled children*. New York: Haworth Press.

Stroud, L., Foster, E., Papandonatos, G., Handwerger, K., Granger, D., Kivlighan, K., et al. (2009). Stress response and the adolescent transition: Performance versus peer rejection stress. *Development and Psychopathology*, *21*, 47–68.

Suomi, S. J. (1995). Influence of Bowlby's attachment theory on research on nonhuman primate biobehavioral development. In S. Goldberg, R. Muir, & J. Kerr (Eds.), *Attachment theory: Social, developmental and clinical perspectives* (pp. 185–201). Hillsdale, NJ: Analytic Press.

Suomi, S. J., & Levine, S. (1998). Psychobiology of intergenerational effects of trauma. In Y. Danieli (Ed.), *International handbook of multigenerational legacies of trauma* (pp. 623–637). New York: Plenum Press.

Susman, E., Dockray, S., Schiefelbein, V., Herwehe, S., Heaton, J., & Dorn, L. (2007). Morningness/eveningness, morning-to-afternoon cortisol ratio, and antisocial behavior problems during puberty. *Developmental Psychology*, *43*(4), 811–822.

Talge, N., Donzella, B., & Gunnar, M. (2008). Fearful temperament and stress reactivity among preschool-aged children. *Infant and Child Development*, *17*, 427–445.

Tyrka, A., Mello, A., Mello, M., Gagne, G., Grover, K., Anderson, G., et al. (2006). Temperament and hypothalamic-pituitary-adrenal axis function in healthy adults. *Psychoneuroendocrinology*, *31*, 1036–1045.

Tyrka, A., Wier, L., Anderson, G., Wilkinson, C., Price, L., & Carpenter, L. (2007). Temperament and response to the Trier Social Stress Test. *Acta Psychiatrica Scandinavica, 115*, 395–402.

Tyrka, A., Wier, L., Price, L., Rikhye, K., Ross, N., Anderson, G., et al. (2008). Cortisol and ACTH responses to the Dex/CRH Test: Influence of temperament. *Hormonal Behavior, 53*(4), 518–525.

van Goozen, S., Matthys, W., Cohen-Kettenis, P., Buitelaar, J. & Van Engeland, H. (2000). Hypothalamic-pituitary-adrenal axis and autonomic nervous system activity in disruptive children and matched controls. *Journal of the American Academy of Child Psychiatry, 39*, 1438–1445.

van Goozen, S., Matthys, W., Cohen-Kettenis, P., Gispen-de Wied, C., Wiegant, V., & Van Engeland, H. (1998). Salivary cortisol and cardiovascular activity during stress in oppositional-defiant disorder boys and normal controls. *Biological Psychiatry, 43*, 531–539.

Weems, C., & Carrion, V. (2007). The association between PTSD symptoms and salivary cortisol in youth: The role of time since the trauma. *Journal of Traumatic Stress, 20*(5), 903–907.

Weems, C., & Carrion, V. (2009). Diurnal salivary cortisol in youth: Clarifying the nature of posttraumatic stress dysregulation. *Journal of Pediatric Psychology, 34*, 389–395.

Weems, C., Pina, A., Costa, N., Watts, S., Taylor, L., & Cannon, M. (2007). Predisaster trait anxiety and negative affect predict posttraumatic stress in youths after Hurricane Katrina. *Journal of Consulting and Clinical Psychology, 75*(1), 154–159.

Weems, C., Saltzman, K., Reiss, A., & Carrion, V. (2003). A prospective test of the association between emotional numbing and hyperarousal in youth with a history of traumatic stress. *Journal of Clinical Child & Adolescent Psychology, 32*, 166–171.

Zobel, A., Barkow, K., Schulze-Rauschenbach, S., Von Widdern, O., Metten, M., Pfeiffer, U., et al. (2004). High neuroticism and depressive temperament are associated with dysfunctional regulation of the hypothalamic-pituitary-adrenocortical system in healthy volunteers. *Acta Psychiatrica Scandinavica, 109*, 392–399.

Understanding and Assessing Traumatic Responses of Guilt, Shame, and Anger among Children, Adolescents, and Young Adults

KENNETH E. FLETCHER

University of Massachusetts Medical School

Most individuals exposed to traumatic events do not develop long-term adverse outcomes such as PTSD or depression. Evidence is accumulating that feelings of guilt, shame, or anger that develop in reaction to the traumatic experience both during and after the event can play an important role in posttraumatic adjustment. What role these feelings might play as traumatic reactions, especially among children, adolescents, and young adults is discussed. Developmental and gender differences are considered. Issues surrounding assessment and available measurement tools are described in detail.

Most children who live through traumatic events do not develop posttraumatic stress disorder (PTSD; Fletcher, 2003). This fact has motivated a search for factors that mediate or moderate the influence of traumatic experience on outcomes. One domain that seems promising concerns the emotions called forth by traumatic experience. Beyond the emotions of anger, fear, and horror included in the definition of PTSD (American Psychiatric Association, 2000), two additional emotions may play important mediational roles between exposure and outcomes: guilt and shame (Bennett, Sullivan, & Lewis, 2005; Spaccarelli, 1994).

Guilt, shame, and anger also play a central role in the proposed symptomatology of complicated traumatic reactions (Herman, 1992; Pelcovitz et al., 1997; van der Kolk, 2005), which is currently undergoing investigation. Complex PTSD is conceived of as a constellation of chronic problems with self-regulation, self-concept, and interpersonal functioning (Ford & Kidd, 1998). The trauma literature suggests that traumatic experiences during childhood, especially those that involve interpersonal violence, can have a profound impact on a child's functioning in all of these areas (Cloitre et al., 2009; Cole & Putnam, 1992). Difficulty regulating emotions, particularly anger, is one of the most salient symptoms of childhood complex PTSD (Cook et al., 2005; Pelcovitz et al., 1997). Attributions of self-blame and the attendant feelings of guilt and shame are prominent indicators of the altered self-perception associated with complex PTSD.

The ability to recognize guilt, shame, and anger among child and adolescent trauma survivors can be critical in developing an understanding of their traumatic experiences, reestablishing their emotional equilibrium, and restoring a sense of self-worth (Cloitre et al., 2009). Possible consequences of traumatic guilt, shame, and anger among children and adolescents are described in this article. Then, an overview of current thinking about each emotion follows, with consideration given to gender and developmental differences. A discussion of issues relevant to assessment of the three emotions concludes the article.

The Nature of Guilt and its Relationship to Trauma

Clinicians and researchers have not always made clear distinctions between the emotions of guilt and shame. Both are self-conscious negative emotions that tend to result from a perceived breach or violation of social norms or standards for social behavior. Beyond that, however, they are distinguishable emotions with distinct etiologies, distinct impacts on the development and maintenance of posttraumatic outcomes, and separate implications for treatment (Ferguson, Stegge, Miller, & Olsen, 1999; Tangney, 1999). Guilt and shame have been reported by survivors of many kinds of traumatic events, such as childhood sexual abuse (Spaccarelli, 1994), physical abuse (Brown & Kolko, 1999; Loader, 1998), serious accidents and burns (Kiecolt-Glaser & Williams, 1987), technological disasters (Joseph, Hodgkinson, Yule, & Williams, 1993), the death of a loved one (McNeil, Hatcher, & Reubin, 1988), violent crime (Andrews, Brewin, Rose, & Kirk, 2000), and war (Leskela, Dieperink, & Thuras, 2002). Trauma survivors frequently report feeling both guilt and shame regarding the same incidents (Hoglund & Nicholas, 1995; Kubany & Watson, 2003).

The Nature of Guilt

Guilt derives from awareness of pain caused to others due to thoughts, feelings, or actions or failures of action that violate internal moral standards concerning interactions with others (Keltner & Buswell, 1996; Kubany & Watson, 2003; Tangney, 1992). Regardless of age or gender, guilty feelings can be very distressing, creating a desire to assuage distress through confession, apology, and acts of restitution (Lewis, 1971; Quiles & Bybee, 1997; Tangney, Burggraf, & Wagner, 1995; Tangney, Wagner, Hill-Barlow, Marschall, & Gramzow, 1996). The possibility of reparation provides some hope of relief from the guilt. Admission of guilt also helps renew social bonds challenged by the individual's wrongful behavior by reaffirming the individual's commitment to moral, empathic behavior (Baumeister, Stillwell, & Heatherton, 1994; Ferguson et al., 1999). Adolescents and young adults who report higher levels of guilt tend to be less aggressive and less likely to engage in acting out or externalizing behavior (Quiles & Bybee, 1997).

Several researchers have argued that "shame-free" guilt (guilt measures from which the correlation with shame has been statistically removed) can lead to positive outcomes, unlike those associated with shame (e.g., Tangney et al., 1996). However, other researchers have taken exception to that view (Ferguson & Crowley, 1997). Harder (1995) summarized findings that "shame-free" guilt was positively associated with "depression, self-derogation, public self-consciousness," and global severity of pathology, among other negative outcomes (Ferguson & Crowley, 1997, p. 428). The apparent discrepancy between the two views of guilt as beneficial or maladaptive might be resolved by a more dynamic conceptualization of guilt as an emotion that changes according to circumstances (Amodio, Devine, & Harmon-Jones, 2007; Ferguson & Crowley, 1997; see "Assessment" section).

Table 1
Developmental differences in guilt

Age range	Effects	Source
2–6 years	Egocentric thinking; Predisposed to see themselves as causes of events.	Piaget (1960); Gray Deering (2000)
5–9 years	Guilt responses increased with age.	Zahn-Waxler, Kochanska, Krupnick, & McNew (1990)
6–11 years	Younger children expressed more guilt over uncontrollable or accidental events; Older children were more likely to express guilt over intentional and controllable events.	Graham, Doubleday, & Guarino (1984)
First, third, and fifth grades	Younger children expressed more fear of detection and punishment; Older children were more likely to • show concern for the victim and • base their guilt responses on internal justice principles.	Hoffman (1982)

Children have less need for the reasons adults associate with their guilt after traumatic events, especially younger children, whose egocentric thinking may predispose them to see themselves as the causes of events (Gray Deering, 2000; see Table 1). For example, children can believe they played an important role in situations adults would consider acts of God and therefore outside anyone's control (Nader, 2008). Situations of interpersonal violence in which irreparable harm or damage is done might be particularly likely to lead to greater feelings of guilt for the parties involved (Brown & Kolko, 1999; Sourander, 1998).

People tend to repeatedly replay unfortunate experiences in their minds, trying to understand what happened and how it might have turned out differently. This can lead them to a kind of faulty thinking known as *hindsight bias* (Hawkins & Hastie, 1990). Accordingly, people may believe that they should have recognized signs or otherwise anticipated and prevented the event (Kubany & Manke, 1995). This leads to such thoughts as "I should have known better" or "I should have helped that injured person" (Kubany et al., 1996, 1997). Hindsight bias may occur fairly frequently among trauma survivors (Kubany, 1997; Kubany & Manke, 1995), giving rise to feelings of guilt (Kubany et al., 1996; Kubany & Watson, 2003; Walster, 1967).

Peritraumatic and Posttraumatic Guilt

Studies of traumatic guilt have often focused on survivor guilt (feeling guilty about surviving when others have not). However, trauma survivors can feel guilty over aspects of their traumatic experiences unrelated to survival. Child survivors might feel guilty for being unable to act due to fear, for simply being afraid, for having hidden instead of helping others, for being unable to defend or assist others, and for a myriad of reasons other than having survived (Kubany et al., 1996; Nader, 2008). Incest survivors, for example, can feel guilty about feeling they deserved their abuse because they had been "naughty" (Kubany et al., 1996). Situations that do not allow resolution of guilt feelings can be particularly problematic, for instance, if a death results and the child views it as his or her fault (Ferguson & Crowley, 1997).

Children's feelings of guilt about what they did or failed to do prior to or during a traumatic experience have been associated with higher levels of PTSD symptomatology (Kinzie, Sack, Angell, Manson, & Rath, 1986; Nader, Pynoos, Fairbanks, & Frederick, 1990; Pynoos et al., 1987). One year after a school sniper attack, "Children reported guilt for being unable to provide aid, being safe when others were harmed, or believing their actions endangered others" (Nader, 2008, p. 375). While a quarter of the children with extreme PTSD symptomatology in that study reported guilt feelings, almost none of those with low-to-mild symptoms reported feeling guilty. In another study of children ages 5–16 who had a history of exposure to interpersonal violence, guilt over acts of commission or omission were highly predictive of PTSD severity (Kletter, Weems, & Carrion, 2009). Children who survived the drowning of the *Herald of Free Enterprise* still had feelings of guilt up to 3 years later, with higher levels of guilt associated with greater distress (Joseph et al., 1993). Guilt over things they failed to do was associated with intrusive symptoms, while guilt over things they did in order to survive were associated with avoidant symptoms.

General guilt has also predicted PTSD symptomatology for childhood sexual abuse (CSA). Among a sample of 69 girl and 21 boy victims of CSA, reports of abuse-related self-blame and guilt predicted more PTSD symptoms (Wolfe, Sas, & Wekerle, 1994). Guilt may be more likely among children not physically coerced into the sexual relations, because in hindsight they may be more likely to consider themselves willing participants (Noll, 2008). Nonsupportive or blaming responses by parents or important others also increase the likelihood that the child will blame him or herself for the abuse (Spaccarelli, 1994).

The Nature of Shame and its Relationship to Trauma

Like guilt, shame results from the perceived violation of social norms or personal standards. Unlike guilt, however, which focuses on specific thoughts, feelings, or acts, shameful experiences are taken to represent failures that reflect on the core or ideal self in an intensely negative way (Babcock & Sabini, 1990; Tangney, 1992; Tangney et al., 1996). While guilt feelings may motivate the individual to approach others in order to make reparations, thus strengthening social bonds (Baumeister et al., 1994), shame involves a sense of painful exposure before a real or imagined audience. There is a tendency to want to withdraw and hide, to shrink in on the self or "into the floor," and to disappear (Tangney et al., 1996), which may be reflected in physical hunching of the body or head looking down, as if to avoid being seen.

Following experiences of shame, people have a sense of being a bad, immoral person; they experience anger and disgust with the self and they feel isolated (Tangney et al., 1996). Shame implies such global "badness" that the best hope for any relief is to hide in order to lessen the sense of exposure associated with the shame (Tangney, Wagner, Fletcher, & Gramzow, 1992). Shame seems more likely than guilt to lead to symptoms of psychopathology, including anger (Bennett et al., 2005), depression, and general dysphoria, whereas "shame-free guilt" does not appear as likely to lead to symptoms of psychopathology and may in fact mitigate such symptoms, as noted earlier (Quiles & Bybee, 1997; Tangney, 1999).

Self-Blame

Shame and guilt are both associated with attributions of self-blame (Janoff-Bulman, 1979; Leskel et al., 2002), which is often considered a maladaptive reaction to trauma. Janoff-Bulman (1979) distinguished between behavioral self-blame, which focuses on specific behaviors, and characterologic self-blame, which focuses on the whole self. Characterologic self-blame can lead to shame, while behavioral self-blame can lead to guilt (Leskel et al., 2002). The behavioral self-blame of guilt can encourage adjustment; however, the characterologic self-blame of shame creates a continuous self-focusing, self-regulatory cycle where the individual sees no way to repair a deeply negative self-image (Pyszcznski & Greenberg, 1987). This results in "intensified negative affect, self-derogation, further negative outcomes, and a depressive self-focusing style in which he or she self-focuses a great deal after negative outcomes but very little after positive outcomes" (Pyszcznski & Greenberg, 1987, p. 122).

Peritraumatic and Posttraumatic Shame

In general, negative self-attributions as a whole, self-blame in particular, and feelings of shame are strongly predictive of negative outcomes such as depression and dissociation, even after controlling for other important predictors (Abramson et al., 2002; Coffey, Leitenberg, Henning, Turner, & Bennett, 1996; Conte & Schuerman, 1987; Feiring & Cleland, 2007; Harvey, 1998; Hazzard, Celano, Gould, Lawry, & Webb, 1995; Morrow, 1991; Spaccarelli, 1994; Whiffen & MacIntosh, 2005). Traumatic experiences that involve behaviors or consequences the community or important others would consider reprehensible, disgraceful, or immoral and that could conceivably lead to stigmatization of those involved are particularly likely to make survivors feel shame. Thus, shame is considered by many to be a core aspect of child maltreatment (Bennett et al., 2005; Loader, 1998). In addition to sexual abuse, physical abuse appears to be particularly shaming to children (Loader, 1998); although emotional abuse can have long-term effects as well (Hoglund & Nicholas, 1995). Furthermore, children do not have to be the direct target of abuse to feel shame. Child witnesses of domestic violence frequently feel shame for multiple reasons including that (a) they cannot defend the abused parent, (b) they simultaneously love and hate the abusing parent, (c) they feel the fighting is due to their own "bad" behavior, and (d) such violence reflects shamefully upon the family (Stiles, 2002). Feeling responsible for traumatic experiences can increase a sense of helplessness and social inadequacy (Silver & Wortman, 1980).

Shame seems particularly likely to develop into a problem after exposure to childhood maltreatment (see Andrews et al., 2000; Leskela et al., 2002), whether it is sexual abuse (Wolfe et al., 1994), physical abuse (Brown & Kolko, 1999; Valle & Silovsky, 2002), neglect, or emotional abuse (Alessandri & Lewis, 1996; Hoglund & Nicholas, 1995). Current research has suggested that characterologic self-blame and shame mediate the connection between abuse and the development and maintenance of PTSD symptomatology (Feiring & Cleland, 2007; Feiring, Taska, & Chen, 2002; Feiring, Taska, & Lewis, 1998, 2002; Runyan & Kenny, 2002; Spaccarelli, 1994; Wolfe et al., 1994).

Shame and guilt associated with stigma have consistently been shown to lead to long-lasting negative outcomes that are resistant to change (Feiring, Taska, & Lewis, 1996, 1998; Finkelhor & Browne, 1985; Negrao, Bonanno, Noll, Putnam, & Trickett, 2005). For children ages 8 to 15 who were interviewed 8 weeks after disclosure of CSA and again 1 year later (Feiring, Taska, & Chen, 2002), accounting for adjustment at abuse discovery, shame was significantly related to higher levels of PTSD and depression and lower levels of self-esteem, while the level of abuse severity was not. Six years later, feelings of shame were still predictive of increased PTSD symptoms (Feiring & Taska, 2005). Shame and self-blame were also significantly associated with sexual difficulties and dating aggression at that time (Feiring, Simon, & Cleland, 2009). Child survivors of CSA tend to show poorer treatment outcomes. Cognitive-behavioral therapies can successfully target shame in treatment; decreases in shame are associated with decreases in PTSD symptomatology (Cohen, Deblinger, Mannarino, & Steer, 2004).

Shame-Rage Spiral

Feelings of shame can lead to depression (Gladstone & Kaslow, 1995; Lewis, 1971). Many individuals attempt to end the seemingly endless cycle of negative self-blame associated with shame by resorting to anger (Lewis, 1971; Tangney et al., 1992). Although the primary focus of shame is on the self, the associated sense of being condemned by others can lead the individual to develop a kind of retaliatory anger that manifests as a lashing out. Such anger is characterized by a humiliated rage that attempts to erase the shame by shifting the rejection from self to the other; although the anger can be held in and unexpressed as well as expressed (Lewis, 1971; Scheff, 1987; Tangney et al., 1992). This tendency for shame to turn into anger is seen consistently, regardless of age or gender (Bennett et al., 2005; Tangney et al., 1996). Rather than curbing aggressive behavior, shame can initiate an irrational and counterproductive form of rage. On some level, the shamed individual realizes the anger is unjustified, and that realization only deepens the sense of shame (Tangney et al., 1992).

The Nature of Anger and its Relationship to Trauma

Anger is a negative emotion in which an individual feels aroused and antagonistic toward someone or something perceived to be the source of deliberate threat or harm to himself or herself or toward someone close to him or her (Novaco, 2008). Anger can be differentiated from aggression, which is intentionally harmful behavior, and from hostility, which is an attitude. Anger is usually experienced as a response to events thought to be wrong (e.g., physical attacks, insults or humiliations, unfair treatment, or intentional prevention of efforts, plans, or desires).

Anger is recognized as a symptom of a range of trauma-response disorders, including PTSD, complex PTSD, dissociative identity disorder, major depressive disorder, borderline personality disorder, and head-trauma dementia. It is also associated with many stress-related physical problems, such as cardiovascular disorders (Novaco, 2008). Meta-analysis (Fletcher, 2003) indicated that 23% of youth exposed to high-magnitude stressors present with symptoms of irritability and anger. Anger may also contribute to the long-term maintenance of PTSD symptomatology (Andrews et al., 2000). As noted, anger can also be aroused by other trauma-related feelings such as shame (Andrews et al., 2000; Bennett et al., 2005; Tangney et al., 1992).

There is evidence that anger mediates the effects of traumatic experience on adjustment (Bennett et al., 2005). Anger also appears to mediate the effects of shame on adjustment (Bennett et al., 2005). Thus, anger that results from maltreatment can lead directly to behavioral problems. At the same time, shame that results from maltreatment can turn into anger and in this way have an indirect impact on behavior problems, while also having a direct effect on adjustment. Mediational paths of shame and anger from maltreatment to behavioral problems may change according to the kind of maltreatment. In one study, physical abuse among boys and girls 3 to 7 years old had only a direct effect on shame, and shame had only a direct effect on anger, which in turn had a direct effect on behavioral problems (Bennett et al., 2005). However, among children in this same study who were victims of neglect rather than physical abuse, maltreatment did not directly affect shame, anger, or behavioral problems. Shame, again, had only a direct effect on anger, which in turn had a direct effect on behavior problems.

Feelings of anger commonly result from exposure to high-magnitude stressors, especially when the stressful events include interpersonal violence and anger (Cloitre et al., 2009; Ford & Kidd, 1998; van der Kolk, 2005). Sexual abuse frequently leads to difficulties regulating anger and aggression (Bal, Van Oost, De Boureaudhuij, & Crombez, 2003; Beitchman, Zucker, Hood, DaCosta, & Akman, 1991). Children and adolescents exposed to community violence frequently respond with anger, aggression, oppositional defiant disorder, and conduct disorder (Schwab-Stone et al., 1999). A recent survey of 1,025 children ages 2 to 17 who had experienced at least one form of victimization in the previous year (e.g., crime, maltreatment, peer and sibling victimization, sexual victimization, or witnessing/indirect victimization) examined the effects of psychological distress—a composite score of anger, depression, and anxiety scales—on later revictimization (Cuevas, Finkelhor, Clifford, Ormrod, & Turner, 2010). The greater their distress over their victimization, the more likely they were to be revictimized during the following year. Distress predicted the total number of victimizations and the likelihood to be revictimized.

Unexpressed Feelings

Shame, guilt, and anger feelings are not always fully expressed by survivors of traumatic events (Herman, 1992; Negrao et al., 2005; Sourander, 1998). Since feelings of shame are associated with threats to one's self-image, the tendency is to hide one's shame and the reasons for it, rather than sharing it with others (Negrao et al., 2005). Guilt feelings can make children hesitant to even discuss their traumatic experiences (Sourander, 1998). Anger associated with shame may discourage outward expression of anger. In addition, open expression of anger is generally socially discouraged. Outward expression of anger may be more likely to occur when the object of the anger is external to the self (Negrao et al., 2005).

The term *emotional coherence* suggests that an emotion is simultaneously experienced and expressed rather than repressed (Negrao et al., 2005). Emotional coherence is generally assumed to facilitate adaptation to challenging life events (Rosenberg & Ekman, 1994). There is some evidence that individuals with PTSD are more likely than those without PTSD to show greater incongruence between self-reports of their experiences and their expression of emotion (Wagner, Roemer, Orsillo, & Litz, 2003). If feelings of shame and guilt remain unacknowledged, over time, a characterological sense of self-blame can develop, making victims feel their traumatic experiences are due in large part to flaws in their character. This increases a sense of helplessness and hopelessness, and these intensified feelings can in turn discourage the sharing of feelings even more, which leads to a vicious cycle (Ferguson, 2005).

However, emotional coherence may not always be beneficial to all survivors of traumatic events (Fernandez-Dols, Sanchez, Carrera, & Ruiz-Belda, 1997; Negrao et al., 2005). Among nondisclosing CSA survivors in one study, coherence predicted more PTSD symptoms, while lack of emotional coherence was associated with better adjustment

(Negrao et al., 2005). The authors suggested that these results might indicate that, although emotional coherence may be adaptive for disclosing CSA survivors, CSA survivors who do not willingly disclose their abuse may be particularly sensitive to their felt emotions. By holding them in check and not directly expressing them, they may be adaptively managing their thoughts and feelings regarding the abuse through minimization or avoidance. So nondisclosing CSA survivors who do express what they feel may actually be demonstrating a breakdown in their defenses, because for them, lack of emotional coherence is more adaptive, at least in the short term.

Developmental and Gender Differences

Self-evaluative emotions such as guilt and shame appear to first develop between the ages of 2 ½ and 3 following the emergence of self-recognition (Lewis, Alessandri, & Sullivan, 1992; Lewis & Sullivan, 2005). Current research suggests that as children develop, feelings of guilt increase in frequency, as does the development of reasons for and expression of the guilt (see Table 1). With sexual abuse, for example, school-aged children may be more vulnerable to shame, while adolescents may be more likely to develop problems with impulsive behavior, conduct problems, and other behavior problems (Cole & Putnam, 1992; Downs, 1993; see Table 2). Most research to date has found that traumatized girls are more likely than boys to report feeling guilty or bad about themselves (see Table 3), and girls seem more likely to exhibit shame than boys (Ferguson & Eyre, 2000; Lewis, Sullivan, Ramsay, & Alessandri, 1992), especially after CSA and physical abuse (Alessandri & Lewis, 1996; Brown & Kolko, 1999; Feiring, Taska, & Lewis, 1999, 2002; Stuewig & McCloskey, 2005; see Table 4).

Research regarding developmental differences in anger is listed in Table 5. In general, the frequency with which anger is experienced and expressed decreases with age, while

Table 2

Developmental differences in shame and self-blame

Age range	Effects	Source
5–7 years	Feelings of shame were found to increase with age among maltreated children.	Bennett, Sullivan, & Lewis (2005)
8–13 years	Younger children were more likely to blame themselves for their abuse.	Hazzard et al. (1995)
8–15 years	CSA[a] is more likely to challenge the self-esteem of adolescent than child victims; No age differences in shame reactions after CSA; No age differences in self-blame attributions were found; Six years after disclosure, perpetrator blame became more common than self-blame among these children and adolescents; Self-blame attributions decreased over time.	Feiring, Taska, & Lewis (1998); Feiring & Cleland (2007)
8–adult	Age at time of abuse was positively correlated with self-blame	Hunter, Goodwin, & Wilson (1992)

[a]CSA = childhood sexual abuse.

Table 3
Gender differences in guilt

Age range	Gender differences	Source
5–9 years	No gender differences were found on guilt scores among children of depressed mothers.	Zahn-Waxler et al. (1990)
5–12 years	Girls high in shame-free guilt showed significantly more symptoms of both internalizing and externalizing behaviors than boys high in shame-free guilt.	Ferguson et al. (1999)
Adolescents	Girls were more likely than boys to report feeling guilty or bad about themselves after traumatic experiences.	Kar & Bastia (2006)
Adolescents	Maltreated girls scored higher on guilt than maltreated boys.	Stuewig & McCloskey (2005)
College	Women scored significantly higher than men on the Global Guilt scale of the Trauma-Related Guilt Inventory	Kubany et al. (1996)

Table 4
Gender differences in shame

Age range	Gender differences	Source
3 years 5–12 years	Girls were more likely to exhibit shame than boys in general	Lewis, Alessandri, & Sullivan, 1992; Ferguson & Eyre, 2000
4–5 years	Maltreated boys showed less shame and less pride than nonmaltreated boys	Alessandri & Lewis, 1996;
Adolescents	Maltreated girls scored more highly on shame than maltreated boys	Stuewig & McCloskey, 2005
Childhood to Adult	Feelings of shame were more likely to lead to symptoms of depression in girls;	Cutler & Nolen-Hoeksema, 1991
	Feelings of shame were more likely to lead to symptoms of rage in boys	Friedrich, Beilke, & Urquiza, 1988; Lewis, 1992; Retzinger, 1987

the control of angry impulses increases (Spielberger, 1999). Research regarding gender differences in the experience and expression of anger is reported in Table 6. For the most part, the data seem to support Harburg, Blackelock, and Roeper's (1979) contention that when angry, females tend to be more likely to try to disengage from their feelings and to find a solution to the problems that gave rise to the anger. Males on the other hand tend to respond more impulsively and aggressively. It has also been suggested that males are more likely than girls to replace shame with anger (Lewis, 1992).

Table 5
Developmental differences in anger

Age range	Effects	Source
Childhood to Adult	The frequency with which anger is experienced and expressed decreases with age; The control of angry impulses increases with age.	Spielberger (1999)
5–9 years	No age differences in hostility themes were found in response to a semi-projective test.	Zahn-Waxler et al. (1990)
2–17 years	Children aged 10–17 years were more likely to react to victimization experiences with aggression than children aged 2–9.	Becker-Blease, Turner, & Finkelhor (2010)
11–16 years	Younger adolescents (11–13 years) reported significantly lower scores on anger control than older adolescents (14–16 years).	Reyes, Meininger, Liehr, Chan, & Mueller (2003)
11–16 years	Hostility was lower among older adolescents (14–16 years) than among younger adolescents (11–13 years).	Reyes et al. (2003)
11–16 years	The reliability of anger scales in general may be lower (unacceptably low for anger—in anger directed at the self—as assessed by the STAXI) among younger adolescents (11–13 years) than among older adolescents (14–16), except perhaps for state anger, which had lower reliability among the older adolescents.	Reyes et al. (2003)
18–25 years	Expressed anger decreases with age among 18- to 25-year-old young men and women.	Galambos, Barker, & Krahn (2006)
Adolescents – Adults	Older adults seem less likely to report experiencing anger than younger adults and adolescents, and when they do, they rate their anger lower in intensity.	Birditt & Fingerman (2005); Blanchard-Fields & Coats (2008); Gross et al. (1997); Schieman (1999)

Assessment

Measures that assess shame, guilt, and anger are listed in Tables 7 through 10. Numerous potential problems exist with current methods of assessing guilt and shame, and possibly anger as well. Many measures fail to distinguish between guilt and shame, for instance, and people have a tendency to confound the two (Tangney, 1996). This is perhaps because shame and guilt can often be felt in response to the same experience (Lewis, 1971). Some measures ask about feelings of shame or guilt in the same items. Methods of item reduction and scale refinement, such as exploratory factor analysis, can lead researchers to conflate one or both feelings with larger domains that subsume them, such as dysphoria. Scales might group together items that ask about guilt or shame with items that ask about moral behavior, standards, beliefs, or attitudes. At other times, only a subset of items is assessed,

Table 6
Gender differences in anger

Age range	Gender differences	Source
5–9 years	No gender differences in hostility themes were found in response to a semi-projective test.	Zahn-Waxler et al. (1990)
Fourth and fifth graders	Boys were more likely to openly express their anger; Girls were more likely to respond to angry feelings with reflection and control.	Jacobs, Phelps, & Rohr (1989)
Adolescents	Girls and boys reported similar levels of anger in response to the 9/11 attacks.	Whalen, Henker, King, Jamner, & Levine (2004)
Older Adolescents	Boys reported more anger-out (anger directed externally) and more overall anger expression but less anger control than girls.	Musante, Treiber, Davis, Waller, & Thompson (1999); Spielberger (1996)

Table 7
Assessment of guilt and shame

Measure	Description
Abuse-Related Beliefs Questionnaire (Ginzburg et al., 2006)	An 18-item assessment of abuse-related beliefs of guilt, shame, and negative self-evaluation.
The Child Attribution and Reaction Survey – Child (C-CARS; Stegge & Ferguson, 1990)	Based on TOSCA; for ages 5–12; includes eight age-appropriate scenarios likely to elicit shame or guilt.
The Differential Emotions Scale (Izard, 1977; Mosher & White, 1981)	Assesses state shame and guilt; key emotion words (e.g., blameworthy, guilty, repentant for guilt) used to rate current feelings.
The Personal Feelings Questionnaire (PFQ2; Harder & Zalma, 1990)	The PFQ2 consists of a 10-item shame subscale and a six-item guilt subscale.
State Shame & Guilt Scale (Marschall, Sanftner, & Tangney, 1994)	Ten items describing subjective experiences of shame and guilt.
TOSCA-A (Tangney, Wagner, Gavlas, & Gramzow, 1991)	Scenarios and responses relevant to adolescents
TOSCA-C (Tangney, Burggraf, Gramzow, & Fletcher, 1990)	For children ages 8–12; 15 illustrated scenarios and responses based on reports of elementary school children.

Note. Includes measures with psychometric statistics that are good to excellent.

such as asking about only survivor guilt. States of guilt or shame have often been confounded with other domains, as well. For instance, Cook's (1989) Internalized Shame Scale (ISS) was created to assess a chronic sense of shame due to feelings of inferiority and inadequacy, internalized as part of an individual's identity, making it difficult to distinguish this

Table 8
Assessment of guilt

Measure	Description
Children's Impact of Traumatic Events Scale-Revised (CITES-R; Wolfe et al., 1991)	A 77-item true-false questionnaire; 11 subscales that assess PTSD and additional cognitive and affective reactions, including a 7-item self-blame/guilt subscale (e.g., "I feel guilty about what happened").
Children's Interpretations of Interpersonal Distress and Conflict (CIIDC; Zahn-Waxler et al., 1988)	A semi-projective measure including four stories with accompanying photographs of ambiguous situations; guilt themes are coded for comments expressing remorse, self-punishment, reparation, apology, and blameworthiness.
Guilt Inventory (GI; Kugler & Jones, 1992)	Forty-five items assessing three domains: trait guilt, state guilt, and moral standards.
Mosher Forced-Choice Guilt Scale (Mosher, 1966)	Two subscales: hostility guilt subscale and a morality-conscience subscale.
Trauma-Related Guilt Inventory (TRGI; Kubany et al., 1996)	Three scales (32 items) assessing affective and cognitive components of trauma-related guilt: global guilt, distress, and guilt cognitions, and subscales assessing hindsight bias/responsibility, wrongdoing, and lack of justification.

Note. Includes measures with psychometric statistics that are good to excellent.

internalized shame from low self-esteem. Even when measures have been created specifically to distinguish guilt from shame, difficulties persist. In particular, there is the problem of distinguishing what is generally referred to as *states* from *traits*. States tend to be transitory and situation specific, while traits or dispositions are generally longer lasting and less amenable to change. Because of the difficulty in assessing situation-specific guilt and shame, more recent measures have tended to focus on "proneness" to shame or guilt, which might be considered a disposition to feel shame or guilt in relevant situations.

The methodology for assessing guilt and shame varies. One approach uses descriptions of situations thought to potentially lead to either feelings of shame or guilt, asking respondents to indicate how anxious, how upset, or how much shame or guilt they or "most people" would feel in each of the situations described. Each situation described is assumed to be theoretically more likely to lead to either shame or guilt, but not to both. A more recent approach uses scenarios based on actual experiences provided by the age group intended to be assessed. Each scenario is followed by several kinds of responses that are intended to capture features related to feelings of shame or guilt without actually using those terms. The scenario approach differs from the situational approach in that, first, the scenarios are based on the kinds of guilt or shame experiences respondents of the relevant age group have actually reported experiencing (e.g., "You get a test in school and you didn't do well"; Tangney, Burggraf, Garmzow, & Fletcher, 1990). A second difference is that rather than explicitly asking respondents to indicate whether they would feel shame or guilt, they are asked to indicate how likely they might be to feel each emotion. This allows respondents to indicate the degree to which they might experience both feelings in response to the same scenario rather than forcing them to make a choice between the two.

Table 9
Assessment of shame

Measure	Description
The Attributions About Abuse Inventory (AAAI; Feiring, Taska, & Chen, 2002)	Designed to differentiate characterological from behavioral attributions of self-blame for CSA (Cole, Peeke, & Ingold, 1996; Dalenberg & Jacobs, 1994; Feiring et al., 2002; Feiring & Cleland, 2007).
Children's Attributional Style Questionnaire (CASQ, also KASTAN; Kaslow, Tannenbaum, & Seligman, 1978) and Attributional Style Questionnaire (ASQ, Peterson & Villanova, 1988)	Forty-eight-item measures of general self-blame attributions (not specifically related to CSA); uses an equal number of scenarios of events with negative and positive outcomes; CASQ: children ages 16 and younger; ASQ: adolescents and adults, 17 and older (Nolen-Hoeksema et al., 1992)
The Children's Cognitive Style Questionnaire (CCSQ; Mezulis et al., 2006)	Six scenarios: 4 negative and 2 positive events; 20 response items for the negative events assessing internal-external, stable-unstable, and global-specific dimensions.
Management of Shame State: Shame Acknowledgement and Shame Displacement (MOSS-SASD; Ahmed, Braithwaite, & Braithwaite, 1996; Ahmed, 2001)	Measures shame-management capacity of children ages 9 and above; two subscales, based on factor analysis, assessing shame acknowledgement and shame displacement, with five questions after each scenario. (Ahmed & Braithwaite, 2004).
Situation-Specific Shame Questions (Feiring et al. 1999, 2002)	Respondents rate themselves on four shame-related items.

Note. Includes measures with psychometric statistics that are acceptable to excellent.

Possible reactions are based on responses others have indicated they had in similar situations. Moreover, responses of shame and guilt are never labeled as such (e.g., for shame, "I'd feel stupid;" and for guilt, "I'd feel that I should have done better. I should have studied more"; Tangney et al., 1990). Another assessment method asks respondents to indicate the degree to which each of a list of supposedly shame- and guilt-related adjectives describes them (e.g., for shame: mortified, embarrassed, feeling ridiculous; for guilt: unethical, culpable, regret). Tangney (1996) identified several problems with this approach. Some of the words used, for example, might be difficult for respondents to define (e.g., culpable).

As noted, many measures designed to assess both guilt and shame have difficulty differentiating guilt responses from shame responses. Very often the two constructs are at least moderately correlated, even among measures specifically designed to differentiate between the two. For example, the PFQ2's Shame and Guilt scales (see Table 7) correlate .52 (Harder & Zalma, 1990), while the TOSCA's Shame and Guilt scales (see Table 7) correlate .45 (Tangney et al., 1995). An even more serious problem with the various measures is that there is growing evidence that many of the measures of shame, guilt, or anger may be assessing different and possibly uncorrelated aspects of the respective feelings. This is perhaps most obvious in the scales designed to assess trait versus state guilt (as in

Table 10
Assessment of anger

Measure	Description
Aggression Questionnaire (AQ; Buss & Perry, 1992)	Four scales (total 29 items): physical aggression, verbal aggression, anger, and hostility (Martin, Watson, & Wan, 2000)
Anger Expression Scale (AX; Spielberger et al., 1985)	Two subscales (total 20 items): anger-in and anger-out
Anger Reaction Indices (ARI-Adolescents, ARI-Children; Tangney et al., 1991; Tangney et al., 1996)	Scenario assessment of anger experience and management; Assesses: (1) anger arousal, (2) intentions, (3) cognitive and behavioral responses, and (4) long-term consequences for self, target, and relationship (Tangney et al., 1996).
Anger Self-Report (ASR; Zelin, Adler, & Myerson, 1972)	Four subscales: anger expression, neuroticism, anger valuation, and cynicism-mistrust
Buss-Durkee Hostility Inventory (BDHI; Buss & Durkee, 1957)	Seventy-five true/false items; six aspects of hostility subscales (66 items): assault, indirect hostility, negativity, irritability, resentment, and suspicion; nine items assess guilt-shame
Cook and Medley Hostility Scale (HO; Cook & Medley, 1954)	Fifty true/false items in five subscales: cynicism, hostile attributions, hostile affect, aggressive responding, and social avoidance
Multidimensional Anger Inventory (MAI; Siegel, 1986)	Yields a composite total for 25 of 38 items and five subscales: anger-arousal, range of situations, hostile outlook, anger-in, and anger-out
The Pediatric Anger Expression Scale (PAES; Jacobs, Phelps, & Rohr, 1989)	A 15-item children's self-report measure of trait anger; four subscales: anger-out (e.g., slams doors); anger-control (e.g., keeps calm); anger-reflection (e.g., tries to calmly settle the problem); and anger-suppression (e.g., holds anger in).
The Positive & Negative Affect Schedule – Expanded Form Hostility Scale (PANAS-X Hostility Scale; Watson & Clark, 1994)	Respondents are instructed to rate how well each of six anger-related affect adjectives, such as "angry" and "irritable," describe their usual feelings.
State-Trait Anger Expression Inventory-2 (STAXI-2; Spielberger, 1999) (administered to children as young as 11 years (Reyes et al., 2003).	Fifty-seven items assessing the experience, expression, and control of anger (ages 16 to 63) in six scales: state anger, trait anger, anger expression-out, anger expression-in, anger control-out, anger control-in; includes an anger expression index and five subscales: state anger/feeling, state anger/verbal, state anger/physical, trait/anger temperament, and trait anger/reaction.
Trait Anger Scale (TAS; Spielberger et al., 1983)	The TAS is composed of 15 items; two 4-item anger subscales can be formed: angry temperament and angry reaction.

Note. Sources: Jones, Thomas-Peter, & Trout, 1999; Martin, Watson, & Wan, 2000; Reyes, Meininger, Liehr, Chan, & Mueller, 2003; Tangney et al., 1996. Only measures with good-to-excellent psychometric properties are included.

the Guilt Inventory; see Table 8) or anger (as in the State-Trait Anger Expression Inventory; see Table 10). However, even measures designed to assess the same domain do not always accomplish this.

Feelings of guilt, shame, and anger may not be simply static states but rather more dynamic experiences that can change over time (Bennett et al., 2005). For example, Ferguson and Crowley (1997) argued that different measures may tap into different aspects of guilt along a continuum that starts with a kind of guilt that motivates an individual to attempt to rectify the situation. If rectification eventually proves impossible, however, the individual may move on to another phase of incessant rumination about the guilt, and if unresolvable guilt experiences accumulate, this can lead to an extreme phase of trait-like guilt.

The assessment of anger, which is a somewhat more mature field than the assessment of guilt and shame, illustrates this phenomenon in that several anger measures assess a wide variety of different aspects of anger (see Table 10). It may be that different measures of guilt and shame actually assess differing phases of the same emotion (see also Amodio et al., 2007). Thus, as mentioned earlier, Cook's (1989) ISS was created to assess a chronic sense of shame that may lie on one extreme of a continuum of shame, much like the continuum of guilt proposed by Ferguson and Crowley (1997). Researchers and clinicians should remain cognizant of the possibility that different kinds of guilt, shame, and anger may exist. Each type might require a slightly different measure to adequately assess it, and perhaps, different kinds of interventions to effectively treat it as well.

Conclusion

Clearly, in addition to the usual symptoms of PTSD, emotions such as guilt, shame, and anger can develop in children's and adolescents' responses to traumatic experiences. These emotions can play an important mediational role between exposure to traumatic events and the development of adverse outcomes. A better understanding of how these feelings can affect other posttraumatic responses should help us evolve better models of individuals' posttrauma experiences and, in turn, inform the development of more effective interventions. Creating better articulated theories and measures of traumatic feelings are prerequisites for explicating and testing the processes whereby traumatic emotions arise and how these emotions influence the course of posttraumatic adjustment.

References

Abramson, L. Y., Alloy, L. B., Hankin, B. L., Haeffel, G. J., MacCoon, D. G., & Gibb, B. E. (2002). Cognitive vulnerability-stress models of depression in a self-regulatory and psychobiological context. In I. H. Gotlib & C. L. Hammen (Eds.), *Handbook of depression* (pp. 268–294). New York: Guilford Press.

Ahmed, E. (2001). Shame management: Regulating bullying. In E. Ahmed, N. Harris, J. Braithwaite, & V. Braithwaite (Eds.), *Shame management through reintegration* (pp. 211–314). Cambridge, England: Cambridge University Press.

Ahmed, E., & Braithwaite, V. (2004). "What, me ashamed?" Shame management and school bullying. *Journal of Research in Crime and Delinquency, 40*, 1–26.

Ahmed, E., Braithwaite, V., & Braithwaite, J. (1996). Management of Shame State: Shame Acknowledgement and Shame Displacement (MOSS-SASD). In *Life at School Survey: Child*

Questionnaire. Unpublished booklet. Research School of Social Sciences at the Australian National University.

Alessandri, S. M., & Lewis, M. (1996). Differences in pride and shame in maltreated and nonmaltreated preschoolers. *Child Development, 67*, 1857–1869.

American Psychiatric Association. (2000). *Diagnostic and statistical manual of mental disorders* (text revision). Washington, DC: Author.

Amodio, D. M., Devine, P. G., & Harmon-Jones, E. (2007). A dynamic model of guilt: Implications for motivation and self-regulation in the context of prejudice. *Psychological Science, 18*, 524–530.

Andrews, B., Brewin, C. R., Rose, S., & Kirk, M. (2000). Predicting PTSD symptoms in victims of violent crime: The role of shame, anger, and childhood abuse. *Journal of Abnormal Psychology, 109*, 69–73.

Babcock, M. K., & Sabini, J. (1990). On differentiating embarrassment from shame. *European Journal of Social Psychology, 20*, 151–169.

Bal, S., Van Oost, P., De Bourdeaudhuij, I., & Crombez, G. (2003). Avoidant coping as a mediator between self-reported sexual abuse and stress-related symptoms in adolescents. *Child Abuse & Neglect, 27*, 883–897.

Baumeister, R. F., Stillwell, A. M., & Heatherton, T. F. (1994). Guilt: An interpersonal approach. *Psychological Bulletin, 115*, 243–267.

Becker-Blease, K. A., Turner, H. A., & Finkelhor, D. (2010). Disaster, victimization, and children's mental health. *Child Development, 81*, 1040–1052.

Beitchman, J. H., Zucker, K. J., Hood, J. E., DaCosta, G., & Akman, D. (1991). A review of the short-term effects of child sexual abuse. *Child Abuse & Neglect, 15*, 537–556.

Bennett, D. S., Sullivan, M. W., & Lewis, M. (2005). Young children's adjustment as a function of maltreatment, shame, and anger. *Child Maltreatment, 10*, 311–323.

Birditt, K. S., & Fingerman, K. L. (2005). Do we get better at picking our battles? Age group differences in descriptions of behavioral reactions to interpersonal tensions. *Journals of Gerontology, Series B: Psychological Sciences and Social Sciences, 60*, P121–P128.

Blanchard-Fields, F., & Coats, A. H. (2008). The experience of anger and sadness in everyday problems impact age differences in emotion regulation. *Developmental Psychology, 44*, 1547–1556.

Brown, E. J., & Kolko, D. J. (1999). Child victims' attributions about being physically abused: An examination of factors associated with symptom severity. *Journal of Abnormal Child Psychology, 27*, 311–322.

Buss, A. H., & Durkee, A. (1957). The measurement of hostility in clinical situations. *Journal of Consulting Psychology, 21*, 343–349.

Buss, A. H., & Perry, M. (1992). The aggression questionnaire. *Journal of Personality and Social Psychology, 63*, 452–459.

Cloitre, M., Stolbach, B. C., Herman, J. L., van der Kolk, B., Pynoos, R., Wang, J., et al. (2009). A developmental approach to Complex PTSD: Childhood and adult cumulative trauma as predictors of symptom complexity. *Journal of Traumatic Stress, 22*, 399–408.

Coffey, P., Leitenberg, H., Henning, K., Turner, T., & Bennett, R. T. (1996). Mediators of the long-term impact of child sexual abuse: Perceived stigma, betrayal, powerlessness, and self-blame. *Child Abuse & Neglect, 20*, 447–455.

Cohen, J. A., Deblinger, E., Mannarino, A. P., & Steer, R. A. (2004). A multisite, randomized controlled trial for children with sexual abuse-related PTSD symptoms. *Journal of the American Academy of Child and Adolescent Psychiatry, 43*, 393–402.

Cole, D., Peeke, L., & Ingold, C. (1996). Characterological and behavioral self-blame in children: Assessment and development considerations. *Development & Psychopathology, 8*, 381–397.

Cole, P. M., & Putnam, F. W. (1992). Effect of incest on self and social functioning: A developmental psychopathology perspective. *Journal of Consulting and Clinical Psychology, 60*, 174–184.

Conte, J. R., & Schuerman, J. R. (1987). Factors associated with an increased impact of child sexual abuse. *Child Abuse & Neglect, 11*, 201–211.

Cook, A., Spinazzola, J., Ford, J., Lanktree, C., Blaustein, M., Cloitre, M., et al. (2005). Complex trauma in children and adolescents. *Psychiatric Annals, 35*, 390–398.

Cook, D. (1989). *Internalized shame scale*. Menomonie, WI: University of Wisconsin-Stout.

Cook, W. W., & Medley, D. M. (1954). Proposed hostility and pharisaic-virtue scales for the MMPI. *Journal of Applied Psychology, 38*, 414–418.

Cuevas, C. A., Finkelhor, D., Clifford, C., Ormrod, R. K., & Tuner, H. A. (2010). Psychological distress as a risk factor for re-victimization in children. *Child Abuse & Neglect, 34*, 235–243.

Cutler, S. E., & Nolen-Hoeksema, S. (1991). Accounting for sex differences in depression through female victimization: Childhood sexual abuse. *Sex Roles, 24*, 424–438.

Dalenberg, C. J., & Jacobs, D. A. (1994). Attributional analyses of child sexual abuse episodes: Empirical and clinical issues. *Journal of Child Sexual Abuse, 3*, 37–50.

Downs, W. R. (1993). Developmental considerations for the effects of childhood sexual abuse. *Journal of Interpersonal Violence, 8*, 331–345.

Feiring, C., & Cleland, C. (2007). Childhood sexual abuse and abuse-specific attributions of blame over 6 years following discovery. *Child Abuse & Neglect, 31*, 1169–1186.

Feiring, C., Simon, V. A., & Cleland, C. (2009). Childhood sexual abuse, stigmatization, internalizing symptoms, and the development of sexual difficulties and dating aggression. *Journal of Consulting and Clinical Psychology, 77*, 127–137.

Feiring, C., & Taska, L. S. (2005). The persistence of shame following sexual abuse: A longitudinal look at risk and recovery. *Child Maltreatment, 10*, 337–349.

Feiring, C., Taska, L. S., & Chen, K. (2002). Trying to understand why horrible things happen: Attribution, shame and symptom development following sexual abuse. *Child Maltreatment, 7*, 26–41.

Feiring, C., Taska, L., & Lewis, M. (1996). A process model for understanding adaptation to sexual abuse: The role of shame in defining stigmatization. *Child Abuse & Neglect, 8*, 767–782.

Feiring, C., Taska, L., & Lewis, M. (1998). The role of shame and attributional style in children's and adolescents' adaptation to sexual abuse. *Child Maltreatment, 3*, 129–142.

Feiring, C., Taska, L., & Lewis, M. (1999). Age and gender differences in children's and adolescents' adaptation to sexual abuse. *Child Abuse & Neglect, 23*, 115–128.

Feiring, C., Taska, L., & Lewis, M. (2002). Adjustment following sexual abuse discovery: The role of shame and attributional style. *Developmental Psychology, 38*, 79–92.

Ferguson, T. J. (2005). Mapping shame and its functions in relationships. *Child Maltreatment, 10*, 377–386.

Ferguson, T. J., & Crowley, S. L. (1997). Measure for measure: A multitrait-multimethod analysis of guilt and shame. *Journal of Personality Assessment, 69*, 425–441.

Ferguson, T. J., & Eyre, H. L. (2000). Engendering gender differences in shame and guilt: Stereotypes, socialization, and situational pressures. In A. H. Fischer (Ed.), *Gender and emotion: Social psychological perspectives* (pp. 254–276). New York: Cambridge University Press.

Ferguson, T. J., Stegge, H., Miller, E. R., & Olsen, M. E. (1999). Guilt, shame, and symptoms in children. *Developmental Psychology, 35*, 347–357.

Fernandez-Dols, J. M., Sanchez, F., Carrera, P., & Ruiz-Belda, M. A. (1997). Are spontaneous expressions and emotions linked? An experiential test of coherence. *Journal of Nonverbal Behavior, 21*, 163–177.

Finkelhor, D., & Browne, A. (1985). The traumatic impact of child sexual abuse: A conceptualization. *American Journal of Orthopsychiatry, 55*, 530–541.

Fletcher, K. E. (2003). Childhood posttraumatic stress disorder. In E. J. Mash & R. A. Barkley (Eds.), *Child psychopathology* (2nd ed., pp. 330–371). New York: Guilford Press.

Ford, J. D., & Kidd, P. (1998). Early childhood trauma and disorders of extreme stress as predictors of treatment outcome with chronic posttraumatic stress disorder. *Journal of Traumatic Stress, 11*, 743–761.

Friedrich, W. N., Beilke, R. L., & Urquiza, A. J. (1988). Behavior problems in young sexually abused boys. *Journal of Interpersonal Violence*, *3*, 21–28.

Galambos, N. L., Barker, E. T., & Krahn, H. J. (2006). Depression, self-esteem, and anger in emerging adulthood: Seven-year trajectories. *Developmental Psychology*, *42*, 350–365.

Ginzburg, K., Arnow, B., Hart, S., Gardner, W., Koopman, C., Classen, C. C., et al. (2006). The abuse-related beliefs questionnaire for survivors of childhood sexual abuse. *Child Abuse & Neglect*, *30*, 929–943.

Gladstone, T. R., & Kaslow, N. J. (1995). Depression and attribution in children and adolescents: A meta-analytic review. *Journal of Abnormal Child Psychology*, *23*, 597–606.

Graham, S., Doubleday, C., & Guarino, P. A. (1984). The development of relations between perceived controllability and the emotions of pity, anger, and guilt. *Child Development*, *55*, 561–565.

Gray Deering, C. (2000). A cognitive developmental approach to understanding how children cope with disasters. *Journal of Child and Adolescent Psychiatric Nursing*, *13*, 7–15.

Gross, J. J., Cartensen, L. L., Pasupathi, M., Tsai, J., Skorpen, C. G., & Hsu, A. Y. C. (1997). Emotion and aging: Experience, expression, and control. *Psychology and Aging*, *12*, 590–599.

Harburg, E., Blakelock, E. H., & Roeper, P. J. (1979). Resentful and reflective coping with arbitrary authority and blood pressure: Detroit. *Psychosomatic Medicine*, *3*, 189–202.

Harder, D. H., & Zalma, A. (1990). Two promising shame and guilt scales: A construct validity comparison. *Journal of Personality Assessment*, *55*, 729–745.

Harder, D. W. (1995). Shame and guilt assessment and relationships of shame and guilt proneness to psychopathology. In J. P. Tangney & K. W. Fischer (Eds.), *Self-conscious emotions: Shame, guilt, embarrassment, and pride* (pp. 368–392). New York: Guilford Press.

Harvey, J. I. (1998). Affective predictors of dissociation II: Shame and guilt. *Journal of Clinical Psychology*, *54*, 237–245.

Hawkins, S. A., & Hastie, R. (1990). Hindsight: Biased judgments of past events after outcomes are known. *Psychological Bulletin*, *107*, 311–327.

Hazzard, A., Celano, M., Gould, J., Lawry, S., & Webb, C. (1995). Predicting symptomatology and self-blame among child sex abuse victims. *Child Abuse & Neglect*, *19*, 707–714.

Herman, J. (1992). *Trauma and recovery*. New York: Basic Books.

Hoffman, M. (1982). Development of prosocial motivation: Empathy and guilt. In N. Eisenberg (Ed.), *The development of prosocial behavior* (pp. 281–313). New York: Academic Press.

Hoglund, C. L., & Nicholas, K. B. (1995). Shame, guilt, and anger in college students exposed to abusive family environments. *Journal of Family Violence*, *10*, 141–157.

Hunter, J. A., Goodwin, D. W., & Wilson, R. J. (1992). Attributions of blame in child sexual abuse victims: An analysis of age and gender influences. *Journal of Child Sexual Abuse*, *1*, 75–89.

Izard, C. E. (1977). *Human emotions*. New York: Plenum Press.

Jacobs, G. A., Phelps, M., & Rohrs, B. (1989). Assessment of anger expression in children: The Pediatric Anger Expression Scale. *Personality and Individual Differences*, *10*, 59–65.

Janoff-Bulman, R. (1979). Characterologic versus behavioral self-blame: Inquiries into depression and rape. *Journal of Personality and Social Psychology*, *37*, 1798–1809.

Jones, J. P., Thomas-Peter, B. A., & Trout, A. (1999). Normative data for the Novaco Anger Scale from a non-clinical sample and implications for clinical use. *British Journal of Clinical Psychology*, *38*, 417–424.

Joseph, S. A., Hodgkinson, P., Yule, W., & Williams, R. (1993). Guilt and distress 30 months after the capsize of the *Herald of Free Enterprise*. *Personality and Individual Differences*, *14*, 271–273.

Kar, N., & Bastia, B. K. (2006). Post-traumatic stress disorder, depression and generalized anxiety disorder in adolescents after a natural disaster: A study of comorbidity. *Clinical Practice and Epidemiology in Mental Health, 2*. Retrieved from http://www.pubmedcentral.nih.gov/picrender.fcgi?artid=1563462&blobtype=pdf

Kaslow, N. J., Tannenbaum, R. L., & Seligman, M. E. P. (1978). *The KASTAN-R: A children's attributional style questionnaire (KASTAN-R-CASQ)*. Unpublished manuscript, University of Pennsylvania.

Keltner, D., & Buswell, B. N. (1996). Evidence for the distinctness of embarrassment, shame, and guilt: A study of recalled antecedents and facial expressions of emotion. *Cognition and Emotion*, *10*, 155–172.

Kiecolt-Glaser, J. K., & Williams, D. A. (1987). Self-blame, compliance, and distress among burn victims. *Journal of Personality and Social Psychology*, *53*, 187–193.

Kinzie, J. D., Sack, W. H., Angell, R. H., Manson, S., & Rath, B. (1986). The psychiatric effects of massive trauma on Cambodian children: I. The children. *Journal of the American Academy of Child Psychiatry*, *25*, 370–376.

Kletter, H., Weems, C. F., & Carrion, V. G. (2009). Guilt and posttraumatic stress symptoms in child victims of interpersonal violence. *Clinical Child Psychology and Psychiatry*, *14*, 71–83.

Kubany, E. S. (1997). Thinking errors, faulty conclusion, and cognitive therapy for trauma-related guilt. *National Center for Post-Traumatic Stress Disorder Clinical Quarterly*, *7*, 6–8.

Kubany, E. S., Haynes, S. N., Abueg, F. R., Manke, F. P. Brennan, J. M., & Stahura, C. (1996). Development and validation of the Trauma-Related Guilt Inventory (TRGI). *Psychological Assessment*, *8*, 428–444.

Kubany, E. S., Haynes, S. N., Abueg, F. R., Manke, F. P. Brennan, J. M., & Stahura, C. (1997). Development and validation of the Sources of Trauma-Related Guilt Survey—War-zone version. *Journal of Traumatic Stress*, *10*, 235–258.

Kubany, E. S., & Manke, F. P. (1995). Cognitive therapy for trauma-related guilt: Conceptual bases and treatment outlines. *Cognitive and Behavioral Practice*, *2*, 23–61.

Kubany, E. S., & Watson, S. B. (2003). Guilt: Elaboration of a multidimensional model. *The Psychological Record*, *53*, 51–90.

Kugler, K., & Jones, W. H. (1992). On conceptualizing and assessing guilt. *Journal of Personality and Social Psychology*, *62*(2), 318–327.

Leskela, J., Dieperink, M., & Thuras, P. (2002). Shame and posttraumatic stress disorder. *Journal of Traumatic Stress*, *15*, 223–226.

Lewis, H. B. (1971). *Shame and guilt in neurosis*. New York: International Universities Press.

Lewis, H. B. (1992). *Shame, the exposed self*. New York: The Free Press.

Lewis, M., Alessandri, S. M., & Sullivan, M. W. (1992). Differences in shame and pride as a function of children's gender and task difficulty. *Child Development*, *63*, 630–638.

Lewis, M., & Sullivan, M. W. (2005). The development of self-conscious emotions. In A. Elliot & C. Dweck (Eds.), *Handbook of competence and motivation* (pp. 185–201). New York: Guilford.

Lewis, M., Sullivan, M. W., Ramsay, D. S., & Alessandri, S. M. (1992). Individual differences in anger and sad expressions during extinction: Antecedents and consequences. *Infant Behavior & Development*, *15*(4), 443–452.

Loader, P. (1998). Such a shame—A consideration of shame and shaming mechanisms in families. *Child Abuse Review*, *7*, 44–57.

Marschall, D., Sanftner, J., & Tangney, J. P. (1994). *The State Shame and Guilt Scale*. Fairfax, VA: George Mason University.

Martin, R., Watson, D., & Wan, C. K. (2000). A three-factor model of trait anger: Dimensions of affect, behavior, and cognition. *Journal of Personality*, *68*, 869–897.

McNeil, D. E., Hatcher, C., & Reubin, R. (1988). Family survivors of suicide and accidental death. *Suicide and Life Threatening Behavior*, *18*, 137–148.

Mezulis, A., Hyde, J., & Abramson, L. Y. (2006). The developmental origins of cognitive vulnerability in depression: Temperament, parenting, and negative life events in childhood as contributors to negative cognitive style. *Developmental Psychology*, *42*, 1012–1025.

Morrow, K. B. (1991). Attributions of female adolescent incest victims regarding their molestation. *Child Abuse & Neglect*, *15*, 477–483.

Mosher, D. L. (1966). The development and multi-trait-multi-method matrix analysis of three measures of guilt. *Journal of Consulting Psychology*, *30*, 25–29.

Mosher, D. L., & White, B. B. (1981). On differentiating shame and shyness. *Motivation and Emotion*, *1*, 61–74.

Musante, L., Treiber, F. A., Davis, H. C., Waller, J. L., & Thompson, W. O. (1999). Assessment of self-reported anger expression in youth. *Assessment*, *6*, 225–233.

Nader, K. (2008). *Understanding and assessing trauma in children and adolescents: Measures, methods, and youth in context*. New York: Routledge, Taylor & Francis Group.

Nader, K., Pynoos, R., Fairbanks, L., & Frederick, C. (1990). Children's PTSD reactions one year after a sniper attack at their school. *American Journal of Psychiatry*, *147*, 1526–1530.

Negrao, C., II, Bonanno, G. A., Noll, J. G., Putnam, F. W., & Trickett, P. K. (2005). Shame, humiliation, and childhood sexual abuse: Distinct contributions and emotional coherence. *Child Maltreatment*, *10*, 350–363.

Nolen-Hoeksema, S., Girgus, J. S., & Seligman, M. E. P. (1992). Predictors and consequences of childhood depressive symptoms: A 5-year longitudinal study. *Journal of Abnormal Psychology*, *101*, 405–422.

Noll, J. G. (2008). Sexual abuse of children—Unique in its effects on development? *Child Abuse & Neglect*, *32*, 603–605.

Novaco, R. W. (2008). Anger. In G. Reyes, J. D. Elhai, & J. D. Ford (Eds.), *The encyclopedia of psychological trauma* (pp. 27–29). Hoboken, NJ: John Wiley & Sons.

Pelcovitz, D., van der Kolk, B., Roth, S., Mandel, F., Kaplan, S., & Resick, P. (1997). Development of a criteria set and structure interview for disorders of extreme stress (SIDES). *Journal of Traumatic Stress*, *10*, 3–16.

Peterson, C., & Villanova, P. (1988). An expanded attributional style questionnaire. *Journal of Abnormal Psychology*, *97*, 87–89.

Piaget, J. (1960). *The child's conception of the world*. Totowa, NJ: Littlefield.

Pynoos, R., Frederick, C., Nader, K., Arroyo, W., Eth, S., Nunez, W., et al. (1987). Life threat and posttraumatic stress in school age children. *Archives of General Psychiatry*, *44*, 1057–1063.

Pyszcznski, T., & Greenberg, J. (1987). Self-regulatory perseveration and the depressive self-focusing style: A self-awareness theory of reactive depression. *Psychological Bulletin*, *102*, 122–138.

Quiles, Z. N., & Bybee, J. (1997). Chronic and predispositional guilt: Relations to mental health, prosocial behavior and religiosity. *Journal of Personality Assessment*, *69*, 104–129.

Retzinger, S. R. (1987). Resentment and laughter: Video studies of the shame-rage spiral. In H. B. Lewis (Ed.), *The role of shame in symptom formation* (pp. 151–181). Hillsdale, NJ: Erlbaum.

Reyes, L. R., Meininger, J. C., Liehr, P., Chan, W., & Mueller, W. H. (2003). Anger in adolescents: Sex, ethnicity, age differences, and psychometric properties. *Nursing Research*, *52*, 2–11.

Rosenberg, E. L., & Ekman, P. (1994). Coherence between expressive and experiential systems in emotion. *Cognition & Emotion*, *8*, 201–229.

Runyan, M. K., & Kenny, M. (2002). Relationship of attributional style, depression, and post-trauma distress among children who suffered physical or sexual abuse. *Child Maltreatment*, *7*, 254–264.

Scheff, T. J. (1987). The shame-rage spiral: A case study of an interminable quarrel. In H. B. Lewis (Ed.), *The role of shame in symptom formation* (pp. 109–149). Hillsdale, NJ: Erlbaum.

Schieman, S. (1999). Age and anger. *Journal of Health and Social Behavior*, *40*, 273–289.

Schwab-Stone, M., Chen, C., Greenberger, E., Silver, D., Lichtman, J., & Voyce, C.(1999). No safe haven II: The effects of violence exposure on urban youth. *Journal of the American Academy of Child and Adolescent Psychiatry*, *38*, 359–367.

Siegel, J. M. (1986). The Multidimensional Anger Inventory. *Journal of Personality and Social Psychology*, *51*, 191–200.

Silver, R. L., & Wortman, C. B. (1980). Coping with undesirable life events. In Garber, J. & Seligman, M. E. P. (Eds.), *Human helplessness: Theory and applications* (pp. 279–340). New York: Academic Press.

Sourander, A. (1998). Behavior problems and traumatic events of unaccompanied refugee minors. *Child Abuse & Neglect*, *22*, 719–727.

Spaccarelli, S. (1994). Stress, appraisal, and coping in child sexual abuse: A theoretical and empirical review. *Psychological Bulletin*, *116*, 340–362.

Spielberger, C. D. (1996). *State-Trait Anger Expression Inventory-2: Professional manual*. Odessa, FL: Psychological Assessment Resources.

Spielberger, C. D. (1999). *State-Trait Anger Expression-2: Professional manual*. Odessa, FL: Psychological Assessment Resources.

Spielberger, C. D., Jacobs, G., Russell, S., & Crane, R. S. (1983). Assessment of anger: The State-Trait Scale. In J. N. Butcher & C. D. Spielberger (Eds.), *Advances in personality assessment* (Vol. 2, pp. 161–189). Hillsdale, NJ: Lawrence Erlbaum.

Spielberger, C. D., Johnson, E. H., Russell, S. F., Crane, R. J., Jacobs, G. A., & Worden, T. J. (1985). The experience and expression of anger: Construction and validation of an anger expression scale. In M. A. Chesney & R. H. Rosenman (Eds.), *Anger and hostility in cardiovascular and behavioral disorders* (pp. 5–30). Washington, DC: Hemisphere.

Stegge, H., & Ferguson, T. J. (1990). *Child-Child Attribution and Reaction Surveys (C-CARS)*. Logan, UT: Utah State University.

Stiles, M. M. (2002). Witnessing domestic violence: The effect on children. *American Family Physician, 66*, 2052–2067.

Stuewig, J., & McCloskey, L. A. (2005). The relation of child maltreatment to shame and guilt among adolescents: Psychological routes to depression and delinquency. *Child Maltreatment, 10*, 324–336.

Tangney, J. P. (1992). Situational determinants of shame and guilt in young adulthood. *Personality and Social Psychology Bulletin, 18*, 199–206.

Tangney, J. P. (1996). Conceptual and methodological issues in the assessment of shame and guilt. *Behaviour Research and Therapy, 34*, 741–754.

Tangney, J. P. (1999). The self-conscious emotions: Shame, guilt, embarrassment and pride. In T. Dalgleish & M. Power (Eds.), *Handbook of cognition and emotion* (pp. 541–568). New York: John Wiley.

Tangney, J. P., Burggraf, S. A., Gramzow, R., & Fletcher, C. (1990). *The Test of Self-Conscious Affect for Children* (TOSCA-C). Fairfax, VA: George Mason University.

Tangney, J. P., Burggraf, S. A., & Wagner, P. E. (1995). Shame-proneness, guilt-proneness, and psychological symptoms. In J. P. Tangney & K. W. Fischer (Eds.), *Self-conscious emotions: The psychology of shame, guilt, embarrassment, and pride* (pp. 343–367). New York: Guilford Press.

Tangney, J. P., Wagner, P., Fletcher, C., & Gramzow, R. (1992). Shamed into anger? The relation of shame and guilt to anger and self-reported aggression. *Journal of Personality and Social Psychology, 62*, 669–675.

Tangney, J. P., Wagner, P.E., Gavlas, J., & Gramzow, R. (1991). *The Test of Self-Conscious Affect for Adolescents* (TOSCA-A). Fairfax, VA: George Mason University.

Tangney, J. P., Wagner, P. E., Hill-Barlow, D., Marschall, D. E., & Gramzow, R. (1996). Relation of shame and guilt to constructive versus destructive responses to anger across the lifespan. *Journal of Personality and Social Psychology, 70*, 797–809.

Valle, L., & Silovsky, V. (2002). Attributions and adjustment following child sexual and physical abuse. *Child Maltreatment, 7*, 9–25.

van der Kolk, B. (2005). Developmental trauma disorder: Toward a rational diagnosis for children with complex trauma histories. *Psychiatric Annals, 35*, 401–408.

Wagner, A. W., Roemer, L., Orsillo, S. M., & Litz, B. T. (2003). Emotional experiencing in women with posttraumatic stress disorder: Congruence between facial expressivity and self-report. *Journal of Traumatic Stress, 16*, 67–75.

Walster, E. (1967). "Second guessing" important events. *Human Relations, 20*, 239–249.

Watson, D., & Clark, L. A. (1994). *The PANAS-X: Manual for the Positive and Negative Affect Schedule – Expanded Form*. Iowa City: University of Iowa.

Whalen, C. K., Henker, B., King, P. S., Jamner, L., & Levine, L. (2004). Adolescents react to events of September 11, 2001: Focused versus ambient impact. *Journal of Abnormal Child Psychology, 32*, 1–11.

Whiffen, V. E., & MacIntosh, H. B. (2005). Mediators of the link between childhood sexual abuse and emotional distress: A critical review. *Trauma, Violence and Abuse*, *6*, 24–39.

Wolfe, V. V., Gentile, C., Michienzi, T., Sas, L., & Wolfe, D. (1991). The Children's Impact of Traumatic Events Scale: A measure of post-sexual abuse PTSD symptoms. *Behavioral Assessment*, *13*, 359–383.

Wolfe, D., Sas, L., & Wekerle, C. (1994). Factors associated with the development of post-traumatic stress disorder among child victims of sexual abuse. *Child Abuse & Neglect*, *18*, 37–50.

Zahn-Waxler, C., Kochanska, G., Krupnick, J., & Mayfield, A. (1988). *Coding manual for Children's Interpretations of Interpersonal Distress and Conflict*. Rockville, MD: National Institute of Mental Health, Laboratory of Developmental Psychology.

Zahn-Waxler, C., Kochanska, G., Krupnick, J., & McNew, D. (1990). Patterns of guilt in children of depressed and well mothers. *Developmental Psychology*, *26*, 51–59.

Zelin, M., Adler, G., & Myerson, P. G. (1972). Anger self-report: An objective questionnaire for the measurement of aggression. *Journal of Consulting and Clinical Psychology*, *39*, 340.

An Update on Proposed Changes in DSM-5 and other Trauma-Related Issues

Kathleen Nader, D.S.W.

In adulthood, 70–80% of individuals report lifetime exposure to one or more traumas (Breslau, 2009; Gabert-Quillen, Fallon, & Delahanty, 2011; Nader & Fletcher, in press). Childhood traumas are linked to risk of a variety of adult disorders including increased risk of PTSD with adult exposure to traumas. Multiple childhood traumas increase the likelihood of multiple problems (Briere, Kaltman, & Green, 2008; Finkelhor, Ormrod, & Turner, 2007a, b). Polyvictimized youth and adults are more likely to have a number of forms of psychopathology (e.g., PTSD, dissociation, substance abuse; internalizing, externalizing) (Bolger & Patterson, 2003; Fergusson & Horwood, 2003; Nader, in press; Walter & LaFreniere, 2007), more complicated forms of trauma (Briere et al., 2008), and chronic health problems in adulthood (Anda et al., 2006).

A number of changes are proposed and in process for DSM-5. Although these changes take into account earlier concerns and findings, not all concerns have been addressed. Among questions still to be explored are those regarding the distinction between complex trauma and PTSD as well as the influence of individual factors on reactions. For example, trauma influences individual neurobiology, and neurobiology influences post-trauma reactions. It is likely that future revisions of DSM-PTSD will consider the importance of genetics and will include additional developmental differences.

Structure and Nature of PTSD in DSM-5

As indicated in Chapter 1, researchers have assessed the structure and dimensionality of PTSD. In place of the three symptom criteria of DSM-III and IV, proposed DSM-5 PTSD (PTSD-V) includes four symptom criteria (B–E): intrusion, avoidance, negative alterations in cognitions and mood, and alterations in arousal and reactivity. Changes in PTSD proposed for DSM-5, follow.

DSM-5 PTSD Criteria

As noted in Part I of this book, a great deal of debate has continued over DSM-IV Criterion A. In PTSD-V, instead of increasing the number of peritraumatic emotions, Criterion A no longer requires an intense or observable reaction (DSM-IV Criterion A2)—fear, helplessness or horror—at the time of the event. Instead, it includes specific exposures—*death or threatened death, actual or threatened serious injury, or actual or threatened sexual violation*—under one of four circumstances—experiencing, witnessing, learning of a close person's exposure to threat, or nonmedia repeated exposure to the details of events (APA, 2012).

In the assessment of PTSD, although PTSD-V no long requires peritraumatic emotions for Criterion A trauma exposure, the importance of intense peritraumtic emotions to reactions necessitates their continued evaluation (Nader, 2010). For adults and youth, evidence suggests that, in addition to the effects of variables such as peritraumatic dissociation and distress, subjective perception rather than objective assessment of injury severity is a more consistent predictor of acute and chronic traumatic stress symptoms after a traumatic event (Gabert-Quillen et al., 2011). Some clinician-researchers have observed that a child's accurate or inaccurate perception that a significant other has been endangered in a potentially traumatic event may be sufficient to result in PTSD or traumatic grief (Cohen et al., 2002; Nader, 1997; Chapter 5 in this volume). In PTSD-V Criterion A, learning of actual events with violent or accidental threat to a close relative or friend meets exposure requirements (APA, 2012). For children, loss of a parent or other attachment figure has been considered for inclusion in Criterion A. As Chapter 10 suggests, such loss is particularly important for young children.

PTSD-V Criterion B (*intrusion symptoms* rather than *reexperiencing)* is similar to DSM- IV B with some important wording changes. For example, in the proposed disorder, B-3 becomes *dissociative reactions* that may occur on a continuum, which at its most extreme includes a complete loss of awareness of present surroundings (e.g., *flashbacks*). Similar to DSM-IV, for children, trauma-specific reenactment may occur in play, which may be an indicator of B-1 (intrusion) or B-3 (dissociative reactions).

DSM-IV Criterion C is to be divided into two criteria in PTSD-V: C (avoidance of internal and/or external reminders) and D (changes in mood and cognition). In contrast to C, D does not require triggered emotional states (i.e., states brought on by reminders of the trauma) (Scheeringa, Myers, Putnam, & Zeanah, 2012). Proposed D includes aspects of DSM-IV C (i.e., C3, C4, C5). D also includes some altered aspects of DSM-IV C: C-6 (*restricted range of affect*) becomes *pervasive negative emotional states*; C-7 becomes negative expectations of self, others and the world (D-2). Distorted self-blame or blame of others for the trauma—considered a symptom of complicated trauma—has been added.

DSM-IV D (arousal) symptoms are PTSD-V E (arousal and reactivity). In addition to the retained DSM-IV arousal symptoms (irritability, hypervigilance, exaggerated startle response, concentration problems, and sleep disturbance), in E aggressive behaviors are combined with irritability. Reckless or self-destructive behavior is included for individuals over age 6 and is considered for young children. Intentional self-harm is difficult to confirm in very young children (Scheeringa et al., 2012). Although the PTSD-V symptom list is now even longer than that for DSM-IV (i.e., 20 versus 17 core symptoms), the number of symptoms required in each criterion is often reduced for children. Unless changed before publication, contrary to recommendations (Chapter 2), a combined three symptoms from the DSM-5 C and D lists are still required for 6 to 12 year olds. Future research will demonstrate whether the changes in symptom wording and/or nature in DSM-5 PTSD will make a difference.

A Developmental Perspective: DSM-5 PTSD in Preschoolers

Although children aged 8 and older are generally the best reporters of their own symptoms, as noted in Chapter 1, when assessing youth, using combined reports (e.g., youth and caregiver, perhaps plus teacher) has provided relatively stronger predictive power, suggesting the importance of aggregating data across informants (Meiser-Stedman et al., 2009; Scheeringa et al., 2006). Research has demonstrated the need for separate criteria for preschool children (De Young, Kenardy, & Cobham, 2011; Scheeringa, Chapter 2, this volume; Scheeringa et al., 2012). Although as noted, some debated issues have not been resolved for PTSD in children, DSM-5 has addressed some of the differences between child and adult PTSD by proposing a diagnosis of *PTSD in preschool children*. Scheeringa et al. (2012) found that assessing the newly proposed DSM-5 PTSD in preschoolers resulted in significantly more cases of PTSD than DSM-IV PTSD. The additional cases were all highly symptomatic and impaired. Scheeringa et al. (2012) studied PTSD in children aged 3 to 6 using DSM-IV PTSD, alternative algorithm PTSD, DSM-5 proposed PTSD in preschoolers, and the DSM-5 diagnosis with two additional symptoms under consideration. Proposed criteria found high agreement on the presence of PTSD but low agreement on the absence of PTSD. Misclassified cases were highly symptomatic.

Complicated Traumatic Reactions

Because of its relationship to complicated reactions, a discussion of polyvictimization precedes that of complex traumatic reactions. Traumatic grief may also complicate or increase traumatic symptom levels, and trauma is among variables that may complicate grieving (Pearlman, Schwartz, & Cloitre, 2010).

Polyvictimization

When more than one type of traumatic event is assessed, many survivors report exposure to multiple categories of trauma (Finkelhor et al., 2007a, b; Greif Green et al., 2010; Kessler, 2000; Martin, Cromer, DePrince, & Freyd, 2011). The assessment of numbers of types of trauma exposure is essential to accurate findings in the study of posttrauma outcomes. Research demonstrates that *polyvictimized* children exhibit disturbances in self-regulation across several domains of functioning including affective, behavioral, cognitive, relational, and somatic, domains. These disturbances include associated problems with self-image; dissociation; conflict, attachment disorganization, and dependency in relationships; and impulse control, aggression, self-harm, and risk taking (Turner, Finkelhor, & Ormrod, 2010). Such symptoms may persist well into adulthood (Briere et al., 2008; Turner et al., 2010). Finkelhor et al. (2007a) found that the number of victimizations—including many presumed less salient kinds of victimization, such as theft, vandalism, sibling assault, and burglary—appears much more predictive of outcomes than any one particular kind of victimization. By the same token, across 3 years for a large sample of adolescents, Cisler et al. (2012) found that cumulative interpersonal violence exposure may operate as a generalized risk factor for subsequent depression, binge drinking, PTSD symptoms, and delinquency. They found that non-interpersonal violence traumas were only weakly related to such future outcomes. *Polyvictimized* children with or without a PTSD diagnosis benefit from treatments that address the adverse impact of victimization on self-regulation and interpersonal functioning (Ford et al., submitted).

Complicated Trauma

Ford et al. (submitted) point out a body of evidence that 10 to 30% of polyvictimized youth trauma victims are at risk of developing sequelae not fully captured by a diagnosis of PTSD (see Chapter 4). Such children exhibit disturbances in self-regulation—including somatic, affective, cognitive, behavioral, and relational domains—and associated problems with self-image, attachments and relationships, conflict, impulse control, aggression, risk taking, dissociation, and self-harm. These problems may persist into adulthood; the number of types of exposure are directly linked to the severity of adult psychological and medical problems (Briere et al., 2008; Ford et al., submitted; Vranceanu, Hobfoll, & Johnson, 2007). Ford et al. (submitted) conducted a forced choice questionnaire and vignettes—based on a theoretical formulation of DTD—with clinicians from the US and several other countries. Symptom criteria in the assessment scale can be found in Table 12.1.

Complicated Grief

Characteristics of the griever can have profound effects on grieving and treatment outcomes (Bonanno, Boerner, & Wortman, 2008; Doughty, 2009; Joyce, Ogrodniczuk, Piper, & Sheptycki, 2010; Martin & Doka, 2000; Chapter 5 in this volume). As noted in Chapter 5, traits such as grieving style or trajectory, relationship to the deceased, adaptive functioning, personality (e.g., introvert vs. extrovert), and resilience can influence course of grief and recovery. Environmental factors such as family support and attachment also influence recovery. For adult therapy patients, Joyce et al. (2010) demonstrated the importance of attachment security to treatment success; attachment insecurity demonstrated a strong inverse association to post-treatment improvement. Proposed for DSM-5, the diagnosis of adjustment disorder—development of clinically significant emotional or behavioral symptoms in response to an identifiable stressor(s) occurring within 3 months of the stressor and resulting in functional impairment—may include a subcategory of the diagnosis, *adjustment disorder related to bereavement*, that is a possible diagnosis for complicated grief. The proposed disorder includes intense yearning or longing for the deceased, intense sorrow and emotional pain, and/or preoccupation with the deceased or the circumstances of the death (APA, 2012). Symptoms may also include difficulty accepting the death, intense anger related to the loss, a diminished sense of self, feeling that life is empty, and/or difficulty engaging in planning for the future, activities, or relationships. As noted in Chapter 1, there are multiple forms of complicated grief proposed by different researchers. That is, a number of circumstances and conditions may complicate grieving. A bereavement -related disorder is to undergo additional study. For children with posttrauma symptoms, a number of treatments have proved successful at relieving posstrauma symptoms and addressing posttrauma grief reactions, including school-based group treatment (Pearlman et al., 2010; Salloum, Garside, Irwin, Anderson, & Francois, 2009), cognitive behavioral and narrative therapies, and coping skills training (Salloum & Overstreet, 2012).

Table 12.1 Symptom criteria of DTD undergoing testing.

Criteria	Description	Areas tested
Criterion B Affective and physiological dysregulation	Inability to tolerate or modulate extreme affective states Sensitivity to sound or quiet; sensitivity to touch Sense body hurts or is not working right Dissociation/diminished awareness (e.g., numbness) Alexithymia—difficulty identifying and describing one's emotions	Anger outbursts and irritability Inability to recover/dysphoria Inability to feel positive affect Impaired expressive emotion Avoidance of emotion expression Eating or urination/defecation Somatoform pain Aversion to touch
Criterion C Attentional or behavioral dyssregulation	Attentional bias toward or away from potential threats Lack of self-protection (e.g., risk taking, thrill seeking) Maladaptive attempts at self-soothing Self-harm Lack of goal directed behavior	Preoccupation with threats Reactive aggression Avoidance due to perceived threat Risk taking or reckless behavior Non-suicidal self-harm Maladaptive self-soothing
Criterion D Self- and relational dysregulation	Negative self-perception/self-loathing Attachment and relationship difficulties Biased expectations Distrust or defiance Reactive aggression Boundary problems; insecurity Dependence Lacking or excessive empathy	Belief that self was damaged Belief self permanently damaged Expectancy of betrayal Expectancy of victimization Indiscriminate physical contact Over-identification with others' distress Expectancy of irresolvable loss

Sources: Ford et al. (submitted); Ford, & the Developmental Trauma Disorder Work Group (2012).

Associated Variables and the Future of PTSD

The effects of specific adverse events are not confined to any one class of disorders (Kessler, 2000; Kessler et al., 1997). The nature of posttrauma reactions is influenced by a number of personal and event variables. A few strong predictors of resilience or risk as well as of type or intensity of reactivity—e.g., attachment, genetics, peritraumatic emotions—are discussed.

Attachment

Attachment patterns are considered to be adaptive responses based on earlier experiences between caregiver and infant (Allen, 2011). Such experiences influence the child's exploratory behavior and form the foundation for and nature of internal working models (IWMs). These IWMs dictate subsequent perceptions of self, others, and interpersonal interactions. Because attachment style has robustly predicted resilience or vulnerability as well as coping and interpersonal style (Chapter 7), it is important to include attachment as a variable in the assessment of trauma. In a study of women abused as children, Stovall-McClough and Cloitre (2006) found that individuals with trauma-based unresolved or disorganized attachment patterns were 7.5 times as likely to be diagnosed with PTSD than participants without this classification. Social stressors and negative life events (e.g., abuse, death of a relative, changes in living arrangements, parental divorce) are associated with instability of attachment patterns (Del Giudice, Ellis, & Shirtcliff, 2011). That is, stressors increase the likelihood that secure attachment styles will change to insecure attachment styles. This may be, at least in part, because attachment classification is associated with coping style.

In relationship to attachment, for infants and young children, the emphasis is on proximity seeking to the caregiver. For school-aged children, emphasis moves to maintaining the availability of a caregiver, which ultimately results in greater physical distance and autonomy (Allen, 2011; Ammaniti, van Ijzendoorn, Speranza, & Tambelli, 2000). By school age, early attachment classifications influence child characteristics such as sense of security, readiness to engage others, and patterns of emotion and behavior regulation (Bowlby, 1969/1982; Moss, Pascuzzo, & Simard, 2012; Nader & Nader, 2012). IWMs assist the child with goal-directed behavior, self-evaluation, emotion regulation, assessing the safety of relationships, as well as with other self- and interpersonal functions (Allen, 2011; Bowlby 1969/1982). Such factors are important in the assessment of complicated trauma reactions. Although both insecure organized (avoidant or ambivalent/resistant) attachments and disorganized attachments have been associated with increased risk of psychopathology, disorganized attachments (D; often associated with traumatization) have proven an especial risk (Moss et al., 2012). For the purposes of assessment, three D subtypes have been identified (Moss et al., 2004). *Controlling–punitive* children use hostile and directive behavior toward parents that may humiliate. *Controlling–caregiving* children direct parents' behavior and conversation in a helpful, emotionally positive manner. *Behaviorally disorganized* or insecure–other children display no organized patterns of interacting with a caregiver. As noted in Chapter 1, recognizing subcategories is important to accurate assessments/diagnoses.

Genetics

The study of genetics is likely to influence future definitions of PTSD and its assessment. Studies have demonstrated the heritability of PTSD (Chapter 9). Koenen (2007) found that PTSD is approximately 30% heritable (see also Gillespie, Phifer, Bradley, & Ressler, 2009). Neurobiology (genetics) may influence posttrauma reactions, and trauma may influence neurobiology (see Nader & Fletcher, in press, for a summary of findings). Specific FKBP5 polymorphisms have been associated with PTSD, suicidality, and elevated peritraumatic dissociation (Binder et al., 2008; Gillespie et al., 2009) as well as with incomplete normalization of stress-induced cortisol secretion (Ising et al, 2008; Willour et al, 2009). High FKBP5 is associated with glucocorticoid receptor (GR) resistance in individuals without PTSD but with GR sensitivity in individuals with PTSD (Binder et al., 2008). Additionally, childhood traumatic exposure has been linked to shorter telemere length (a measure of biological aging) (Tyrka et al., 2010).

Stress Sensitivity

Evidence-based theories also suggest that variations in stress sensitivity/vulnerability exist among individuals and that genes play a role in these variations (Caspi et al., 2010; Del Giudice et al., 2011) (see Table 12.2). Notably, individuals with specific serotonin (short allele 5-HTTPLR) and dopamine polymorphisms appear to be more sensitive to their environments. The 5-HTTPLR and dopamine polymorphisms have been linked to PTSD (Xie et al., 2009) and/or its symptoms (Bakermans-Kranenburg & van Ijzendoorn, 2008; Drury, Theall, Keats, & Scheeringa, 2009; Moss et al., 2012; Nader, in press; Table 12.2). Genetic studies have shown differences in findings depending on the study methods used. For example, direct interview methods rather than non-face-to-face child self-reports have revealed that a serotonin genotype moderates the effects of adverse environments (Bakermans-Kranenburg, Dobrava-Krol, & van Ijzendoorn, 2011).

Genetics and the Nature of Posttrauma Response

Because specific genetic polymorphisms are related to specific types of posttrauma/adversity reactions, future versions of PTSD may include or take into account gene-specific reactions. For example, evidence links 5-HTTLPR to increased levels of many symptoms that are also among trauma-related symptoms (Nader & Fletcher, in press) including depression (proposed PTSD D-7), posttrauma suicide attempts (proposed E-2; Roy et al., 2007), conditioned fear reactions (proposed E-3; Lonsdorf et al., 2009), auditory startle response (proposed E-4; Armbruster et al., 2009), sympathetic reactivity to others' pain (Crisan et al., 2009), aggressive reactions (proposed E-4; laboratory assessed; Verona, Joiner, Johnson, & Bender, 2006), stress-linked alcohol consumption (proposed C or E-2; Covault et al., 2007), substance use (proposed E-2; Brody et al., 2009), emotion-induced retrograde amnesia (proposed D-1; Strange, Kroes, Roiser, Tan, & Dolan, 2008), anxiety sensitivity (proposed E3; Stein, Schork, & Gelernter, 2008), and stress-related sleep disturbance (proposed E-6; Brummett et al., 2007; Caspi et al., 2010). In addition, 5-HTTLPR has been linked to biased information processing (proposed D-2; e.g., a threat-related attentional bias; a negative information processing

Table 12.2 Vulnerability/sensitivity: biological type and phenotype findings.

	Type/ genetics	Predictions/associations
Biological sensitivity to context (Del Giudice et al., 2011; see also Belsky & Pleuss, 2009)	**Sensitive**	• Predicted high PNS responsivity; moderate SNS responsivity: high trait anxiety, and an overly sensitive fight–flight response (not needed in a safe, protected environment); a highly responsive HPA system promotes sensitivity to social feedback, and the mobilization of metabolic and psychological resources • Sensitive children and adults are described as reflective, self- and other-conscious, and engaged with the environment; high in inhibitory control, executive function, and delay of gratification
	Buffered	•Predicted to develop preferentially in conditions of moderate environmental stress; a moderately unresponsive SRS would partially filter out cues of danger and environmental unpredictability •Predicted to be lower in anxiety and aggression, less risk prone, more sensitive to social feedback and more oriented to long-term couple relationships
	Vigilant	•Predicted to develop in stressful contexts; high responsivity and basal activity in HPA and sympathetic systems, and low parasympathetic tone and responsivity • Predicted heightened attention to threats and high trait anxiety; may also display freezing in severe challenges (Porges, 2007); may exhibit slower HPA recovery to baseline and slower habituation (see Gunnar and Vazquez, 2006; Netter, 2004; Pruessner et al., 1997). •Subtypes: may manifest as a vigilant–agonistic pattern more typical of males—"fight" responses predominate; or a vigilant–withdrawn pattern, more typical of females—protective "flight" behavior predominates; both should involve lower serotonergic activity
	Unemotional pattern	•Predicted low responsivity in total SRS system •Behavioral correlates may depend on the action of sex hormones and may differ between the genders—low serotonergic and dopaminergic activity are also expected to be associated with unresponsive phenotypes, especially when associated with aggression and risk taking; when displayed, aggression is often instrumental/proactive and cold blooded
GENETIC RISK	**STATB5 and MHC class II**	• A direct inhibitor of the nuclear translocation of activated GR; downregulated in PTSD individuals; major histocompatibility complex (MHC) Class II gene is compatible with abnormally reduced cortisol levels (Yehuda et al., 2009)
	Serotonin (5	Studies using interview rather than self-report methods have

	HTT)	found that, while the short (*s*) allele genotypes have shown high levels of adverse effects (e.g., emotional problems), the long (*ll*) allele genotype has shown the lowest levels of problems (Bakermans-Kranenburg et al., 2011; Kumsta et al., 2010) **Stress sensitivity** ***s* allele** 5-HTTPLR associated with increased stress sensitivity and reactivity (Caspi et al., 2003, 2010); increased and more rapid amygdala reactivity to stress (Dannlowski et al., 2007; Furman, Hamilton, Joormann, & Gotlib, in press; Hariri et al., 2003); increased HPA axis reactivity to aversive or threatening stimuli (Caspi et al., 2010; Mueller, Brocke, Fries, Lesch, & Kirschbaum , 2010), elevated depression and suicidality in response to trauma and/or chronic stress (Caspi et al., 2003, 2010; Roy, Hu, Janal, & Goldman, 2007); poorer outcomes with poor parenting (Barry et al., 2008); relatively decreased amygdala and medial prefrontal cortex gray matter volume (Pezawas et al., 2005) and altered connectivity between the two regions (Pacheco et al., 2009), greater acquisition of conditioned fear responses (Lonsdorf et al., 2009), greater auditory startle response (Armbruster et al., 2009), and increased sympathetic reactivity when observing someone receiving shock (Crisan et al., 2009); linked to depression and other stress-reactive phenotypes, including PTSD (Xie et al., 2009), posttrauma suicide attempts (Roy et al., 2007), laboratory assessed aggressive reactions (Verona, Joiner, Johnson, Bender, 2006), stress-linked alcohol consumption (Covault et al., 2007), substance use (Brody et al., 2009), emotion-induced retrograde amnesia (Strange, Kroes, Roiser, Tan, & Dolan, 2008), and stress-related sleep disturbance (Brummett et al., 2007; Caspi et al., 2010); also linked to biased information processing—e.g., a threat-related attentional bias and a negative information processing bias (Caspi et al., 2010); 5-HTTLPR *s* allele children with poor attachment relationships to parents exhibit poor self-regulation of negative affect (Barry, Kochanska, & Philibert, 2008; Fox et al., 2005; Kochanska, Philibert, Barry, 2009; Pauli-Pott, Friedl, Hinney, & Hebebrand, 2009), which in turn predicts a number of adult psychiatric disorders (Caspi et al., 2010) **L_G allele** is also associated with a low rate of HTT transcription, functionally similar to the *s* allele (Hu et al., 2006; Roy et al., 2007) ***Long (l)* allele** may be protective against some of the adverse effects of environments, e.g., institutionalized upbringing (Bakermans-Kranenburg, Dobrava-Krol, & van

		Ijzendoorn, 2011) and poor parenting (Barry et al., 2008)
	Monoamine oxidase A (MAOA)	• Linked to externalizing disorders such as antisocial personality (Kim-Cohen et al., 2006) • Low MAO activity in platelets has been associated with suicidal behavior, impulsive aggression, bipolar disorder, alcoholism, with monotony avoidance, sensation seeking, and impulsiveness (Byrnes, 2001; Nader, 2008)
	FKBP5	**GR activation, cortisol binding, and facilitation of transcription of stress response genes** are moderated by a large molecular complex that includes FKBP5 (Roy, Gorodetsky, Yuan, Goldman, & Enoch, 2010); SNPs associated with incomplete normalization of stress-induced cortisol secretion (Ising et al., 2008), with response to antidepressants, recurrence of depressive episodes (Binder et al., 2004), and suicide attempts in bipolar patients (Willour et al., 2009) **PTSD**: for individuals without PTSD, the alleles associated with high FKBP5 protein/mRNA expression are associated with GR resistance (i.e., FKBP5 inhibits GR); this association appears to be switched for patients with PTSD symptoms, who exhibit increased GR sensitivity (Binder et al., 2008). FKBP5 and major histocompatibility complex (MHC) Class II have state markers (Sarapas et al., 2011), with reduced expression in PTSD, consistent with enhanced GR responsiveness (Yehuda et al., 2009); with PTSD severity, FKBP5 expression has been predicted by cortisol in regression analysis and has been reduced for individuals with PTSD (Yehuda et al., 2009); four SNPs (rs3800373, rs9296158, rs1360780, and rs9470080) significantly interacted with childhood trauma to predict adult PTSD (African American sample), even after controlling for other variables (Binder et al., 2008); the four SNPs interacting with child abuse were associated either with higher FKBP5 protein levels or a stronger induction of FKBP5 mRNA by cortisol in healthy individuals (rs1360780 and rs3800373) or in strong linkage disequilibrium with the SNPs (rs9296158 and rs9470080); SNPs associated with the highest FKBP5 mRNA induction in peripheral blood mononuclear cells by cortisol associated with greatest vulnerability to PTSD symptoms following child abuse and significantly associated with greater PTSD severity in individuals exposed to two types of child abuse but not in a larger group exposed to one type of abuse; homozygosity for any of the four risk-related polymorphisms predicted FKBP5 expression that mediated indirect effects of genotype on plasma cortisol (hypercortisolemia) and PTSD severity (Sarapas et al.,

		2011); associated with elevated **peri-traumatic dissociation** in medically injured children (Gillespie et al., 2009; Koenen et al., 2005) **Suicide**: for those with high levels of childhood trauma and variants of FKBP5 haplotype-tagging SNPs (rs3777747, rs4713902, and rs9470080 and interactive effects of rs3800373, rs9296158, and rs1360780) increased risk for attempting suicide (Roy et al., 2010); may be related to whether HPA axis dysregulation is blunted or sensitized
	Dopaminergic system	The dopaminergic systems are involved in the reward systems and affect modulation; are intermediate in the synthesis of epinephrine; instigate growth spurts in neurons, glia, and blood vessels; and relate to endogenous opiates, which are elevated during dissociative states and are diminished with ADHD and hyperactivity with schizophrenia (Byrnes, 2001; Stein & Kendall, 2004). Meta-analysis confirms that dopamine related genes (DRD2, DAT, and DRD4) serve as moderators of the association between positive and negative environmental factors with developmental outcomes in children up to age 10 (Bakermans-Kranenburg & van Ijzendoorn, 2009). Like the short allele 5HTT polymorphism, youth with less efficient dopamine-related genes function more poorly in negative environments than comparisons and also benefited most from positive environments **Impulsive behavior**: study of CD and SA, TaqIA SNP located near the dopamine receptor D2 (DRD2) gene, might be related to a non-specific vulnerability to a wide range of impulsive and reward-inducing behaviors **PTSD**: conflicting results related to DRD2 and PTSD (Koenen, 2007); positive association between DRD2A1 and PTSD for only a subset of individuals who engaged in harmful drinking (Young et al., 2002); positive association between chronic PTSD and the dopamine transporter SLC6A3 (DAT1) 3' polymorphism (Segman et al., 2002); for post-Hurricane Katrina preschool children, a relationship between PTSD symptoms—primarily arousal symptoms—and a dopamine (*DA)* polymorphism (Drury, Theall, Keats, & Scheeringa, 2009) **Parenting**: children with the DRD4 7 repeat allele exhibit greater sensitivity to parenting changes in maternal discipline (Bakermans-Kranenburg, van Ijzendoorn, Pijlman, Mesman, & Juffer, 2008b); children with the DRD4 7-repeat allele and insensitive mothers showed significantly more externalizing behaviors than without the DRD4 7-repeat allele (regardless of maternal sensitivity); with the DRD4 7 repeat allele and sensitive mothers showed the *lowest* levels of externalizing

		problems (Bakermans-Kranenburg, Van IJzendoorn, Pijlman, Mesman, & Juffer, 2008; Moss et al., 2012) **Stress sensitivity**: increased sensitivity to environment Bakermans-Kranenburg et al., 2008b; Bakermans-Kranenburg & van IJzendoorn, 2009)
	Cortico-tropin-releasing hormone (CRH)	Polymorphisms within the CRH receptor (CRHR1) gene may influence risk for depression, PTSD, and suicidality (Gillespie et al., 2009; Roy et al., 2012); persistent hyperactivity of HPA axis following developmental stress exposure is mediated, in part, by a hyperactive CRHR1 system (Gillespie et al., 2009; Lupien et al., 2009); HPA axis dysregulation includes dysregulation of CRH and AVP resulting in increased release of plasma ACTH and cortisol, which may be coupled with glucocorticoid receptor (GR) insensitivity resulting in impairment of the negative feedback loop (Roy et al., 2010) **PTSD**: elevated cerebrospinal fluid concentrations of CRH have repeatedly been reported in patients with depression and with combat-related PTSD (Gillespie et al., 2009) **Suicide**: interaction effect on suicidal behavior for CRHBP SNP rs7728378 and childhood traumatic experiences score (African Americans; Roy et al., 2012); greater risk of suicide attempts for schizophrenic rs1875999 heterozygotes (De Luca et al., 2010); additive effect of CRHBP and FKBP5 variation interaction with childhood trauma predicting risk for suicide attempt—almost double (0.58) for those who carried both major homozygotes, and highly trauma-exposed individuals with neither major homozygote had rates equivalent to individuals with no childhood trauma. The non-ancestral allele of CRHR1 rs9900679 (unique to African ancestry) was protective against suicide attempt **Other disorders**: CRHBP SNPs rs7728378 and rs10474485 associated with anxiety disorders in Plains Indians and alcohol-use disorders in Caucasians (Enoch et al., 2008; Roy et al., 2012); rs10474485 associated with remission of depressive symptoms (primarily for anxious depression) (Binder et al., 2010) and with depressive symptoms in alcoholics (Kertes et al., 2010); rs10055255 has moderated heavy drinkers' stress-induced alcohol craving (Ray, 2011)
	Brain-derived neurotrophic factor (BDNF; functional variant of BDNF gene, val66met)	**Stress**: acute and chronic stress inhibit hippocampal BDNF synthesis (Savitz et al., 2007; Tsankova et al., 2006) **Memory**: **low activity methionine (Met) allele:** associated with memory dysfunction (Savitz et al., 2007) and poorer memory and disruption of a normal hippocampal disengagement pattern during memory task (Egan et al., 2003; Hariri et al., 2003; Savitz et al., 2007); mediates

		neural plasticity in response to aversive social experiences and neurotoxins (Berton et al., 2006; Tsankova et al., 2006); Met/Met homozygotes memory scores decreased sharply with increasing sexual abuse (SA) scores (Savitz et al., 2007) **Val allele**: believed associated with bipolar disorder, schizophrenia, and reduced cognitive performance (Fan et al., 2005; Savitz et al., 2007); *val/val* homozygotes (with no Met alleles) demonstrated no decline in memory score with increases in SA scores (Savitz et al., 2007); high-activity BDNF *val* allele might partially counteract the stress-induced inhibition of BDNF synthesis and the adverse cortisol-related effects on hippocampal function **Apolipoprotein E (ApoE: ε*4* allele)**: risk for Alzheimer's disease and later life impaired cognition; memory scores were the same with no SA but rapidly decreased with increasing SA scores (Savitz et al., 2007) **Dissociation**: with or without abuse, low-activity (**Met**) allele and **Met/Met allele** associated with lower levels of self-reported dissociation (Savitz, van der Merwe, Newman et al., 2007); functional catechol-O-methyltransferase Val158Met polymorphism interacted with total abuse scores to influence perceived dissociation; **Val/Val** genotype was associated with increasing levels of dissociation in participants exposed to more childhood trauma

Notes: GR = glucocorticoid receptor; HPA = hypothalamic-pituitary-adrenal; PNS = parasympathetic nervous system; SNS = sympathetic nervous system; SRS = stress response system.

bias such as biases toward perceiving and expecting negative outcomes) (Caspi et al., 2010; Williams et al., 2009). 5-HTTLPR *s* allele children with poor attachment relationships to parents exhibit poor self-regulation of negative affect (proposed D-3; Barry, Kochanska, & Philibert, 2008; Kochanska, Philibert, Barry, 2009; Pauli-Pott, Friedl, Hinney, & Hebebrand, 2009), which, in turn, predicts a number of adult psychiatric disorders (Caspi et al., 2010). The dopaminergic systems, by way of contrast, are involved in reward systems and affect modulation (Nader, in press; Nader & Fletcher, in press). Their elevations are associated with dissociative states. Specific dopamine polymorphisms appear to be related to non-specific vulnerability to a wide range of impulsive and reward-inducing behaviors (Hoenicka et al., 2007). Differences in the reactions of individuals (e.g., without full PTSD) with functional impairment suggest a need to additionally investigate trauma's effects on individuals with specific genetic polymorphisms and their combinations.

Guilt, Shame and Anger

As discussed in Chapters 6 and 11, intense peritraumatic emotions—e.g., guilt, shame and anger—have been linked to increased posttrauma reactions. In DSM-5, anger, guilt, and shame are proposed for criterion D—D4: *pervasive negative emotional states* —for example: *fear, horror, anger, guilt, or shame* (APA, 2012)—as well as part of complicated traumatic reactions.

As noted, traumatic experiences contribute to IWMs related to self-image and self-regulation. Guilt, shame, and other adverse emotions associated with negative representations of the self can interfere with affect regulation and the ability to cope with painful emotions (Briere & Runtz, 1993; Sandberg, Seuss, & Heaton, 2010). Lee, Scragg, and Turner (2001) suggest that PTSD can be either guilt based or shame based. Accordingly, individuals with high shame may attribute the trauma to their own weakness or inadequacy. After trauma exposures, shame may result from feelings of personal inadequacy (e.g., related to the inability to cope or prevent harm). Potentially guilt-inducing experiences—such as failure to prevent things that happened during the event, inaction, or actions taken during the trauma (e.g., killing/harming another person or other undesirable actions forced by threat/fear of harm) (Hundt & Holohan, 2012; Nader, 2008)—that are inconsistent with one's self-view may also result in shame (Hundt & Holohan, 2012; Stone, 1992). One theory of shame suggests that attacking others—that is, using insults, ridicule, contempt, or even physical violence to feel better about oneself by reducing the self-esteem of another person—is among several possible methods people use to defend themselves against strong feelings of shame (Cook, 1994; Chapter 11). Hundt and Holohan (2012) found that, although shame, guilt, depression, and PTSD symptoms were all associated with perpetration of intimate partner violence (IPV), shame mediated the relationship between PTSD and IPV committed by veterans. Some evidence suggests that guilt without shame is not strongly associated with psychopathology (Hundt & Holohan, 2012; Tangney & Dearing, 2002). Significance varied depending on whether depression was taken into account and may also be influenced by variables not assessed (e.g., antisocial tendencies; genetic variables). Studies that have found an association between guilt and PTSD have not always assessed shame (Nader et al., 1990; Pynoos et al., 1987). More study is needed.

Conclusions

DSM-5 is to include more of the symptoms suggested for complex traumatic reactions in the symptom criteria of PTSD. It is possible that, in future, complicated traumatic reactions will become a subset of PTSD reactions or will be covered in the severity of reactions. Future definitions of PTSD may also recognize individual differences in the impact of traumatic exposure. For example, a number of the symptoms included in DSM-5 PTSD are associated with stress-linked outcomes of genetic polymorphisms. Short allele serotonin polymorphisms have been linked to negative expectations of self and others, negative emotional states, increased auditory startle response, emotion-induced amnesia, sleep disturbance, and social withdrawal. Some dopaminergic system polymorphisms (e.g., TaqIA SNP located near the dopamine receptor D2 gene) might be related to a non-specific vulnerability to a wide range of impulsive and reward-inducing behaviors. Youth with poorer transcription of serotonin or dopamine have evidenced greater sensitivity to positive and to negative environmental conditions. Inasmuch as the likelihood of gene-related specific dysfunction is reduced without a trigger (e.g., trauma or other adversity; Lau & Pine, 2008), future iterations of PTSD may take into account dysfunction related to individual variations in traumatic response. That is, because many of the symptoms of PTSD seem to assess specific gene related dysfunction, future DSM versions of PTSD conceivably could suggest gene-related versions of the disorder.

References

Allen, B. (2011). The use and abuse of attachment theory in clinical practice with maltreated children, Part I: Diagnosis and assessment. *Trauma, Violence, & Abuse*, *12*(1), 3–12.

American Psychological Association (APA) (2012). *G 05 posttraumatic stress disorder*. Downloaded 4/4/12 from www.dsm5.org/proposedrevision/PAGES/ TraumaandStressorRelatedDisorders. aspx.

Ammaniti, M., van Ijzendoorn, M., Speranza, A., & Tambelli, R. (2000). Internal working models of attachment during late childhood and early adolescence: An exploration of stability and change. *Attachment and Human Development*, *2*, 328–346.

Anda, R., Felitti, V., Bremner, J., Walker, J., Whitfield, C., Perry, B. et al. (2006). The enduring effects of abuse and related adverse experiences in childhood: A convergence of evidence from neurobiology and epidemiology. *European Archives of Psychiatry and Clinical Neuroscience*, *256*, 174–186.

Armbruster, D., Moser, D., Strobel, A., Hensch, T., Kirschbaum, C., Lesch, K. et al. (2009). Serotonin transporter gene variation and stressful life events impact processing of fear and anxiety. *International Journal of Neuropsychopharmacology*, *12*, 393–401.

Bakermans-Kranenburg, M., Dobrava-Krol, N., & van Ijzendoorn, M. (2011). Impact of institutional care on attachment disorganization and insecurity of Ukrainian preschoolers: Protective effect of the long variant of the serotonin transporter gene (5HTT). *International Journal of Behavioral Development*, *36*(1), 11–18.

Bakermans-Kranenburg, M., & van Ijzendoorn, M. (2008). Oxytocin receptor (OXTR) and serotonin transporter (5-HTT) genes associated with observed parenting. *Social Cognitive and Affective Neuroscience*, *3*, 128–134.

Bakermans-Kranenburg, M., & van Ijzendoorn, M. (2009). Oxytocin receptor (OXTR) and serotonin transporter (5-HTT) genes associated with observed parenting. *SCAN*, *3*, 128–134.

Bakermans-Kranenburg, M., van Ijzendoorn, M., Pijlman, F., Mesman, J., & Juffer, F. (2008). Experimental evidence for differential susceptibility: Dopamine D4 receptor polymorphism

405 (DRD4 VNTR) moderates intervention effects on toddlers' externalizing behavior in a randomized controlled trial. *Developmental Psychology, 44*, 293–300.

Barry, R., Kochanska, G., & Philibert, R. (2008). G x E interaction in the organization of attachment: Mothers' responsiveness as a moderator of children's genotypes. *Journal of Child Psychology and Psychiatry, 49*, 1313–1320.

Belsky, J. & Pleuss, M. (2009). Beyond diathesis stress: Differential susceptibility to environmental influences. *Psychological Bulletin, 135*(6), 885–908.

Berton, O., McClung, C., DiLeone, R., Krishnan, V., Renthal, W., Russo, S. et al. (2006). Essential role of BDNF in the mesolimbic dopamine pathway in social defeat stress. *Science, 311*, 864–868.

Binder, E., Bradley, R., Liu, W., Epstein, M., Deveau, T., Mercer, K. et al. (2008). Association of FKBP5 polymorphisms and childhood abuse with risk of posttraumatic stress disorder symptoms in adults. *JAMA, 299*(11), 1291–1305.

Binder, E., Salyakina, D., Lichtner, P., Wochnik, G., Ising, M., et al. (2004). Polymorphisms in FKBP5 are associated with increased recurrence of depressive episodes and rapid response to antidepressant treatment. *Nature Genetics, 36*, 1319–1325.

Bolger, K., & Patterson, C. (2003) Sequelae of child maltreatment: Vulnerability and resilience. In S. S. Luthar (Ed.), *Resilience and vulnerability: Adaptation in the context of childhood adversities* (pp. 156–181). New York: Cambridge University Press.

Bonanno, G., Boerner, K., & Wortman, C. (2008). Trajectories of grieving. In M. Stroebe, R. O. Hansson, H. Schut, & W. Stroebe (Eds.), *Handbook of bereavement research and practice: Advances in theory and intervention* (pp. 287–308). Washington, DC: APA Books.

Bowlby, J. (1969/1982) Attachment and loss. Vol. 1. *Attachment*, 2nd ed. New York: Basic Books.

Breslau, N. (2009). The epidemiology of trauma, PTSD, and other posttrauma disorders. *Trauma, Violence, and Abuse, 10*(3), 198–210.

Briere, J., Kaltman, S., & Green, B. L. (2008). Accumulated childhood trauma and symptom complexity. *Journal of Traumatic Stress, 21*(2), 223–226.

Briere, J., & Runtz, M. (1993). Childhood sexual abuse: Long-term sequelae and implications for psychological assessment. *Journal of Interpersonal Violence, 8*, 312–330.

Brody, G., Beach, S., Philibert, R., Chen, Y., Lei, M., Murry, V. et al. (2009). Parenting moderates a genetic vulnerability factor in longitudinal increases in youths' substance use. *Journal of Consulting and Clinical Psychology*, 77, 1–11.

Brummett, B., Krystal, A., Ashley-Koch, A., Kuhn, C., Zuchner, S., Siegler, I. et al. (2007). Sleep quality varies as a function of 5-HTTLPR genotype and stress. *Psychosomatic Medicine, 69*, 621–624.

Byrnes, J. P. (2001). *Minds, brains, and learning*. New York: Guilford Press.

Caspi, A., Hariri, A., Holmes, A., Uher, R., & Moffitt, T. (2010). Genetic sensitivity to the environment: The case of the serotonin transporter gene and its implications for studying complex diseases and traits. *American Journal of Psychiatry, AIA*, 1–19.

Caspi, A., Sugden, K., Moffitt, T., Taylor, A., Craig, I., Harrington, H. et al. (2003). Influence of life stress on depression: moderation by a polymorphism in the 5-HTT gene. *Science, 301*, 386–389.

Cisler, J., Begle, A., Amstadter, A., Resnick, H., Danielson, C., Saunders, B. et al. (2012). Exposure to interpersonal violence and risk for PTSD, depression, delinquency, and binge drinking among adolescents: Data from the NSA-R. *Journal of Traumatic Stress, 25*, 33–40.

Cohen, J., Mannarino, A., Greenberg, T., Padlo, S., & Shipley, C. (2002). Childhood traumatic grief: Concepts and controversies. *Trauma, Violence & Abuse, 3*, 307–327.

Cook, D. R. (1994). *Internalized Shame Scale: Technical manual*. North Tonawanda, NY: Multi-Health Systems, Inc.

Covault, J., Tennen, H., Armeli, S., Conner, T., Herman, A., Cillessen, A. et al. (2007). Interactive effects of the serotonin transporter 5-HTTLPR polymorphism and stressful life events on college student drinking and drug use. *Biological Psychiatry, 6*, 609–616.

Crisan, L., Pana, S., Vulturar, R., Heilman R., Szekely, R., Druga, B. et al. (2009). Genetic contributions of the serotonin transporter to social learning of fear and economic decision making. *Social Cognitive and Affective Neuroscience*, *4*, 399–408.

Dannlowski, U., Ohrmann, P., Bauer, J., Kugel, H., Baune, B., Hohoff, C. et al. (2007). Serotonergic genes modulate amygdala activity in major depression. *Genes Brain and Behavior*, *6*, 672–676.

Del Giudice, M., Ellis, B. & Shirtcliff, E. (2011). The Adaptive Calibration Model of stress responsivity. *Neuroscience and Biobehavioral Reviews*. 35(7), 1562-92.

De Luca, V., Tharmalingam, S., Zai, C., Potapova, N., Strauss, J., Vincent, J. et al. (2010). Association of HPA axis genes with suicidal behaviour in schizophrenia. *Journal of Psychopharmacology*, *24*, 677–682.

De Young, A., Kenardy, J., & Cobham, V. (2011). Diagnosis of posttraumatic stress disorder in preschool children. *Journal of Clinical Child and Adolescent Psychology*, *40*(3), 375–384.

Doughty, E. (2009). Investigating adaptive grieving styles. *Death Studies*, *33*, 462–480.

Drury, S., Theall, K., Keats, B., & Scheeringa, M. (2009). The role of the dopamine transporter (DAT) in the development of PTSD in preschool children. *Journal of Traumatic Stress*, 22(6), 534–539.

Egan, M., Kojima, M., Callicott, J., Goldberg, T., Kolachana, B., Bertolino, A. et al. (2003). The BDNF val66met polymorphism affects activity-dependent secretion of BDNF and human memory and hippocampal function. *Cell*, *112*, 257–269.

Enoch, M-A., Shen, P-H., Ducci, F., Yuan, Q., Liu, J., White, K. et al. (2008). Common genetic origins for EEG, alcoholism and anxiety: the role of CRH-BP. *PLoS One*, *3*(10), e3620.

Fan, J., McCandliss, B., Fossella, .J, Flombaum J., & Posner M. (2005). The activation of attentional networks. *Neuroimage*, *26*, 471–479.

Fergusson, D., & Horwood, L. (2003). Resilience to childhood adversity: Results of a 21-year study. In S. S. Luthar (Ed.), *Resilience and vulnerability: Adaptation in the context of childhood adversities* (pp. 130–155). New York: Cambridge University Press.

Finkelhor, D., Ormrod, R., & Turner, H. (2007a). Poly-victimization: A neglected component in child victimization. *Child Abuse & Neglect*, *31*, 7–26.

Finkelhor, D., Ormrod, R., & Turner, H. (2007b). Re-victimization patterns in a national longitudinal sample of children and youth. *Child Abuse & Neglect*, *31*, 479–502.

Ford, J. & the Developmental Trauma Disorder Work Group (2012). Developmental Trauma Disorder Structured Interview for Children (DTDSI-C) 10.4. Available by contacting jford@uchc.edu .

Ford, J., Grasso, D., Greene, C., Levine, J., Spinazzola, J., & van der Kolk, B. (submitted). Clinicians' views of the clinical significance of developmental trauma exposure and symptoms: An international survey.

Fox, N., Henderson, H., Marshall, P., Nichols, K., & Ghera, M. (2005). Behavioral inhibition: Linking biology and behavior within a developmental framework. *Annual Review of Psychology*, *56*, 235–262.

Furman, D., Hamilton, P., Joormann, J., & Gotlib, I. (in press). Altered timing of amygdala activation during sad mood elaboration as a function of 5-HTTLPR. *Biological Psychiatry*.

Gabert-Quillen, C., Fallon, W., & Delahanty, D. (2011). PTSD after traumatic injury: An investigation of the impact of injury severity and peritraumatic moderators. *Journal of Health Psychology*, *16*(4), 678–687.

Gillespie, C., Phifer, J., Bradley, B., & Ressler, K. (2009). Risk and resilience: Genetic and environmental influences on development of the stress response. *Depression and Anxiety*, *26* (11), 984–992.

Greif Green, J., McLaughlin, K., Berglund, P., Gruber, M., Sampson, N., Zaslavsky, A. et al. (2010). Childhood adversities and adult psychiatric disorders in the National Comorbidity Survey Replication. I: Associations with first onset of DSM–IV disorders. *Archives of General Psychiatry*, *67*, 113–123.

Gunnar, M., & Vazquez, D. (2006). Stress neurobiology and developmental psychopathology. In D. Cicchetti & D. Cohen (Eds.), *Developmental psychopathology, vol. 2.* Hoboken, NJ: Wiley.

Hariri, A., Goldberg, T., Mattay, V., Kolachana, B., Callicott, J., Egan M. et al. (2003). Brain-derived neurotrophic factor val66met polymorphism affects human memory-related hippocampal activity and predicts memory performance. *Journal of Neuroscience, 23*, 6690–6694.

Hoenicka, J., Ponce, G., Jimenez-Arriero, M., Ampuero, I., Rodriguez-Jimenez, R., Rubio, G. et al. (2007). Association in alcoholic patients between psychopathic traits and the additive effect of allelic forms of the CNR1 and FAAH endocannabinoid genes, and the 3' region of the DRD2 gene. *Neurotoxicity Research, 11*, 51–59.

Hu, X., Lipsky, R., Zhu, G., Akhtar, L., Taubman, J., Greenberg, D. et al (2006). Serotonin transporter promoter gain of function genotypes are linked to obsessive-compulsive disorder. *American Journal of Human Genetics, 78*, 815–826.

Hundt, N., & Holohan, D. (2012). The role of shame in distinguishing perpetrators of intimate partner violence in U.S. veterans. *Journal of Traumatic Stress, 25*, 191–197.

Ising, M., Depping, A., Siebertz, A., Lucae, S, Unschuld, P., Kloiber, S. et al (2008). Polymorphisms in the FKBP5 gene region modulate recovery from psychosocial stress in healthy controls. *European Journal of Neuroscience, 28*, 389–398.

Joyce, A., Ogrodniczuk, J., Piper, W., & Sheptycki, A. (2010). Interpersonal predictors of outcome following short-term group therapy for complicated grief: A replication. *Clinical Psychology and Psychotherapy, 17*, 122–135.

Kertes, D., Kalsi, G., Prescott, C., Kuo, P., Patterson, D., Walsh, D. et al. (2010). Neurotransmitter and neuromodulator genes associated with a history of depressive symptoms in individuals with alcohol dependence. *Alcoholism: Clinical and Experimental Research, 5*(3), 496–505.

Kessler, R. (2000). Posttraumatic stress disorder: The burden to the individual and to society. *Journal of Clinical Psychiatry, 61*, 4–12.

Kessler, R., Davis, C., & Kendler, K. (1997). Childhood adversity and adult psychiatric disorder in the US National Comorbidity Survey. *Psychological Medicine, 27*, 1101–1119.

Kochanska, G., Philibert, R., & Barry, R. (2009). Interplay of genes and early mother and child relationship in the development of self-regulation from toddler to preschool age. *Journal of Child Psychology and Psychiatry, 50*, 1331–1338.

Koenen, K. (2007). Genetics of posttraumatic stress disorder: Review and recommendations for future studies. *Journal of Traumatic Stress, 20*(5), 737–750.

Koenen, K., Saxe, G., Purcell, S., Smoller, J., Bartholomew, D., Miller, A. et al. (2005). Polymorphisms in FKBP5 are associated with peritraumatic dissociation in medically injured children. *Molecular Psychiatry, 10*, 1058–1059.

Kumsta, R., Stevens, S., Brookes, K., Schlotz, W., Castle, J., Beckett, C. et al. (2010). 5HTT genotype moderates the influence of early institutional deprivation on emotional problems in adolescence: Evidence from the English and Romanian adoptee (ERA) study. *Journal of Child Psychology and Psychiatry, 51*, 755–762.

Lau, J., & Pine, D. (2008). Elucidating risk mechanisms of gene–environment interactions on pediatric anxiety: integrating findings from neuroscience *European Archives of Psychiatry and Clinical Neuroscience, 258*, 97–106.

Lee, D., Scragg, P., & Turner, S. (2001). The role of shame and guilt in traumatic events: A clinical model of shame-based and guilt based PTSD. *British Journal of Medical Psychology, 74*, 451–466.

Lonsdorf, T., Weike, A., Nikamo, P., Schalling, M., Hamm, A., & Öhman, A. (2009). Genetic gating of human fear learning and extinction: Possible implications for gene-environment interaction in anxiety disorder. *Psychological Science, 20*, 198–206.

Lupien, S., McEwen, B., Gunnar, M., & Heim, C. (2009). Effects of stress throughout the lifespan on the brain, behaviour and cognition. *Neuroscience, 10*(1), 1–12.

Martin, C., Cromer, L., DePrince, A., & Freyd, J. (2011). The role of cumulative trauma, betrayal, and appraisals in understanding trauma symptomatology. *Psychological Trauma: Theory, Research, Practice, and Policy.* Advance online publication.

Martin, T., & Doka, K. (2000). *Men don't cry . . . women do: Transcending gender stereotypes of grief.* Philadelphia, PA: Brunner Mazel.

Meiser-Stedman, R., Smith, P., Bryant, R., Salmon, K., Yule, W., Dalgleish, T. et al. (2009). Development and validation of the Child Post-Traumatic Cognitions Inventory (CPTCI). *Journal of Child Psychology and Psychiatry, 50*, 432–440.

Mueller, A., Brocke B., Fries, E., Lesch, K., & Kirschbaum, C. (2010). The role of the serotonin transporter polymorphism for the endocrine stress response in newborns. *Psychoneuroendocrinology, 35*, 289–296.

Moss, E., Cyr, C., & Dubois-Comtois, K. (2004). Attachment at early school age and developmental risk: Examining family contexts and behavior problems of controlling–caregiving, controlling–punitive, and behaviorally disorganized children. *Developmental Psychology, 40*(4), 519–532.

Moss, E., Pascuzzo, K., & Simard, V. (2012). Treating insecure and disorganized attachments in school-aged children. In Nader, K. (Ed.), *School rampage shootings and other youth disturbances: Early preventive interventions.* New York: Routledge.

Nader, K. (1997). Childhood traumatic loss: The intersection of trauma and grief. In C. Figley, B. Bride, & N. Mazza (Eds.), *Death and trauma: The traumatology of grieving* (pp. 17–41). London: Taylor & Francis.

Nader, K. (2008). *Understanding and assessing trauma in children and adolescents: Measures, methods, and youth in context.* New York: Routledge.

Nader, K. (2010). Children and adolescent's exposure to the mass violence of war and terrorism: Role of the media. In Webb, N.B. (Ed.), *Helping Bereaved Children* (3rd edition, pp. 215-239). New York: Guilford.

Nader, K. (in press). Assessing childhood traumatic reactions: The variables that influence reactions and methods of assessment. In P. Clements & S. Seedat (Eds.) *Mental health issues of child maltreatment.* St. Louis, MO: STM Learning, Inc.

Nader, K., & Fletcher, K. (in press). Childhood posttraumatic stress disorder. In E. Mash & R. Barkley (Eds.) *Child psychopathology*, 3rd ed. New York: Guilford Press.

Nader, K., & Nader, W. (2012). Youth at risk: Targeted shootings, other school violence, and suicides. In K. Nader (Ed.), *School rampage shootings and other youth disturbances: Early preventive interventions* (pp. 33–70). New York: Routledge.

Nader, K., Pynoos, R., Fairbanks, L., & Frederick, C. (1990). Children's PTSD reactions one year after a sniper attack at their school. *American Journal of Psychiatry, 147*, 1526–1530.

Netter, P. (2004). Personality and hormones. In R. Stelmack (Ed.), *On the psychobiology of personality* (pp. 343–377). Ottawa, Canada: Elsevier.

Pacheco, J., Beevers, C., Benavides, C., McGeary, J., Stice, E., & Schnyer, D. (2009). Frontal-limbic white matter pathway associations with the serotonin transporter gene promoter region (5-HTTLPR) polymorphism. *Journal of Neuroscience, 29*, 6229–6233.

Pauli-Pott, U., Friedl, S., Hinney, A., & Hebebrand, J. (2009). Serotonin transporter gene polymorphism (5-HTTLPR), environmental conditions, and developing negative emotionality and fear in early childhood. *Journal of Neural Transmission, 116*, 503–512.

Pearlman, M., Schwartz, K., & Cloitre, M. (2010). *The varied manifestations of grief: Assisting a child and caregiver after the loss of a parent.* Washington, DC: APA.

Pezawas, L., Meyer-Lindenberg, A., Drabant, E., Verchinski, B., Munoz, K., Kolachana, B. et al. (2005). 5-HTTLPR polymorphism impacts human cingulate-amygdala interactions: A genetic susceptibility mechanism for depression. *Nature Neuroscience, 8*, 828–834.

Porges, S. W. (2007). The polyvagal perspective. *Biological Psychology, 74*, 116–143.

Pruessner, J., Gaab, J., Hellhammer, D., Lintz, D., Schommer, N., & Kirschbaum, C. (1997). Increasing correlation between personality traits and cortisol stress responses obtained by data aggregation. *Psychoneuroendocrinology, 22*, 615–625.

Pynoos, R., Frederick, C., Nader, K., Arroyo, W., Eth, S. et al. (1987). Life threat and post-traumatic stress in school age children. *Archives of General Psychiatry, 44*, 1057–1063.

Ray, L. (2011). Stress-induced and cue-induced craving for alcohol in heavy drinkers: Preliminary evidence of genetic moderation by the OPRM1 and CRH-BP genes. *Alcoholism: Clinical and Experimental Research, 35*, 166–174.

Roy, A., Hu, X., Janal, M., & Goldman, D. (2007). Interaction between childhood trauma and serotonin transporter gene variation in suicide. *Neuropsychopharmacology, 32*, 2046–2052.

Salloum, A., Garside, L., Irwin, C., Anderson, A., & Francois, A., (2009). Grief and trauma group therapy for children after Hurricane Katrina. *Social Work with Groups*, 32, 64–79.

Salloum, A., & Overstreet, S. (2012). Grief and trauma intervention for children after disaster: Exploring coping skills versus trauma narration. *Behaviour Research and Therapy, 50*, 169–179.

Sandberg, D., Seuss, E., & Heaton, J. (2010). Attachment anxiety as a mediator of the relationship between interpersonal trauma and posttraumatic symptomatology among college women. *Journal of Interpersonal Violence, 25*(1), 33–49.

Sarapas, C., Cai, G., Bierer, L., Golier, J., Galea, S., Ising, M. et al. (2011). Genetic markers for PTSD risk and resilience among survivors of the World Trade Center attacks. *Disease Markers, 30*(2–3), 101–110.

Savitz, J., van der Merwe, L., Stein, D., Solms, M., & Ramesar, R. (2007). Genotype and childhood sexual trauma moderate neurocognitive performance: A possible role for brain-derived neurotrophic factor and apolipoprotein E variants. *Biological Psychiatry*, 62, 391–399.

Scheeringa, M., Myers, L., Putnam, F., & Zeanah, C. (2012). Diagnosing PTSD in early childhood: An empirical assessment of four approaches. *Journal of Traumatic Stress, 25*, 359–367.

Scheeringa, M., Wright, M., Hunt, J., & Zeanah, C. (2006). Factors affecting the diagnosis and prediction of PTSD symptomatology in children and adolescents. *American Journal of Psychiatry, 163*, 644–651.

Segman, R., Cooper-Kazaz, R., Macciardi, F., Goltser, T., Halfon, Y., Dobroborski, T. et al. (2002). Association between the dopamine transporter gene and posttraumatic stress disorder. *Molecular Psychiatry, 7*, 903–907.

Stein, M., Schork, N., & Gelernter, J. (2008). Gene-by-environment (serotonin transporter and childhood maltreatment) interaction for anxiety sensitivity, an intermediate phenotype for anxiety disorders. *Neuropsychopharmacology, 33*, 312–319.

Stein, P., & Kendall, J. (2004). *Psychological trauma and the developing brain: Neurologically based interventions for troubled children*. New York: Haworth Press.

Stone, A. M. (1992). The role of shame in post-traumatic stress disorder. *American Journal of Orthopsychiatry, 62*, 131–136.

Stovall-McClough, K., & Cloitre, M. (2006). Unresolved attachment, PTSD, and dissociation in women with childhood abuse histories. *Journal of Consulting and Clinical Psychology, 74*, 219–228.

Strange, B., Kroes, M., Roiser, J., Tan, G., & Dolan, R. (2008). Emotion-induced retrograde amnesia is determined by a 5-HTT genetic polymorphism. *Journal of Neuroscience, 28*, 7036–7039.

Tangney, J., & Dearing, R. (2002). *Shame and guilt*. New York: Guilford Press.

Tsankova, N., Berton, O., Renthal, W., Kumar, A., Neve, R., & Nestler, E. (2006). Sustained hippocampal chromatin regulation in a mouse model of depression and antidepressant action. *Nature Neuroscience*, 9, 519–525.

Turner, H. A., Finkelhor, D., & Ormrod, R. (2010). Poly-victimization in a national sample of children and youth. *American Journal of Preventive Medicine, 38*(3), 323–330.

Tyrka, A., Price, L., Kao, H-T., Porton, B., Marsella, S., & Carpenter, L. (2010). Childhood maltreatment and telomere shortening: Preliminary support for an effect of early stress on cellular aging. *Biological Psychiatry*, *67*(6), 531–534.

Verona, E., Joiner, T., Johnson, F., & Bender, T. (2006). Gender specific gene-environment interactions on laboratory-assessed aggression. *Biological Psychology*, *71*, 33–41.

Vranceanu, A., Hobfoll, S., & Johnson, R. (2007). Child multi-type maltreatment and associated depression and PTSD symptoms: The role of social support and stress. *Child Abuse and Neglect*, *31*(1), 71–84.

Walter, J., & LaFreniere, P. (2007). Preschoolers' avoidance in a mishap paradigm: Implications for emotional adjustment, guilt, and shame. *North American Journal of Psychology*, 9(1), 111–130.

Williams, L., Gatt, J., Schofield, P., Olivieri, G., Peduto, A., & Gordon, E. (2009). "Negativity bias" in risk for depression and anxiety: Brain–body fear circuitry correlates, 5-HTT-LPR and early life stress. *Neuroimage*, *47*, 804–814.

Willour V., Chen, H., Toolan, J., Belmonte, P., Cutler, D., Goes, F. et al. (2009). Family-based association of FKBP5 in bipolar disorder. *Molecular Psychiatry*, *14*, 261–268.

Xie, P., Kranzler, H., Poling, J., Stein, M., Anton, R., Brady, K. et al. (2009). The interactive effect of stressful life events and serotonin transporter 5-HTTLPR genotype on PTSD diagnosis in two independent populations. *Archives of General Psychiatry*, 66, 1201–1209.

Yehuda, R., Cai, G., Golier, J., Sarapas, C., Galea, S., Ising, M. et al. (2009). Gene expression patterns associated with posttraumatic stress disorder following exposure to the World Trade Center attacks. *Biological Psychiatry*, *66*, 708–711.

PAGE 183Young, B., Lawford, B., Noble, E., Kanin, B., Wilkie, A., Ritchie, T. et al. (2002). Harmful drinking in military veterans with posttraumatic stress disorder: Association with the D2 dopamine receptor A1 allele. *Alcohol and Alcoholism*, *37*, 451–456.

Index